THE JEWISH POLITY

JEWISH POLITICAL AND SOCIAL STUDIES

Daniel J. Elazar and Steven M. Cohen, Editors

Jewish Political Organization

THE JEWISH POLITY

from Biblical Times to the Present

DANIEL J. ELAZAR

AND

STUART A. COHEN

Indiana University Press

Bloomington

Manufactured in the United States of America

Elazar, Daniel Judah.
The Jewish polity.
(Jewish political and social studies)
Includes index.
1. Jews—Politics and government.   2. Politics in the
Bible.   3. Jewish councils and synods.   I. Cohen, Stuart.
II. Title.   III. Series.
DS140.E396   1984   320'.089924   83-48648
ISBN 0-253-33156-0

*This book is dedicated with affection and respect
to the memory of Katherine Sonneborne Falk (1904–1983),
whose own life represented a continuation
of a grand tradition.*

CONTENTS

Part Four: MODERNITY AND THE RESTORATION OF STATEHOOD

PREFACE

Jewish political studies is a field just now emerging within Jewish studies, on the one hand, and political science, on the other. Although it has been articulated as a field for little more than a decade, it has already developed a core of scholars who see themselves as working within it. Nevertheless, and perhaps precisely because of its novelty, the field lacks most of the basic tools necessary for disciplined study, teaching, and research. One of the major projects of the Jerusalem Center for Public Affairs is the development of such tools. In recent years, the Center has been in the forefront of the development of Jewish political studies through its Center for Jewish Community Studies and, we dare say, has been the single most important source of its emerging literature. This volume is presented as another such contribution. It puts together for the first time an overall picture of the political system of the Jewish polity and the various regimes which have served the Jewish people—as a whole and as subdivided into communities—in a systematic way, epoch by epoch, in Eretz Israel and in the diaspora. It provides data on the structure of each regime and its offices, the constitutional framework within which it functioned, the constitutional issues it confronted, and the camps and parties which emerged to define and contest those issues to the extent that such data are available. It does all this within the context of the constitutional history of each epoch, utilizing the prevailing political terminology, Hebrew or other, of the epoch.

This volume is a product of over twenty-five years of research, beginning with the work of Daniel Elazar in the late 1950s. Nearly fifteen years of this research was conducted at the Center for Jewish Community Studies or its predecessor, the Jewish Community Studies Group. The present work is an expansion of the *Gazetteer of Jewish Political Organization* published by the Center in 1981. That effort sharpened our understanding of what materials were—and are—needed to advance the field, including a comprehensive overview of the Jewish polity from its biblical beginnings to the present.

We present this volume with full knowledge of the lacunae which need to be filled, the fog which surrounds major as well as minor events, issues, and institutions in various epochs of Jewish history, and the necessity to draw conclusions based upon partial and even inadequate knowledge. Although there is no comparable source presenting the materials contained within it, the gaps in our knowledge are painfully apparent to us and will be to the reader as well. Entire epochs and whole communities remain unexplored for lack of accessible sources. Even where outlines of knowledge are available, details often are lacking. Where we have had to exercise judgment we have done so on the basis of serious review of the available evidence and scholarly discussions of that evidence as put forth by the leading students of each epoch and community; but, of course, in the final analysis, the conclusions are our own. In exercising our critical faculties in this way, we are no different from our colleagues in Jewish history and classical Jewish studies who must, perforce, do the same.

We believe that this volume establishes a framework and an outline which can be filled in more fully as our knowledge increases. Fortunately, the great expansion of research in Jewish studies in our time promises regular additions to the store of data, information, and knowledge available to us. Even in the brief interim between the compilation of the *Gazetteer* and the preparation of this volume, we have been able to clarify certain matters on the basis of new knowledge. Hence we look forward to the publication of future editions of this book which will incorporate even more complete delineations of the Jewish polity in all its facets.

In the meantime, we hope that this volume will set both the agenda and the direction of research in the field of Jewish political studies. Hence, we offer the present edition as a teaching tool *par excellence*. We are confident that it can be used with great success in university-level courses in Jewish history and in the growing number of courses in Jewish political studies, in the professional education of Jewish civil servants, as an introduction to the teaching of Jewish civics in Jewish schools, in leadership development programs, and for adult education whether in formal courses or study groups.

In the course of our preparation of this book, we were aided by various students and colleagues. Research assistants who contributed to the gathering of the raw material for the original *Gazetteer* included Ruth Gil, Adina Weiss Liberles, Avraham Shapiro, and Avi Weinstein. Sarah Mayer contributed to the refinement of the initial outline which led to the *Gazetteer*. We have benefited from the work of the Workshop in the Covenant Idea and the Jewish Political Tradition cosponsored by the Center for Jewish Community Studies and the Bar-Ilan University Department of Political Studies and from the assistance of Ruth Gil and Meir Kasirer, the Workshop coordinators.

Partial support for preparing the initial *Gazetteer* came from the Israel Ministry of Education as part of its funding of the Center to prepare a course in "The Jewish Political Tradition and the State of Israel" for Israeli high schools. Bar-Ilan University provided partial support for its publication through the Senator N. M. Paterson Chair on Intergovernmental Relations. Nevertheless, the major share of the funding for this project came from the Jerusalem Center for Public Affairs and its loyal supporters. Particularly welcome at the final stages of this enterprise was the encouragement which we received from our colleague, Stephen M. Cohen, and from Robert Mandel of Indiana University Press.

We owe a special debt of gratitude to Judy Ann Cohen and Sarah Lederhendler, of the Jerusalem Center for Public Affairs, for their work in preparing the manuscript for publication.

D.J.E.
S.A.C.
Jerusalem
Sivan 5743-May 1983

A Note on Hebrew Terminology and the Diagrams

In order to introduce the reader to the Jewish political tradition in the most authentic way possible, Hebrew political terminology has been used throughout. In every case, the terms are defined where they are first introduced as well as in the glossaries at the end of each chapter. Transliteration follows the system used in the *Encyclopedia Judaica* with certain modifications for greater readability.

The following conventions are used in the diagrams:

1. *Keter Torah* officers and institutions are placed on the right axis of the triangle.

   Keter Malkhut officers and institutions are placed on the left axis of the triangle.

   Keter Kehunah officers and institutions are placed on the bottom axis of the triangle.

2. Solid-line axes indicate that the relevant *keter* possessed identifiable officers and institutions.

   Broken-line axes indicate that the officers and institutions cannot presently be identified or are assumed not to have existed.

3. Patterns of influence, authority, and communication are indicated as follows:

   $- - - \rightarrow$ intermittent and/or indirect

   $\longrightarrow$ continuous and/or direct

THE JEWISH POLITY

An Introduction to the Jewish Political Tradition

THE JEWISH POLITICAL TRADITION

The Jewish national revival of our times led first to the restoration of Jewish political consciousness, then to the reestablishment of a Jewish state. Paradoxically, however, the operational resurgence of the concept of a Jewish polity has not been accompanied by an awareness of its historical parallels and roots. Concentrating their focus on what is novel in their present political situation, Jews have tended to ignore what is traditional. Virtually unrecognized are the striking similarities in the structure of Jewish institutions in Israel and the diaspora, past and present; equally obscured is the evidence which indicates that contemporary Jewry functions—for the most part unconsciously—in the political arena in no small measure on the basis of certain fundamental beliefs and practices which are embedded in Jewish culture. There has been very little regard for the fact that the present behavioral patterns of the Jewish political world, revolutionary though some of them might seem,[1] are in essence extensions and modifications of what can only be described as a Jewish political tradition.

For there does indeed exist a Jewish political tradition, with all that the term implies in the way of a continuous dialogue regarding proper modes of political behavior and acceptable institutional forms and political norms. In part, this tradition has been expressed formally, in the political ideas of Jewish thinkers; far more fully, however, has it been articulated in the institutional and behavioral dimensions of Jewish political and communal life, sometimes set down on paper and sometimes not. That, indeed, is what makes it a tradition rather than a systematic body of knowledge or wisdom. It can best be understood, not by seeking the works of individual thinkers, but by identifying the principles and modes of action which have animated the activities of Jewish political practitioners and by exploring the ways in which Jewish political institutions have embodied those principles and modes over the long course of Jewish history. The present volume is designed to facilitate that exploration.

The Jewish political dialogue began over 3200 years ago, with the emergence of the Jewish people as a body politic. According to the biblical account, it was then that the Children of Israel developed common (and distinctive) responses to emergent situations in the political realm, as well as in others. That dialogue has continued ever since. Admittedly, the lines of progression have not followed a single linear pattern. Periods of intense political expression, when the Jewish political dialogue resonated strongly, have alternated with those of a more muted kind. But the persistence of the Jewish attempt to maintain and enhance that dialogue nevertheless remains one of its most striking characteristics; it is also a testimony to the fact that the Jewish political tradition constitutes an integral segment of the entire fabric of Jewish civilization. The constancy of political concern within Judaism has throughout reflected an implicit understanding—albeit sometimes obscured—that the validity of Jewish teaching can best find expression in a political setting, through a polity in which Jews bear the responsibility for creating the "kingdom of heaven" (Hebrew: *malkhut shamayim*)—the good commonwealth—on earth.[2]

Ironically, after experiencing constitutional changes and surviving changes of regime, exile, and dispersion, the Jewish political tradition has been nearly lost in our time, precisely at the moment of the renewal of full Jewish political life. The emancipation of the Jews in the modern era, bought at the price of virtually abjuring Jewish corporate identity, almost brought it to a close; but precisely at its weakest moment it was revived operationally as the political character of the Jewish people became clear once again. Now its intellectual dimension needs to be recovered by systematic effort so that it may fill a vital and needed role in contemporary Jewish life—both in Israel and in the diaspora.

As in the case of other peoples whose grounding is not philosophic or ideological, tradition has always occupied an extremely important role in Jewish life. (The Hebrew word for tradition, *masoret*, literally means bond and is closer to the original meaning of the word *religion*, whose Latin root also means bond.) The Jewish political tradition is an integral part of the whole fabric of Jewish tradition, a *sine qua non* of that tradition given the Jewish commitment to peoplehood and the attainment of redemption through the creation of the good commonwealth on earth.[3]

What is perhaps most compelling about the need to rediscover the Jewish political tradition is the fact that Jews continue to function in the political arena in no small measure on the basis of their political tradition, albeit without conscious awareness that they are functioning within a living tradition of their own or any tradition at all. The striking similarities in the structure of Jewish institutions in Israel and the diaspora, present and past, the basic characteristics of Jewish political behavior, the fundamental beliefs and practices embedded in Jewish political culture, all attest to the persistence of a Jewish political tradition that remains for the most part unrecognized.[4]

Because Judaism emphasizes God's sovereignty, Jewish peoplehood, and the building of the holy commonwealth, political motifs permeate Jewish ideas and ways and are often found where modern man would least expect them. Thus the exploration of the Jewish political tradition requires the re-examination of familiar materials with new eyes as much as it does the exploration of unfamiliar sources and data. This volume is designed to facilitate that exploration.

SOME ELEMENTS OF THE JEWISH POLITICAL TRADITION

Every political tradition rests upon certain assumptions about the nature of man, government, and politics; the character and role of law; and what justice is. Central to the dialogue that informs every political tradition are such questions as what constitutes political authority and obligation, what is political responsibility, who governs and who gets what, when, and how from the polity, and a terminology in which those questions are phrased. Both the questions and the terminology have many ramifications which need exploration in order to understand any particular political tradition. The exploration itself is an exceedingly ambitious task. In order to facilitate that task, this volume summarizes the political organization of the Jewish people through the various epochs of Jewish history. It focuses on eight dimensions of political concern as they were manifested in each epoch:

1. The dominant events of political significance
2. A constitutional survey of the epoch and of the manner whereby its principal features relate to one another
3. The constitution under which the Jewish people functioned as a body politic, including both
   3.1 The principal constitutional issues and
   3.2 The principal political camps and the parties within each camp
4. The governmental structure, functions, and lines of authority of the *edah* (nation as a whole)
5. The governmental structure, functions, and lines of authority of the *medinot* or *aratzot* (the principal constituent units of the *edah*)
6. The governmental structure, functions, and lines of authority of the *kehillot* (local communities within the various *medinot*)
7. A representative selection of the politically significant personalities
8. The principal political terms, especially new ones introduced and old ones transformed

Before turning to the design and detail of Jewish political organization, it is desirable to have some understanding of the conceptual basis upon which it rests and the ends toward which it is directed.

Man, Government, and Politics

From the Jewish perspective, humans are partners with the Sovereign of the Universe (*Ribbon ha-Olam*) in the development and governance of this world, which partnership is established by covenant (*brit*). Humans have both good and evil inclinations (*yetzer ha-tov* and *yetzer ha-ra*). Because they have inclinations to evil, they require laws to guide them. Because they are more good than bad, their behavior can be improved by proper institutions (especially good laws). At the same time, people, when unrestrained, are capable of utilizing government and politics for the institutionalization of their evil inclinations, thereby greatly increasing their capability to do evil.

Government and, concomitantly, politics are necessary parts of human existence in every case but, necessary and important as they are, government and politics are merely tools for the achievement of more sacred goals and not ends in themselves. Politics is a universal and serious human activity but only as a means to achieve holy purposes (*tikkun olam*—reformation of the world). Since politics is part and parcel of the way of man (*derekh ha-adam*), it is a mixture of the petty as well as the grand. Its importance must be recognized but always with a certain ambivalence given its propensities to serve unwarranted ambition. In the last analysis, however, full achievement of the goals of political activity is dependent upon God's intervention to redeem (*geulah*) humanity. Hence it is necessary to look to a better future in the messianic age (*yemot ha-mashiah*).

Law and Justice

Law, in the sense of the Divine constitutional teaching (the *Torah*), provides the foundation of human polity. Divine law is comprehensive and immutable, but properly constituted human agency has been granted broad powers of interpretation. This strong commitment to constitutionalism and the rule of law tends to elevate judges to a position of special authority within the body politic. In its most narrow application, this commitment tends to encourage hairsplitting legalism. On the other hand, it can be coupled with an equally strong operational commitment to the idea that every individual must ultimately decide for himself to what extent particular laws apply in his case, i.e., a kind of rule of law by repeated acts of consent. In certain ways, law is understood as a norm to be attained as much as a fixed rule or boundary.

Justice is intimately associated with Divine law, but the association extends beyond a simple one-to-one relationship to involve practical considerations of covenant obligation (*hesed*) and mercy (*rahamim*). This often leads to a paradoxical condition whereby legal support for doing justice exacts the strongest penalties for unjust acts, which penalties are rarely if ever applied on grounds of tempering justice with mercy.[5]

Political Authority and Obligation

The universe and all its parts is under Divine sovereignty (*malkhut shamayim*) and hence all human institutions possess only delegated authority and powers. That is the essence of Jewish theocracy. In fact, the good political order is a complex of interlocking authorities whose legitimacy is derived from the covenant-established partnership between God and man.[6] In some cases the former elects and the latter ratifies, and in others the process is reversed, but in every one the two sides of the partnership are somehow represented. This can lead to power-sharing at its best or, in extreme manifestations, to near-anarchy. Part of the theocratic character of the Jewish political tradition is reflected in a constant tension between the Divine (*shamayim* or *theo*) and rule (*malkhut* or *cratos*) which must be reconciled by federal or covenantal linkage.[7]

The basis for political authority is invariably covenantal, and political obligation flows from that covenantal base.[8] Covenanting makes Divine sovereignty concrete and human self-government possible in this world, but removal of the former can lead to the institutionalized expression of Faustian ambition on the part of humans.[9]

The Polity (Especially the Jewish People)

A legitimate polity (*kibbutz medini*) is an extension of the covenantal relationship, constituted consensually by compact, as a partnership or metapartnership of its constituents. There is no "state" in the Jewish political tradition, in the sense of a reified political entity complete in and of itself. The contemporary Hebrew term for state, *medinah*, refers to a political unit with its own jurisdiction (*din*) within a larger entity, e.g., a province. While the term *medinah* is today used for politically sovereign states, its classical echoes still remind us that "polity" would be a better translation. The latter term offers wider and narrower expressions of meaning consistent with the Hebrew original—wider in that all entities with their own political-legal jurisdiction are polities (cf. the Arabic *medinah* meaning "city") and narrower in that no polity exists apart from its component elements nor does it possess absolute sovereignty. Both dimensions are vital elements in the Jewish political tradition. In fact, the Jewish political tradition does not recognize state sovereignty in the modern sense of absolute independence. No state—a human creation—can be sovereign. Classically, only God is sovereign and He entrusts the exercise of His sovereign powers to the people as a whole, mediated through His Torah-as-constitution as provided through His covenant with Israel.[10]

The Jewish people (*Am Yisrael*) is a polity of equals, a commonwealth (*edah*), with all that implies for the organization and conduct of Jewish political affairs.[11] While no single form of political organization is mandated by Jewish law or tradition, any form chosen must embody this basic republican (*res publica*=a public thing) principle.[12] Jewish regimes have not always been democratic republics; because of the emphasis on the Divine role, they have aristocratic tendencies that often have degenerated into oligarchic patterns of rule. But with rare exceptions, they have not been autocratic in character. The republican foundations of the Jewish political tradition have prevented that.

A proper Jewish polity is one which embodies a proper set of political relationships rather than any particular structure or regime.[13] This emphasis on relationships is particularly relevant to a covenantal polity and helps reinforce Jewish republicanism, but it can also lead to ignoring structures unless confronted by extreme difficulties with them.

The Jewish people as an *edah* takes as its point of departure a strong commitment to bargaining as the basic mode of political decision-making. In its best sense, this leads to negotiated cooperation based upon covenant obligation; in its worst, to willingness to subject everything to haggling with minimum regard for norms or accepted procedures.[14]

Political Responsibility

The basis of Jewish political responsibility rests upon the collective self-perception that the Jews are a special people; that they are shaped by their combined religio-political character which, in a certain sense, transcends time and space, although it is always focused on the Land of Israel as the only place where complete Jewish individual and collective self-fulfillment is possible. At best, this has facilitated the maintenance of the unity and survival of a people in exile for millenia and dispersed throughout the world. It has also led to periodic attempts to deny the political dimension of Jewishness.[15]

Responsible policy-making rests upon the collective self-perception which the Jewish people shares as a perpetually small minority, usually isolated from the larger world when its own interests are involved, which must develop and pursue survival strategies accordingly. This set of perceptions encourages a wide variety of strategies, both accommodationist and hostile, integrationist and isolationist.[16]

Research indicates that each of these elements recurs in one form or another in every period of Jewish history; in fact, the changing modes of their expression can be used to identify and demarcate the various epochs of Jewish history from a political perspective.[17]

POLITICAL TRADITION AND THE
LANGUAGE OF POLITICAL DISCOURSE

A very useful starting point for understanding the Jewish political tradition is the language of political discourse among Jews, the recurring basic terminology that creates the conceptual and perceptual framework for considering and dealing with public affairs. In Kadushin's terms, the exploration of this dimension of Jewish tradition is possible through the identification and explication of *value concepts*, in this case terms and phrases bearing political content.[18] Many of the basic terms of discourse are offered in the preceding pages. The body of this volume contains a more comprehensive lexicon of Jewish political terminology and indicates some of the implications of that terminology for understanding the Jewish political tradition.[19]

The Bible is rich in political terminology, as any close reading of the text in context reveals. Indeed it remains the prime source of Hebrew political terms, many of which have been transmitted with no or minimum change in meaning over the millenia. The terminology as such and in context has substantial implications for understanding the sources of the Jewish political tradition and deserves full treatment on its own. Among those terms and phrases are several that are of special importance because they give meaning to fundamental political relationships and the regimes they shape. In essence, they are the Hebrew equivalents of the classic political terminology of ancient Greek and Latin.

The classic character of this political terminology can be illustrated through the device of the "mapping sentence" devised by Louis Guttman as the basis for hypothecation in social research.[20] The classic Jewish political worldview can be summarized as follows:

The family or kith (*moledet*) of tribes (*shevatim*) descended from Abraham, Isaac, and Jacob which God raised up to be a nation (*goy*) became the Jewish people (*Am Yisrael*) through its covenant (*brit*) with God, which, in turn, laid the basis for the establishment of a Jewish commonwealth (*edah*) under Divine sovereignty (*malkhut shamayim*) and hence bound by the Divine constitutional teaching (*Torah*). The *am* so created must live as a community of equals (*kahal*) whose locus is the Land of Israel (Eretz Israel), under the rule of law (*ḥukah, ḥok*) which applies to every citizen (*ezrah*), defined as a partner to the covenant (*ben-brit*). Every citizen is linked to his neighbor (*rea*) by covenant obligation (*ḥesed*). Within these parameters there is latitude in choosing the form of government or regime as long as the proper relationships between the various parties just referred to are preserved. That, in turn, requires a system of shared authorities (*reshuyot*)—what today would be termed "checks and balances." These *reshuyot* are combined under three authoritative categories (*ketarim*): the authority of Torah (*keter torah*), the authority of civil governance (*keter malkhut*), and the authority of the priesthood (*keter kehunah*), each of which plays a role in the government of the *edah* through a system of shared powers. At any given time, different religious and political camps (*mahanot*) and parties (*miflagot*) within those camps compete for control of the governing institutions of the *edah*. Moreover, since the full achievement of its religio-political goals requires reformation of the existing order (*tikkun olam*) and redemption (*geulah*), the Jewish political worldview is messianic in orientation, looking toward a better future rather than a golden past.

What is important about Jewish political terminology is not only that it exists in such abundance, had its origins in the very earliest epochs of Jewish history, and has remained extraordinarily consistent in meaning for some three millenia, but that it is so thoroughly rooted conceptually in the covenantal worldview which pervades the Jewish political tradition. Not only are there so many obvious covenantal terms of political import (e.g., *brit* and *hesed*—see later text), but other terms whose covenantal dimension is not usually recognized until they are examined more deeply also abound (e.g., *edah*, *haver*, *va'ad*—see later text). In other words, Hebrew is permeated with covenantal echoes, and nowhere more so than in its political vocabulary.[21]

Brit and *Hesed*: The Covenant or Federal Base

The Jewish political tradition, like every other political tradition, is concerned with the question of power and justice, but it differs from the political traditions growing out of classic Greek thought in that it begins with a concern for relationships rather than structures. More specifically, it is less concerned with the best structure for the best regime than with the proper relationships between power and justice, the governors and the governed, and God and man. This orientation is embodied in the principle of covenant that lies at the root of the Jewish political tradition and gives the tradition its form. A covenant in its very essence deals with the definition of relationships; hence the Jewish covenantal orientation properly serves as the basis for defining all political relationships within the Jewish tradition.[22]

Covenant theology has become sufficiently common coin in the last two decades in Jewish circles that the idea itself is hardly foreign even to those who were brought up in a different generation of Jewish intellectual endeavor when that vital aspect of the biblical teaching was overlooked.[23] What is suggested here is that there is a strong political dimension to the covenant idea and that covenants themselves have consistently served as the principal instruments for shaping Jewish political institutions and relationships.

Like all great ideas, the basic simplicity of the covenant idea masks important complexities. The term *brit* (covenant) conveys the sense of both separation and linkage, cutting and binding.[24] A covenant creates a perpetual (or at least indefinitely continuing) bond between parties having independent but not necessarily equal status. That bond is based upon mutual obligations and a commitment to undertake joint action to achieve certain defined ends which may be limited or comprehensive, under conditions of mutual respect in such a way as to protect the fundamental integrity of all parties involved.

A covenant is much more than a contract—though our modern system of contracts is related to the covenant idea—because it involves a pledge of loyalty beyond that demanded for mutual advantage, often involving the development of a certain kind of community among the partners to the covenant, and ultimately based upon a moral commitment. In its classic form, it is also more than a compact because God is either a party to it or its witness and guarantor. In that sense, a covenant creates a holy or Divinely sanctioned community or partnership based upon a firm, constitutionally defined relationship delineating the authority, power, and integrity of each of the partners.

The prophet Ezekiel referred to *masoret ha-brit*—the covenant tradition (or bond)—as the central thread of Jewish existence (Ezek. 20:35–37). In his highly sensitive commentary to the Bible, the *Malbim* (Meir Loeb ben Yeḥiel Michael, 1809–1879) offers us a good summary of the covenantal relationship between God and Abraham described in Genesis 17:

> This covenant will be "between Me and thee," meaning that the binding obligation rests on both parties to the covenant, because Abraham also obligated himself to be a partner with God in the act of creation by perfecting what was created and by participating in its improvement. [*Ha-Torah ve-ha-Mitzvah*, I, 68]

This deceptively simple idea is of great importance because of what it offers in the way of building relationships. The Bible posits, describes, and develops a whole system of relationships based upon covenants, some of which, it is suggested, were actual covenants between God and mankind and some of which seem to be figurative covenants between God and inanimate objects such as the heavenly bodies.[25] Inevitably present within the covenant idea is the sense of a contractual partnership in which the partners must, by definition, share in the implementation of certain common tasks and at the same time are able to preserve their respective integrities while doing so. In some cases the partners are equals. In some cases they are unequals. Obviously covenants between God and man, even between God and Israel, ultimately are covenants among unequals, but the very idea that a covenantal relationship can be established between God and man is quite radical. The covenant idea inevitably suggests that God limits Himself drastically by recognizing the freedom of humans to contract an obligation with Him and to maintain their own integrities while doing so, not simply to obey Him but to hearken to His word as covenant partners. The implications of this are developed in the biblical and rabbinic literature to suggest that, in matters of *tikkun olam*, God and man are equal, under the terms of the *brit*. Indeed, covenanted people are then required to choose whether or not to live up to the terms of the covenant.

The Puritans understood this when they developed their interpretation of the covenantal basis of the biblical worldview as the *federal theology* ("federal" is derived from the Latin term *foedus*, meaning "covenant"), which emphasizes that the same covenant that tightly binds man to God, on one hand, also radically emancipates humanity and enables it to act on its own accord.[26]

The covenant as a political instrument resembles the social compact of the seventeenth-century philosophers except that it is not secular in character. Indeed, the seventeenth-century philosophers developed the social compact theory by taking the covenant idea and secularizing it. Both represent initial political acts which create the conditions of polity under which constitutions and regimes can be instituted. The Sinai covenant, for example, transformed the Jewish people from a family of tribes into a body politic which could then proceed to develop a constitution and a regime. Chapters 18–20 of the Book of Exodus provide us with a clear picture of this process. On one hand, they describe the covenant that institutionalized the fundamental relationship between God and Israel which was necessary actually to create a new body politic in which God assumed the responsibility for direct rule over Israel. On the other hand, the organization of the regime is portrayed as coming from a distinctly non-Divine source. It came partly from the inherited tradition of tribal government and partly from Jethro, Moses' father-in-law, who suggested the organization which the national government should take.

That these two stories are intertwined and placed parallel to one another suggests that the political basis for the constitution is the covenant, which is the equivalent of a social compact. But the covenant did not dictate or establish the organization of the regime. The latter was derived from a human source who was not even Israelite, on the basis of necessity and convenience. This is the pattern of interaction between regime and covenant throughout Jewish political history. On one hand there is the continuity of the fundamental covenant and the constitution which flows from it, the Torah, with the oral Torah building the body of constitutional law. On the other hand, within the latitude established by the Torah, Jews are free to adopt the regime they wish and have adapted themselves to different historical situations and conditions accordingly. Thus, the interaction between the two elements is a continuing one. The model of this post-Sinai interaction is to be found in the Book of Joshua, chapters 8 and 24, where covenanting acts take place and the regime is reestablished after the conquest of the land. The Bible itself contains at least five others.

Jewish political institutions and behavior reflect this covenantal base in the way they give expression to the concepts of political relationships as the embodiment of a partnership based upon a morally grounded compact and, like all partnerships, oriented toward decision- and policy-making through negotiation and bargaining. Here the concept of *hesed* (covenant obligation) plays

a crucial role in providing the basis for the operational dynamics of the covenant relationship, requiring a wide and generous response among *bnei brit*
(covenant partners) and blocking a natural human inclination in contractual
situations to interpret contractual obligations as narrowly as possible. The requirement that covenant partners act with *hesed* to one another is presented in
the Bible as beginning with God's relationship to Israel. Humans who display
the same characteristics become known, in Jewish tradition, as *hasidim* if they
are Jews and *hasidei ummot ha-olam* (*hasidim* of the nations of the world) if
they are not.

Beyond that, wherever the possibility has existed, Jews have organized their
political institutions on a federal basis, whether in the form of the ancient
tribal confederacy; the Hellenistic politeuma and the loose confederation of
diaspora communities in the Roman Empire: the medieval confederations of
local communities; the Council of the Four Lands; the communal federations
of the contemporary diaspora based on country-of-origin communities, the
internal political structure of their countries of residence, or federations of
functional agencies; or the party and settlement federations in modern Israel—
to cite only a few of the most prominent examples.[27]

Thus the Jewish political tradition can be said to be federal in its fundamental orientation.[28] For that reason, a variety of structures are animated and informed by federal principles. Jewish history attests to this. In many cases,
these structures were characterized by a lack or minimum of central institutions but this did not prevent a great deal of unified action because of common interests and, most important, a shared law, constitution, and political
tradition. Federal arrangements are, by their very nature, multicentered and
do not rely upon the kind of centralized mechanisms associated with the modern nation-state.[29]

Edah and *Kahal*: The Republican Base

The covenant not only transformed a *goy*—primarily a kinship group with its
own land and culture—into an *am*—kinship groups united through some vocation—but the *'am* became an *edah*—a body politic based on consent. The
term literally implies an assembly of all citizens that meets at regular times or
frequently. Even in the earliest period it became the Hebrew equivalent of
"commonwealth" or "republic" (in the original sense of *res publica*—a public
thing—rather than the private preserve of any person), with strong democratic
overtones. The idea of the Jewish people as an *edah* has persisted ever since.

Weinfeld has argued that the term *edah* actually described the regime prior
to the introduction of the monarchy.[30] In this respect it parallels (and historically precedes) similar phenomena such as the *landesgemeinde* in Switzerland, the Icelandic *althing*, and the town meeting in the United States. What
is crucial is that it continued to be used to describe the Jewish body politic in

every period down to the present. Only in contemporary Israel has the term lost its authentic meaning to become a sociological expression intentionally devoid of political content.

The characteristics of the original *edah* can be summarized as follows:

1. Political equality existed for those capable of bearing arms.
2. Decisions were made by an assembly that determined its own leaders.
3. The *edah* was portable and transcended geography.
4. Nevertheless, for it to function completely, the *edah* needed Eretz Israel.
5. The Torah was the constitution of the *edah*.

These basic characteristics have been preserved with a minimum of modification over the centuries. At one point, the arms-bearing measure of political equality gave way to one of Torah study and today is in flux as a referent. The principles of assembly, leadership, and decision-making have remained the same although modes of assembling, leadership recruitment, and leaders' roles and responsibilities have changed from time to time. The portability of the desert-born *edah* is as notable a characteristic as is its attachment to Zion. And, as will be shown in this volume, the Torah has persisted as constitution however interpreted. Indeed, the central theme of this book is the tracing out of the practical application of these characteristics in different epochs and locales.

The documentary literature of every age is full of the classic usage of the term *edah*. Moreover, that body was invariably defined as including all adult males as participants in fundamental decision-making. At the very least, the *edah* as a whole was responsible for actions of a constitutional character whether electing kings in ancient Israel, constituting the Council of the Four Lands in medieval Poland, or forming communities in the modern United States. The *edah* offered a variety of adaptations of covenantal principles, with a new one for each new era of Jewish political adjustment. A high point was reached in the Jewish communities of the Middle Ages. The congregational form itself—the *kahal* or *kehillah*—is a subsidiary product of the linkage of the covenant and the *edah*. Any ten male Jews may come together to form a *kahal* by covenanting among themselves to create a local framework (within the larger framework of the Torah) for the conduct of their religious, social, and political life. Even the terminology of congregational organization reflects its covenant orientation. Among Sephardic communities, for example, the articles of agreement establishing congregations are known as *askamot*—a term that has an explicitly covenantal derivation and significance. Thus the term *kahal*, used almost synonymously with *edah* in the Bible, became the terminological subsidiary of *edah*—the *edah* in its constituted local dimension.

The fundamental equality of the *edah* should not obscure the fact that the Jewish political tradition has a strong aristocratic current, not in the sense of aristocracy as a political structure but as a relationship whereby those who hold powers of government are trustees for both the people and the Torah, selected on the basis of some qualifications to be trustees—Divine sanctification, scholarship, lineage, or wealth. In the last analysis, however, the Jewish political tradition is based upon what S. D. Goitein has termed "religious democracy," using the term *religious* in its original sense of "binding" (cf. *masoret ha-brit*). It emphasizes a tripartite division of powers: between God (through His spokesmen or deputies), the citizenry, and the human governors empowered under the particular regime in operation at the time.[31]

Edah, Medinah, and *Kehillah*:
The Arenas of Jewish Political Organization

From earliest times, the Jewish polity has been organized in three arenas: generally definable as national, regional or intermediate, and local. The Bible delineates the first form in which these three arenas were constituted, nationally in the form of the *edah*, which was constituted by the *shevatim* (*shevet*= tribe), each with its own governmental institutions. Each *shevet* was, in turn, a union of *batei av* (*bet av*=extended household). After the Israelite settlement in Canaan, the most prominent form of local organization was the *ir* (city or township) with its own assembly (*ha-ir*) and council (*sh'ar ha-ir* or *ziknei ha-ir*).

This threefold division into separate arenas of governance, once formulated in early Israelite history, has remained a permanent feature of Jewish political life. This is so despite frequent changes in the forms of organization of the several arenas and in the terminology used to describe them. Thus just as the *bet av* gave way to the *ir*, the latter gave way to the *kehillah* (local community) in later epochs. In turn, the *kehillah* became the molecular unit of organization for all postbiblical Jewry, especially since one could be established by any ten adult Jewish males who so constituted themselves. While the *kehillah* survives in the diaspora, in contemporary Israel it has once again reemerged as an *ir*.

Similarly, the breakdown of the traditional tribal system (a phenomenon which long preceded the first exile) resulted in the replacement of the *shevet* by the *medinah* (properly rendered as autonomous jurisdiction or province in its original usage), a regional framework which embraces a congeries of *kehillot* which it unites within an organizational structure, as in *Medinat Yehud* (Judea in the Persian Empire). In the diaspora, *medinah* became virtually interchangeable with *eretz* (country) to describe the intermediate arena, as in *Eretz Lita* (the organized Jewish community in late medieval Lithuania). In modern times, the term came to mean a politically sovereign state and is presently used in connection with *Medinat Yisrael* (the State of Israel).

The most obvious difference between the three arenas of government here outlined lies in their contrasting geographic dimensions. By definition, no *kehillah* can encompass an area of jurisdiction larger than that of its own *medinah*; neither can any single *medinah* be broader than the *edah*. More difficult to define, however, is the precise nature of the relationship between these arenas. Actions of constitutional import taken by and for the *edah* as a whole are binding on every one of its constituent parts. One illustration of this rule is provided by the connected biblical narratives relating to the settlement of the two and a half tribes on the eastern bank of the Jordan (Num. 32 and Josh. 22). It is significant that the initial approach, by the Reubenites and Gadites, was to Moses, Elazar the priest, and the *nesi'im* tribal magistrates (Num. 32:2). Similarly, it was in the name of *Adat Adonai*, "The Congregation of the Lord," that the two and a half tribes were subsequently upbraided for the construction of an altar on their way home from Joshua's wars. At issue, as Josh. 22:16–20 makes explicit, was the contention that the original commitment to worship the one God had been undertaken by the entire *edah* and that the entire *edah* would be held responsible for any violation—even if it be on the part of a minority. The system is not, however, a hierarchy and certainly not centralized—in the sense that all the important lines of political communication and decision-making are controlled by a unitary government transmitting its directives through a clearly stratified system of regional and local instruments. Rather, the *edah* is a framing institution which, among its various tasks, establishes boundary rules for the pursuit of political objectives but leaves to its constituent parts considerable leeway in the conduct of their political affairs. Individual *medinot* and *kehillot* are not merely creatures of the *edah*. Like the *edah*, they derive their authority directly from the series of covenants periodically entered into by God and the entire Jewish people. That is why, to quote another biblical example, Divine sanction could be granted for secession from an overweening centralized monarchy[32] and why, during the High Middle Ages, individual communities could enact highly particularistic *takkanot ha-kahal* (communal ordinances). Moreover, and notwithstanding the very special place alloted to Eretz Israel in all Jewish thought, the preeminence of that *medinah* in matters constitutional has never been taken for granted. On the contrary, it proved to be a bone of serious contention in talmudic times, as in our own.[33]

Of the many implications of this organizational framework, the most important is that the traditional system of Jewish government might best be described as a matrix rather than a pyramid. It does not posit "high" and "low" power centers, with gradations of power flowing down from the top (or out from the center). Rather, it forms a matrix of larger and smaller arenas of authority, linked through common adherence to a single recognized constitutional framework and through formal and informal lines of mutual communication. Furthermore, it is the texture of the lines of communication between and within the various arenas which has, over the long haul, provided the Jewish system of government with the flexibility necessary to its stability and resilience. Since the system was not dependent on the rigid maintenance of any single central institution, it did not disintegrate the moment any individual locus of power was destroyed (as happened when the first two Jewish commonwealths were destroyed) or withered away (the fate of the subsequent *Nesi'ut* in Eretz Israel and the *Ga'onut* of Bavel [Babylonia]). These were undoubtedly severe blows to the Jewish polity, but they did not prove fatal because the *edah*'s survival had never been dependent on such mechanisms.

As much was indicated, to take a more positive example, during the eleventh epoch of Jewish constitutional history (eleventh–fourteenth centuries CE), when the older seats of jurisdiction in Bavel and Eretz Israel lost all authority outside their immediate geographic perimeter and before the newer centers of Sepharad (the Iberian Peninsula) and Ashkenaz (West-Central Europe) had developed substitute widely embracing organizational frameworks. The fact that institutional authority was in this epoch vested almost exclusively in the *kehillah* did not vitiate the continuity of the *edah*. The "nerves" of the system, which are ultimately far more important prerequisites of its successful functioning, continued to exist. Indeed, it was precisely during this epoch that they flourished, with *halakhic* (legal-religious) correspondence between individual *posekim* (literally, "arbiters"; authorities) serving as a communications network of extraordinary efficiency and repute.

This organizational framework thus differs from the models of centralization and decentralization dominant in much of the current literature of political science. Instead, it posits the appropriate adoption of the perspective of noncentralization, which has been found to be characteristic of all federal systems based—as in the Jewish tradition—on the notion of a covenantal relationship between its partners. In this scheme of things, the diffusion of power is not a matter of grace (dependent upon the whim—or weakness—of a central authority); rather it is a matter of right. The rank order of the several arenas of government is deliberately left flexible, allowing the system as a whole to adapt to the changing political circumstances of its environment.[34] The history of the Jewish polity indicates that some concentration of governmental power in the founding institutions of the *edah* may have been permissible; it was never mandatory. Far more entrenched is the tradition whereby authority is spread widely (even if not in equal proportions) among a range of regional authorities, each with the right to independent self-expression.

As a tool of analysis, the matrix model presented here may serve two primary functions. At one level, it can supply a means of monitoring the respective weights of the individual arenas during the various epochs of Jewish constitutional history, helping to explain the forces which affected the balance of power between them and facilitating an examination of the constitutional devices employed in order to sharpen their relationships. Secondly, it helps underscore the flexibility of the Jewish system of governmental organization which—over the long haul—has contributed to its survival.

Reshuyot and *Ketarim*: Delegation and Separation of Powers

The diffusion of power characteristic of the organizational structure of the *edah* is to a large extent mirrored (and amplified) by the traditional insistence on its distribution within the various arenas of government. Here, too, a concentration of political authority (together with the privileges and prerogatives that go with it) is abjured. Every covenantal system true to its fundamental principles will respond in the same way. Whichever the constitutional epoch chosen for examination—and whichever the arena of government within that epoch—its maxim seems to remain the same. Constitutional omnipotence is occasionally and implicitly refused even to God; it is permanently and explicitly denied to man.[35] In principle, the concentration of power is to be avoided and denigrated; its diffusion among various legitimate (or legitimated) government and authorities (*reshuyot*) is to be encouraged and praised.

From the time of the foundation of the *edah* in Sinai, these *reshuyot* have been clustered into three sets of authoritative combinations, each with its own direct source of Divine authority. In the period of the Second Commonwealth, these three authoritative combinations were designated *ketarim*, literally "crowns," an expression of the theory that each represented a separate grant of authority from God through its own covenant.[36]

Following the traditional texts, the Sinai covenant can be understood to have delineated the *keter torah* which passed from the *Eved Adonai* (God's chief minister, e.g., Moses) to the *nevi'im* (prophets) to the *hakhamim* (sages) and *rabbanim* (masters). The covenant with the sons of Aaron established the *keter kehunah* (priesthood) which was located in various Aaronite families until after the destruction of the second temple and which then had to find other vehicles for expression as well. The covenant with David gave the *keter malkhut* (kingship and civil rule), which had been lodged with the *zekenim* (elders) and *nesi'im* (magistrates—lit. those raised up) of the *edah* from earlier times, a natural focal point in the form of a *Melekh* (king), referred to by the *nevi'im* as *Nagid* (God's high commissioner). The history of this *keter* is one of shifting back and forth between a single focal point—a *Melekh*, *Nasi*, or *Rosh* (head)—and one of collective leadership.

The immediate manifestations of the *ketarim* are easily apparent, but each should be understood in its larger significance as well. The *keter torah* is the means of giving programmatic expression to Israel's Divine constitutional teaching. The *keter kehunah* is the means of bringing God and the *edah* into close proximity through shared rituals and symbolic expressions. The *keter malkhut* is the vehicle for civil authority to exercise power within the *edah*. The first tends to flow from God to the people through mediating institutions such as the *navi* (prophet), Torah, or Talmud. The second tends to involve human initiatives directed heavenward. The third emphasizes human political relationships with other humans.

The Mishnaic formulary, our first documentary evidence to identify these three domains as *ketarim*, did not invent a system. Rather, it provided appropriate terminology to a classification which (as the biblical texts indicate) had been in existence ever since the Israelites' sojourn in the desert. That, indeed, is the understanding of subsequent rabbinic sources—several of which frequently and persistently apply the term as an explanatory device when expounding relevant biblical passages.[37] As thus understood, each of the *ketarim* might be seen as a distinct domain of government, with prerogatives laid down in various sets of law-making enunciations. In this scheme, the *keter torah* constitutes the vehicle whereby God's teachings to Israel are interpreted, specified, and transmitted; the *keter kehunah*, the conduit whereby God and the *edah* are brought into constant contact; the *keter malkhut*, the legitimately empowered means whereby civic relationships are structured and regulated in accordance with the covenantal stipulations of the Divinely ordained constitution.

This unique tripartite division of authority allows the Jewish polity to encompass far more than the narrow functions of contemporary political systems. In effect, it embraces means of governance usually associated with tribal societies and voluntary associations, as well as states. Through the three *ketarim*, the multifaceted character of the Jewish people finds political as well as religious expression in a way that constitutionalizes power-sharing. Each *keter* has a share in the governance of the *edah* through institutions and officers empowered by it. Each, however, does so from a different base. Demarcating these combinations are not differences of functions, but of orientation. Indeed, what distinguishes the division of authority among the *ketarim* from conventional separation of powers systems is that the *ketarim* address themselves first to the source, character, and purpose of authority, and only then to issues of function (e.g., executive, legislative, judicial). The latter are usually shared by two or more of the *ketarim* by design, whose distinctions therefore lie less in the needs they each serve than in the perspectives which each of them brings to bear on political activities. Each *keter* is regarded as a mediating institution between God and the *edah* in possession of a distinct focus. This facet enables each *keter* to act as a particular prism on the constitution of the polity and entitles it to exercise a constitutional check on the others.

Of the many implications of this system for a study of Jewish political behavior, two require particular attention: the autonomy of each of the *ketarim* and the interdependence of the tripartite system as a whole. The first finds expression in those texts which stress the intrinsic "sovereignty" of each *keter* (a concept itself nicely conveyed by the generic title). They depict each as wielding—under God—independent authority within its own sphere of jurisdiction. This is the theme underlying the talmudic insistence that none but the *Kohen Gadol* (High Priest), the principal instrument of the *keter kehunah*, may enter the Holy of Holies; that only officers of the *keter malkhut* can lead the *edah* into a battle classified as *milkhemet reshut* (permitted war); and that no constitutional interpretation is valid unless it receives the sanction of accredited representatives of the *keter torah*. The clear implication is that no *keter* possesses a constitutional right to impinge upon the domain of the others, far less to deprive them of their proper constitutional franchises. As much is indicated by the attested circumstances of their creation. These distinctions were further hallowed by the ordained differences in the internal structure of each *keter*.[38] From the first, each possessed its own hierarchy of officers; each, furthermore, instituted its own procedures in order to determine the manner of their legitimate appointment and succession.[39]

Interdependence—the second characteristic of the *ketaric* arrangement—is no less marked a feature of the system. Essentially, this principle conveys the idea that no Jewish polity is constitutionally complete unless it contains representatives of all three *ketarim* in one form or another. They are, indeed, the governmental extensions of the three pillars upon which all society must rest; remove any one and the entire edifice is bound to collapse.[40] They are not, therefore, perceived as severely compartmentalized spheres of jurisdiction, with one (or more) being responsible for matters secular and the other (or others) for matters religious. On the contrary, what characterizes the system in its entirety—indeed, what transposes it into a system—is the insistence that they be seen jointly to participate in the most crucial areas of Jewish governmental life: judicial as well as legislative, military as well as sacerdotal. That is why authorized officers of all three *ketarim* must combine in order to give constitutional effect to acts of political significance—minor as well as major.[41] The proper Jewish polity, is the implication, is that which contains fully articulated and functioning institutions in all three *ketarim*. The good Jewish polity is that in which, furthermore, the balance between the *ketarim* is both buttressed and respected.

In practice, of course, history rarely obliged by conforming to such neat categorization. Consequently, it is difficult—although not altogether impossible—to find examples of occasional moments of ketaric equilibrium.[42] It is far easier to discern lengthy periods of inter-*keter* conflict, when accredited representatives of the *ketarim* vied for a preponderance of political power and the preeminence of their own facet of constitutional interpretation. What has to be noted, nevertheless, is that not even the regularity of such conflicts served to undermine the essential framework of the tripartite structure. For all the vicissitudes of Jewish public life, the basic parameters of the triad seem constantly to have reasserted themselves. Throughout every epoch of Jewish constitutional history, and within virtually every arena of political organization—in the diaspora as well as in Eretz Israel—each of the *ketarim* can be seen to have found some form of expression.

The resilience of the Jewish polity must, in some measure, be attributed to the flexibility and adaptability of all three *ketarim*. Each has, at various points in the course of Jewish constitutional history, effected multiple changes in its institutional structures and operational procedures, inventing and utilizing a rich variety of terms to describe its activities and officers and developing new means of expression within its original terms of reference. Equally important, however, have been the bounds of propriety, maintained by all three *ketarim*—even at periods of great antagonism between them. According to the sources, even when instruments of a particular *keter* have achieved dominance over the others, the dominant *keter* has been careful to maintain the others' existence. There is no record of a single instance of the utter destruction of one *keter* by another (or by a combination of the other two); neither, for that matter, do the sources reveal any real attempt on the part of one *keter* to challenge the legitimate existence or necessity of any other.[43]

What can be discerned, rather, are numerous examples of an attempted process of co-option. Principal instruments of one *keter* attempted (sometimes, and for limited periods, successfully so) to attain commanding authority within the *edah* by posing as the repositories of two domains. By thus amalgamating prerogatives and wearing, as it were, two crowns they have contrived to neutralize the constitutional influence of the third and subject its officers to their own will. It is, however, characteristic of the system that—in so doing—they have provided their opponents with the constitutional ammunition necessary to justify their resistance to such a concentration of political power.[44] Spokesmen for the *keter* which felt itself to be dangerously isolated could specifically appeal to the constitutionally enshrined principles of proper balance. Such was the argument employed, most explicitly, by the Pharisaic opponents of Alexander Yannai; "Suffice yourself with the *keter malkhut*," they exhorted him in a classic exposition of the thesis, "and leave the *keter kehunah* to the descendants of Aaron."[45]

To suggest that such conflicts form part of a wider pattern is not, of course, to ignore the unique circumstances by which each was generated. It is, however, to indicate that they might also be seen as extensions and expressions of a wider pattern, and thus as witnesses to the continuity of Jewish governmental forms and expressions over long periods and across cultural watersheds. Hence the study of the three *ketarim*, the relationships between them, and the changes within them is necessary to gain an understanding of the workings of the Jewish political tradition in its entirety. Indeed, by encouraging the shift of attention from an examination of the immediate motives of particular constitutional conflicts to an understanding of their underlying structure, the concept can be employed as a means of accounting for the recurrence of constitutional tensions which have historically underlined such a large proportion of the intricate gyrations of Jewish politics, both sectional and national.

Significantly, the two great constructive phenomena of twentieth-century Jewry, the reestablishment of a Jewish state in the Land of Israel and the establishment of the great Jewish community in North America, represent interesting and highly significant adaptations of the *brit* and *ketarim* within the *edah*. If one looks at the foundation of the early institutions and settlements of the new *yishuv* (Jewish settlement) in Eretz Israel, one finds that their basis in almost every case was covenantal. Borrowing from the established patterns of congregational *askamot*, they established partnerships and created associations on the basis of formal compacts and constitutional documents. This continued to be the standard form of organization in the Jewish *yishuv* even after the British became the occupying power in the country. The *yishuv* was governed internally through a network of covenants and compacts until the emergence of a centralized state in 1948.[46] Moreover, the Zionist movement implicitly recognized the existence of at least the *keter malkhut* and the *keter torah* even though it sought to capture the former and radically reduce the role of the latter.

In the United States, the organization of congregations follows the traditional form even though the congregations themselves may be untraditional in their religious practices. They continue to embrace the *keter torah* and the *keter kehunah*, if at times in uneasy combination. Similarly, the organization of social agencies and educational institutions and their coming together in local Jewish federations or countrywide confederations as expressions of the *keter malkhut* is simply another extension of what has been the standard pattern of Jewish organization for several millenia.[47] One would be hard put to prove that in either the Israeli or the American case there was an explicit or conscious desire to maintain a particular political tradition. Rather, it was a consequence of the shared political culture of the Jews involved that led to the continuation of the traditional patterns in new adaptations.

Contemporary Israeli and Jewish politics reflect the Jewish political tradition, in its virtues and its vices, good and bad. It is more than a little ironic that in the United States, where the government does not care how Jews organize themselves, so long as they do not try to go beyond certain fundamental constitutional restrictions, this pattern has been able to express itself most fully under contemporary conditions whereas in Israel, where there was a necessity, as it were, to create an authoritative state on the model of the reified nation-state of modern Europe, this process has run into something of a dead-end at the state level, stifled by the strong inclination toward centralized control of every aspect of public life brought by the state's molders and shapers from their European experience.[48]

THE CONSTITUTIONAL PERIODIZATION
OF JEWISH HISTORY

Constitutionalism in the Jewish Political Tradition
Implicit in the foregoing discussion and otherwise a matter of commonsense knowledge is that the *edah* has gone through periodic regime changes in the

course of Jewish history. The key to understanding those changes is to be found in the pattern of constitutional development of the Jewish people and its polity. Indeed, it is not too bold to suggest that Jewish history can be read as the progression of the generations through a series of historical epochs, each marked by the unfolding and subsequent undoing of its own constitutional synthesis within the overall framework of the Torah, leading in turn to a new epoch and the necessity for a new constitutional synthesis. It has been the genius of the Jews as *am* and *edah* to keep the flow of generations intact via those periodic reconstitutions, through exile and dispersion. Hence the issue of constitutionalism and constitutional change is central to the study of Jewish political history in its entirety and provides a base for its periodization. Basically, this is because the Jewish constitution has differed from modern constitutions, most significantly because of its all-embracing character. It is not confined to the delineation of the political power of a secular society, but extends into virtually all phases of life. A study of constitutionalism in Jewish history, accordingly, must embrace far more than the record of specific fundamental political laws. A reconstruction of the communal constitution of any particular period of Jewish history must come to terms with the entire range of communal living during that time and thereby provide a framework that can encompass virtually all aspects of Jewish civilization.[49]

The Torah is, in this respect, both an exemplar and a touchstone. It contains all the characteristics of organic and all-embracing law; it has also (for the vast majority of Jewish history and by the vast majority of the Jewish people) been perceived to be of Divine origin. On both counts, the Torah must be regarded as the basic and foremost constitutional document of Jewish history. Its subsequent modifications and/or amplifications must, therefore, be considered to have been necessitated by overwhelming pressures for constitutional change. All subsequent constitutional referents claim, whether explicitly or implicitly, to maintain the traditions embodied in the Torah; but all nevertheless do so in a manner which supplements and redirects the original in line with the pressures of contemporary conditions. The *Mishnah, Gemara,* and the great halakhic codes (to cite only a few such documents) thus constitute indices for the identification and analysis of such adjustments and an explanatory device for relating the change from one epoch to another. Indeed, the Torah-as-constitution can be understood as a kind of nucleus to whose original core have been added layers of additional material, each of which becomes compacted into the original to the point where it is bonded to it permanently and there is no operational difference between earlier and later materials even where it is possible to distinguish between them.

At the same time, the Torah is a uniquely Jewish constitution in that it is first and foremost a teaching, as the word Torah itself indicates. Although binding on Jews through the Sinai covenant, as a teaching it is based on the recognition that, in a covenantal system, its binding character still requires consent. Jews must hearken to their constitutional teaching, and since hearkening begins with hearing, they must be rendered open to hearing. In Jewish tradition, this openness comes as a result of learning, not by nature or grace. This characteristic of the Jewish constitution is reflected, inter alia, in the use of terms which refer to teaching to describe the most important constitutional referents, e.g., *Torah, Mishneh Torah* (Deuteronomy), *Mishnah, Gemara, Talmud.*

The idea of Jewish history as constitutional history is not new, just as explicit reference to the Torah as the fundamental constitution of the *edah* is at least as old as Philo and Josephus.[50] Applying this idea in the special way in which the constitution of the Jewish people embraces more than fundamental political law, it is possible to discuss meaningfully constitutions and constitutionalism in Jewish history. Indeed, the principal value of the constitutional approach to the study of Jewish history lies in its ability to provide a framework that can embrace virtually every aspect of Jewish life without either deemphasizing or overemphasizing the political dimension.

What is distinctive about this approach is its deliberate emphasis on the political facet of Jewish history. Accordingly, it is not bound by conventional historiographical categories. Most conspicuously is this so in the thorny matter of chronological divisions. The traditional breakdown into "ancient," "medieval," and "modern" periods is superseded by a more refined typology based on the rhythm of political life; so, too, is the less obtuse (but hardly more helpful) division into standard subperiods: "biblical," "postbiblical"; "talmudic," "post-talmudic"; "premodern," "modern," and the like.

Patterns of Constitutional Development

We begin, then, by distinguishing periods of constitution-making and constitutional change in the course of Jewish history on the basis of the Jewish response, or series of connected responses, to challenges from within or without the *edah*. In doing so, we can rely first on recognized constitutional texts and the benchmarks of Jewish political history and constitutional development, noting how they relate to one another. Out of those relationships temporal patterns emerge, with each period representing a particular rhythm of challenge and response. Once that rhythm is identified, the framework within which it moves—and which it modifies—can be identified as well. Each epoch is not only characterized by its constitutional synthesis but also by particular institutional expressions of that synthesis. Each is set off by founding, climactic, and culminating events which set its constitutional agenda, bring that agenda to whatever degree of fruition is achieved, and tie off the epoch's loose ends in such a way as to start the movement toward a new constitutional agenda for a new epoch.

Constitutions are changed or modified only as the necessity for change becomes overwhelming. In the Jewish polity this is particularly true because of the traditionally Divine nature of Jewish fundamental law. Hence these epochal transitions occur relatively infrequently. By tracing the subsequent constitutional modifications of the Torah which supplemented and redirected the original Torah in line with the demands of later ages, we posit that Jewish history can be divided into fourteen constitutional epochs, each of approximately three centuries' duration and each of which can be seen to possess a distinct political character of its own, as follows:

1. *Ha-Avot*/The Forefathers	c. 1850–c. 1570 BCE	
2. *Avdut Miẓrayim*/Egyptian Bondage	c. 1570–c. 1280 BCE	
3. *Adat Bnei Yisrael*/The Congregation of Israelites	c. 1280–1004 BCE	
4. *Brit ha-Melukhah*/The Federal Monarchy	1004–721 BCE	
5. *Malkhut Yehudah*/The Kingdom of Judah	721–440 BCE	
6. *Knesset ha-Gedolah*/The Great Assembly	440–145 BCE	
7. *Ḥever ha-Yehudim*/The Jewish Commonwealth	145 BCE–140 CE	
8. *Sanhedrin u-Nesi'ut*/The Sanhedrin and the Patriarchate	140–429 CE	
9. *Ha-Yeshivot ve-Rashei ha-Golah*/The Yeshivot and Exilarchs	429–748 CE	
10. *Yeshivot ve-Geonim*/Yeshivot and the Geonim	748–1038 CE	
11. *Ha-Kehillot*/The *Kehillot*	1038–1348 CE	
12. *Ha-Va'adim*/Federations of the *Kehillot*	1348–1648 CE	
13. *Hitagduyot*/Voluntary Associations	1648–1948 CE	
14. *Medinah ve-Am*/State and People	1948– CE	

Table 1 lists the fourteen constitutional epochs of Jewish history as delineated in accordance with the above criteria, also supplying the dates of each epoch, its principal constitutional referents, and dominant events of political significance.

The thirteen epochs that have been completed were remarkably uniform in duration. Each epoch extended over nine historical generations (the years available to mature humans for participation in public affairs), between 25 and 40 years in length. The shortest epochs were approximately 280 years in length and the longest 320. This seems to indicate rise and decline of historical epochs within a similar general pattern. Each of these epochs corresponds with parallel periods of general history which had their impact on the Jewish people, but what is of the essence in this scheme is the Jewish response to whatever challenges are posed, external as well as internal. Indeed, its emphasis on the internal Jewish rhythm of events is one of the marks of its authenticity. Significantly, the pattern itself is suggested in the Torah, which marks off epochs on a similar basis, i.e., ten generations from Adam to Noah

Table 1 The Constitutional Periodization of Jewish History

Epoch	Dates BCE	Constitution	Founding Events	Climactic Events	Culminating Events
1. *Ha-Avot*/ The Forefathers	c. 1850–c. 1570	Abraham's covenant	Abraham migrates to Canaan	Jacob becomes Israel	Descent to Egypt
2. *Avdut Mizrayim*/ Egyptian Bondage	c. 1570–c. 1280	Patriarchal covenant as reaffirmed	Settlement in Goshen	Egyptian slavery	Exodus
3. *Adat Bnei Yisrael*/ The Congregation of Israelites	c. 1280–1004	Mosaic Torah	Sinai	Gideon rejects kingship	David accepted as king
4. *Brit Ha-Melukhah*/ The Federal Monarchy	1004–721	Covenants of kingship	David's kingship	Division of kingdom	Destruction of Israel
5. *Malkhut Yehudah*/ The Kingdom of Judah	721–440	Deuteronomy	Judean rule consolidated	Josianic reform	Abortive restoration of monarchy
6. *Knesset Ha-Gedolah*/ The Great Assembly	440–145	Ezra/Nehemiah Covenant	Ezra restoration	Shift to Hellenistic world	Hasmonean revolt
7. *Ḥever Ha-Yehudim*/ The Jewish Commonwealth	145 BCE– 140 CE	Oral tradition (Torah)	Hasmonean kingship	Destruction of Temple	Bar Kochba Rebellion

	CE				
8. Sanhedrin U-Nesi'ut/ The Sanhedrin and the Patriarchate	140–c. 425	Mishnah	Organization of Mishnah/Renewal of Exilarchate	Christian ascendancy established anti-Jewish policy	End of Patriarchate
9. Ha-Yeshivot ve-Rashei Ha-Golah/ The Yeshivot and Exilarchs	c. 425–c. 750	Gemara	Completion of Gemara	Jews come under Islam	Reunification of Jews under Islamic rule
10. Yeshivot ve-Geonim/ Yeshivot and Geonim	c. 750–1038	Talmud and codes	Geonim and first codes	Last Israel-Babylonian controversy	End of Gaonate
11. Ha-Kehillot/ The Kehillot	1038–1348	Constitutional responsa	Passage of hegemony to Europe	Kabbalah in Spain. Reestablishment of Jewish settlement in Jerusalem	Black Death massacres
12. Ha-Va'adim/ Federations of Kehillot	1348–1648	Arba'ah Turim	Polish Jewry's charters. Council of Aragonese community	Spanish expulsion and aftermath	Sabbatean movement
13. Hitagduyot/ Voluntary Associations	1648–1948	Shulhan Arukh	Rise of Modernism	Emancipation	The Holocaust
14. Medinah Ve-Am/ State and People	1948–	?	Establishment of state of Israel	?	?

(nine preflood and then the generation of the new founding), ten more from Noah to Abraham, 322 years from the birth of Abraham to the death of Jacob, ten generations in Egyptian bondage, and ten more from Moses to David.

The Generational Rhythm

The structure of each constitutional epoch reflects the generational rhythm of human affairs. Man's own biological heritage provides him with a natural measure of time. We often use the concept of the generation in a common-sense way for just that purpose, as when we talk about the "lost generation" or the "generation gap." In fact, social time does move in sufficiently precise generational units to account for the rhythm of social and political action. If we look closely and carefully, we can map the internal structure of each generation in any particular civil society and chart the relations among generations so as to formulate a coherent picture of the historical patterns of its politics.[51]

During a period rarely, if ever, less than twenty-five and rarely, if ever, more than forty years, averaging thirty to thirty-five, most people will move through the productive phase of their life cycles and then pass into retirement, turning their places over to others. Every individual begins life with childhood, a period of dependency in which his role as an independent actor is extremely limited. Depending upon the average life expectancy of his society, he begins to assume an active role as a member of society sometime between the ages of sixteen and thirty—at which point he has between twenty-five and forty years of "active life" ahead of him during which he is responsible for such economic, social, and political roles as are given to mature men and women in his society. Sometime between the ages of sixty and seventy-five, if he is still alive, he is relieved of those responsibilities and is by convention, if not physically, considered ready for retirement.

Human political life reflects this generational pattern on both an individual and a collective basis. For the first eighteen or more years of life, an individual is essentially powerless from the political point of view. Most people reach their thirties before assuming positions of responsibility of any significance on the larger political scene. It is only then that they become serious contenders for political power and, with good fortune, are able to replace incumbent power holders who depart from the scene as a result of physical or political death (which may be defined as the ending of one's serious political career without suffering actual death). By and large the years from one's thirties into one's sixties represent the period in which the potential for political influence is at its maximum. A few people begin to exercise influence earlier and some very exceptional people remain political leaders longer, but rare indeed is a political career that exceeds forty years of meaningful influence past one's apprenticeship.

Because political beginnings occur in history from time to time, they establish a much greater regularity of generational succession in social and political life than the random processes of human biology. Biology taken alone should lead to a constant "changing of the guard" because births and deaths constantly occur. In fact, the biological basis for the progression of generations is modified by historical and social processes—what may be termed factors of geo-historical location. These regularities reflect the influence of founding— of peoples, civil societies, and polities—on human events. Stated simply, foundings as beginnings establish a more or less orderly pattern of generational succession because founders are generally people at the threshhold of their public careers. In the course of founding the new entity, they not only establish the institutions, offices, and roles to be filled but become the first incumbents, remaining in those positions of authority and power until retirement, a generation later. Only when they vacate their positions can a new generation occupy them and, since they generally start together, their retirement tends to come at the same time, thereby opening the way for beginning the process all over again. Given sufficient data, we could probably trace the generational cycles and patterns back to the very foundations of organized society. In the United States, for example, a society whose foundings are recorded in detail, we can do just that.

Such changes as occur in any society are intimately tied to the progression of historical generations. Each new generation to assume the reins of power is necessarily a product of different influences and in a historical society (as distinct from a preliterate or primitive one), is shaped to respond to different problems, heightening the impact of the change and encouraging new political action to assimilate the changes into their lives. At the same time, the fact that three or (at the most) four biological generations are alive at any given time creates certain linkages between generations (e.g., the influence of grandparents on grandchildren) that ensure a measure of intergenerational contacts and social continuity and also help shape every generation's perception of its past and future.

Here we come to the linkage between generations of people and generational patterns of events. Any particular event is the end product of the coming together of myriad causal chains; yet a careful and systematic review of history reveals that, for whatever reasons, those end products of similar contextual import which at first glance seem to be "accidents" occur at appropriate points within the generational time-forms.

Within each generation, there is a more or less regular progression of political events revolving around the development of a particular set of challenges and responses that gives the generation its particular character. While the shape of the challenges may be determined by external—or environmental— forces, the mode of handling those challenges and the shape of the response is primarily determined internally. A generalized map of the pattern of challenge and response within each generation will look something like this: the "border" between the old and the new generations is marked by several decisive political actions, often involving constitutional change, whose characteristic feature is the simultaneous completion of the major responses of the old generation and the opening of new directions, challenges, and opportunities for the new one. The first half of the new generation is a time for recognizing the new challenges, confronting them and the issues they raise, and developing and testing proposals for political action to meet them. At the same time, it is a period of population change—perhaps five years into the new generation the people who have reached majority after it began outnumber those who had reached majority in the previous generation. Moreover, previous leaders pass from the scene of political activity and new ones come into it. During that period, there occur the generation's expressions of public will that point it in the direction which the responses will take, generally by raising leaders to office who have indicated that they are ready to respond to the generation's developing challenges. In fact, the responses build up in a diffuse way in various public quarters while the challenge is coming to public attention, and only after it has been tested in many quarters does it emerge as a concentrated national effort.

The second half of the generation begins with a great effort to respond to the now-recognized challenges. That effort lasts for three to five years. The remainder of the generation is then occupied with digesting the results of that response, modifying those results so that they will achieve greater success, and at the same time integrating them into the polity's overall fabric. The end of the generation is marked by political acts that both ratify and codify its accomplishments while also serving to open up the issues of the next generation. By that time, voices calling for political responses to new challenges are already beginning to be recognized.

As suggested above, individual generations not only have their own integrity but combine to become the building blocks of historical epochs. Each epoch follows a process of constitutional development which parallels the intragenerational process of political change. A review of Jewish constitutional history indicates how this process works. A specific constitutional framework—at first the Torah and in subsequent epochs structured elaborations or restatements of the Torah—emerges at the beginning of the epoch, based on a Jewish response to the needs of the age and locale, usually embodied in a critical series of events. With the exception of the second, each of the first seven epochs was inaugurated in its first generation by a formal covenant involving the people, their leader or leaders, and God, which, beginning with Epoch III, was then followed (approximately a generation later) by the acceptance of a text of constitutional character (Table 2). All but one of the next six epochs were inaugurated by the introduction of a code in some form (see Table 1). This constitutional framework becomes the basis for action and interpretation during the historical period in which it is dominant. The epoch itself unfolds

Table 2   Epochs, Covenants, and Constitutions in Ancient Israel

Epoch	Covenant	Constitution
1. *Ha-Avot*	*Brit bein ha-Betarim* (Abraham's Covenant)	—
2. *Avdut Miẓrayim*	—	*Masoret he-Avot* (Patriarchal Tradition)
3. *Adat Bnei Yisrael*	*Brit Sinai* (Sinai Covenant)	*Torat Moshe* (Mosaic Law)
4. *Brit ha-Melukhah*	*Brit* between David and *Am* before God	*Torat Moshe* and *Mishpat ha-Melekh* (Law of Kingship)
5. *Malkhut Yehudah*	Covenant renewed on *Pesaḥ* by Hezekiah	*Torat Moshe* and *Mishpat ha-Melekh* and Prophetic works
6. *Knesset ha-Gedolah*	*Amanah* (Covenant) of Ezra and Nehemiah	*Torat Moshe* and *Takkanot Ezra ve-ha-Soferim* (Ordinances of Ezra and the Scribes)
7. *Ḥever ha-Yehudim*	*Brit* between Simon the Hasmonean, the *Zekenim*, and the *Am*	*Torat Moshe* and *Torah she-b'al Peh* (Oral Torah)

through a series of generations until, about midway through it, a generation of climactic events occurs. Those events bring out the character and thrust of the epoch and usually are of constitutional significance. The remaining generations in the epoch basically follow the patterns established by the climactic events and the entire epoch comes to an end with a series of culminating events.

During the epoch, a body of interpretations of the Torah, as understood through the constitutional framework established at the epoch's beginning, is developed, reaching its apogee in the climactic generations and thereafter. Then after some three hundred years, new challenges of time and place demand a more thorough revision of the framework. Utilizing the body of interpretations developed since the preceding constitutional revision (some of which already set forth guidelines for the new era), a revision emerges that provides a basis for meeting the new conditions. Then the process begins again. In the course of the epoch, each new revision becomes universal in its application, not confined to the part of the world in which it originated. So far as the local differences need to be considered, they are provided for in the interpretative process, but within the constitutional framework of the time.

Constitutional Architects, Statesmen, and Commentators
While it is tempting to portray the sweep of Jewish political history in the relatively abstract terms of critical events and epochal trends, history is made and constitutions shaped by people. This volume suggests that there are three key types of leadership in matters of constitutional design and development:

1. Constitutional architects: those who played a critical rolé in designing the various constitutional referents and systems of the Jewish polity (e.g., Moses, Ezra, Hillel, R. Meir of Rothenberg)
2. Statesmen: those who implement the constitution and maintain the polity (e.g., Joshua, the Hasmoneans, the leaders of the Zionist movement)
3. Constitutional commentators: those who influence the application of constitutional principles through their discussion of constitutional principles and commentary on the polity's constitutional texts (e.g., most of the prophets, the *tannaim* and *amoraim*, Rashi, Moses Mendelssohn)

Each epoch has produced its own architects, statesmen, and commentators. Indeed, one of the ways in which an epoch is demarcated is through the appearance and work of its constitutional architects, the style and concerns of its statesmen, and the orientation of its constitutional commentators. In the following pages, we can do no more than highlight a few outstanding examples in each category for each epoch.

This brief outline of the constitutional approach to understanding Jewish history has merely touched upon the highlights of Jewish constitutionalism. Much work remains to be done to fill it out. Dates within each epoch must be clarified. Specific constitutional documents and traditions must be placed in proper context. The interaction between the *edah*-wide constitutional framework and the structuring of *medinot* or *aratzot* and local Jewish communities must be explored further. Despite these, and other, remaining difficulties, an understanding of Jewish constitutionalism as the basis for Jewish responses to the stimuli of history will not only shed light on the Jewish past but should provide guidelines for the Jewish future. What follows is a first effort to map the constitutional framework of Jewish political organization, the structure and functions of the *edah*, and its components throughout all the epochs of Jewish history based upon this constitutional perspective.

The Epochs in Outline
The first two epochs, which are by far the most obscure, reflect the biblical traditions of the Patriarchs and the Egyptian bondage. The first (roughly the nineteenth–sixteenth centuries BCE) begins with the covenant with Abraham which marks the first emergence of the Jews as a distinctive entity and culminates with the descent of Jacob's family into Egypt. Under this original covenant, it might be said that the family which later became the Jewish people first began to function as Jews. The operative elements of the constitution

were probably an unwritten set of tribal traditions rather than a written code. This does not lessen its importance as a fundamental organic law which could be, and was, applied and developed as the basis of Jewish life until the time of Moses and the Exodus. The second (roughly the sixteenth–thirteenth centuries BCE) embraces the generations of slavery in Egypt where the descendants of Jacob retained their identity and traditional tribal organization.

The third epoch (c. 1280–1000 BCE) marks the emergence of the Jewish people in its first "national" stage, as an *edah*—a tribal confederacy—and as a religious civilization based on a fundamental organic law, or constitution, the original Mosaic Torah (*Torat Moshe*) that was promulgated at Sinai after the covenant there. Under *Torat Moshe*, the Jewish people conquered Canaan, became conscious of a basic common identity and destiny, and embarked on the road toward national unity under the monotheistic Jewish religious civilization with all that it entailed.

The fourth epoch (1000–722 BCE) begins with the emergence of the first major revision of the Mosaic constitution, the establishment of a federal state under a constitutional monarchy at the time of David. The constitutional form used in this period was the covenant between the people through their tribes and the king before God. Apparently, each new ascendant to the throne had to bind himself to maintain that covenant, which was designed, among other things, to protect the Torah as constitution and the traditional liberties of the tribes.

The division of the kingdom after the death of Solomon changed the framework of the monarchic covenant but did not change its basic constitutional form, particularly since both David and Solomon actually reigned over two separate entities, Judah and Israel. The monarchic constitution continued as a dual one, as it were, existing as the organic law of two related kingdoms, with each developing its own operational variants (e.g., dynastic consistency in Judah). The Bible itself provides illustrations of how the common heritage of the Jewish people was maintained in the twin kingdoms.

The real end of the fourth epoch came with the destruction of the northern kingdom and the formal end of the tribal confederacy. In the southern kingdom, the Davidic dynasty was completely entrenched in a unitary state, whose boundaries were extended by Hezekiah and his successors to include significant portions of Israel. Hezekiah himself acted to reunify the people through a renewal of the *Pesaḥ* (Passover) observance in Jerusalem, a covenantal act. The consolidation of the monarchy and the centralization of political power coincided with the rise of the prophetic tradition in its second form, as a counterweight to king, court, and temple. It was this somewhat revised prophetic tradition which was used by the prophets to review and modify the revised organic law, establishing the fifth epoch (721–440 BCE) as the period in which the Prophetic Torah took form.

The climactic event of the fifth epoch was the Josianic Reform. This important event followed on the heels of a period in which the old constitution had been persistently violated and even abandoned by the powerholders in Judah. It involved a recovenanting between the king, the people, and God under the auspices of the high priest. When the opportunity came for the restoration of the fundamental law, its restorers were able to capitalize on the chaotic situation to revise the constitution so as to include the body of prophetic doctrine that had been progressively developed under the Prophetic Torah. The account of this constitutional reform is embodied in the biblical discussion of the rediscovery of the Book of Deuteronomy. It was this Deuteronomic constitution, as interpreted by the later prophets, which formed the basis for the maintenance of Jewish national existence during the transition from a rooted nation in Judea to an exiled people in Babylonia and back to a new form of nationhood in Judea again. Constitutionally, then, the destruction of the Temple did not mark the end of the epoch. Rather, it enabled the prophets to establish their constitution more firmly without the heavy counterweights of an enthroned king and a temple. The offices of king and high priest continued to exist in exile but lost most of their real power.

It was only with the restoration of the national home in Judea under Persian rule that conditions became sufficiently different from those of the previous epoch to require another constitutional revision, particularly once it became clear that the monarchy would not be restored. Ezra and Nehemiah introduced a fourth revision of the fundamental law as embodied in the Torah and in doing so formally brought the Jewish people into a sixth historical epoch (440–145 BCE). Its founding act was the *Sukkot* (Tabernacles) covenant described in the Bible. The body of interpretations that had developed around the Deuteronomic Constitution to enable it to meet the new national needs was incorporated into the new framework, which was further developed through the *takkanot* (ordinances) of Ezra, the *soferim* (lit. "scribes"), and the *Knesset ha-Gedolah* (Great Assembly). Under the Ezra Torah, new approaches and interpretations were developed to make possible the preservation of the greatest degree of Jewish autonomy feasible under foreign imperial rule.

This constitution and its practical application were sufficient until the Seleucid oppressions that led to the Hasmonean Revolt. That event was, in great part, the result of a constitutional crisis stemming from the attempt by the Seleucids and the Hellenizing Jews to substitute the constitution of a Greek polis for traditional Jewish organic law. In the process of overthrowing Seleucid domination and reestablishing an independent Jewish commonwealth, the sixth modification of the Jewish constitution emerged, established by Simon the *Nasi* by covenant with the people as described in 1 Maccabees, marking the beginning of the seventh epoch in Jewish history (145 BCE– 140 CE). This was the era of the Hasmoneans and the *tannaim*. It was marked by Hasmonean political control so long as Jewish independence continued and the rise of the several Tannaitic parties (the Hasidim, the Pharisees, etc.)

to a position of power in national life and particularly in regard to the constitutional process. By the time the monarchs of the Hasmonean dynasty ceased to reign (some time after they had ceased to rule), Jewish organic law was well concentrated in the hands of the *tannaim* (lit. "masters of teaching"), particularly as they were constituted in the judicial-legislative body known as the *Sanhedrin*. The political upheavals of the epoch led to various regime changes during its course and had far-reaching constitutional implications for the Jewish people. Nevertheless, they were tied together by a coherent and continuous constitutional superstructure throughout.

In this respect, the destruction of the Second Temple may have been the climactic event of the epoch, but was not, in itself, a constitutional change. It provides a good example of how, within the general framework of every epoch, there occur historical events of the highest significance. It is only when such events and the developments surrounding them significantly alter the framework itself that constitutional revision becomes necessary and a new period can be said to replace the old one. Events such as the destruction of the Temple must be understood in that context, even if that reduces their dramatic quality somewhat.

The seventh epoch lasted until the Bar Kokhba revolt put an end to the possibility of a Jewish state, even within the framework of the Roman Empire. At that time, the interpretations of the *tannaim* were put into a systematic framework by R. Akiva which became the basis of the *Mishnah*, which was added to the corpus of Jewish constitutional law early in the eighth epoch (140–429 CE). The new epoch under the Mishnaic constitution featured rule by the *Nesi'im* (mistranslated Patriarchs) and the Sanhedrin. During this epoch, the Jewish community in Eretz Israel came under Byzantine control and began to decline. The Mishnaic constitution served as the basis which eased the transfer of the center of Jewish life and authority to Babylonia and whose interpretations in the process led to the compilation of the Gemara.

The abolition of the office of *Nasi* marked the end of the eighth epoch, while the completion of the Gemara (c. 500 CE) ushered in the ninth (429–748 CE). During the more than three hundred years of this epoch, the definitive text of the Talmud was completed and was applied in a new way, to a diaspora-centered Jewish national life. The completion of the Talmud marked the last all-embracing textual change in the constitutional documents. Subsequent epochs are marked by the development of codes based on the Talmud that included progressively less in the way of basic constitutional modifications.

The first of these periodic codal revisions was embodied in the two codes compiled in the middle of the eighth century in Babylonia, the *Halakhot Pesukot* and the *Halakhot Gedolot*. These two codes have been overlooked as constitutional documents. Despite their modest character as codes, they mark an epochal change in the character of constitutional revision, initiating a thousand years of codes. With them, the period of debate over fundamentals seems to have ended. As the national homeland became more a memory of the past and a hope for the future only, the Jewish constitutionalists felt the need for definitive statements, not permissive discussions. They represent the first constitutional revisions based entirely on a diaspora-centered Jewry, encompassing the interpretations of the early talmudic period and preparing the way for the epoch of the *Geonim* and *Yeshivot* (c. 748–1030 CE). Hence, for the first time, the laws concerning Eretz Israel are omitted while the 613 commandments first appear in that form.

European Jewry, which inherited the mantle of leadership from the Babylonian community, was the source of the next major constitutional revision, which came in the middle of the eleventh century. The first landmark of this revision, which also marked the beginnings of the middle talmudic period, was the *Sefer ha-Halakhot* of R. Isaac Alfasi, the first comprehensive codification of Jewish law. The epoch's high point was marked by the *Mishneh Torah* of Maimonides and the controversy surrounding it. This eleventh epoch lasted from 1038 to 1348 CE.

This epoch brought with it the development of the *kehillah* and a set of constitutional devices used throughout European Jewry to provide a basis for Jewish self-government in the absence of overarching national or even regional political institutions. One of the principal constitutional devices to emerge was the rabbinical responsum as a vehicle for constitutional interpretation. Both were authentically Jewish responses to the new conditions of the High Middle Ages in which the Jews found themselves. In principle, each new *kehillah* was organized as a partnership with the authority of a *bet din* (court authorized to enact ordinances) on the basis of a local covenant which followed a standard halakhic mold.[52]

The twelfth epoch (1348–1648 CE) began with the communal reconstitutions required in the aftermath of the dislocations generated by the Black Death (1348). The principal documentary expressions of the new constitutional epoch were the *Arba'ah Turim*, which established the organization used in all subsequent codifications, including the *Shulḥan Arukh*, and the codifications of communal ordinances in Spain which brought together the basic constitutional framework for Jewish self-government. The Iberian expulsions represented its climactic events. They actually infused new life into Sephardic Jewry, which created its own diaspora including the centers in Safed, Salonika, and Constantinople. By the late seventeenth century, however, the real decline did set in. From that point on, the leadership of world Jewry began to pass to the Ashkenazim.

The culminating events of the epoch revolved around the Sabbatean movement, which brought an end to medieval forms of messianism, on one hand, and opened up new avenues for the succor of individual Jews in new lands, on the other. This transition was marked by another constitutional revision, the last to take place fully within the traditional halakhic framework. It signified

the beginning of the thirteenth epoch in Jewish history (1648–1948 CE), parallel to the modern epoch in world history. Though it is common to date
modern Jewish history from the middle of the eighteenth century, a closer examination of the history of recent centuries strongly indicates that a more accurate reckoning will place the change in the middle of the seventeenth century, when the Jews began to enter western society. Its culmination is to be
found in the Holocaust and the rise of Israel.

The completion of the *Shulḥan Arukh* by R. Joseph Caro and the *Mapah*,
its Ashkenazic modification, by R. Moses Isserles in the latter quarter of the
sixteenth century provided the code for the new epoch, for those who remained within the fold of tradition. These twin documents also marked the
culmination of significant constitutional revision in the halakhic pattern since
they virtually abolished the amending process. This closed pattern was reflected in the period it served, both in the normative Judaism of the era and its
challengers. One result of this was that, parallel to the continued life of the
majority of Jews, Sephardim and Ashkenazim alike, within the framework of
halakhah, there emerged a growing share of world Jewry who lived outside the
framework of *halakhah* and who had to be bound to the Jewish community, if
at all, by different constitutional devices and forms. Emancipation, the climactic event of this period, provided the new direction for more and more
Jews. Moreover, the emancipated Jews increasingly dominated the cutting
edge of Jewish life.

The rise of modern Zionism provided the basis and the actions necessary
for the task. In bringing together the various currents of the nineteenth century and providing a means for reconstitution of the Jewish people in a meaningfully Jewish way to meet the challenges of the modern age, the Zionist
movement initiated a constitutional revolution that is still under way. The
establishment of the State of Israel marked the initiation of a new constitutional and historical epoch in Jewish life, parallel to the postmodern epoch in
world history which began at the same time. For the first time since the collapse of the Second Commonwealth, the basis for inclusion in the Jewish
body politic was something other than *halakhah*; in this case it became Jewish
peoplehood.

It is not yet clear what kind of constitution will emerge from this revolution, but it is likely to take the form of a new covenant of peoplehood. Though
the term is borrowed from Mordecai M. Kaplan, who actually advocated a
formal constitutional convention of world Jewry and the creation of a single
constitutional document on that basis, such a covenant of peoplehood is not
likely to turn on a single constituting event or written document. Rather it is
developing through a series of pacts and procedures which are already becoming identifiable and are given expression through a developing institutional
framework. The results produced by the application of this new constitution
already are visible in Israel and the world Jewish community. Today we are

living in the early stages of the fourteenth epoch of Jewish history, a period which shows every sign of being one of great constitutional and historical change. Nevertheless, revolutionary as it may be, it involves a revision, not an abandonment, of the old constitution.

THE VIRTUES OF THE CONSTITUTIONAL APPROACH TO JEWISH TRADITION

The constitutional approach to Jewish tradition not only reveals a dimension of Jewish life long concealed, real as it has been, but also has the virtue of increasing our overall understanding of Jewish history, law, and tradition. The intellectual constructs of political science applied to the same body of knowledge examined through other disciplines often reveal elements otherwise overlooked for lack of appropriate tools. Thus the framework of analysis applied here allows us to draw out a generally accurate delineation, epoch by epoch, arena by arena, *keter* by *keter*, even where all the details may be lacking in any particular case.

The successful application of these tools is another reflection of the way in which Jewish tradition is prismatic—that is to say, it can be looked at from many perspectives, each revealing its own reality but every one ultimately revealing a common core. It is the very act of looking at all the various planes of the prism which reflects its richness. Conversely, neglect of any of those planes robs us all of a full comprehension of the prism in its entirety.

NOTES

1. The argument of much Zionist history and historiography: see, e.g., H. Fisch, *The Zionist Revolution* (London: Weidenfeld and Nicolson, 1978).
2. There is no classic Jewish text that does not make this point in one way or another. Among the twentieth-century works that illustrate it by reliance on classical sources are Martin Buber, *Kingship of God* (third edition, translated by R. Scheimann; New York: Harper and Row, 1967). Chayim Hirschensohn, *Aileh Divrei ha-Brit* (Hebrew: Biblical Covenants, Their Terms and Their Force), 3 vols. (Haibri Press, 1926–1928). Ella Belfer, *Am Israel u-Malkhut Shamayim—Iyunim ba-Musag ha-Teokratia ha-Yehudit* (Hebrew: The People of Israel and the Kingdom of Heaven—Studies in Jewish Theocracy; Ramat-Gan: Bar-Ilan University, Department of Political Studies, Covenant Working Paper No. 11, 1981).
3. Emanuel Rackman, *One Man's Judaism* (New York: Philosophical Library, 1970). The classical biblical discussion of this idea is to be found in Ezekiel 37.
4. See Daniel J. Elazar, *Israel: From Ideological to Territorial Democracy* (New York: General Learning Press, 1970); "Kinship and Consent in the Jewish Community: Patterns of Continuity in Jewish Communal Life," *Tradition*, vol. 14, no. 4 (Fall 1974), pp. 63–79; and *Covenant as the Basis of the Jewish Political Tradition* (Ramat-Gan: Bar-Ilan University, Department of Political Studies, Covenant Working Paper

No. 1), also in Elazar (ed.), *Kinship and Consent, The Jewish Political Tradition and its Contemporary Manifestations* (Ramat-Gan: Turtledove Publishing, 1981), pp. 21–56. See also Shlomo Avineri, "Israel, Two Nations?" *Midstream*, vol. XVIII, no. 5 (1972).

5. Menachem Elon, *Ha-Mishpat ha-Ivri: Toldotav, Mekorotav, Ekronotav* (Hebrew: Jewish Law: History, Sources, Principles), vol. I (Jerusalem: Magnes Press, 1973), introduction. On the concept of *ḥesed* see, most recently, Katherine Doob Sakenfeld, *The Meaning of Hesed in the Hebrew Bible* (Harvard Semitic Monographs, 17: Missoula, Montana: Scholars Press, 1978).

6. Rabbi Adin Steinsaltz elaborated on these arrangements in a series of still-unpublished lectures delivered at the Van Leer Institute in Jerusalem during 1974–1975. See also Daniel J. Elazar, "Government in Biblical Israel," *Tradition* (Spring-Summer 1973), and *The Kehillah* (Ramat-Gan: Bar-Ilan Department of Political Studies, Covenant Working Paper No. 6, 1977); M. Elon, "On Power and Authority: Halakhic Stance of the Traditional Community and its Contemporary Implications," in Elazar, *Kinship and Consent*, pp. 183–213.

7. Belfer, *Am Israel u-Malkhut Shamayim*.

8. Elazar, *Covenant as the Basis*; Ilan Greilsammer, *Notes on the Concept of Brit* (Ramat-Gan: Bar-Ilan Department of Political Studies, Covenant Working Paper No. 4, 1977); Gordon M. Freeman, "The Rabbinic Understanding of the Covenant as a Political Idea" in Elazar (ed.), *Kinship and Consent*, pp. 59–86.

9. Harold Fisch, *Jerusalem and Albion* (New York: Schocken Books, 1964) and *Covenant with the Devil* (Ramat-Gan: Bar-Ilan Department of Political Studies, Covenant Working Paper No. 9, 1978).

10. Buber, *Kingship of God*, pp. 99–107; Rackman, *One Man's Judaism*; Eliezer Schweid, "The Attitude toward the State in Modern Jewish Thought before Zionism" in Elazar, *Kinship and Consent*, pp. 127–147.

11. Robert Gordis, "Democratic Origins in Ancient Israel—The Biblical Edah," *Alexander Marx Jubilee Volume*, ed. S. Lieberman (New York: Jewish Theological Seminary, 1950), pp. 369–388. Moshe Weinfeld, "From God's Edah to the Chosen Dynasty: The Transition from the Tribal Federation to the Monarchy," in Elazar, *Kinship and Consent*, pp. 151–166.

12. Leo Baeck, *This People Israel: The Meaning of Jewish Existence* (Philadelphia: Jewish Publication Society of America, 1964). Daniel J. Elazar, "Government in Biblical Israel."

13. We are indebted to Gordon Freeman for clarifying this point and its significance.

14. Norman Henry Snaith, "The Covenant Love of God" in *The Distinctive Ideas of the Old Testament* (New York: Schocken Books, 1964), chapter 5.

15. Jacob Katz, *Out of the Ghetto* (Cambridge, Mass.: Harvard University Press, 1973); Michael A. Meyer, *The Origins of the Modern Jew* (Detroit: Wayne State University Press, 1967). Michael Selzer, *The Wineskin and the Wizard: The Problem of Jewish Power in the Context of East European Jewish History* (New York: Macmillan, 1970); Emil Marmorstein, *Heaven at Bay* (Oxford: Clarendon Press, 1969).

16. Cf. Ismar Schorsch, *On the History of the Political Judgment of the Jew* (New York: Leo Baeck Institute, 1979).

17. See Daniel J. Elazar, *The Constitutional Periodization of Jewish History* (Jerusalem: Center for Jewish Community Studies, 1980), and the files of the Jerusalem Center for Public Affairs, Jerusalem.

18. Max Kadushin offers an excellent exposition of Jewish modes of thought in *The Rabbinic Mind* (second edition, New York: Blaidsell Publishing Co., 1965) and *Organic Thinking: A Study in Rabbinic Thought* (New York: Jewish Theological Seminary, 1938).

19. The Jerusalem Center is presently exploring Jewish political terms and their development from the biblical period to the present with a view toward developing a lexicon of Jewish political terminology.

20. Louis Guttman, "An Additive Metric from All the Principal Components of a Perfect Scale," *British Journal of Statistical Psychology*, vol. VIII, part I (1955), pp. 233–278.

21. Cf., for example, Daniel J. Elazar, *The Vocabulary of Covenant* (Philadelphia: Center for the Study of Federalism, 1981).

22. See, e.g., Daniel J. Elazar, *The Covenant Idea in Politics* (CJCS Working Paper No. 22, Jerusalem, 1983).

23. Eugene B. Borowitz, "Covenant Theology," *Commentary*, July 1962, and "Covenant Theology—Another Look," *Worldview*, March 1973.

24. Ruth Gil, *The Covenant in the Bible—Collected Sources*, and Ruth Gil and Yehiel Rosen, *The Covenant in the Tannaic Literature—Collected Sources* (Ramat-Gan: Bar-Ilan Department of Political Studies, Covenant Workshop). See also Moshe Weinfeld, "Covenant," in *Encyclopedia Judaica*, 5:1012–1022.

25. Gil, *The Covenant in the Bible*.

26. Perry Miller, *The New England Mind* (Boston: Beacon Press, 1961), 2 vols., particularly vol. I, book IV, and Appendix B.

27. This argument will be elaborated and illustrated in the course of ensuing chapters. Initial information is scattered throughout Salo W. Baron, *The Jewish Community* (3 vols., New York: 1942); Haim Hillel Ben Sasson (ed.), *A History of the Jewish People* (London: Weidenfeld and Nicolson, 1976); L. Finkelstein, *Jewish Self-Government in the Middle Ages* (New York: Jewish Theological Seminary, 1924).

28. Elazar, "Government in Biblical Israel"; "Covenant as the Basis of the Jewish Political Tradition." Also, P. Ramsay, "Elements of Biblical Theory," *Journal of Religion*, vol. 29 (1949), pp. 258–283.

29. Daniel J. Elazar, *The Ends of Federalism* (Jerusalem: Jerusalem Institute for Federal Studies, J11, 1978).

30. Weinfeld, "From God's Edah to the Chosen Dynasty." The most explicit traditional description of the political dimension of the term is to be found in the biblical commentary by Meir Loeb ben Jehiel Michael (the *Malbim*), *Ha-Torah veha-Mitzvah*, (first edition, Bucharest, 1860), II:241 (commentary to Lev. 4:13).

31. S. D. Goitein, "Political Conflict and the Use of Power in the World of the Geniza," Elazar (ed.), *Kinship and Consent*, pp. 169–182.

32. For a typical reference to this in the traditional literature, see Barukh Epstein, *Torah Temimah*, on Deut. 16:18: "It therefore appears that beside the Sanhedrin appointed for each municipality (*ir*), another Sanhedrin is appointed for each tribe, and they supervise the matters of the members of the tribe—even though they are scattered amongst several municipalities. Thus, every man of Israel has two judges: one from his city, the other from his tribe."

33. See, e.g., the "exchange of views" between David Ben Gurion (prime minister of Israel) and Jacob Blaustein (president of the American Jewish Committee) in *American Jewish Year Book*, 1952 (Philadelphia: Jewish Publication Society, 1952), pp. 564–568.

34. The matrix model and the concept of rim centralization have been developed more fully by Daniel J. Elazar in connection with the study of federalism. See his *Federalism and Political Integration* (Ramat-Gan: Turtledove Publishing, 1979) and *American Federalism, A View from the States*, third edition (New York: Harper and Row, 1984). See also Martin Landau, "Federalism, Redundancy and System Reli-

ability," and Vincent Ostrom, "Can Federalism Make a Difference," in Daniel J. Elazar, ed., *The Federal Polity* (New Brunswick: Transaction Books, 1974), pp. 137–146 and 197–238.

35. Hence Abraham can invoke jurisprudential principles when haggling over the fate of Sodom (Gen. 18:25); Moses can refer to basic rights when attempting to avert God's wrath (Num. 16:22); the *tannaim* can insist that the Torah is "not in heaven" (Babylonian Talmud [henceforth, T.B.] *Baba Meẓiah* 59a–b); and the *amoraim* can reject that the notion that the covenant was forced upon an unwilling and virgin people at Sinai (T.B. *Shabbat* 88a and *tosafot*).

36. The most succinct, and probably best known, statement of this thesis is to be found in *Mishnah:Avot* 4:13: "Rabbi Simeon said: 'There are three crowns: the crown of the *torah*, the crown of *kehunah*, and the crown of *malkhut*; but the crown of a good name excels them all.'" See also the commentary to this saying in *Avot de Rabbi Natan*, chapter 41. Also of interest is T.B. *Kiddushin* 66a and *Sifrei*, chapter 119.

37. Most explicitly in the sixteenth-century commentary, *Torat Mosheh*, to the governmental provisions outlined in Deut. 17 and 18, by Moses Alshekh of Safed (esp. commentary to Deut. 18:1). See also the use of the term in Rashi's explanation of the term *zirin* (lit. "wreaths") to T.B. *Yoma* 72b.

38. *Avot de Rabbi Natan*, chapter 41; for an early comparison of the "priestly" and "royal" covenants see Ecclus. 45:24–25, to which might be added the rabbinic comment: "Until David came all Israel were eligible for the kingship; once David was chosen, all Israel were exempt" (*Mekhilta of R. Ishmael* to portion *Bo*; paragraph 4).

39. As is the case in all political systems, the issue of legitimate succession poses problems of a particularly thorny nature. These are too intricate to be detailed here. Briefly stated, the Jewish political tradition requires that prospective candidates for appointment to office (*minui*) fulfill at least two of the following three criteria: appropriate lineage (*yihus*); popular selection and/or recognition (*haskamah*); and the enactment of a constitutionally recognized ceremony of induction into office (*meshihah*—"anointment"—or *semikhah*—"ordination"). The point to be made here is that the "mix" between these various requirements varies from *keter* to *keter*, with no two *ketarim* demanding identical qualifications. As much is evident, to take but one example, from the Deuteronomic passage referred to in note 37 above: *melekh*, in that case, derives his power from a process which combines both popular selection and Divine approval (in later coronation ceremonies symbolized by both acclamation and *meshihah*); the position of the *kohanim* is made principally dependent on genetic circumstances; the *Navi* is "raised up from among his brethren" by virtue of his Divinely inspired understanding of God's will (which can be given formal recognition within the *keter* by a process of *semikhah*—the method employed in the case of Joshua, who was thus ordained by Moses: Num. 27:15–23).

40. E.g., Joshua Falk Katz, *Persishah to Tur, Ḥoshen Mishpat*, I, 1a, commentary to *Mishnah:Avot* 1:2.

41. The presence of representatives of all three *ketarim* in such major constitutional actions as the designation of the *melekh* is profusely illustrated in the Bible (e.g., 1 Kings 1). More interesting, because less obviously necessary, is the requirement that any extension of the city limits of Jerusalem, or of the boundaries of the Temple, similarly requires their joint presence. See *Mishnah:Shavuot* 2:2.

42. The three *ketarim* can be described as manifestly articulated entities during the ancient periods of independent Jewish statehood. Most obviously was this so during the First Commonwealth (here designated epochs III–V). The biblical account suggests that, after an initial period of gestation, the system then settled into what might

be described as a "classic" pattern: the prophets constituted the principal instruments of the *keter torah*; the high priests those of the *keter kehunah*; and the kings those of the *keter malkhut*. The era of the Second Commonwealth promised to bring about the emergence of a similar pattern, with the offices being occupied by (respectively) the sages, the high priests, and—after the Maccabean revolt—the ethnarch. See chapter 7.

43. What we do find, on the other hand, are several attempts to posit a hierarchy of the *ketarim*. All of these place the *keter torah* at the top of the list—not surprisingly since the relevant texts are of rabbinic origin and hence compiled by persons with an obvious stake in that *keter*. See, e.g., *Mishnah: Avot* 4:12; *Sifrei* to Numbers, chapter 119; Maimonides, *Mishneh Torah*; *Hilkhot Talmud Torah*, 3:1.

44. For a fuller discussion of the theoretical implications of this model, see S. A. Cohen, "The Concept of the Three Ketarim: Its Place in Jewish Constitutional Thought and its Implications for a Study of Jewish Constitutional History," *Association for Jewish Studies Review* (forthcoming: 1984).

45. T.B. *Kiddushin* 66a; precisely the same constellation seems to have emerged during the First Commonwealth. Although the kings did not call themselves high priests, they certainly turned the *keter kehunah* into an instrument of royal tutelage, thus isolating the *keter torah*. It was in response to this threat that the *nevi'im* developed a distinctly "prophetic code," posing as the repositories of the *edah*'s moral conscience. (See, e.g., Amos 7:10–17.)

46. S. N. Eisenstadt, *Israeli Society* (New York: Basic Books, 1967).

47. Daniel J. Elazar, *Community and Polity: The Organizational Dynamics of American Jewry* (Philadelphia: Jewish Publication Society, 1976); Ernest Stock, "In the Absence of Hierarchy," *Jewish Journal of Sociology* vol. XII (2), (December 1979).

48. E. Guttman and Y. Landau, "The Political Elite and National Leadership in Israel," in George Lenczowski (ed.), *Political Elites in the Middle East* (Washington, D.C.: American Enterprise Institute, 1975); Daniel J. Elazar, "The Compound Structure of Public Service Delivery Systems in Israel," in Vicent Ostrom and Francis Bish (eds.), *Comparing Urban Service Delivery Systems, Structure and Performance*, vol. 12, Urban Affairs Annual Reviews (Sage, 1977).

49. This discussion draws heavily on the political science literature on constitutionalism. Standard works on the subject include James Bryce, *Constitutions* (New York: Oxford University Press, 1905); Carl J. Friedrich, *Constitutional Government and Politics: Nature and Development* (Boston: Ginn and Co., 1937) and "Constitutions and Constitutionalism," in David L. Sills (ed.), *International Encyclopedia of the Social Sciences*, vol. 3 (New York: Macmillan and Free Press, 1968), pp. 318–326; Charles H. McIlwain, *Constitutionalism, Ancient and Modern* (Ithaca, N.Y.: Cornell University Press, 1947); and M. J. C. Vile, *Constitutionalism and the Separation of Powers* (Oxford: Clarendon Press, 1967). Although otherwise problematic for a system whose origins are in a divine covenant, Hans Kelsen's constitutional theory is particularly helpful in this connection, cf. his *General Theory of Law and State* (New York: Russell and Russell, 1961).

50. Cf. Josephus Flavius, *Antiquities of the Jews*, Book IV, Chap. 8, especially paragraphs 196–198 and Philo, *De Specialibus Legibus*, Book IV "De Constitutione Principum." For an analysis of Philo's political thought, with frequent references to Josephus and to classical Jewish sources, see Harry Austryn Wolfson, *Philo: Foundations of Religious Philosophy in Judaism, Christianity, and Islam* (revised edition; Cambridge, Mass.: Harvard University Press, 1962) vol. 2, chapter 13 "Political Theory," pp. 322–437.

51. For a more complete exposition of this thesis see Daniel J. Elazar, "The Generation Rhythm of American Politics" in *American Politics Quarterly*, vol. 6, no. 1 (January 1978). After developing this theory out of his work in American political history, Elazar discovered the European literature on the subject which thoroughly parallel his own conclusions. Chief proponents of the generational thesis include Aguste Comte, Karl Mannheim, Julian Marias, John Stuart Mill, and Jose Ortega y Gasset. Comte was the first to suggest the historical process of generational succession. Mill developed Comte's idea of social generations and Ortega y Gasset added the dimension of multigenerational epochs as the macrostructure of history based on the generation as the microstructure. For an overview of their thought, see Julian Marias, "Generations: The Concept" in Sills (ed.), *International Encyclopedia of the Social Sciences*, vol. 6, pp. 88–92, and his *Generations: A Historical Method* (translated by H. Raley; New York: OUP, 1970).

52. See, for example, the model covenant in R. Judah ha-Barceloni, *Sefer ha-Shtarot*, published in the eleventh century.

PART ONE

The Classic Biblical Epochs

EPOCH I

c. 1910–c. 2190 AM (c. 1850–c. 1570 BCE)

Ha-Avot

The Forefathers

1. DOMINANT EVENTS

1.1 Founding Events
Migration of Abram to Canaan (Gen. 12)   c. 1850 BCE*
Covenant between God and Abraham (Gen. 15 and 17)

1.2 Climactic Events
Birth of Jacob's sons (Gen. 29 and 30)   c. 1680 BCE*
Jacob's struggle with the angel and change of name to Israel (Gen. 32)

1.3 Culminating Events
Descent of Israelites to Egypt   c. 1570 BCE*
Jacob's sons identified as fathers of distinct tribal units (Gen. 46)

2. CONSTITUTIONAL HISTORY

Epoch I deals essentially with the prehistory of the Jewish people and as such is shrouded in the mist of oral tradition not otherwise corroborated. Here we have chosen to focus on the biblical account as the authoritative Jewish national understanding of its own origins. The Bible itself focuses on the history of a limited number of individuals and is more concerned with their personal traits than with their political development. Nevertheless, on close examination, the Book of Genesis proves to be a particularly rich source for the study of the political terminology and constitutional ideas which were to have an

---

*All dates are conjectural, based upon most reasonable estimates in light of biblical account and very limited archeological evidence.

abiding impact on the Jewish political tradition. Even if the account before us has been organized to teach or provide paradigms for later generations, it is instructive in its presentation of the founding epoch of the Jewish kith. Despite the limits of our knowledge, we can fairly conclude that the epoch is in this sense of seminal importance: it embraces the emergence of a distinctive patriarchal household as a political fact to which is attributed a language and structure of constitutional discourse which were particularly its own.

The boundaries of the epoch are clearly delineated in the biblical text. Prior to the migration of Abram, the Bible does not record any notion of a specific covenantal relationship between God and any particular portion of mankind. Earlier covenantal promises (as in the case of that made to Noah, Gen. 9:8–17) had been entered into with humanity as a whole. The constant and intensely personal relationship between Abram (soon Abraham) and God resulted in the founding of a people divorced from both the territorial base (*eretz*) and kith network (*moledet*) in which Abraham was reared. By the time Jacob and his sons descended from Canaan to Egypt, however, the mainline descendants of Abraham stood in a unique religious and constitutional relationship with God. In the process, they had also laid the foundations for the later emergence of Israel as a nation within a twelve-tribe constitutional framework. Jacob and his sons descended to Egypt as *Bnei Yisrael* (the Children of Israel)—a name which was itself allocated at the climax of the epoch during an episode of highly charged and direct contact between Jacob and the angel of the Lord.

What bound the *Bnei Yisrael* together in the epoch was already more than their self-evident family affiliations mentioned in Gen. 42:11. The crucial element in their affiliation was the fact that they were all *bnei brit*, children of the covenant concluded between God and each of the patriarchs. Indeed, it is the cluster of covenants recorded in Genesis which together comprise the constitutional basis of the emergent polity. Three elements are common to these covenants: first, the Divine promise to make of Abraham's seed "a great nation" through whom "all the nations of the earth shall be blessed" (Gen. 12:3); second, the allocation of the land of Canaan as a territorial base for the new nation; and third, the undertaking by the human partners to the covenant to worship God, trust Him, and hearken to His words. Thus the combination of kinship and consent as the twin foundations of Jewish peoplehood was present from the very beginning.

From these fundamental referents a number of constitutional consequences immediately followed. One was the investiture of the rite of circumcision with unequivocal constitutional importance. Circumcision constituted a mark of citizenship, a sign of the consent of the family of the circumcised to the terms of the covenant. The circumcised was henceforth to be designated a *ben brit* and clearly distinguished from the *arel* (uncircumcised), who stood outside the covenantal framework (Gen. 17:14). Another was the designation of the

line of constitutional descent. Significantly, each of the patriarchs violated—
in most cases wittingly—the rule of the primogeniture (*bekhorah*) when conferring his blessing (*berakhah*) on his offspring: Isaac—not Ishmael—was to
inherit the covenant with Abraham (Gen. 17:21); Jacob (not Esau), that with
Isaac (Gen. 27); Judah (not Reuben), Jacob's mantle (Gen. 49:8); and Ephraim
attained precedence over Menasseh (Gen. 48:19). Apparently personal ap-
propriateness, not precipitate birth, was construed to be the criterion for political leadership of the new nation.

The functions which these leaders themselves performed (and were expected to perform) further underline the particularity of the political unit at
whose center they stood. Within the groundrules of the constitution (as laid
down in the covenant) the patriarchs are presented as performing in person all
of the functions appropriate to the three separate *ketarim* which were later to
form the basis of the structure of the Jewish polity. In this respect—as in others—their position was unique. Constitutional authority was never again to
be so concentrated, with one person alone dominating the sacerdotal, governmental, and instructional spheres of Jewish political life. As the attached diagram illustrates, it was only in the domain of the *keter malkhut* that the
patriarchs may have been intermittently assisted by functionaries (such as
Eliezer of Damascus); otherwise, their influence was both exclusive and (be-
neath that of God) hegemonic.

What is more, Abraham, Isaac, and Jacob were simultaneously constitutionalists and statesmen. Besides transmitting the terms of the covenant to
their households, they also conducted the internal and external business of
the polity. Not until the last generation of the epoch did a possible distinction
of functions emerge, with Reuben, Judah, and Joseph assuming the role of
statesmen rather than constitutionalists.

To say all this is not to imply that the *Bnei Yisrael* can be classified as a fully
fledged political entity by the end of Epoch I. The seventy "souls" (*nefesh*)
who descended to Egypt are not therefore to be described as an *edah* (in fact,
the term itself does not appear in the entire book of Genesis). They did, however, unquestionably constitute an embryonic *edah*. They possessed a unique
code of constitutional behavior, a distinct territorial attachment (in itself buttressed by the purchase and repeated use of the sepulchre at Machpelah), and
even a form of internal political subdivision. At one level, this is indicated by
the political aspirations and consequent conflicts which set Joseph apart from
his brothers. At another, it is apparent from the sharpening of the unique
identities of each of Jacob's sons. By the end of the epoch, twelve distinct family subunits (later to become tribes) had begun to emerge—within which the
head of the household (*bet av*) could wield prescriptive authority (Gen.
42:37).

3. CONSTITUTION

Covenant between God and Abraham plus customary law

3.1 Constitutional Issues

Founding of a new nation through a unique relationship with God
    The original covenant with Abraham (Gen. 15, 18) was reconfirmed with
    Isaac (Gen. 26:23–24) and Jacob (Gen. 28:10–22).
Circumcision
    A sign of citizenship via consent to constitution (Gen. 17:9–22)
Birthright and accompanying blessing
    Devolved not by primogeniture but by criterion of personal appropriateness
    to lead new nation (Gen. 48:18–19)
Relationship to land of Canaan
    Covenantal promise of land of Canaan (Gen. 13:14–16 and 35:12)
    Treaties with neighbors (e.g., Gen. 14:18–20; 21:22–34)
    Purchase of sepulchre at Machpelah (Gen. 23)

3.2 Camps and Parties

Joseph and his brothers

4. CONSTITUTIONAL STRUCTURE
OF THE *EDAH*

Israel was not yet an *edah* (term is therefore not to be found in book of Gene-
    sis) nor was it subdivided. It is best defined as a proto-*edah*, commencing as
    a *bet av*. However, by the end of the epoch, emergence of *Bnei Yisrael* with
    12 proto-tribes (Gen. 46).
Functions of all three *ketarim* were present, but all were performed by pa-
    triarchs who might, however, be assisted in sphere of *keter malkhut* by
    functionaries (e.g., Eliezer of Damascus).

7. REPRESENTATIVE PERSONALITIES

7.1 Constitutional Architects

Abraham: (Originally Abram), the first human with whom God covenanted
            on a dynastic (rather than personal or universal) basis; the first to
            hearken to God's words which stressed his family's special rela-
            tionship with God; the first to be singled out as the conduit of a
            Divine message to his descendants. In his capacity as patriarch
            (*av*) was principal instrument of all three *ketarim*

Isaac: Abraham's designated heir. Covenanted with God and transmit-

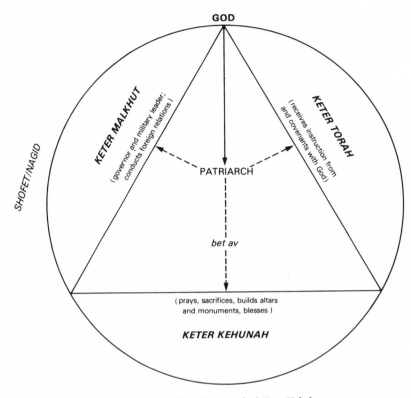

FIGURE I-1. The Patriarchal Pre-*Edah*

ted blessing to his own designated heir. In his capacity as *av*,
principal instrument of all three *ketarim*

Jacob/   Covenanted (and wrestled) with God. Transmitted blessing to
Israel: each of his sons. In his capacity as *av*, principal instrument of all
three *ketarim*. It was with him that the family of Hebrews became
a tribe

7.2 Statesmen (in Addition to the *Avot*)

Reuben: Firstborn son of Jacob; eponymous ancestor of tribe bearing his
name. Attempted to uphold constitutional practice in case of
Joseph (Gen. 37:21–22); breached constitutional norms in case
of his father's concubine and was punished accordingly (Gen.
35:22)

Judah: Fourth of Jacob's sons; eponymous ancestor of tribe bearing his
name. Spokesman for entire family (Gen. 44:18, 46:28)

Joseph: Eleventh of Jacob's sons. Achieved power and authority in Egypt
             and ultimately used both to the advantage of his family

8. TERMS

Alah (covenant), here used in secular sense (Gen. 26:28)

Am (people), a generic description, not specifically applied to the Jewish
       people (Gen. 11:6)

Ba'al brit, confederate (Gen. 14:13)

Bekhorah (birthright), constitutional means of succession (Gen. 25:31)

Ben brit, member of community (Gen. 15:3)

Ben nechar (stranger), one outside the kith network (Gen. 17:27, 31:15)

Berakhah (blessing), means whereby Divine legitimization of succession was
       transmitted (Gen. 27:38)

Bet av (household), the molecular unit of the community (Gen. 46:31)

Brit (covenant), used in both religious and secular sense (Gen. 6:18, 21:27)

Eretz (land), territorial base (Gen. 17:8)

Ger (resident alien) (Gen. 23:4)

Goy (nation), an ethnic group with its own culture (Gen. 12:2)

Mishpaḥah (family) (Gen. 24:38)

Moledet, kith network (Gen. 14:1–2)

Naḥalah, inheritance (Gen. 31:14)

Nasi (elevated one), recognized leader (Gen. 23:6)

Rado (v.inf. *lirdot*), to rule dictatorially over an unequal (e.g., Gen. 1:26)

9. BIBLIOGRAPHY

The following are general works to be consulted for the biblical period (Epochs I–V).

W. F. Albright, *The Biblical Period from Abraham to Ezra: An Historical Survey* (New
    York: Harper, 1968).
S. W. Baron, *A Social and Religious History of the Jewish People,* vol. I (second edition;
    revised and enlarged; Philadelphia: Jewish Publication Society of America, 1952).
J. Bright, *A History of Israel* (third edition; Philadelphia: Westminster Press, 1982).
A. Malamat, "Origins and the Formative Period," in H. H. Ben-Sasson (ed.), *A His-
    tory of the Jewish People* (Cambridge, Mass.: Harvard University Press, 1976),
    pp. 3–87.

On specific topics in both Epoch I and Epoch II see:
E. Isaac, "Circumcision as a Covenant Rite," *Anthropos* 59 (1964), pp. 444–456.
H. Kohn, "Israel and Hellas" in *The Idea of Nationalism* (New York, 1961), pp. 27–47.
B. Mazar (ed.), "The Patriarchs," *The World History of the Jewish People,* vol. I (New
    Brunswick, 1970).
G. E. Mendenhall, "Ancient Oriental and Biblical Law," *The Biblical Archeologist* 17
    (2), 1954, pp. 26–46.
N. H. Snaith, "The Covenant-Love of God" in *The Distinctive Ideas of the Old Testa-
    ment* (New York, 1964), pp. 94–127.

E. A. Speiser (ed.), "Genesis," *The Anchor Bible,* vol. I (New York, 1964).

R. de Vaux, "Introduction," in *Ancient Israel. Volume One: Social Institutions.* (New York, 1965), pp. 3–15.

M. Weinfeld, "Berit-Covenant vs. Obligation," *Biblica* 56 (i), 1975, pp. 109–128.

EPOCH II

c. 2190–c. 2480 AM (c. 1570–c. 1280 BCE)

Avdut Miẓrayim

Egyptian Bondage

1. DOMINANT EVENTS

1.1 Founding Events
Settlement in Goshen (Gen. 47:11–12)   c. 1570 BCE*

1.2 Climactic Events
Enslavement (Exod. 1:5–14)—an obvious transformation of the political status of the *Bnei Yisrael*, whose political life was thus influenced by external ruler   c. 1450 BCE*

1.3 Culminating Events
The exodus from Egypt and the circumstances surrounding it   c. 1280 BCE*

2. CONSTITUTIONAL HISTORY

Epoch II is an unknown chapter in Jewish history and must be considered with all the caveats mentioned in connection with Epoch I. Even in the biblical account, its dominant constitutional characteristic—the emergence of the *Bnei Yisrael* as an *am* (people)—gains expression only in its last generation. Hitherto, the term had been used in the Pentateuch in only a generic sense (Gen. 11:6) and without specific reference to the Israelites. However, by the time the *Bnei Yisrael* emerged from slavery it had also acquired a clearly circumscribed connotation of a nation bound to some transcendent power and defined by a vocation. The term was employed by both the Egyptians and the

---

*All dates are conjectural, based upon most reasonable estimates in light of biblical account and available archeological evidence.

biblical text itself with particular reference to the Israelites (note the repetition of the word in Exod. 13:17–22 and 14:1–31). The change thus indicated, it is here suggested, was one of form and content—as well as of numerical size. The *Bnei Yisrael* whom Moses led forth from Egypt comprised an intrinsically different political conglomeration from those whom Joseph had settled in the land of Goshen. They were distinctive not only because of their origins (as *ivrim*—Hebrews; Exod. 2:6), but also because of their political cohesion and the framework which endowed their affiliation with purpose and strength. As such, they must be distinguished from other *amim* (such as the Egyptians, to whom the term is also applied) and from the *erev rav* (mixed multitude, Exod. 12:38).

Changing attitudes toward the covenants between God and the patriarchs provide one clear example of the process of development which had transpired, not least because they are so pointedly recollected in the early chapters of Exodus. These patently remained fundamental constitutional referents throughout the epoch; in essence, their terms did not change. Nevertheless, during the course of the epoch they underwent a shift of emphasis. For one thing, Israel's precedence in God's eyes over all other nations was for the first time made explicit (Exod. 4:22). For another, the Divine promise to make Israel a "great nation" necessarily imposed upon Him the obligation to deliver them from bondage. In order to accomplish that task, moreover, God had to demonstrate the extent of His own power. It was precisely in order to free His people and to bring them to their promised inheritance (now referred to as *morashah*, Exod. 6:8—compare the earlier use of the term *ahuzah* in Gen. 17:8), that He had both to harden Pharaoh's heart and then to inflict upon the Egyptians the ten plagues. Henceforth, the *Bnei Yisrael* were to know God as the force who brought them out of the land of Egypt (Exod. 6:7).

The experience of slavery (here identified as the climactic phase of the entire epoch) produced two further constitutional consequences. The first, and most obvious, was that it brought the *Bnei Yisrael* under the direct influence of a polity external to the covenantal relationship between themselves and God. It was the Egyptians who set taskmasters (*sarei misim*) over the slaves and who issued explicit directives to their officers (*shoterim*; Exod. 5:6ff). In so doing, they aggregated to themselves policy-making and major administrative functions of the *keter malkhut*, over which independent Israelite control can have been very limited.

Nevertheless, as the text of Exodus makes plain, the *Bnei Yisrael* did not thereby lose their distinctiveness. On the contrary, the second constitutional consequence of the period of enslavement was that it provided the *Bnei Yisrael* with precisely the kind of common historical experience which assisted their development as a separate corporate body. Thus it was that at the very end of this epoch they first acquired the characteristics (though not the constitution) of an *am* with particular traditions, beliefs, and—not least—rules of collective procedure (see Exod. 3:15–18). The sense of unique identity which these imparted was again reinforced by the rite of circumcision (Exod. 4:25); it was further strengthened during the period of the ten plagues. Goshen was not affected by the ninth, nor the first-born Israelites by the tenth. Furthermore, on the eve of the last plague the *Bnei Yisrael* took additional steps to signify their national distinctiveness by daubing their lintels with the blood of the paschal lamb—an act which at once delineated both the territorial boundaries of the *am*'s domain and the citizenship of its members.

The precise nature of the internal structure of the *Bnei Yisrael* during this epoch must largely remain a matter of conjecture. It may be assumed that the *ziknei yisrael* (elders of the Israelites) attempted to maintain traditional governance in as far as was possible and that it was during this period that the twelve tribes emerged as extensions of separately articulated familial groupings (Exod. 2:1). The arrangements prescribed for the celebration of the Passover sacrifice (Exod. 12) also suggest the autonomy of smaller units, the *batei av* (households), which can be considered the precursors of later *kehillot*.

Following the biblical account, it was Moses who orchestrated the activities of the entire people, under the guidance of God. By the end of the epoch—but not before—he had established himself as the leader of the entire community of the *Bnei Yisrael*. Two points need to be made about his leadership prior to that occurrence. First, Moses was in this epoch not in any way a constitutionalist, but a statesman. His achievement lay in that he ultimately attained the recognition and acclaim of both the *Bnei Yisrael* and the Egyptians (Exod. 11:3). But his function, throughout, was merely that of a spokesman (in which capacity he relied strongly on the help of his brother Aaron). Moses neither created nor interpreted law—he merely transmitted Divine commands.

Secondly, and moreover, Moses' right to do so was Divinely ordained. There is no evidence whatsoever that the *am* had itself developed a mechanism capable of conferring national leadership upon a single individual. The fact that Moses was in many respects an outsider who was not a member of the senior tribe or even the firstborn of his own family merely emphasizes the dimension of choice and consensus in his selection. The clear implication is that already the right to wield authority in the polity of the *Bnei Yisrael* did not pass through inheritance. Beyond that, the point is made that leadership is initially conferred by Divine selection and then must be confirmed by popular acclaim.

3. CONSTITUTION

Customary law plus (in a latent way) patriarchial covenant as reaffirmed (Exod. 6:3–9)

3.1 Constitutional Issues
Maintenance of separate corporate structure (Exod. 5:1–21)
Source of authority of leadership (Exod. 5:20–23)

Hitherto, leadership was hereditary. Moses and Aaron represent the first instance of Divinely appointed leadership from within the *am* without reference to their descent.

3.2 Camps and Parties
Unknown; possibly groupings of sons of Leah and Rachel and their respective handmaidens

4. CONSTITUTIONAL STRUCTURE
OF THE *EDAH*

The only officers recorded are *zekenim* and *shoterim*. Both categories operated from the *keter malkhut*; they were subject to the foreign suzerain, whose influence was a crucial factor, both globally and in terms of appointment.

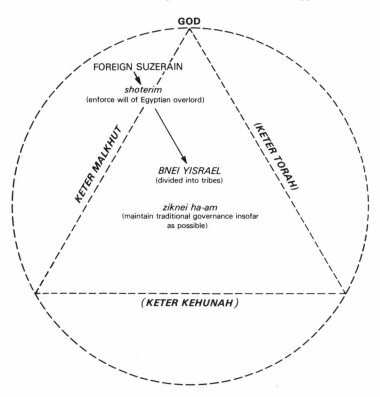

FIGURE II-1. The Proto-*Edah* in Egyptian Bondage

5. *MEDINOT*

Tribes as extensions of separately articulated households (e.g., Exod. 2:1, 6:14–17)

6. *KEHILLOT*

Batei av (households)
   The details of the structure are not apparent in the text; however the ordinances of the Passover rite (Exod. 12, 13) certainly provide several indications of the existence of a structure.

7. REPRESENTATIVE PERSONALITIES

7.2 Statesmen
Moses: In this epoch his principal function was to transmit in God's name the demand that the Israelites be freed from bondage and to negotiate their exodus. Ultimately, his activities gained both Israelite recognition of his authority and Egyptian admiration (Exod. 11:3)
Aaron: Elder brother of Moses; recruited by God to assist Moses in his representations before Pharaoh

8. TERMS

8.1 New
Ahuzah (holding), a place of settlement (Gen. 47:11–12)
Erev rav (mixed multitude), an unorganized mass (Exod. 12:38)
Morashah (inheritance), as of right—applied to *Bnei Yisrael*'s claim to Canaan (Exod. 6:8)
Sar, one who wielded executive authority delegated to him by a human superior (Exod. 1:11)
Shofet (judge), one who wielded authority through administering the law (Exod. 2:14)
Shoter (officer), a subordinate official whose task was to enforce the policies of the government (Exod. 5:14)
Zaken (elder), constitutionally recognized leader and representative of a people, tribe, and/or group of households (Exod. 3:16)

8.2 Old—Those Which Have Undergone Change in Meaning and/or Application
Am, a nation defined through its ties to a transcendent power (in this epoch

used with specific reference to the *Bnei Yisrael,* although also used to define other peoples)

9. BIBLIOGRAPHY

See bibliography to Epoch I.

EPOCH III

c. 2480–2756 AM (c. 1280–1004 BCE)

Adat Bnei Yisrael

The Congregation of Israelites

1. DOMINANT EVENTS

1.1 Founding Events

Crossing of the Red Sea (Exod. 14:26–31)	c. 1280 BCE
Covenant at Sinai (Exod. 19, 20)	c. 1280 BCE
Settlement of Canaan and covenant at Shechem (Josh. 24)	c. 1240 BCE

1.2 Climactic Events

Deborah and Barak broke the back of last major Canaanite resistance (Judg. 4)
c. 1125 BCE

Gideon declined kingship out of respect for constitution (Judg. 8:22–23)
c. 1100 BCE

1.3 Culminating Events

Samuel's failure to preserve Israel's republican regime in which the prophet-judge played the principal role. In response to popular demand for a *Melekh* (King), he appointed Saul—whose qualifications for office he recognized to be military—as a *Nagid* (appointed one) (1 Sam. 8:1–10:26). The experiment failed, and at the end of the epoch David was designated *Nagid* by God and anointed *Melekh* through covenants with the tribe of Judah and the *zekenim* of the tribes of Israel in sequence (2 Sam. 2:4, 5:1–3).
c. 1020 BCE–c. 1004 BCE

2. CONSTITUTIONAL HISTORY

The dominant constitutional characteristic of Epoch III is the emergence of *Torat Moshe* as the constitutional expression of the covenant between God

and *Bnei Yisrael*. The biblical account emphasizes the constitutional processes involved. The Ten Commandments, enunciated at Sinai, were enscribed on *shnei luḥot ha-brit* (the two tablets of the covenant), while the remainder of the laws transmitted to the polity via Moses were collectively
known as *Sefer ha-Brit* (Book of the Covenant—Exod. 24:7). Together, these
codes called into being Israel as a *goy kadosh* (holy nation) or *am* in the sense
of a people whose identity is bound up with its ties to its Divine patron, with
the *edah* as its organized manifestation.

By any standards, Epoch III must stand as the most crucial of all the constitutional epochs in Jewish history. It witnessed the formation of *Bnei Yisrael* as
a people and polity and the enunciation of *Torat Moshe* as the constitution of
Adat Bnei Yisrael (the Congregation of Israelites). Henceforth the body of
laws contained in what became known as the Torah was to be the basic constitutional referent for the entire *edah* throughout its history. All subsequent
constitutions would claim to do no more than elucidate and explicate this first
classic text.

Three factors distinguish *Torat Moshe* from the covenantal arrangements of
the two previous epochs. First, the constitution embodied in it represents a
covenant concluded between God and the entire *edah*—whose members collectively consented to its terms. At Sinai, a public oath was taken to enact "all
that God has said" (Exod. 19:8), and this declaration was subsequently reaffirmed by similar public assemblies attended by "every man in Israel" (Deut.
29:9–25, Josh. 4:4–14, Josh. 24).

Secondly, the Bible indicates that *Torat Moshe* (as its name implies) was not
transmitted directly from God to the *edah*. Rather (and initially at the express
wish of the *edah*), it was Moses who acted as the human channel through
which God's will was made known (Exod. 20:19). Admittedly, God did not
entirely withdraw from direct communication with the *edah*. Even after the
episode of the golden calf (when God began to reduce His direct role and delegated some of His functions to a *malakh*—"angel," Exod. 33:2–3), He continued to reside in its midst and, from time to time, to direct its affairs via
Moses. That is evident from the presence of a cloud over the *ohel mo'ed* (tent
of meeting—Exod. 33:9); from His occasional explicit directives of a constitutional, political, military, and judicial nature; and—more often—by sporadic indications of His favor or wrath. Nevertheless, after Sinai, God never
again addressed the entire *edah* directly. Instead, His chosen instruments
served as the conduits of God's words. The process had begun whereby those
instruments were to become the exclusive communicators of the Divine will.

Finally, it was *Torat Moshe* which for the first time specified who those
chosen instruments were to be and which functions they would perform.
Thus, besides setting down the constitutional content of the covenant between God and the *edah*, it also designated the necessary elements for a
proper regime (albeit without specifying any single regime as the only proper

one). It was thus that the three *ketarim* first appeared as separate spheres of constitutional authority and interpretation, each of which involved the performance of distinct functions by individuals either Divinely designated or Divinely recognized.

The Bible has God as the sole and explicit source of original authority. He designated Aaron as *Kohen Gadol* and conferred that office, through covenant, upon Phineas and his descendants (Num. 25:13). He provided a classificatory scheme for distinguishing between true and false prophets (Deut. 18:15–22) and demonstrated the legitimacy of Moses' claim to be the leader of the entire *edah* (Num. 16:23–35). Only in the case of the *keter malkhut* did God recognize previously established authority which continued from the original covenants with the *avot* (patriarchs). Nevertheless, within those parameters, a crucial break with previous constitutional practice was entailed in the delegation of constitutional power to a particular body of priests (*keter kehunah*), prophets (*keter torah*), and civil officials, the *nesiim* and *shofetim* (*keter malkhut*).

Henceforth, not only was authority to be divided (as is illustrated in the accompanying diagram), it was also to be granted to prescribed offices and officeholders. Koraḥ and his family could thus be accused of seeking an unconstitutional extension of their domain (Num. 16:10). The Bible presents two of Aaron's sons as being killed by Divine act for overstepping the bounds of their functions (Lev. 10:1–2). With apparently less good cause, Eldad and Medad were threatened with imprisonment for having "prophesied throughout the camp" (Num. 11:26–29).

The constitutional structure thus outlined was perforce loosely coordinated (although explicitly defined) during the first generation of the epoch. During the course of succeeding generations, however, it attained increasing form and force. That is why Gideon's refusal to arrogate to himself a position of hegemony (by refusing hereditary rulership, Judg. 8:22–23) marks the climactic event of the epoch; his action confirmed the extent to which the constitution was in force. Israelites were still to be governed by God and not by any human who had other than delegated powers. It was only an externally generated crisis, the Philistine invasion and conquest, which led to demands for basic constitutional change, namely the constitution of a national power strong enough to expel the invader. Samuel's inability to resist popular demand for a king who could do just that announced the onset of a constitutional crisis, whose resolution brought the epoch to a close.

Until that time, however, the *edah* managed to retain its prescribed framework. During Epoch III it also attained organizational characteristics which enabled it to function for religious, military, political, and judicial purposes. Thus, during the course of the epoch the judicial system (first established in the desert on Jethro's advice, Exod. 18:13–27) became formalized (Deut. 16:18), and the military organization (which initially functioned on what appears to have been an *ad hoc* basis, Exod. 17:9) became standardized with the introduction of a regulated system of tribal levies and a standard order of battle. In such respects, the experience of territorial conquest and settlement in Canaan proved decisive. In addition to providing the *edah* with a permanent territorial base, it also imposed on the *edah* the need to develop instruments capable of dealing with such diverse matters as territorial inheritance (Josh. 17:3–4), treaties with neighbors (e.g., the Gibeonites—Josh. 9), and defense against endemic incursions (e.g., the Midianites).

Altogether, then, by Samuel's generation what had begun as a somewhat amorphous conglomeration (*Am Yisrael*) had been transformed into a clearly defined political unit (*Adat Bnei Yisrael*), each of whose citizens possessed distinctive rights and duties within the parameters of the uniformly accepted constitution. In the process, it also developed distinct instruments of authority and governance, a unique code of rewards (*berakhot*) and punishments (*kellalot*), and—as is most apparent from the texts—a political terminology which is peculiarly, and richly, its own. The fierce determination of the *edah* to retain these constitutional forms and practices was demonstrated on several occasions during the course of the epoch. Rebels (such as Korah) were ousted; miscreants (such as Aḥan) were severely punished; instances of suspiciously sectarian tendencies (as in the case of the altar erected on the Jordan by the two and a half tribes) were hastily investigated and clarified in the direction of maintaining national unity under a common constitution, however divided its administration.

It was this transformation which accounted for, and justified, the repeated description of the tribes as an *edah* throughout the epoch. Citizenship was very important in this regard. Members of the *edah* were explicitly enjoined to preserve their distinctiveness by not following the heathen ways of the Egyptians and the Canaanites (Lev. 18) and by not intermarrying with the Ammonites and Moabites (Deut. 23:4). Persons who were not full members of the *edah* were excluded from the celebration of the Passover rite, while failure to participate on the part of those who were *ezraḥim* (citizens) incurred the penalty of *karet* (death by Divine punishment; Exod. 12:43–45). Similarly, when at one juncture suspicions were aroused that the two and a half tribes settled east of the Jordan were rebelling against the true faith, steps were taken to verify the meaning of their action and to avert secession from the confederacy—if necessary by force (Josh. 22:9–34). Finally, it must be noted that in this epoch, too, circumcision regained its constitutional significance, with the renewal of the practice upon entry into Canaan signifying a reaffirmation of mutual trust between God and the *edah* (Josh. 5:2–9).

The unity of the *edah* was graphically symbolized during this epoch by the central location of its place of worship. The *mishkan* (tabernacle) and *ohel mo'ed* (tent of assembly) resided in the center of the Israelite camp during their wanderings in the wilderness (Num. 2:17). After the entry into Canaan, the ark of the Lord (although still without a permanent shrine) was generally located in an area roughly equidistant from the major regions of settlement. Wherever sited, it became the seat of the tribal confederacy (Gilgal—Josh. 4:19, 1 Sam. 7:6; Shiloh—Josh. 18:1 and 19:51, Judg. 21:19–21; Mitzpeh—1 Sam. 7:5–12; Ophrah—Judg. 6:11–32; Dan—Judg. 18:30–31).

Nevertheless, it is also clear that the constituent elements of the *edah* attained individual identity during this epoch. Each of the tribes retained both its independent lineage and—to a large degree—its political independence. The tendency to do so measurably increased once most of the tribes attained separate territorial bases (by which they are sometimes known; e.g., Gilead, Judg. 5:17) upon which they could further nurture their separate institutions of communal government. It is this development which justifies the reference to each of the *shevatim* as separate *medinot* (in our terms) and the description of the *edah* as a whole as a tribal confederacy, the constituent members of which could often pursue their individual interests without apparent regard for the common good (hence the strictures in Judg. 5:15–18).

The centripetal tendencies at work within the *edah* must not, however, be exaggerated. Throughout the period, the *edah* did possess common leaders. Most obviously was this so in respect to the *keter kehunah*, whose principal office (that of the *Kohen Gadol*) remained in the possession of a single family (the Aaronides) and passed in succession from Phineas, the son of Elazar, the son of Aaron. In other domains, too, a unified line of authority was generally retained. Thus, during the early generations of the epoch, first Moses and then Joshua occupied the position of *Eved Adonai* (the Minister of the Lord or, better, Prime Minister) in which capacity they combined the principal functions of both the *keter torah* and the *keter malkhut*. Even after their deaths, national leadership appeared in the persons of those who are conventionally known as the *shofetim* (magistrates), particularly those who receive the briefest mention. From the biblical text it is apparent that those men who were not heroes deemed worthy of elaborate attention are mentioned precisely because they exercised authority over wide portions of the *edah*. National authority was clearly in evidence at the very end of the epoch when Samuel (as a *ro'eh*—seer—and national representative of the *keter torah*) anointed Saul to be *Nagid* of the entire *edah*.

During this formative epoch, individuals could function from several bases, and indeed were often expected to do so. The same personality could act as prophet, judge, and legislator, and would hence be entitled *Nagid*, *Shofet*, *Navi*, and *Ro'eh* accordingly. It was only during the culminating generations of the epoch, when institutional distinctiveness became increasingly articulated, that clear divisions of function (and hence of title) occurred. It is in this sense that the anointment of Saul to be *Nagid* heralded the close of this epoch and the emergence of a monarchy which was to be the distinctive constitutional characteristic of the next epoch.

3. CONSTITUTION

Torat Moshe (Mosaic Torah), founded on the covenant between God and the entire *edah*

The ten commandments constitute the founding covenant, which called into being the *am* (people) as a holy nation and the *edah* as its organized manifestation (Exod. 19).

The covenant was reaffirmed in subsequent assemblies of the *edah* (Deut. 29:9–25, Josh. 8:31 and 23:6).

The constitution took form as *Sefer ha-Brit* (Exod. 20), later as *Sefer Torat Moshe* (Josh. 8:31 and 23:6).

3.1 Constitutional Issues

The composition of the *edah* and the defense of Israel's uniqueness, as defined in

the Passover sacrifice, from which were excluded those not in the *edah* (Exod. 12:43–45), and the nonobservance of which incurred the penalty of being cut off from the *edah* (*nikhrata ha-nefesh*)

admonitions against intermarriage with Ammonites and Moabites and against following the "heathen ways" of the Canaanites and Egyptians (e.g., Lev. 18)

The organization of the edah, necessitating

the establishment of a system which enabled the *edah* to function as a body politic in matters constitutional (e.g., Num. 11:16–18), in matters judicial (e.g., Exod. 18:13–27), in matters military (e.g., Num. 2), and in matters sacerdotal (e.g., Exod. 40:12–16)

the establishment of mechanisms for conferring leadership and succession—e.g., *semikhah* (ordination—Num. 27:18) and *meshihah* (anointing—Exod. 29:7), popular demand and Divine appointment (e.g., 1 Sam. 8:7), jurisdictional authority (Deut. 16:18)

the establishment of mechanisms of enforcement of the laws (Deut. 17:8–13)

The settlement of Canaan

The conquest and division of the land illustrates the key role of the *edah* in allocating tribal territories; it enabled the transposition of governmental institutions to a territorial base (e.g., the establishment of *arei miklat* (cities of refuge—Deut. 19, Josh. 20).

The issue of national unity and the preservation of the tribal confederacy— e.g., the transjordanian settlement by two and one-half of the tribes (Num. 32; Josh. 13:8ff), appeals by various *shofetim* for multitribal responses to various external threats (Judg. 4:10), and the preservation of the twelve-tribe system after the civil war with the tribe of Benjamin (Judg. 20:16ff)

3.2 Camps and Parties

Authorized leadership vs. its opponents—e.g., Datan and Abiram (Exod. 33) and *Korah ve-adato* (Num. 16 and 17)

Anti-monarchists vs. monarchists—e.g., Gideon (Judg. 9) and Samuel (1 Sam. 9 and 10)

Groups which retained distinctiveness within the *edah*—e.g., Kenites (Judg. 1:16; 4:11, 17) and *Bnei ha-nevi'im* (1 Sam. 19:20)

4. CONSTITUTIONAL STRUCTURE OF THE *EDAH*

The *Edah* as a Confederation of the Twelve Tribes of Israel

In this epoch, God was presented as inaugurating or ratifying the authoritative roles of each of the three *ketarim*. At certain decisive moments, He was also an active moving force in their respective spheres of influence, initiating critical decisions of a constitutional, political, judicial, and military nature.

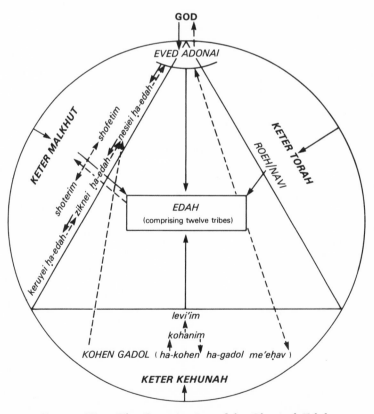

FIGURE III-1. The Organization of the Classical *Edah*

The *edah* was a tribal confederacy, whose unity was symbolized by the central location of the *ohel mo'ed* (tent of assembly) in which the *luḥot ha-brit* (tablets of the covenant) were housed. At times the term used, *ohel ha-edut* (tent of the covenant witnessing, e.g., Num. 17:22), is replaced by the *mishkan* (tabernacle, e.g., Exod. 33:7–11 and Num. 7).

The unity of the *edah*, forged in the wilderness, tended to break down with the attainment of separate tribal bases (hence Moses' fears in Num. 32). Nevertheless, the epoch witnessed only one serious instance of internecine warfare (Judg. 20).

4.1 Principal Instruments, Officers, and Functions

Eved Adonai (God's Prime Minister): A personal appointment by God, subsequently ratified by the *edah* whose members accepted him as their leader (Exod. 14:31). The *Eved Adonai* transmitted constitution to *edah* (Exod. 20:15 and Num. 27:1–11), exercised and delegated national political authority (Exod. 18:25–26), supervised issues of military and territorial relevance (Num. 32, Josh. 17:14–19:51), and acted as spokesman for *edah* before God (Exod. 32:11–14). The office was based on the premise that God played a direct role in the governance of the *edah*; hence the *Eved Adonai* combined the principal functions of both *keter malkhut* and *keter torah*. A major function of the office was constitutional design. Perhaps that is why the office existed only during the founding generations of the epoch. After the death of Joshua, the office lapsed with its *keter malkhut* functions being exercised by *shofetim* (magistrates). Many of the latter exercised pan-*edah* influence in their capacity as jurists and arbiters (e.g., lists in Judg. 10:1–5 and 12:8–15) when acting in military capacity (e.g., Judg. 8:29–32 and 12:7) referred to as *moshiah* (savior)—but on an irregular basis (Judg. 3:9). During culminating generations of epoch, the functions once those of the *Eved Adonai* were more clearly separated by *keter*, those of *keter torah* being exercised by the *Ro'eh* (seer) and then *Navi* (prophet) and those of *keter malkhut* by the *Nagid* (syndic or chief executive).

KETER TORAH

Ro'eh: (seer)	A personal appointment by God, subsequently recognized by the *edah* (1 Sam. 9:9–10). The *Ro'eh* interpreted constitution to *edah* on basis of divine communication.
Navi: (prophet)	Interpreted constitution to *edah* on basis of Divine communication (Deut. 13:2)
	Exercised national political authority in his sphere and designated *Nagid* as principal officer of *keter malkhut* (1 Sam. 10:1)

KETER KEHUNAH

Kohen Gadol: (high priest)	God's covenant with Phineas established right of Aaronides to succession (Num. 25:12). *Kohen gadol* was:

  —principal sacerdotal officer (Lev. 21:10)

  —witness at important national constitutional acts (Josh. 19:51)

  —neutral arbiter between national authorities, tribes, and households (Josh. 22:13–14)

  —activator of use of *urim* and *tummim* (appurtenances used to "inquire of the Lord"; Exod. 28:30; Num. 27:21; 1 Sam. 14:41–42, 23:9ff, 30:7ff)

  —military functionary in time of war (e.g., blessed troops— Deut. 20:2–4 and brought Divine presence into battlefield via Ark of Lord—Num. 10:35–36, 1 Sam. 4)

Kohanim : Subordinate or local sacerdotal functionaries (e.g., Judg.
Leviim 18:5)

Participated in national judicial system (Deut. 17:8–13)

Adjudicated interfamilial and intercommunal controversies (Deut. 21:1–9)

Blessed *edah* in fixed formulary (Num. 6:22–27)

KETER MALKHUT

Shofet: Appointed by *Eved Adonai* or *Navi* when such existed; other-
(national wise appointed by God (Judg. 3:9–10, 4:7, 6:14, 6:34,
magistrate) 11:29, 13:5, 13:25, 14:6, 9). The *shofet* interpreted and defended constitution and served as military leader.

Nagid: The *Nagid* performed both functions but (unlike *Shofet*) did
(syndic, so on a comprehensive nationwide basis. His constitutional
chief title aside, he was considered a *Melekh* by the people from
executive) the first. It is indicative of the constitutional crisis of the very
   last years of the epoch that the distinction between *Nagid* and
   Melekh was blurred. Saul acted in a typically kingly fashion,

  —initiating military reforms (1 Sam. 14:52)

  —offering tax exemptions to his champions (1 Sam. 17:25)

  —creating a new social class (1 Sam. 22:7)

  —coming into conflict with instruments of *keter kehunah* (1 Sam. 22:16–18) and *keter torah* (1 Sam. 15:20–21)

Shoterim: Executive functionaries of the *keter malkhut* and appointed by its authority. They, e.g., carried out court orders and e.g., supervised exemptions from military service (Deut. 20:5–9).

Nesiei Permanent heads of individual tribes, by whom they were
ha-edah: appointed. Here functioning in a federal capacity and representing interests of their tribes when participating in acts of national concern (e.g., dedication of *mishkan*—Num. 7:2–11 and treaty with Gibeonites—Josh. 9:15)

Ad hoc officers, appointed by tribes to represent their individual interests in matters of national constitutional importance (Num. 13:3–15, Josh. 18:1–10)

Ziknei *ha-edah*:	Senate of tribal representatives, apparently selected by *Eved Adonai*, whom they assisted in transmitting constitution (Exod. 34:31). They also ratified actions of national constitutional importance.
Keruyei *ha-edah*: (commis- sioners)	*Ad hoc* officers appointed to represent the tribe on specific issues (e.g., Num. 1:16 and the twelve spies—Num. 13:3–15).

5. *MEDINOT*

Individual *shevatim* (tribes) retained their distinctiveness and internal autonomy. Indeed, the latter increased once they achieved territorial uniqueness. Nevertheless, they were bound together by their common allegiance to the composite bonds of the constitution (hence suspicion of two and one-half transjordanian tribes in Josh. 22:9–34).

Shevatim were governed by

Nasi	Magistrate ("raised up") head of the tribe and its representative before other constituents of the *edah*
Zekeñim	Council of elders—heads of households; dealt with day-to-day affairs of tribal concern
Ha-Shevet	The tribal council consisting of all males above the age of twenty, i.e., those liable for military service within the framework of the tribe as a *mateh* or *degel* (e.g., Num. 2:2).

Pelagot were possible political factions within the *shevet* (e.g., Judg. 5:15).

6. *KEHILLOT*

Batei av (households), kinship units, as signified by laws relating to blood vengeance (Deut. 10:2, Josh. 22:2)

Arim (townships)

Both were subdivisions of the *shevet*.

Kehillot were governed by *ziknei ha-ir* (elders of the township), often referred to in their collective capacity as *sha'ar ha-ir* (lit. gate of the township where they sat as a council), who would be called up to adjudicate and administer matters of local concern (e.g., Deut. 21:1–9, Ruth 3), and *ha-ir*, the assembly of those entitled to participate in local government.

7. REPRESENTATIVE PERSONALITIES

7.1 Constitutional Architects

Moses:	*Eved Adonai*, in which capacity he served as principal instrument of *keter torah* and *keter malkhut* for entire *edah*. Transmitter to *edah* of Divine Torah, the basic constitutional referent for all succeeding generations; also statesman and commentator

Samuel: During course of his career acted (variously) as *Navi, Ro'eh, Shofet,* and apprentice and appointer of priests, hence almost as an *Eved Adonai.* Initially attempted to uphold republic, but eventually presided over establishment of a constitutional kingship (1 Sam. 10:25). Also statesman and commentator

7.2 Statesmen

Moses: Military leader, diplomat, and spokesman for entire *edah*

Joshua: *Eved Adonai,* military leader, diplomat, and spokesman for the entire *edah.* His principal contribution lay in his role in transforming the *edah* into a settled polity through the conquest of the land of Canaan, its division among the tribes, and the subsequent renewal of the covenant, all of which implemented the prescriptions presented in *Torat Moshe*

Samuel: After establishment of kingship, principal spokesman for *keter torah*

Saul: *Nagid;* principal instrument of *keter malkhut*

Aaron: First *Kohen Gadol*

Phineas: *Kohen Gadol;* zealous defender of constitution

Caleb: *Nasi* of Judah; advocate (with Joshua) before entire *edah* of early conquest of Canaan

Korah: Led revolt against centralization of powers of *ketarim* in hands of the brothers Moses and Aaron

Shofetim: (Othniel, Ehud, Deborah, Abimelekh, Tola, Yair, Jephtha, Ibzan, Elon and Abdon, Samson) acted as military leaders, magistrates, and guides for entire *edah,* or segments thereof

7.3 Constitutional Commentators

Moses: Transmitted and interpreted Torah; argued in defense of *edah* before God by referring to constitutional principles

Joshua: Interpreted *Torat Moshe* as part of implementation of its prescriptions for settling the *edah* in Canaan

Samuel: defended principle of God as king

8. TERMS

8.1 New

Degel (flag), tribe as constituted for war (Num. 2:2)

Edah (congregation or assembly), entire people as politically constituted (Exod. 12:3)

Edot (testimonies), constitutionally ordained actions which bear witness to the covenant (Deut. 6:20)

Edut (testimony), synonym for covenant (Deut. 4:45)

Eved Adonai (servant of God), God's Prime Minister (Num. 12:8)

Ezraḥ (citizen), member of the *edah* (Lev. 23:43)

Gibbor he-Ḥayyil, authorized leader or champion (Judg. 6:12)

Hakhale, a convocation for political/constitutional purposes (Deut. 31:13)

Ḥesed (covenant-love or obligation), the dynamic dimension of covenant, namely, going beyond the letter of the law as a result of covenantal obligation to act lovingly toward one's neighbor (Josh. 2:14)

Ḥok, constitutional law (Deut. 4:25)

Ḥukah, body of constitutional laws (Exod. 13:10)

Kahal (congregation or assembly), generic term for polity, often synonymous with *edah* (Num. 15:15)

Keruyei ha-Edah, commissioners (Num. 1:16)

Kohen (priest), now used in specifically Israelite context (Lev. 21:1)

Kohen Gadol (high priest), constitutional empowered authority in arena of *keter kehunah* (Lev. 21:10)

Lehamrot, to disregard Divine constitutional ordinances (e.g., Num. 20:10) or the words of His appointed instrument (e.g., Josh. 1:18)

Limrod, to rebel against Divine constitutional ordinances (e.g., Num. 14:9, Josh. 22:19)

Mashol, to govern (legitimately) as a governor (Judg. 8:22ff); previously used in non-Jewish context (e.g., Gen. 1:16, 24:2, 45:6)

Mateh (staff), symbol of tribal unity and authority (Num. 1:4)

Melekh (king), first used in this epoch in a specifically Israelite context (Deut. 17:14)

Mesharet, personal assistant to *Eved Adonai* (Exod. 24:13)

Meshiḥah (anointment), process of leadership conferment by Divine sanction (Exod. 28:41, 1 Sam. 15:17); hence *Mashiaḥ* (one who holds his office by virtue of anointment) (e.g., Lev. 4:3, 1 Sam. 24:6)

Mishpat, statute or case law (Deut. 4:45)

Mitzvah, constitutional command, originating with God (Exod. 24:12)

Nagid, chief executive and military leader (1 Sam. 9:16)

Nasi (magistrate or chief magistrate), one constitutionally raised up to lead or represent his *shevet* (Exod. 34:31)

Navi (prophet), conduit of Divine commands (Deut. 13:2)

Ohel mo'ed (tent of assembly), the focal point of the meetings of the *edah*, or its representatives, for governmental purposes

Pelagot, possible groupings within *shevet* (Judg. 5:15)

Pinot kol ha-am, leaders of the people (Judg. 20:2)

Rashei alfei yisrael (heads of the hosts of Israel), designation of constitutionally recognized leaders of tribes (Num. 1:16)

Ro'eh (seer), conduit of Divine will and hence constitutionally authorized leader of *edah* in sphere of *keter torah* (1 Sam. 9:9–10)

Sar, minister (Num. 22:7)

Semikhah (ordination), process whereby leadership is constitutionally conferred (Deut. 34:9)

Shevet (tribe), constituent unit of *edah* (Exod. 28:21)

Torah (teaching), corpus constituting constitution of *edah* (Exod. 24:12)

8.2 Old—Changed Meaning

Rado, to rule dictatorially, now used in sense of one people to another (e.g.,
Lev. 26:17)

9. BIBLIOGRAPHY

A. Alt, "The Formation of the Israelite State" in *Essays on Old Testament History and Religion*, translated by R. A. Wilson (New York, 1966).

R. G. Bowling and G. Ernest Wright (eds.), "Joshua," *The Anchor Bible*, vol. 5 (New York: 1982); "Judges," *The Anchor Bible*, vol. 6 (New York 1980).

M. Buber, *Moses: The Revelation and the Covenant* (New York, 1959).

R. Gordis, "Democratic Origins in Ancient Israel—The Biblical Edah," in *The Alexander Marx Jubilee Volume* (New York, 1967), pp. 373–388.

W. A. Irwin, "Saul and the Rise of the Monarchy," *American Journal of Semitic Languages and Literatures* 58 (1941), pp. 113–138.

Flavius Josephus, "The Polity Settled by Moses" in *The Works of Flavius Josephus, Antiquities of the Jews*, vol. I, translated by W. Whiston (Philadelphia, 1958), pp. 261–284.

Y. Lever, "Shivtei Yisrael" in *Ha-Historiah Shel Am Yisrael*, ed. M. Mazor (Jerusalem, 1962), vol. 2, pp. 247–262.

B. Lindars, "Gideon and the Kingship," *Journal of Theological Studies* 16 (1965), pp. 315–326.

A. Malamat, "Shivtei Yisrael" in *Ha-Historiah Shel Am Yisrael*, pp. 218–233.

P. K. McCarter, "I Samuel," *The Anchor Bible*, vol. 7 (New York, 1980).

G. E. Mendenhall, "The Census Lists of Numbers 1 and 26," *Journal of Biblical Literature* 65 (1946), pp. 45–49.

M. Noth, "The Confederation of the Tribes of Israel" in *The History of Israel* (New York, 1958), pp. 85–97.

H. M. Orlinsky, "The Tribal System of Israel and Related Groups in the Period of the Judges," *Oriental Antiquities* 1 (1962), pp. 11–20.

E. A. Speiser, "Background and Functions of the Biblical Nasi," *Catholic Biblical Quarterly* 25 (1965), pp. 111–117.

C. Umhau Wolf, "Terminology of Israel's Tribal Organization," *Journal of Biblical Literature* 65 (1946), pp. 45–49.

R. de Vaux, "The Free Population," in *Ancient Israel. Volume One: Social Institutions* (New York, 1965), pp. 68–74.

M. Weinfeld, "Judge and Officer in Ancient Israel and in the Ancient Near East," *Israel Oriental Studies* 7 (1977), pp. 65–88.

EPOCH IV

2756–3039 AM (1004–721 BCE)

Brit ha-Melukhah

The Federal Monarchy

1. DOMINANT EVENTS

1.1 Founding Events
Accession of David to kingship   c. 1004 BCE
  His coronation (2 Sam. 5, 6)
  Conquest of Jerusalem (and its establishment as capital and, under Solo-
    mon, as site of sole house of God)
  Unification of tribes under his rule
  Defeat of Philistines (2 Sam. 8)
  Foundation of Davidic dynasty

1.2 Climactic Events
Division of *edah* into two kingdoms (1 Kings 12:1–24)   c. 928 BCE
Transfer of political power from tribes to royal instrumentalities

1.3 Culminating Events
Destruction and conquest of northern kingdom, which resulted in final collapse of tribal system (2 Kings 17:1–6)   721 BCE

2. CONSTITUTIONAL HISTORY

The establishment of a dynastic kingship at the beginning of Epoch IV
marked a fundamental break with previous Jewish constitutional practice. By
welding the Israelites into a unified national unit, the monarchy superseded
the tribal confederacy as the form of government for the entire *edah*. The
transition was not a smooth one. Several of the rebellions which studded
David's reign can be interpreted as tribal reactions to royal centralization

(hence the deliberate contrast in the texts between "the men of Israel" and David's servants). Overweening centralization under Solomon led to the division into two kingdoms which followed Solomon's death (and which constitutes the epoch's climactic event).

The northern kingdom sought a synthesis that combined kingship and tribal authority in a federal monarchy. One result of this effort was the failure to establish a stable means of dynastic succession, which, in turn, was one of the prime causes for the chronic run of political crises which plagued that polity's internal history. By the end of the epoch, however, even there the principle of kingship had firmly taken root. The fall of Israel to the Assyrians (the culminating event of the epoch) merely confirmed the collapse of the tribal structure dominant during the previous epoch. Long before, in both Judah and Israel, royal instrumentalities—and royal terminology—had replaced tribal officers as the effective instruments of national government, thereby replacing confederation with federation under a *Melekh/Nagid*.

Significantly, and in strict accordance with the entire course of the Jewish political tradition, the kingship was established by covenant. Indeed, it was the *brit ha-melekhuh* (the covenant of kingship between God, the king, and the people) which supplemented the *Torat Moshe* as the basic constitutional referent for the *edah* throughout the epoch. This was a development of revolutionary proportions, whose consequences upon the balance among the three *ketarim* were immediately apparent. Hitherto, the terms of *keter malkhut* had been subsumed within the general framework of the Torah; as much was made explicit by the *parshat ha-melekh* (laws relating to kingship) in Deut. 17:14–20. Moreover, the founding covenant of that *keter* had been concluded, not with any single person, but with the people—who were empowered to appoint a king if they so chose. The introduction of a physical *Melekh* and the establishment of a royal dynasty radically changed the balance of forces. As early as the first generation of the epoch, royal dominance of the *keter malkhut* became firmly institutionalized and (with the enunciation of the dynastic principle) the preserve of a single family.

The authority and political power thus wielded by the *Melekh* was further augmented by David's transfer of the Ark of the Covenant to Jerusalem and his designation of the Zadokites to be the dominant priestly family, thereby placing the principal bearers of the *keter kehunah* under royal patronage. This process was substantially completed by Solomon, who constructed the Temple in Jerusalem and designated it the sole house of God. This act did not entirely succeed. Other shrines (*bamot*) continued to exist throughout the monarchy, with the centrality of the cult remaining a bone of constitutional contention. Nevertheless, the construction of the Temple did consolidate the process whereby the instruments of national government were centralized in the capital.

At the same time, it also strengthened the *keter malkhut*. Instruments of the *keter kehunah* were henceforth in fact (and often in name) royal servants—financially secure but politically subordinate. Within its new circumscribed condition, the *keter kehunah* did remain a balancing force in the constitutional system, particularly in times of internal political crisis, but more than ever, the ability to maintain that *keter* as a co-equal branch of the polity was contingent on the personal strength of the *Kohen Gadol*. Thus, only as outstanding a *Kohen Gadol* as Jehoiada, who organized and led the palace revolt against a usurper to the throne in order to restore the constitution, could give substance to the claims of the *keter kehunah* to constitute a co-equal branch of the polity.

More often, however, the counterweight to hegemonic royal influence was to be located in the *keter torah*. Indeed, now that the *keter malkhut* had become the exclusive demesne of a man of flesh and blood, constitutional dynamics themselves appeared to demand a strengthening of the *keter torah* as a separate branch of the polity. Accordingly, it was during the course of this epoch that the latter's sphere of influence was progressively expanded. The *Navi* (a Divine appointee who, while capable of serving the *Melekh*, was not necessarily dependent upon him) now emerged as the principal check upon kingly absolutism. It was Samuel who anointed David and Nathan who reprimanded him when he overstepped prescribed constitutional boundaries.

Once the pattern had been set during the early generations of the epoch, it was hardly affected by subsequent developments. Neither the division of the kingdom nor the fall of Israel altered the balance of the three *ketarim* within the *brit ha-melukhah*. The constitutional significance of these events lies elsewhere, in their influence on the corporate structure of the *edah*. This, too, altered substantially—albeit gradually—as the epoch unfolded. Even before David's accession, some tribes had begun to lose their individuality; others had become decidedly prominent. Judah clearly stood apart from the others even in Saul's time, its troops being numbered separately from the rest of the house of Israel (1 Sam. 11:8). The loyalty of that tribe to the Davidic house after Solomon's death must therefore be viewed as an extension of an earlier trend, rather than an entirely new development. The tribal structure continued to exist throughout the epoch in both kingdoms, especially for purposes of local government, but the tribes were drastically weakened as sources of national power from the time of David. After the division of the kingdom, Jerusalem became the almost exclusive center of state power in Judah although Benjamin apparently preserved its distinctiveness for local purposes and internal government in the kingdom as a whole was quite decentralized. The tribes retained greater power in the northern kingdom until relatively late in its history and Israel can be deemed a federal monarchy in that sense until its final conquest.

The political division of the kingdom must remain an event of central constitutional significance. The *edah* still possessed a sense of corporate unity:

members of both kingdoms could address each other as *aheikhem* (your brothers) *bnei yisrael*. But for the first time they owed allegiance to distinct political entities, both of which developed recognized and recognizable institutions of self-government and neither of which accepted the authority of any other state framework. What tied them together was the common recognition of God's sovereignty and *Torat Moshe* as defended and interpreted by the *nevi'im* who crossed the borders of the two polities on an essentially unrestricted basis. Thus the *keter torah* constituted the principal instrument of the unity of the *edah*.

3. CONSTITUTION

Torat Moshe and covenant of kingship (between God, king, and people)—
    2 Sam. 5:1–3 (David), 1 Chron. 28:1–10 (David and Solomon), and
    2 Chron. 6 (Solomon)
Mishpat ha-Melukhah (constitutional law binding king)—1 Sam. 10:25

3.1 Constitutional Issues
Status of tribes within new kingship system
Centrality of cult at Jerusalem
Relations between two kingdoms as segments of one nation
Legitimacy of dynastic succession

3.2 Camps and Parties
New royal supporters, dependents, and bureaucracy ("David's servants") vs. traditional structure—e.g., "people of Israel" in case of Absalom (2 Sam. 18:7)
Groups which retained distinctiveness within *edah*—e.g., *bnei ha-nevi'im* (2 Kings 2) and Kenites (Judg. 1:16; 4:11, 17)

4. CONSTITUTIONAL STRUCTURE OF THE *EDAH*

A federation of tribes consisting of two distinct entities, Israel and Judah, with strong national institutions. These two segments were distinct even during reigns of David and Solomon (whose regimes were constituted virtually as "dual monarchies"); their political separation became complete after the latter's death.

4.1 Principal Instruments, Officers, and Functions
KETER MALKHUT
Judah: A limited monarchy, in the sense that the *Melekh*, sometimes still referred to as *Nagid* (e.g., 2 Sam. 7:8), was still subject to the origi-

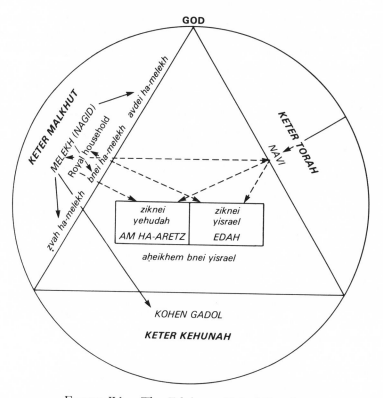

FIGURE IV-1. The *Edah* as a United Kingdom

nal *Torat Moshe* and to the popular will. Hence the coronation ceremony consisted of: anointment, acclamation, and enthronement. In
addition, when a major constitutional development occurred, the
king had to recovenant with the *edah* before God (e.g., Solomon at
dedication of Temple—1 Kings 8).

Israel: In the northern kingdom, the dynastic principle did not function well
in practice because the tribes sought to maintain their traditional
powers while the *Melekh* lacked independent constitutional legitimacy. The constitutional problem which arose was that no means
was discovered to create a system of succession which would both sta-
bilize the regime and preserve the rights of the *edah*.

The *Melekh/Nagid* attained office through dual process of Divine appointment (anointed by the *Navi*) and popular ratification (through covenant or,
when no constitutional question arose, by acclamation). Though referred to
as *Melekh* by the people, the title-holder officially remained *Nagid* in constitutional theory and in the eyes of the prophets. In Judah, the Davidic house
was accepted as the legitimate holder of crown, which passed by succession.

The *Melekh* was the principal human repository of national executive and military authority.

The establishment of the monarchy generated the emergence of a royal household (*benei ha-melekh*, e.g., 1 Chron. 27:32). It also gave rise to the creation of a royal court (*beit ha-melekh*) and bureaucracy (*avdei ha-melekh*), whose wide-ranging functions and powers were often reflected in their titles. Thus, the *beit ha-melekh* included officers such as the following:

Al ha-tzavah, commander-in-chief

Al ha-bayit, chamberlain (1 Kings 4:6)

Kohen le-David, court priest (2 Sam. 20:26)

Mazkir, royal herald

Rai'a David, "the king's friend" (i.e., counsellor, 2 Sam. 15:37)

Sofer, scribe

Yoetz, counsellor (2 Sam. 15:12)

Among the *avdei ha-melekh* were the following:

Al ha-kreiti ve-ha-pleitie, military officers

Al otzrot ha-melekh

Al ha-mas

Al ha-keramim

Al shebakramim (otzrot ha-yayin)　　　　　　　　}　exchequer officials

Al ha-zeitim

Al otzrot ha-shemen

Al ha-bakar; al ha-gemalim; al ha-atonot; al ha-tzon

Al osei melekhet hasadeh, public works officials

Sarei ha-rekhush asher lamelekh (1 Chron. 27:25–32), officials of the royal demesne

Soharei ha-melekh (1 Kings 10:28–29), commercial officials

KETER TORAH

Once the *keter malkhut* was dominated by a king of flesh and blood, there was a perceived need to strengthen the independent authority of the *keter torah*. This was accomplished by expanding the office of *Navi* (prophet), who anointed the *Melekh* and whose clashes with royal authority became endemic.

Navi:　　　　A personal appointment by God

　　　　　　　—evaluated performance of *Melekh* and *edah* in light of *Torat Moshe*

　　　　　　　—interpreted constitution to *edah* on basis of Divine communication and, in so doing, acted as counterweight to authority of *Melekh*

　　　　　　　—acted as political counselor (e.g., Nathan, 2 Sam. 12:1ff, and 1 Kings 12:22ff, 22:5–28)

　　　　　　　—anointed *Melekh*, thus conferring or denying legitimacy (thus Elisha anointed Jehu during Ahab's reign, 2 Kings 9:1ff)

Bnei ha-neviim: Disciples of the *Navi* who served him (e.g., 2 Kings 2)

KETER KEHUNAH

With the establishment of the kingship, the *keter kehunah* declined in power and came under the patronage of the *keter malkhut*. Conversely, the *melekh* now performed some sacerdotal functions (e.g., Solomon played sacerdotal role at dedication of the Temple—1 Kings 8). Indeed, with the construction of the Temple in Jerusalem by Solomon (although the idea for the project originated with David), all *kohanim* were linked to it by the Davidic house, to which they inevitably became subordinate. In return, their sacerdotal role was expanded, the priesthood was bureaucratized, and *kohanim* were given greater economic security.

Centralization of the cult also had political overtones, affecting relations between two kingdoms (as appreciated by Jeroboam, 1 Kings 12:27–33).

In Judah, the principle of Aaronic descent of the bearers of the *keter kehunah* was retained, thereby furnishing some independent basis for a continued constitutional role for the *Kohen Gadol*. In Israel, however, it was abandoned. There, *kohanim* were entirely the *Melekh*'s creatures (1 Kings 12:28–32).

Kohen Gadol: Appointment continued on basis of Aaronic covenant, although *Melekh* now had power to determine incumbent.

Priestly functions were generally limited to maintaining Temple service, although at times the *Kohen Gadol* played a decisive role in restoring a legitimate king to the throne and/or binding him to the Torah (e.g., Jehoiada, 2 Kings 11:17, and Ḥilkiah in the days of Josiah, 2 Kings 22).

Thus he remained, despite the changes in his office, the head of a presumably co-equal branch of the polity and could be independently influential, at least in times of crisis. No doubt the *Kohen Gadol* played an advisory role at other times as well.

5. *MEDINOT*

Twelve *shevatim* retained their distinctiveness (e.g., census lists in 2 Sam. 24:1–9 and David's monarchy in Judah, 2 Sam. 2:1–11), but as federated entities within kingdom. As such, they were combined with royal bureaucratic divisions (e.g., Solomon's appointment of twelve *niẓavim*, 1 Kings 4:7–19, and Ahab's *medinot*, 1 Kings 20:14), by which they were sometimes superseded.

After the division of the kingdom, there were two main *medinot*:

Israel, where ten *shevatim* continued as before (but note Ahab's organization of *medinot*, 1 Kings 20:14) with responsibilities for (1) participation

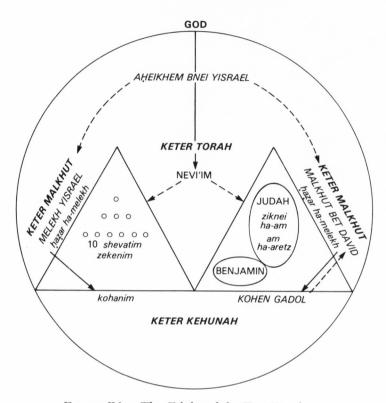

FIGURE IV-2. The *Edah* and the Two Kingdoms

in the royal army and payment of royal taxes and (2) sharing of administrative responsibilities determined by royal government

Judah, where Benjamin apparently maintained some measure of separate
identity (Jer. 17:26, 32:8) but was essentially merged with Judah insofar
as the kingdom was concerned

The two *medinot* were linked as an *edah* (referred to as *aheikhem bnei
yisrael*, 1 Kings 12:24, although the term is older—see Judg. 20:13) through
cult, emphasis on common ancestry, and common *nevi'im*.

6. *KEHILLOT*

Local communities, urban and rural

Continued to be governed by *shaarei ha-ir*, *ziknei ha-ir*, and *ha-ir*, but the
period witnessed increasing influence of local magnates, the extent of
whose political and economic power had no constitutional sanction (e.g.,
Amos 1:7)

7. REPRESENTATIVE PERSONALITIES

7.1 Constitutional Architects

David: First *Melekh*, established dynasty; first to conceive of permanent shrine; also statesman

Jeroboam: Architect of secession of northern tribes and their first *Melekh*, also statesman

7.2 Statesmen

David: Military leader, diplomat

Nathan: *Navi*, representative of *keter torah* vs. infringements of constitution by David; also commentator

Solomon: Diplomat and magistrate; constructed permanent Temple

Jeroboam: First *Melekh* of northern kingdom

Jehoiadah: *Kohen Gadol* in Judah during reigns of Athaliah and Josiah; led popular resistance to Athaliah; instituted new administrative procedures in Temple; rescued Josiah and enthroned him after Athaliah killed, thus preserving both the dynastic principle and the constitution

Elijah: *Navi* in northern kingdom in reigns of Ahab and Aḥizah, defender of Israelite monotheism and social justice elements in constitution, also commentator

Omri: Most powerful *Melekh* of northern kingdom; built new capital in Samaria

Ahab: Son of Omri, *Melekh* of northern kingdom which, during his kingship, attained economic prosperity but suffered religious strife

7.3 Constitutional Commentators

(All emphasized moral dimensions of *Torat Moshe* as counterbalance to kingly "pragmatism.")

Ahijah   *Navi* in time of Solomon and his successors; foretold split in
ha-Shiloni: *edah* (1 Kings 11:29–39)

Nathan: *Navi* in time of David, emphasized that *Melekh* was bound by Torah

Elijah: *Navi*

Amos: *Navi* in northern kingdom; originated in south

Hosea: *Navi* in northern kingdom

8. TERMS

8.1 New

Am ha-aretz, term used to describe assembly of entire *medinah* of Judah

Eved, now used in sense of a royal minister (*eved ha-melekh*, 2 Sam. 18:29)

Gevirah, queen mother

Kreitie and *Pleitie*, mercenaries (2 Sam. 8:18)

Mamlakhah, kingdom; now used in reference to Israelites (1 Sam. 28:17)

Mazkir, secretary to the court (2 Sam. 8:16)

Melukhah, kingdom (1 Kings 21:7)

Memshalah, kingdom (1 Kings 9:19)

Medinot, regional divisions (1 Kings 20:14); tended to supersede tribes

Moshel, governor (1 Kings 5:1)

Nizavim, regional administrators, representatives of the royal bureaucracy without apparent tribal affiliations; originally, term applied to non-Israelite administration (e.g., 2 Sam. 8:6), later adapted for Israelite use by Solomon (1 Kings 4:7–14)

Yoetz, royal counsellor (2 Sam. 15:12)

8.2 Old—Change in Meaning

Alah, now used in sense of contract between humans (1 Kings 8:31)

Agudah, organizing concept, group within polity (2 Sam. 2:25)

Rado, to rule beyond constitutional limits; now in sense of dictatorial power within Jewish polity (e.g., 1 Kings 5:4)

Nasi, now used as prefix to nontribal unit; e.g., *nesiei ha-avot* (1 Kings 8:1), indicative of breakdown of tribal system

Sar, royal minister (1 Kings 4:2)

Zedakah, equity; now in sense of royal justice (2 Sam. 8:15)

9. BIBLIOGRAPHY

W. F. Albright, "Tribal Rule and Charismatic Leaders" in *The Biblical Period from Abraham to Ezra* (New York, 1968), pp. 35–52.

S. H. Blank, "The Dissident Laity in Early Judaism," *Hebrew Union College Annual* 19 (1945–1946), pp. 1–42.

M. Buber, *Kingship of God* (third edition, translated by R. Scheimann; New York, 1967), chapter one: "The Gideon Passage," pp. 59–65.

M. M. Cohen, "The Role of the Shilonite Priesthood in the United Monarchy of Ancient Israel," *Hebrew Union College Annual* 36 (1965), pp. 59–98.

R. W. Corney, *The Reigns of Omri and Ahab* (unpublished Ph.D. thesis; Union Theological Seminary, 1970).

B. Halpern, *The Constitution of the Monarchy in Israel* (Harvard Semitic Monographs No. 25, 1981).

E. W. Heaton, *Solomon's New Men. The Emergence of Ancient Israel as a Nation State* (London, 1974).

Y. Kaufman, "The Monarchy" in *The Religion of Israel* (Chicago, 1960), pp. 262–270.

J. Levenson, "The Davidic Covenant and its Modern Interpreters," *Catholic Bible Quarterly* 41 (ii), 1979, pp. 205–219.

A. Malamat, "Organs of Statecraft in the Israelite Monarchy," *The Biblical Archeologist* 28 (2), 1965, pp. 34–50.

J. Muilenberg, "The 'Office' of the Prophet in Ancient Israel" in J. P. Hyatt (ed.), *The Bible in Modern Scholarship* (1966), pp. 79–97.

H. Tadmor, "'The People' and the Kingship in Ancient Israel: The Role of Political Institutions in the Biblical Period," *Journal of World History* 11 (1968), pp. 46–68.

S. Talmon, "Kingship and Ideology of the State" in *The World History of the Jewish People*, vol. 4, part 2 (Jerusalem, 1979), pp. 3–26.

R. de Vaux, "The Administration of the Kingdom" in *Ancient Israel. Volume One: Social Institutions* (New York, 1965), pp. 133–142.

G. Widengreen, "King and Covenant," *Journal of Semitic Studies* 2 (i), 1957, pp. 1–27.

M. Weinfeld, "The Transition from Tribal Rule to Monarchy and its Impact on the History of Israel" in *Kinship and Consent: The Jewish Political Tradition and its Contemporary Uses*, ed. Daniel J. Elazar (Ramat-Gan, 1981), pp. 151–166.

EPOCH V

3039–3320 AM (721–440 BCE)

Malkhut Yehudah

Kingdom of Judah

1. DOMINANT EVENTS

1.1 Founding Events

Fall of the northern kingdom, destruction of tribal system   721 BCE

Inheritance by Kingdom of Judah of remnants of Israel through absorption of refugees and territorial expansion northward and eastward and reinstitution of *edah*-wide rites in Jerusalem Temple

1.2 Climactic Events

Josiah's reforms (2 Kings 22,23; 2 Chron. 34,35).   639–609 BCE

These embodied measures which initiated a process of constitutional reconstruction, as well as religious regeneration. Both characteristics survived the later destruction of the First Temple and continued to exercise a dominant influence in the Babylonian diaspora.

Conquest of Judah by neo-Babylonians and ensuing Babylonian captivity (2 Kings 25:1–21)   586 BCE

1.3 Culminating Events

Failure to restore the Kingdom of Judah in its original form after the Babylonian exile. This imposed a need for the reconstitution of the *edah* (2 Kings 25:22–26; Jer. 40:7–43:7).   C.450 BCE

2. CONSTITUTIONAL HISTORY

The fall of the northern Kingdom of Israel in 721 BCE opened a new epoch in Jewish constitutional history. Not only did that event severely reduce the population of the *edah*; it also completed the demise of the *shevet* as a distinct governmental entity. The history of Epoch V, therefore, essentially revolved around the fate, fortunes, and activities of the southern Kingdom of Judah which extended its rule over much of the territory and most of the survivors of the northern kingdom, thereby restoring national unity.

Within that polity, the epoch began with a program of reform and reconstruction. This was a process in which Hezekiah, King of Judah at the time of the fall of the northern kingdom, played a central role. The biblical account (2 Chron. 29–31) stresses both his fidelity to *Torat Moshe* and his righteousness (for which attribute he is compared to David). His most important diplomatic achievement was his declaration of Judea's independence from Assyria—a status which (with apparently miraculous Divine assistance) he managed to retain even when Sennacherib swept down upon Jerusalem "like a wolf on the fold." His most important constitutional achievement was the restoration of the centrality of worship in the Temple in Jerusalem for the entire *edah* through the convocation of a Passover ceremony which (although held somewhat belatedly) included remnants of the northern tribes.

It is significant that Hezekiah's reforms were carried out with the help of principal instruments of both the *keter kehunah* (who were restored to something like their classical status) and the *keter torah* (Hezekiah's personal relationship with the *Navi* Isaiah was particularly close). Indeed, one of the characteristics of the epoch as a whole was the retention of the balance among the three domains. The Josianic reform, which marked one of the epoch's climactic events, reflected an equal degree of inter-*keter* cooperation and indeed did much to further that tradition.

Not even the physical and cultic calamity of the fall of Jerusalem in 586 BCE affected the resilience of this structure. The *Navi* remained the principal instrument of the *keter torah* (with Jeremiah being succeeded by Ezekiel, the second Isaiah, Zachariah, and Ḥaggai) and the *Kohen Gadol* that of the *keter kehunah*, although his role was in abeyance for nearly two generations. Royal status was retained by the Davidic line even during the Babylonian exile, with the family of the *Melekh* located at the neo-Babylonian court, thus also indicating the continuity of the *keter malkhut*. Nevertheless, it is worthy of note that the prophesies of Ezekiel and the second Isaiah refer to the principal instrument of this domain by the older title of *Nasi* rather than *Melekh*, thus portending the shift in authority away from the *keter malkhut* and toward the *keter torah* which was to become so marked a feature of the succeeding epoch.

Equally significant were the constitutional developments which took place in two other areas: in the basic constitutional referent of the *edah*, and in its corporate structure. The change in constitutional referent itself proceeded upon two parallel lines. One consisted of the Josianic reforms, which explicitly reinforced the constitutional status of *Torat Moshe*. The other was the advancement of the prophetic covenant (whose genesis is to be found in the previous epoch) to full constitutional status. Unlike the Josianic reforms, which were inaugurated under the auspices of the *keter malkhut*, the prophetic covenant was initiated (as its name implies) by the *nevi'im* in their capacities as instruments of the *keter torah*. It was they who provided the polity with a moral base and supplied it with an ideological formulation which was to enable it to continue to function under conditions of exile after the destruction of the Temple.

The latter event accelerated the second significant constitutional development of the epoch: the restructuring of the *edah*. This also proceeded along two parallel lines—first, the demise of the tribes as governmental entities with the destruction of the northern kingdom and, second, the emergence of organized diaspora communities. Limited and scattered exiled settlements existed in Asia Minor during the early generations of the epoch—immediately after the fall of the northern kingdom. Only during the latter half of the epoch, however, did this phenomenon become permanent and solidified, with diasporas of note and importance emerging in Egypt and—after the destruction of the Temple—in Bavel. By the close of the epoch, the constitutional legitimacy of such diasporas had been made manifest through prophetic sanction, enabling them to function in a corporate fashion within the *edah*. At the same time, the weight of these *medinot* in the *edah* had also grown. Judea remained by far the most important, the focus of Jewish national and religious aspirations and therefore the goal of Zerubavel's attempt at national restoration in c.522 BCE. During the latter half of the epoch, however, the limited territory under Jewish jurisdiction did not encompass the majority of the *edah*. In fact, some of the more seminal constitutional developments of the latter generations occurred in the diaspora.

Most crucially was this so in the case of Bavel. It was there that local *kehillot* created institutional replacements for the Temple and its service. The emergence of the *bet knesset* as a locus of communal assembly, instruction, and devotion is—by any standards—a development of major constitutional importance. It was the *bet knesset*, also referred to by Ezekiel as a *mikdash me'at* or miniature temple, which furnished local communities with means of significant constitutional existence even when distant from Judah and Jerusalem.

3. CONSTITUTION

Torat Moshe, including *Sefer ha-Brit* (Deuteronomic Code)

The latter was formally readopted as the constitution of the entire *edah* during an assembly at which the king, elders, priests, prophets, and all the people "from small to great" covenanted to accept and abide by the Deuteronomic Code (2 Kings 22,23 and 2 Chron. 34,35). The new covenant explicitly aimed to restore the centrality of *Torat Moshe*—hence the symbolic significance of the restoration of the Passover rite, where specific references are made to the compliance with ordinances first transmitted through Moses (e.g., 2 Chron. 35:6,12).

The Deuteronomic Code included the covenant of kingship as constitutionalized and was informed by the emphasis on social justice, thus incorporating the contribution of the *nevi'im* as well. The latter element had been present during the previous epoch but now became increasingly prominent and provided the polity with a sharpened moral basis (Mic. 6:1–9, Jer. 7:1–15, Ezek. 20:35–37). At the same time, however, the prophetic covenant also enabled the *keter torah* to attain status as an instrument of popular resistance to kingly absolutism.

3.1 Constitutional Issues

The reforging of national unity—including the incorporation of exiles from and territory of the northern kingdom (Isa. 8:4, Ezek. 37)

The prerogatives of the *Navi* vis-a-vis the *Melekh* (Jer. 27)

The reestablishment of the Deuteronomic Code (2 Chron. 34,35)

The maintenance of continued Jewish existence in conditions of exile (Jer. 29:5–9, 44:14)

The restoration of Jewish jurisdiction in Eretz Israel (2 Kings 25:22–24)

3.2 Camps and Parties

CAMPS

Religious reformers vs. those who "defiled the house of God" (e.g., 2 Chron. 36:14)

Polarization with regard to possible foreign policy orientations (e.g., Jer. 27)

PARTIES WITHIN CAMPS

Rival court factions (e.g., 2 Kings 11, 2 Kings 21:23)

Rivalry between true and false prophets and their respective followings (e.g., Jer. 28 and 29:21–22)

4. CONSTITUTIONAL STRUCTURE OF THE *EDAH*

Limited monarchy, in which the tribal system had been effectively eliminated as a factor in government

4.1 Principal Instruments, Officers, and Functions

Remained the same as in Judah in the previous epoch. Significantly, the destruction of the Temple did not affect the basic internal structure of the *edah*. The three *ketarim* retained their classical status and institutions, with incumbents in each generation of the exile to fill the necessary roles, even if in a limited or subordinate way. The Bible even provides us with their names.

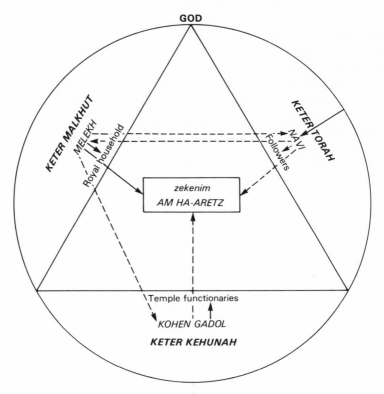

FIGURE V-1. The *Edah* in the Latter Years
of Independent Judah

	Keter Malkhut	Keter Torah	Keter Kehunah
1	Jehoiachin	Jeremiah	?
2	Shezbazar (Sheruzar)	Jeremiah second Isaiah/Ezekiel	?
3	Zerubavel	Zachariah Haggai	Joshua the High Priest

(column at left, rotated: Generation)

KETER MALKHUT

Remained with Davidic line until end of epoch. At climax (580 BCE), Nebuchadnezer transferred the king and his court to Babylon, where—at least from the point of view of the exiles and probably their captors as well—they continued to maintain their prerogatives (2 Kings 25:27–30).

KETER KEHUNAH

Remained with line of Aaron through Zadok. Although deprived of its most important function after destruction of Temple, it also retained its identity and was restored upon rebuilding of Temple (e.g., Zech. 4:1–10; 6:11, 13).

KETER TORAH

Remained with *nevi'im* until end of epoch. During that time, *Navi* continued to function as both voice of Torah and political counselor to *Melekh* (e.g., Jeremiah, even when in prison—Jer. 37:17ff. and 38:14ff.). After exile, represented and enhanced by Jeremiah in Egypt and by Ezekiel in Bavel. Its authority within the *edah* grew, with the *Navi* restating his constitutional right to legitimize appointments in other spheres. Thus, Ezekiel could speak of the restoration of the *keter malkhut* (although the term used is *Nasi*, not *Melekh*— e.g., Ezek. 34:23–24, 45:16, 46:9–18) and of the priesthood (Ezek. 43:18–27, 44:15–31) in a restored tribal federation united by *masoret ha-brit*, the bond or tradition of the covenant.

5. *MEDINOT*

Destruction of tribal system in the northern kingdom eliminated traditional *medinot* (*shevatim*) as a political factor. For a brief period, Judah was the only organized Jewish entity although the exiles from the north were settled in two concentrations in Assyria: Gozan and Medea. The conditions of exile consequent upon the destruction of the first Temple divided the *edah* into three proto-*medinot* (Judah, Bavel, and Yev or Elephantine), each of which began to develop parallel—although not identical—institutions of governance.

6. *KEHILLOT*

During the first half of the epoch, the system of local government in Judah was possibly strengthened by the elimination of the *shevatim*.

After destruction of the Temple, the traditional form of *kehillah* passed to Bavel with virtually no change, the genealogies and organization of *batei av* proving particularly persistent. Although the exiles apparently settled in townships of their own within a discrete region, the *bet knesset* (house of assembly) emerged as focal point to replace the *sha'ar ha-ir*, perhaps a reflection of a different juridical status of Jewish townships under foreign rule as distinct from those in an independent Jewish state. The introduction of the *bet knesset* was a major constitutional development, perhaps the single most significant political adaptation to conditions of dispersion.

There is evidence that older forms of local government may well have persisted in Eretz Israel after the destruction of the Temple, especially in the territory of the tribe of Benjamin (Jer. 17:26, 32:5).

7. REPRESENTATIVE PERSONALITIES

7.1 Constitutional Architects

Jeremiah: *Navi* in both Judah and diaspora; proposed reforms of kingdoms; granted legitimacy to establishment of diaspora communities

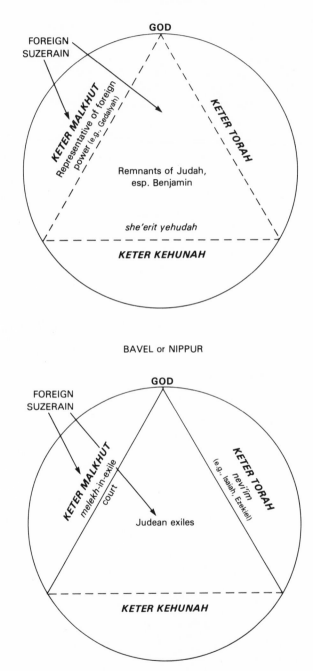

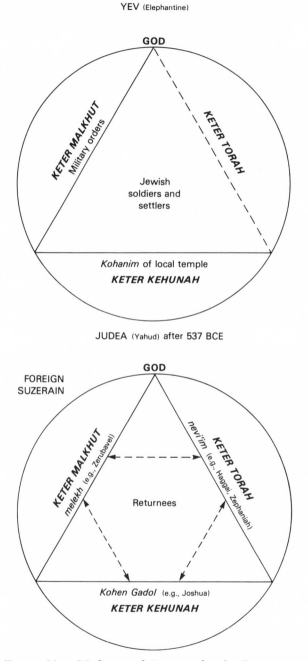

FIGURE V-2. *Medinot* and *Aratzot* after the Destruction
of the First Temple

Hilkhiah: *Kohen Gadol* in reign of Josiah; discovered Deuteronomic scroll and, on Josiah's orders, removed all appurtenances of pagan worship from Temple
Josiah: *Melekh*, principal force behind constitutional reforms, also statesman

7.2 Statesmen

Isaiah: *Navi*; played crucial role in inauguration of new constitutional epoch; his cooperation with Hezekiah essential to the reformulation of the constitution
Josiah: *Melekh*, warrior and diplomat
Hezekiah: *Melekh*; played crucial role in inauguration of new constitutional epoch; instituted religious reforms, ensured survival of one of two Jewish states, and—to an extent—preserved unity of *edah*
Zerubavel   Babylonian Jew, became *pehah* of postexilic Jerusalem
ben   With help of Joshua the *Kohen Gadol*, rebuilt Temple
Shealtiel:

7.3 Constitutional Commentators

Ezekiel: *Navi* in Bavel; his vision contributed to the architecture of the constitution during the epoch that followed

8. TERMS

8.1 New

INDIGENOUS

Golah, exile; a description of the status of the polity as well as its location (Ezek. 1:1)

Mahlakot, miflagot, pelugot, organized groups of families (e.g., 2 Chron. 35:5, 12)

Masoret, bond or tradition (Ezek. 20:37)

Negid bet elohim, chancellor of the House of God; description of *Kohen Gadol*; perhaps indicative of the decline in status of the office (2 Chron. 31:13)

Sarisim (lit. "eunuchs"), royal officials (2 Kings 10:1)

Zemah (branch); designation of God's chosen instrument (Jer. 23:5, Zech. 6:12)

FOREIGN DERIVATIVES

Pehah, governor appointed by foreign suzerain (Hag. 1:1, 2:2)

8.2 Old

CHANGE IN MEANING

Nasi, term revived by Ezekiel, after the office of *Melekh* ceased to be operative, to describe the principal repository of the *keter malkhut* (e.g., Ezek. 34:23–24). In this way he restored the spirit of the classical constitutional structure while incorporating the changes which that structure had been forced to accommodate. Hereafter the term was invariably used in place of *Melekh*.

Sokhen, "steward," wielder of delegated power (Isa. 22:15); originally servant (e.g., 1 Kings 1:2)

Zekenim, now also referred to as *ziknei ha-golah* (Jer. 29:1, Ezek. 1:1); signified attempt to regain traditional form of government in conditions of exile

NEW MEANING

Limrod, to rebel; now against foreign rule (e.g., 2 Kings 18:7; 24:1,20; Jer. 52:3)

9. BIBLIOGRAPHY

A. Alt, "Das Koenigtum in dem Reiches Israel und Judah," *Vetus Testamentum* 11 (1961), pp. 2–22.

J. Bright, "The Monarchy: Crisis and Downfall," in *A History of Israel* (third edition, Philadelphia, 1981), pp. 267–339.

Z. Falk, "The Temple Scroll and the Codification of Jewish Law," *Jewish Law Annual* 2ʼ(1979), pp. 33–44.

M. Galston, "Philosopher-King vs. Prophet," *Israel Oriental Studies* 8 (1978), pp. 204–218.

B. Z. Luria, "Ha-Yaḥasim bein Yehudah le-vein Efraim le-min ha-Ḥalukah ve-ad la-Ḥurban," *Beit Mikrah* 23 (iv), 1978, pp. 411–424.

A. Malamat, "Yirmiyahu u-Malkhei Yehudah ha-Aḥaronim," *Sefer ha-Kinus ha-Rishon le-Madaei ha-Yahadut* (Jerusalem, 1952), pp. 226–230.

N. M. Sarna, "The Abortive Insurrection in Zedekiah's Day (Jer. 27–29)," *Eretz-Israel* 14 (1978), English section, pp. 89–96.

S. Talmon, "Divergence in Calendar Reckoning in Ephraim and Judah," *Vetus Testamentum* 8 (1958), pp. 48–74.

R. de Vaux, "Le Sens de l'expression 'Peuple du Pays' dans l'Ancien Testament et le rôle politique du peuple en Israël," *Revue d'Assyriologie* 58 (1964), pp. 167–172.

———. "The Israelite Concept of the State," in *Ancient Israel. Volume One: Social Institutions* (New York, 1965), pp. 91–99.

J. A. Wicoxen, "The Political Background of Jeremiah's Temple Sermon," *Rylaarsdam* (1977), pp. 151–166.

S. Yavin, "Mishpaḥot u-Miflagot be-Mamlekhet Yehudah," *Mehkarim be-Toldot Yisrael ve-Artzo* (Jerusalem, 1960), pp. 239–251.

PART TWO

The Second Commonwealth
and Its Aftermath

EPOCH VI

Knesset ha-Gedolah
The Great Assembly

1. DOMINANT EVENTS

1.1 Founding Events

Reestablishment of Jewish polity in *Yehudah* (Judea—in Persian terminology,
  Yahud) within framework of the Persian empire   c. 445 BCE
  Reconstruction of the walls of Jerusalem
  Renewal of the covenant by Ezra and Nehemiah (Neh. 8:1–8)
  Refashioning of the political system and establishment of *Anshei Knesset
  ha-Gedolah* as the expression of the *edah*

1.2 Climactic Events

Final break between Samaritans and Jews
Conquest of Eretz Israel by Alexander the Great   332 BCE
Accommodation with Alexander and his heirs which ensured the continuity
  of the order established by Ezra and Nehemiah (e.g., T.B. *Yoma* 69a)

1.3 Culminating Events

The Maccabean revolt; a reaction against the attempt by Antiochus to impose
  the constitution of a polis on Judea, as much as the expression of Jewish
  revulsion against foreign beliefs   166–140 BCE

2. CONSTITUTIONAL HISTORY

The reconstruction of the Temple in Jerusalem and the reestablishment of a
Jewish polity in *Yehudah* (albeit in a protected rather than an independent
form) necessarily affected the corporate structure of the *edah*. As early as the
first generations of the epoch, Jerusalem once again became the principal

nexus of Jewish political life. Residence elsewhere had, from a political point of view, a decidedly attenuated appearance (which is why the Tobiads, despite their powerful territorial base in transjordan, found it necessary to make the capital their principal base of operations). Although at first only a relatively small number of Jews returned to Eretz Israel from the Babylonian exile, by the end of the epoch several million Jews lived in their land and probably formed a majority of world Jewry.

Nevertheless, the legitimacy of other centers of Jewish political life, established during the previous epoch, was now confirmed. Egypt became the locus for local temples constructed at Yev (Elephantine) and Leontopolis, both of which constituted active bases of Jewish political as well as religious life, with institutions and procedures of their own. Little is known about developments in the Babylonian diaspora during this epoch, but it is doubtful whether the community there could have attained its later prominence without strengthening the instruments and offices which it had begun to develop during the previous epoch.

Traditional accounts of the first generation of the epoch tend to highlight Ezra's contribution to the reconstruction of the *edah*. By comparison, Nehemiah's role in the process is somewhat underplayed. This bias is most apparent in the Talmud, which draws distinct parallels between Ezra, the chief representative of the *keter torah*, and Moses (who remains the epitome of all constitutional—and other—excellence), thereby further obfuscating the vital role and personality of Nehemiah, the chief representative of the *keter malkhut*. Whatever may be the reasons for this tendency, a plain reading of the relevant biblical accounts in the books of Ezra and Nehemiah suggests that theirs was a joint effort in which (if anything) Nehemiah played the senior role. It was, after all, he who framed the *amanah* (covenant) which provided the epoch with its distinctive constitutional referent. Not incidentally, in so doing the two also established a precedent for the influence of settlers from the diaspora over the shape and form of government in Eretz Israel which was to be repeated throughout several of the succeeding epochs of Jewish constitutional history.

The principal contribution of the Ezra-Nehemiah covenant lay in the refashioning of the three *ketarim* and the emergence of the *keter torah* as the preeminent domain among the three. This, indeed, is the dominant constitutional characteristic of Epoch VI, even though the *keter kehunah* also gained in power and influence. The *Kohen Gadol*, for instance, besides performing sacerdotal duties in the reconstructed Temple, was also the *ex officio* president of the *Gerousia* (Greek: "Council"), which served as the supreme executive body in *Yahud* (Judea) and, to some degree, for the *edah* as a whole. The *keter malkhut*, although no longer the preserve of a single family once the kingship disappeared, remained in evidence principally through the governors (perhaps mostly Jewish) appointed by the foreign suzerain and local magnates. Nevertheless, it is significant that Ezra, although himself of priestly descent, never attempted to wield influence from the basis of the *keter kehunah* and that the title of *Melekh* fell into disuse.

Our knowledge of this epoch is basically confined to its first and last generations, with no more than snatches of information regarding the intervening ones. Based on that knowledge, it seems that the prime role of the *keter torah* throughout most generations of the epoch was rarely in doubt. The pattern was set early in the epoch when, in a sacred assembly, the *edah* renewed its covenant with God and was thereby reconstituted as an autonomous theocratic republic. Its distinctiveness from all other peoples (and particularly the Samaritans) was thereby ensured; so, too, was its adherence to *Torat Moshe* as interpreted and adapted by the *soferim* (of whom Ezra was the first) as its constitution. This process itself further ensured the preponderance of the *keter torah*.

By the middle generations of the epoch, the *Anshei Knesset ha-Gedolah* (the Men of the Great Assembly—the *edah's* supreme legislative body, heir of the *Am ha-Aretz* of the previous epoch and the *Edah* of yet earlier ones) had clearly established its claim to act as authoritative custodian of the constitutional tradition. In the process, it also moved the *torah she-be'al peh* (oral law) into the realm of constitutional discourse, thereby making that body of oral teaching and interpretation an implicit segment of the constitution itself. At the same time, it also broadened the base from which the *keter torah* recruited its principal officers and instruments. Certainly by the end of the epoch, scholarship rather than any other criterion (including privilege or birth) had become the principal qualification for exercising constitutional authority.

After the epoch's climactic events, the policy of religious toleration as pursued by Alexander the Great and his heirs supplied additional momentum to the process whereby the *keter torah* expanded its jurisdiction and appeal. The later incidence of Hellenizing tendencies among the elitist classes of the population (holding dominant office in both the *keter kehunah* and the *keter malkhut*) finally cemented it. The Maccabean revolt was, among other things, a civil war between two distinct camps within Yehudah, each with a very different view of the desired character of the Jewish polity. The fact that Mattathias (himself a *kohen* who identified with the new role of the *keter torah*) was able to muster such a large following was itself indicative of the extent to which the outlook disseminated through the instruments of the *keter torah* in previous generations had won popular recognition.

3. CONSTITUTION

Torat Moshe (now enshrined as *masoret ha-brit*, the "covenantal tradition," Ezek. 20:35–37) and Ezra-Nehemiah covenant (*amanah*, Neh. 10:1)

3.1 Constitutional Issues

Yiḥusin (lineage) as basis for citizenship, related to Samaritan question

Adaptation of *Torat Moshe* to changed conditions, hence enactment of *tak-kanot* (religious reforms) by Ezra and *Knesset ha-Gedolah* (e.g., Ezra 10)

Relationship with non-Jewish suzerains—Persians, Alexander the Great, Ptolemies, Seleucids

Relationships with diaspora communities

3.2 Camps and Parties

Parties formed by local magnates with strong territorial base, e.g., *Bnei Tuviah* (Tobiads) in southern Galilee

Camps of supporters and opponents of Hellenization

Groups which attained distinctiveness (e.g., *Ḥassidim*—1 Macc. 2:41)

4. CONSTITUTIONAL STRUCTURE OF THE *EDAH*

Restored theocratic republic as autonomous polity within one foreign empire or another. Divided into at least three *medinot* and various *kehillot*, with its center at Jerusalem.

4.1 Principal Instruments, Officers, and Functions

KETER TORAH

It is this epoch which witnessed the initial transfer of the oral law (*torah she-be'al peh*) into the public domain of constitutional discourse, with the *Anshei Knesset ha-Gedolah* as its authorized recipients and transmitters (*Mishnah: Avot* 1:1). In this context, it is significant that two of Ezra's functions were *lidrosh et torat ha-shem* (to interpret the Torah, Ezra 7:10) and—as *sofer*—to appoint *shofetim* and *dayyanim* (Ezra 7:25).

Anshei Knesset ha-Gedolah:	Continuation of the *edah* as supreme constitutional authority with explicit authorization to take custody of the *torah she-be'al peh*. Loosely knit body drawn from all the people of Judea meeting at irregular intervals to pass major enactments, then acting as supreme legislative and executive council
Sofer:	Replaced *Navi* as principal figure of *keter torah*
	Ezra the *sofer*—authorized to act by foreign suzerain; his constitutional authority recognized by *edah*. Renewed constitution via recovenanting and adapted constitution via *takkanot*
	Soferim—continued process of adaptation and reinforced status of *Torat Moshe* by sharpening its focus

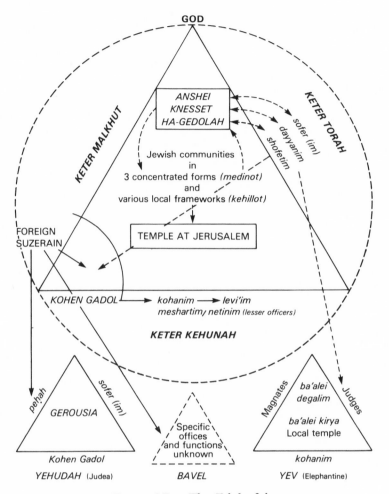

FIGURE VI-1. The *Edah* of the
Anshei Knesset Ha-Gedolah

KETER KEHUNAH

Kohen Gadol: (also referred to as *negid bet ha-Elohim*—Neh. 11:11).
            Sacerdotal functions of this office were revived with recon-
            struction of the Temple of Jerusalem toward the end of the
            previous epoch. With the disappearance of the *Melekh*, the
            governmental functions of the *Kohen Gadol* were also re-
            vived and even expanded, on a shared basis with the *Anshei
            Knesset ha-Gedolah* (hence leading to some friction between

keter kehunah and *keter torah*). The *Kohen Gadol* became the principal officer of the *edah* in Eretz Israel and the diaspora by virtue of the Temple's central *edah*-wide role. He presided over the *Gerousia*, exercised supreme authority over the Temple in Jerusalem, and was responsible for collecting royal taxes for foreign suzerain in Judea. Under the Ptolemies he had the title of *prostates*.

Kohanim:	Priests divided into 24 *mishmarot* (watches) who rotated between field and Temple service
	The Jewish temples in Egypt: This was the only epoch when *kohanim* officiated in a temple in a *medinah* outside of Eretz Israel (e.g., Yev, Leontopolis)
Meshartim/ Netinim:	Lesser priestly officers (Ezra 8:17, 20)

KETER MALKHUT

With the disappearance of the kingship at the end of the previous epoch, single individuals or institutions dominated the *keter malkhut* only intermittently. Instead, its authority and spheres of influence progressively contracted. During the early generations of the epoch, the *keter* was represented by such personalities as Nehemiah, who held office as *pehah* and/or *tarshata* of the foreign suzerain (Neh. 8:9) but who was responsible for constitutional actions of prime importance (whose significance is probably underplayed in the biblical account—possibly because he owed his appointment to the foreign suzerain but also because of the biblical interest in strengthening the position of the *keter torah*). Jurisdiction of the *keter malkhut* was confined to Judea and no internal mechanisms were developed for succession in this sphere. In succeeding generations, consequently, the *keter malkhut* tended to become the preserve of powerful magnates (e.g., the Tobiads) and alternatively (and often simultaneously) externally appointed authorities.

FOREIGN SUZERAIN

Peripherally incorporated into the structure of the *edah* (e.g., tradition of appointing Jews to office of *pehah*—Neh. 8:9—who thereby assumed *keter malkhut* sacrifices offered in the Temple on behalf of foreign suzerain—e.g., T.B. *Yoma* 69a)

5. *MEDINOT*

There were major concentrations of Jews with their own internal organization, bound to *edah* through common sense of nationhood, common cult, and, organizationally, through Temple and Temple tax instituted by Nehemiah.

At the beginning of the epoch there were at least three: Yehudah (Judea),

Bavel (Babylonia and its environs), and Yev (Elephantine). Subsequently, Yev disappeared and was replaced by Mitzrayim (Egypt).

Medinot outside Eretz Israel were recognized as legitimate places of Jewish residence and communal organization. However, *Yahud*/Judea was in a position of superiority to diaspora *medinot* because it was (1) in Eretz Israel, (2) the locus of the Temple, and (3) the seat of governance of the *edah*. Communities elsewhere paid taxes for upkeep of Temple (e.g., one-third shekel tax of Nehemiah, Neh. 10:33).

Judea itself was governed principally by the same institutions which directed the *edah* in its entirety, but it was also served by governing instruments of its own. Principal among these, after the Hellenist conquest, was the *Gerousia* (Greek—Assembly of *Zekenim*)—a standing body representing supreme authority of nation when *Anshei Knesset ha-Gedolah* was not in session and including representatives of all three *ketarim*. Presided over by *Kohen Gadol*, its members included *soferim* and notables.

For national-religious purposes, Judea included Eretz Israel in its entirety, although the other sections of the country were located in different political jurisdictions: Samaria (e.g., Ramathaim), Galilee (e.g., Arbel), coastal cities (e.g., Jaffa), and transjordan (e.g., Tobiad estates). All these areas participated in later Maccabean revolt.

6. *KEHILLOT*

Individual Jewish communities, whose organization followed common principles but with constitutional adaptations to the constitutional structures of each *medinah*, *kehillot* were characterized by *batei knesset* (places of assembly and of worship) and *batei din* (see tradition reported in 2 Macc. 3:46, 48 and T.B. *Menahot* 29a), and they were governed by a local council, consisting of representatives of *batei av*, magnates or elders.

7. REPRESENTATIVE PERSONALITIES

7.1 Constitutional Architects

Ezra *ha-Sofer*, Nehemiah:	Together the principal architects of the reconstitution of Jewish life in Judea; also statesmen

7.2 Statesmen

Nehemiah:	Persian-appointed Governor of Judea
Ezra:	Spokesman for Jewish restoration in Judea
Simon the Just (*Shimon ha-Zaddik*):	*Kohen Gadol* at time of conquest of Judea by Alexander the Great; diplomat and paragon of virtue

Mattathias: First leader of Hasmonean uprising against attempt by Antiochus Epiphanes to impose on Judea the government of a polis

Judah the Maccabee: Third son of Mattathias; first and most notable military leader of the revolt against Syrians

7.3 Constitutional Commentators
Ben Sira: Simeon b. Joshua ben Eleazar (second century BCE); aphorist, sage, and scribe; author of *Ecclesiasticus*

8. TERMS

8.1 New
INDIGENOUS
Amanah, covenant (Neh. 10:1)
Ba'al kirya, civilian citizen, used in Yev
Dayyanim, judges, as appointed by Ezra (Ezra 7:25)
Ḥorim, magnates (Neh. 5:7)
Iggeret, letter of authorization (Neh. 6:5)
Knesset (lit. coming together), from the Aramaic *kinishtu* (assembly), an assembly with constitutional authorization to enact constitutional changes; the equivalent of *edah* (*Mishnah Avot* 1:1)
Netinim, nonpriestly temple officials (Ezra 2:58)
Seganim, magistrates (Neh. 5:7)
Takkanot, constitutional enactments
FOREIGN DERIVATIVES
Gerousia (from Greek, assembly of elders), functioned in Judea as assembly of representatives of all three *ketarim*, where *Kohen Gadol*, *soferim*, representatives of *batei avot*, and magnates combined in order to authorize political decisions (e.g., dispatch of Yosef ben Tuviah to Alexandria)

8.2 Old—Change in Meaning
Mesharet, nonpriestly temple officials (Ezra 8:17)
Sofer, originally an administrative officer (e.g., 2 Sam. 8:17); now also—and increasingly—an instrument of *keter torah* (e.g., Ezra 7:6)

9. BIBLIOGRAPHY

E. Bickerman, *From Ezra to the Last of the Maccabees* (New York, 1962).
J. Bright, "Tragedy and Beyond: The Exilic and post–Exilic Periods," in *A History of Israel* (third edition, Philadelphia, 1982), pp. 341–401.
J. Bright, "The Formative Period of Judaism," *A History of Israel*, pp. 403–426.
Y. Gutman, "Alexander Mokdon be-Eretz Israel," *Tarbitz* 11 (1940), pp. 271–294.
S. B. Hoenig, *The Great Sanhedrin* (Philadelphia, 1953).

B. Z. Luria, *Bimei Shivat Zion* (Jerusalem, 1953).

B. Porten, *Archives from the Jews of Elephantine* (Berkeley, 1968).

M. Snaith, "Nehemiah," in *Palestinian Parties and Politics that Shaped the Old Testament* (New York, 1971), pp. 126–147.

M. Stern, "Hearot le-Sippur Yosef ben Tuvyah," *Tarbitz* 32 (1963), pp. 35–47.

E. Tcherikover, *Hellenistic Civilization and the Jews* (Philadelphia, 1959).

S. Zeitlin, *The Rise and Fall of the Judean State*, vol. 1 (Philadelphia, 1962).

EPOCH VII

Ḥever ha-Yehudim
The Jewish Commonwealth

1. DOMINANT EVENTS

1.1 Founding Events
Attainment of full political independence
Establishment of Hasmonean dynasty
Territorial expansion of Judean state

145–100 BCE

1.2 Climactic Events
Hasmonean civil war and consequent entry of Ptolemy into Jerusalem effectively heralded end of Jewish independence   63 BCE
Herodian rule destroyed full autonomy of the *edah*   37–4 BCE
Destruction of Temple—massive enfeeblement of *keter kehunah*   70 CE

1.3 Culminating Events
Bar Kochba revolt (132–135) and its failure   132–135 CE
Demise of Judea as center of Jewish life
Establishment of the division of the *Mishnah* into *sedarim* (orders) by Akiva (see T.B. *Bava Meziah* 36a and T.B. *Gittin* 67a)
(Note: culminating event in Hellenistic diaspora was the rebellion against the Romans in 115–117 and the destruction of the largest diaspora communities)

2. CONSTITUTIONAL HISTORY

Epoch VII is at once one of the most fruitful and least unified of all Jewish constitutional epochs. It commenced on a note of great triumph (with the attainment of full Jewish independence) and ended on a note of deep tragedy (with the collapse of the Bar Kochba revolt and the end of Jewish hopes for political restoration). The intervening generations—here grouped into four subperiods—experienced a political kaleidoscope of civil strife, foreign wars, increasingly interventionist Roman rule, and abortive rebellions.

Constitutional developments were no more quiescent. The covenant between Simon the Maccabee and the great assembly of priests, people, and elders both called into being the *Hever ha-Yehudim* (Jewish Commonwealth) and added a political layer to the basic constitutional referents of written and oral Torah which had been accepted during the previous epoch. The *keter malkhut*, so quiescent in the previous epoch, was restored and gained great power during the first generation of the new one. Perhaps significantly, the transition was brought about through the agency of a priestly family which continued the earlier combination of the functions of the *keter kehunah* and *keter malkhut* but shifted the formal and informal power to the latter. The office of *Nasi* was revived as the chief magistrate of the *edah* with Simon as first incumbent, but it did not establish a stable regime for long.

The national coalition of anti-Hellenizers which had defeated the old elite and had ensured the Maccabees' success soon broke down. After two generations, the Hasmonean rulers began to assume the powers of royalty and the title of king in their dealings with the nations (although they did not dare to do so before their own people), provoking sharp opposition. Under Herod, the *keter malkhut* became most blatantly dictatorial, thus distinguishing him as one of the only two unabashed dictators in Jewish constitutional history (the other being Menasseh of Israel). Allegiances within the *edah* varied with changes of regime, and constitutional orientations fluctuated in response to the thrust of events over which the Jews possessed almost no control. Consequently, during the course of the epoch, two major camps emerged within the *edah*, the *Perushim* (Pharisees) and the *Zedukim* (Sadducees), each with very different views and outlooks in political and constitutional—as well as other—matters. These were further subdivided into separate parties.

Initially, the Hasmoneans were successful in restoring the borders of the Jewish state to something close to their extent under David and Solomon. This situation persisted (with brief interruptions) until the end of Herod's rule (4 BCE), thereby restoring the Jewish character of much of Eretz Israel. Nevertheless, Judea's independence was steadily undermined. As a result of the struggles within the *keter malkhut*, Rome began to intervene in Judean internal politics, putting an end to the independence of the Judean state after less than a century. At first Roman rule was indirect, but persistent troubles in Judea led to the imposition of direct rule over the major part of the land which, in turn, led to a growing Jewish resistance movement. The end result was the series of disastrous rebellions which destroyed the basis of the Jewish polity established in the previous epoch.

Relationships between the three *ketarim* were similarly volatile. The balance between them, although retained in theory, was constantly infringed in practice. Conflict and tension between them hence became endemic. The early Hasmonean attempt to combine the principal offices of the *keter kehunah* and the *keter malkhut* represented an obvious threat to the authority wielded by the *keter torah* in the previous epoch. The debasement of the *keter kehunah* during and after the middle generations of the epoch merely polarized the conflict. Increasingly, the Sanhedrin of the Pharisees stood in conflict with the royal palace (*Sanhedryon*—privy council); the members of the former body (whose principal officer significantly took the title *Nasi*) developed forms, rules, and procedures whose thrust was to evolve an interpretation of the constitution—as well as an entire political terminology—which was exclusively their own.

It is in this way that the epoch witnessed two divergent tendencies: the consolidation and expansion of the *keter malkhut* and the rise to constitutional influence of the *ḥakhamim* (sages), instruments of the *keter torah* whose claims to authority resided entirely in their contributions to the development of the *halakhah*. Although individual *ḥakhamim* were *kohanim* by ancestry or related to the royal family (as was Simon ben Shetaḥ), as a group they were dependent upon neither royal patronage nor priestly lineage. Instead, they stood as a counterweight to both. As such, they were ideally placed to benefit from the events of 55–70 CE, which destroyed the *keter kehunah* and created a vacuum in the persona of the *keter malkhut*.

During the last generations of this epoch, the *talmidei ḥakhamim* also began to lay the groundwork for the constitutional patterns which were to dominate the succeeding epoch. For one thing, they developed a new form of exegesis (*midrash*) which reaffirmed their authority throughout the *edah*. For another, they began to perform many of the functions which at the beginning of the epoch had been restored to the domain of the *keter malkhut*, resuming the pattern initiated by Ezra. During and after the great rebellion, individual spokesmen for the *keter torah* (now entitled *rabbanim*, e.g., Rabban Yoḥanan ben Zakkai) negotiated with the foreign suzerain, established a new seat of learning at Yavneh, and (in the case of R. Akiva) proclaimed Bar Kochba to be the *Nasi Yisrael*.

To note such instances is not to imply that the *ḥakhamim* thus effected a complete constitutional revolution. During this epoch, such efforts must still be regarded essentially as holding actions, designed to facilitate a subsequent process of readjustment once the notion of independent Jewish statehood had entirely disappeared. It is significant, for instance, that the *ḥakhamim* of Yavneh were not granted jurisdiction in civil matters until the principalship of Gamliel—and even he was entitled the *Nasi* of the Sanhedrin, rather than of the complete house of Israel. The *rabbanim* did constitute a new political elite, but their intrinsic weakness was brutally demonstrated by the ease with which they were subjugated during the wave of Hadrianic persecutions which followed the failure of the Bar Kochba revolt.

Throughout this chronicle of turmoil and change, the corporate status of the *edah* retained its unified appearance. Judea continued to dominate the *edah*; indeed, because of the new political status of the Jewish state, it tended to do so even more strongly than in previous epochs. Religious practice, national sentiment, and occasional migrations all served to bind separate diasporas to Jerusalem. In this respect, the fall of the Temple did not constitute a transformation of the status quo. Thereafter, the calendar continued to be fixed in Judea, the diaspora communities continued to send funds to Judea on the basis of the Temple tax, and the *Nasi* and his court embarked on various missions abroad to maintain and cement the ties between Eretz Israel and the diaspora.

Within the diaspora itself, however, some significant changes were in progress. Jewish settlements outside Judea were spreading geographically and becoming more diversified institutionally throughout the epoch. Parts of Eretz Israel were divided into several proto-*medinot* under the heirs of Herod. In the Hellenistic diaspora, some *kehillot* continued to be governed on traditional lines; others (e.g., Alexandria, Berenike) assumed the characteristics of a polis, whose main institutional form was a politeuma led by either an Ethnarch or Archons. With the single but massive exception of Bavel, none of the regional congeries of local communities yet constituted a *medinah*; but several could be classified as *aratzot*.

3. CONSTITUTION

Torat Moshe and *torah shebe'al peh* (oral tradition, originally probably termed *torah be peh*; see *Sifre* 351) with its political derivative being the covenant between Simon the Maccabee and the great assembly (congregation) of priests and people and *nesiei ha-am* (1 Macc. 14:27–49)

3.1 Constitutional Issues
Foreign intervention and need to comply with foreign rule
Legitimacy and status of Hasmonean dynasty
Civil wars
Paramountcy of oral tradition
Proselytization (e.g., by Hyrcanus and Herod)
Enactment of *takkanot* (e.g., by Hillel and Yohanan ben Zakkai)

3.2 Camps and Parties
Camps
Zedukim (Sadducees)

Perushim (Pharisees, also called *Haverim*)
Essi'im (Essenes) and other sectarians
PARTIES
Patriots vs. Collaborators
Bet Hillel vs. *Bet Shammai*
R. Yohanan ben Zakkai and his supporters vs. supporters of the revolt
Desert sectarians
Zealot parties

All three camps emerged as such at the beginning of the epoch and two of the three disappeared before it ended. The leading families of the previous epoch and their parties disappeared from the scene during the Hasmonean revolt. The formation of the *Zedukim* and *Perushim* was a result of the dissolution of the Hasmonean coalition. The leaders of the *Perushim* were known as *hakhamim*. Their rivalry with the priesthood, which was under the control of the Hasmonean rulers who were *kohanim*, was summarized in their self-determined designation as *talmidei Aharon* (disciples of Aaron) rather than *bnei Aharon* (descendants of Aaron), which reflected the differences in the *ketarim* from which the authority of each was derived. All but the *Zedukim* were strongly influenced by the ideology of *malkhut shamayim* (the kingdom of Heaven), namely that only God should rule over the Jewish people. This was an important contributory factor to the revolts.

All three camps and the parties within each contended with each other in all three domains, but the *Zedukim* were particularly dependent upon the existence of a strong *keter malkhut* and a state apparatus for their survival since their Judaism was preeminently a civil religion revolving around state and Temple. Thus the destruction of both spelled their end as a distinctive camp. The *Essi'im*, who ideologically eschewed both in favor of an isolated communal society, in fact were dependent upon the existence of a state for protection; hence their communities were destroyed or dispersed once that protection was removed. Only the *Perushim*, whose power resided primarily in the *keter torah*, continued to exist after the destruction of the state and the Temple.

4. CONSTITUTIONAL STRUCTURE OF THE *EDAH*

The polity constituted by the *Hever ha-Yehudim* and its institutional manifestations was based on the premise that Judea would be politically independent and the center of the *edah* comprised of Jews living both there and in diaspora *medinot*.

Because of its new political status, Judea came to dominate the *edah* far more than in the previous epoch. Its hegemony was reinforced by the fact that only one other concentration of Jews, that of Bavel (now under Parthian rule) was organized as a *medinah* with governing institutions of its own (though these, too, were subordinate to those of Judea-as-*Ḥever ha-Yehudim*). Thus, Hyrcanus and even Herod were recognized as spokesmen for the entire Jewish community, and diaspora congregations continued to pay half-shekel contributions for the upkeep of the Temple (*Mishnah: Ḥallah* 4:11) which also remained the object of frequent diaspora pilgrimages (*Mishnah: Pesaḥim* 5:5–7).

While organized Jewish settlement in the Hellenistic world and Roman Empire was spread more widely than ever before, the constitution of each city as a polis meant that the Jewish communities within those cities were organized separately with no overarching regional frameworks. Hence their principal ties were to Judea and Jerusalem, rather than to each other.

These ties continued to be of importance after the fall of the independent Jewish state and in certain spheres even assumed greater significance. The continuation of diaspora aspirations with regard to Eretz Israel was most acutely demonstrated during the Trajanic rebellions of 115–117. These con-

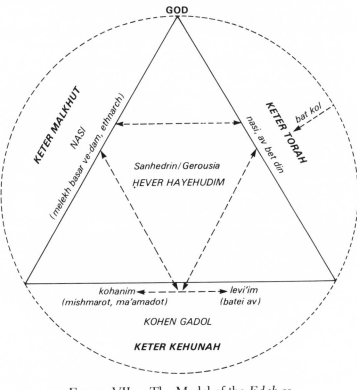

FIGURE VII-1. The Model of the *Edah* as
Constitutionally Specified

stituted a truly national uprising, inspired by hopes of a messianic restoration of Jewish independence and the defeat of Roman rule. The rebellions encompassed Jewish communities in Libya, Cyrenaica, Egypt, Cyprus, and Bavel.

Under more normal circumstances, diaspora ties to Eretz Israel were signified by religious practice (e.g., pilgrimages from diaspora to Jerusalem—*Mishnah: Pesaḥim* 5:5–7; calendar fixed in Judea—*Mishnah: Rosh ha-Shanah* 4:4; consultations with diaspora—*Tosefta: Eruvin* 9:5, *Ḥullin* 3:10; and standardized liturgy—e.g., *haggadah*) and by national-political ties (e.g., Hyrcanus and Herod recognized as spokesmen for all Jews; appointment of diaspora figures to Sanhedrin, high priesthood; journey to diaspora by *Nasi* and his court; half shekel to Jerusalem (*Mishnah: Ḥallah* 4:11); and later use of *sheliḥim* (leading members of Sanhedrin who visited diaspora communities regularly to teach, apply *halakhah* to local issues, and even play a role in determining leadership in those communities).

In regard to dynamics of political change within the *edah*, the epoch can be divided into four periods: (1) three generations of Hasmonean ascendancy (145–63 BCE), (2) two generations of Herodian ascendancy (63 BCE–6 CE), (3) two generations of direct Roman rule in Judea (6–66 CE), and (4) two generations of rebellions (66–135 CE). Each had its own variant of the constitutional model.

The unification of the leadership of the *keter malkhut* and the *keter kehunah* within the single personage of the Hasmonean ruler upset the balance of the constitutional mode. Hence tension between the King-Priest and the Sages was endemic—all too often becoming violent conflict. The two sides crystallized into the *Ẓeduki* (Sadducean) and *Perushi* (Pharisaic) camps.

Although the appointment of Antipater and his descendants to supreme authority in the *keter malkhut* by the Roman suzerain restored the separation between the *keter malkhut* and *keter kehunah* (Antipater's family—Edomite converts—were not of priestly descent), it did not restore the constitutional balance. The High Priesthood became a puppet of the *keter malkhut*, with the candidates for the office being drawn from a small circle of aristocratic families who were all dependent upon the favor of the royal court. The debasement of the *keter malkhut* and *keter kehunah* during these generations thus further widened the rift between the *Perushim* and the state.

The imposition of direct Roman rule over Eretz Israel in 6 CE threw the entire system into confusion. The new situation ultimately tended to augment the intra-Jewish authority of the *keter torah*, which remained the only fully Jewish domain and, as such, was actively extending its sphere of authority outside the formal political structure. No Judean personage now held the principal position of the *keter malkhut* (although the political unity of the *medinah* was buttressed by Julius Caesar's proclamations that it constituted a single province). This *keter* remained in the hands of the Herodians, foremost among whom was Agrippa I who, because of his friendship with the Emperor,

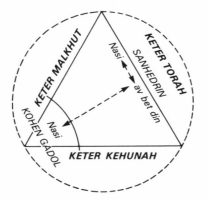

FIGURE VII-2. The Hasmonean State (from Simon the
Maccabee to Hyrcanus/Aristobulus)

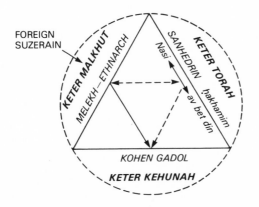

FIGURE VII-3. Roman Protectorate (from Antipater to
Agrippas I)

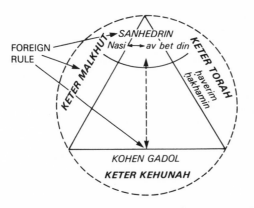

FIGURE VII-4. Roman Province (after Agrippas I—66 CE)

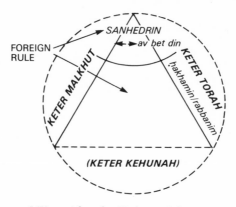

FIGURE VII-5. After the Failure of the Great Rebellion
in 70 CE

was actually restored as king of Judea and the adjacent provinces (virtually all of Eretz Israel) for a brief period. The *kohanim*, who still constituted the nexus of a group of aristocratic and wealthy families, were clearly discredited in the eyes of the populace because of their corruption and assimilationist orientation.

The confused and competitive situation which resulted transformed the great rebellion into a civil war as much as a struggle for national liberation. The Sicarii, for instance, proclaimed their own monarch (Menasheh of Galilee), and the Zealots provided Simon bar Giora with royal titles. Increasingly, representatives of the *keter torah* were looked to for guidance in matters civil as well as religious and thus were invited to take upon themselves functions traditionally reserved to the *keter malkhut*.

The destruction of the Temple and the fall of Jerusalem created a power vacuum, which the representatives of the *keter torah* were ideally placed to fill. The members of the Sanhedrin now groped toward full authority in matters civil as well as religious, with the *Nasi* of that body assuming the office of the representative of the entire community in its dealings with the foreign suzerain. The extent to which power had shifted is demonstrated by the fact that it was representatives of the *keter torah* (especially R. Akivah) who proclaimed Bar Kochba to be the *Nasi* of Israel.

4.1 Principal Instruments, Officers, and Functions
KETER TORAH
CHARACTERISTICS
Persistent attempts to establish an interpretation of the constitution which legitimized consolidation of power in hands of *keter torah*—even to the point of veto on *bat kol* (T.B. *Bava Meẓiah* 59a–b; also *Tosefta: Sanhedrin* 7:1)

Hence increasing conflicts with *keter malkhut* (see later text)

Establishment by representatives of *keter torah* of forms, rules, and procedures whose thrust was to give it monopoly of constitutional interpretation
and application (e.g., development and use of *takkanot*—such as that of
prozbul, eighteen enactments of conclave of 65–66 —T.B. *Sanhedrin*
17a–b); standardization of hermeneutical rules—such as *baraita* of Rabbi
Yishmael (*Sifre*, intro.); development of *semikhah* as device of *keter torah*
(T.B. *Sanhedrin* 5b)

REPRESENTATIVES

Sanhedrin:	Continuation of *Gerousia* under new name and with locus fully in the *keter torah* as its authoritative body; comprising seventy (or seventy-one) leading scholars who themselves were part of an intellectual meritocracy drawn from a widely popular base. It acted as a high court with the power of law enforcement (although, after the middle of the epoch, not of capital punishment), interpreted the constitution and sharpened it by enactment of *takkanot* and participated in certifying actions of constitutional import (e.g., date of new moon)
Nasi:	President of the Sanhedrin
Av Bet Din:	Chairman of the court; shared with *Nasi* in work of the Sanhedrin
Bat Kol:	A heavenly or Divine voice which revealed God's will, choice, or judgment to man, thus replacing prophecy (T.B. *Yoma* 9b); decisive in determining that the *halakhah* was in accordance with views of *Bet Hillel* rather than *Bet Shammai* (T.B. *Eruvin* 13b), but toward the end of the epoch rejected as a constitutional device (T.B. *Bava Meẓiah* 59a–b)

KETER MALKHUT

CHARACTERISTICS

Hasmonean attempt to concentrate constitutional power by combining principal roles of *keter kehunah* and *keter malkhut* (opposed by representatives of *keter torah*; T.B. *Kiddushin* 66a—an exception being Agrippas in
Mishnah: Sotah 7:8)

Growth of royal bureaucracy

Dependence on Roman suzerainty/rule, which acquired power, successively,
to guarantee Judean independence, to ratify or choose between Jewish
claimants to *keter malkhut*, to appoint bearer of principal office of *keter
malkhut* (e.g., Herod), and to usurp functions of *keter malkhut* (e.g., by
appointment of procurators).

REPRESENTATIVES

Nasi: Principal instrument of *keter malkhut*.

Appointed by people through covenant with Simon, thereafter dynastic, eventually dependent on Roman sanction. Exercised virtually

undisputed authority in military and foreign affairs, but his constitutional and actual authority in domestic affairs a matter of dispute between various incumbents and Sanhedrin.

The office revived by Hasmoneans for those holding kinglike powers, using classical term as redefined by the *Navi* Ezekiel (see epochs V and VI). Sometimes referred to by Greek term *Ethnarch* as on coins (although obverse—in Greek—uses the title "king"), or in talmudic sources as *melekh basar ve-dam* (king of flesh and blood).

After the death of Herod, the line of *nesi'im* presumably continued through his heirs but only Agrippas I was so recognized by the Jews.

The title *Nasi* also adopted by Bar Kochba, who was the last representative of the *keter malkhut* to do so.

KETER KEHUNAH

CHARACTERISTICS

Lost much of its independence under Hasmoneans as Hasmonean *Nasi* assumed high priesthood by right of priestly descent

Hereditary principle fell into abeyance (e.g., under Herod, a Babylonian, Ḥanamel, appointed to office—*Mishnah: Pe'ah* 3:5)

Retained sacerdotal functions (e.g., *Mishnah: Yoma* 1:1), but *kohanim* fell into increasing disrepute (e.g., *Mishnah: Yoma* 3:11 and T.B. *Pesaḥim* 57a; cf. earlier idealization of *Kohen Gadol* in Ecclesiasticus 50:1–6)

Temple officials now included *strategos, amarcalim* (overseers), and *gabbayim*

With destruction of Temple, *keter kehunah* as a whole largely fell into abeyance. The idea of the *Kohen Gadol* as an equal partner in governance remained alive until the end of the epoch as reflected by the immediate appointment of a *kohen* to share authority with Simon bar Kosiba (Bar Kochba) during the revolt of 132–135 (coins struck by the Judean authorities bear the inscription Simon bar Kosiba *ha-Nasi* and Elazar *ha-Kohen*) but that is the last known expression of the office

5. *MEDINOT*

Medinot with overarching organizational frameworks

Judea-as-*medinah*: dominant, divided into three major districts (*aratzot* in *halakhah*—e.g., *Mishnah: Shevi'it* 9:2–3)—Judea, Galilee, and Perea. Gabinius divided into five administrative/fiscal districts

Bavel: the only other region organized as a *medinah*, presumably with *Resh Galuta*, although precise form of that organization not known. Included Babylonia, Persia, Media, and Elam

Aratzot, congeries of *kehillot* within recognized geopolitical entities but without overarching organizational frameworks

Egypt: an *eretz* comprising a congeries of autonomous *kehillot*, chief of which was Alexandria; Jews resided in virtually every city and town

Cyrenaica: an *eretz* with major *kehillot* in Cyrene and Berenice as well as extensive settlement in rural areas

Syria: an *eretz* with major *kehillot* in Antioch, Damascus, and Apamea and settlements in other cities and towns

Asia (Asia Minor): *kehillot* in major cities, especially on Anatolian littoral

Cyprus: Jewish settlements on island

Achea (southern Greece): principal *kehillot* in Athens, Corinth, and Delphi with settlements in all the main districts

Macedonia: principal *kehillah* in Thessalonika

Regnam Bospori (north shore of Black Sea): Jewish settlements

Italia: Jewish settlements in city of Rome and Italian towns

Lands with Scattered Settlements

Hispania

Gaul

Pannonia

Kingdoms with Jewish Ruler

After the conquest of Judea by Rome, certain branches of the Hasmonean royal family came under Roman patronage and, in due course, were given provinces of Eretz Israel to rule as protected kingdoms under Roman suzerainty. These protectorates, which flourished in the years following Herod's rule after the Hasmoneans had become Herodians, were located in the Galilee, the Golan, and transjordan and on the Judean coast (Philistia). They were not as demographically homogeneous as was almost exclusively Jewish Judea, but either had Jewish majorities or very strong concentrations of Jews, principally settled in cities and towns of their own. In a certain sense, they can be seen as *medinot*, the last of which, under Agrippas II, persisted until c. 95 CE.

Adiabene, a vassal kingdom within the Parthian Empire, ruled by Izates (36–60), who converted to Judaism (*Genesis Rabbah* 46:11; *Tosefta Megillah* 4:30)

6. *KEHILLOT*

Principal *kehillot* included the following:

Eretz Israel

Judea-Jerusalem, ruled by a community council on traditional pattern (*Sanhedria* or *Gerousia*); executive in hand of *Bouleterion* (state council) (T.J. *Pe'ah* 1:1)

Galilee—e.g., Tiberias, a *polis* with a community council and popular assemblies, which sometimes convened in the synagogue. Led by *Archon* and *Archonomus*, and *Bouleterion*

Bavel
  Nehardea
  Nisibis
  Mahoza   } all Jewish cities, governed and garrisoned by Jews
  Pumbedita
Egypt
  Alexandria—the classic polieuma and major Jewish community of the
    Hellenistic diaspora; headed by Ethnarch (*Nasi*) and later by Council of
    Elders (*Gerousia*). Until 70 CE site of a temple, Beit Ḥonyo, thereafter
    closed (T.B. *Menaḥot* 109B)
Cyrenaica
  Cyrene
  Berenike (Benghazi)—a politeuma like Alexandria but led by *archeons*
Syria
  Antioch—had charter of communal rights inscribed on copper tablets
  Damascus
  Apamea
Asia Minor
  Ephesus
  Miletus
  Pergamum
  Sardis
Greek islands
  Delos
  Melos
  Other islands
Achea
  Athens
  Corinth
  Delphi
Macedonia
  Thessalonika
Regnum Bospori
Italia
  City of Rome—no overarching organization, each synagogue a *kehillah*
    unto itself; leaders entitled *pater synagoguus, archisynagogue, mater syn-*
    agogae, etc.
Hispania

7. REPRESENTATIVE PERSONALITIES

7.1 Constitutional Architects

Simon the Maccabee:
(d. 135 BCE), founder and architect of the Hasmonean polity, also statesman

Hillel the Elder:
(late first century BCE–early first century CE), *Nasi* of Sanhedrin, principal authority of *keter torah*, founder of school (*Bet Hillel*) and of dynasty, architect of *takkanot* (e.g., *prozbul*) and of rules of biblical exegesis

Shammai the Elder:
(c. 50 BCE–c. 30 CE), principal authority of *keter torah*, colleague of Hillel, also founder of school (*Bet Shammai*)

Akiva:
(c. 50–135 CE), outstanding *tanna*, exerted decisive influence on development of constitution by both his authoritative rulings and his arrangement of the *torah shebe'al peh* according to subjects, also statesman

7.2 Statesmen

KETER MALKHUT

Jonathan the Maccabee:
(d. 143 BCE), youngest of Mattathias's sons, successfully completed revolt; appointed *Kohen Gadol* and governor of Judea, thus becoming first Hasmonean to combine principal functions of *keter kehunah* and *keter malkhut*

Simon the Maccabee:
(d. 135 BCE), first Hasmonean to be acclaimed *Nasi* and Ethnarch, with title and offices passing to his heirs

Alexander Yannai:
(c. 126–76 BCE), first Hasmonean to employ title of *Melekh*; his combination of authority of *keter kehunah* and *keter malkhut* provoked fierce opposition of Pharisees

Herod:
(c. 73–4 BCE), soldier, administrator, builder, diplomat, constitutional violator; as King of Judea, attempted to destroy internal organization of Jewish community and to bring *medinah* into Roman-Hellenistic orbit

Joḥanan ben Levi:
(*Gush Ḥalav*); principal leader of revolt against Rome, 66–70 CE

Simon bar Giora:
Principal leader of revolt against Rome 66–70 CE

Joḥanan ben Ḥizkiyah:
Principal leader of revolt against Rome 66–70 CE

Simon Bar Kochba:
(*Bar Kosiba*, d. 135 CE), leader of revolt against Rome, 132–135 CE; proclaimed *melekh mashiaḥ* by R. Akiva and referred to as *Nasi*, the last as such from *keter malkhut*

KETER TORAH

Simon ben
(first century BCE), one of *zugot*, probably *Nasi* of Sanhedrin,

Shetaḥ:	leader of Pharisee camp, principal spokesman for *keter torah* against *keter malkhut* during reign of Alexander Yannai
Joḥanan ben Zakkai:	(first century CE), deputy *Nasi*, created *yeshiva* of Yavneh, and thus facilitated reconstruction of *edah* during next epoch
Gamaliel ha-Zaken:	(first century CE), *Nasi*, grandson of Hillel, author of several *takkanot*
Akiva:	Attempted to confer sanction of *keter torah* on Bar Kochba's revolt
Gamaliel II:	(first–second centuries CE), succeeded Joḥanan ben Zakkai as *Nasi* c. 80 CE; attempted to strengthen his office and unify halakhic process under auspices of *keter malkhut*. His firmness and exploitation of power led to severe struggle with representatives of *keter torah*; for a time removed from office

7.3 Constitutional Commentators

| Philo Judaeus: | (c. 20 BCE–50 CE), sought to reconcile his understanding of stoic philosophy with Judaism, influenced Christianity more than Judaism |
| Yosef ben Matityahu: | (Josephus Flavius, c. 38–after 100 CE), historian; first Jew to attempt to describe history and development of his people to Gentile world |

8. TERMS

8.1 New

INDIGENOUS

Amarcal, fiscal officer of the *keter kehunah* (e.g., *Mishnah: Shekalim* 5:2)

Av bet din, president of the Sanhedrin; second in importance to *Nasi* (*Mishnah: Ḥagigah* 2:2)

Avot ha-edah, fathers of the congregation (e.g., in Scroll of the Sons of Light, 2:1)

Bat kol, a heavenly or Divine voice, revealing God's will to man (e.g., T.B. *Eruvin* 13b; *Bava Meẓiah* 59a–b)

Bet Din Gadol, high court

Bet Midrash, seat of exposition of the *Torah* (*Mishnah: Berakhot* 4:2)

Galut, exile, now a description of punishment (*Mishnah: Avot* 1:11)

Gezerah, decree possessing constitutional force (T.B. *Megillah* 17a)

Gizbar, fiscal officer of the *keter kehunah* (*Mishnah: Shekalim* 5:2)

Halakhah (lit. "way"), system of laws of the Torah, or at times specific law derived from the Torah (*Mishnah: Peah* 4:1–2)

Halakhah le-Moshe mi-Sinai (a law given to Moses at Sinai), constitutional device giving effect to laws for which there is no scriptural support (e.g., *Mishnah: Peah* 2:6)

Hora'at ha-Sha'ah (lit. "order of the hour"), constitutional device entitling
   kehillah to enact emergency legislation (T.B. *Yoma* 69b)

Horayot, rulings of Sanhedrin or *Kohen Gadol* (*Mishnah: Horayot* 1:1)

Keter (crown), domain of constitutional authority (e.g., *Mishnah: Avot* 4:13)

Malkhut Zadon (*harashah*), domain of iniquity (T.B. *Shabbat* 15a)

Rabbanut, authority (*Mishnah: Avot* 1:10)

Rabbi (master of the law), recognized instrument of *keter torah*; title used for
   those constitutionally ordained (*musmakhim*) by R. Johanan ben Zakkai
   (T.B. *Bava Metziah* 85a)

Rashut, government (e.g., *Mishnah: Avot* 1:10), authority

Shlihim, emissaries of Judea to diaspora

Va'ad, council, court (T.J. *Berakhot* 2:5)

Yeshiva, place of assembly and academy of learning (T.J. *Shabbat* 10:12)

FOREIGN DERIVATIVES

Agronomus, supervisor of markets

Archon, communal officer of the independent Jewish community in Greek
   and Roman spheres; an executive officer of the *Gerousia*, generally appointed for one year

Ethnarch, ruler (1 Macc. 41:47)

Gerousia, assembly (e.g., *The Book of Judith* 15:8)

Politeuma, political association with its own constitution located within another polity

Sanhedrin, assembly (*Mishnah: Sanhedrin* 1:1)

8.2 Old—Change in Meaning

Ger, now used to describe proselyte (e.g., T.B. *Berakhot* 47b)

Haver (partner, companion), now used to describe a recognized authority in
   domain of *keter torah*; originally an associate (e.g., Judg. 20:11, 2 Chron.
   20:35)

Hever, commonwealth, especially in the sense of partnership; originally an
   alliance (e.g., Gen. 14:3) or bond (e.g., Hos. 6:9); now a form of political
   organization, hence *Hever ha-Yehudim*

Hakham, learned man, now used to describe one fitted to interpret constitution as instrument of *keter torah* (e.g., *Mishnah: Avot* 1:11)

Nasi, description of *both* principal instrument of *keter malkhut* and the president of the Sanhedrin (e.g., *Mishnah: Hagigah* 2:2)

9. BIBLIOGRAPHY

G. Alon, *Jews, Judaism and the Classical World* (Translated by I. Abrahams; Jerusalem, 1977).

S. W. Baron, "The Palestinian Municipality," in *The Jewish Community. Its History
   and Structure to the American Revolution* (Philadelphia, 1942), pp. 31–54.

Y. Blidstein, "Lekorot ha-Munaḥ 'Torah shebe'al Peh,'" *Tarbitz* 42 (1973), pp. 496–498.

Y. Engelard, "Tanuro shel Akhnai: Perushah shel Aggadah," *Shnaton ha-Mishpat ha-Ivri* 1 (1975), pp. 45–53.

L. Finkelstein, *The Pharisees: The Sociological Background of Their Faith* (third edition, New York, 1962).

B. Gartner, *The Temple and the Community in Qumram* (Cambridge, 1965).

M. Grant, *Herod the Great* (New York, 1971).

———. *The Jews in the Roman World* (London, 1973).

H. D. Mantel, "The High Priest and the Sanhedrin in the Time of the Second Temple," in *The World History of the Jewish People*, First Series, vol. 7: "The Herodian Period" (ed. M. Avi-Yonah; New Brunswick, 1975), pp. 264–282.

J. Neusner, *Judaism: The Evidence of the Mishnah* (Chicago, 1981).

———. *A Life of Yohanan ben Zakkai. C.I.–80 C.E.* (Leiden, 1970).

S. Rhoads, *Israel in Revolution, 6–74 CE. A Political History Based on the Writings of Josephus* (Philadelphia, 1976).

E. Rivkin, "Defining the Pharisees: The Tannaitic Sources," *Hebrew Union College Annual* 40–41 (1970), pp. 205–250.

M. Stern, "Ha-Manhigut bikevutzot Loḥamei ha-Ḥerut besof Yemei Bayit Sheni" in *Ha-Ishiut ve-Doro* (Jerusalem 1964), pp. 70–78.

E. M. Smallwood, *The Jews Under Roman Rule* (Leiden, 1979).

S. Zeitlin, *The Rise and Fall of the Judean State*, vols. 2–3 (Philadelphia, 1969–1978).

EPOCH VIII

3900–c. 4185 AM (140–c. 425 CE)

Sanhedrin u-Nesi'ut

The Sanhedrin and the Patriarchate

1. DOMINANT EVENTS

1.1 Founding Events

Reconstitution after failure of Bar Kochba revolt
Revival of Sanhedrin under dynastic *Nasi* with its seat in the Galilee

c. 140 CE

Emergence of strong *Resh Galuta* in Bavel
Final redaction of the *Mishnah* by Yehudah ha-Nasi, whose work was based
on that of previous compilations   c. 210 CE

1.2 Climactic Events

Decline of Jewish settlement in Eretz Israel (economic decline, demographic
decline and emigration, and division of Roman province of Palestine into
three by Diocletian)   4th century CE
Christian ascendancy and beginnings of anti-Jewish policies   325 CE
Failure of rebellion against Gallus in Eretz Israel   351 CE
Fixing of calendar which lessened diaspora dependence on Sanhedrin in
Eretz Israel   358 CE
Completion of *Talmud Yerushalmi*   c. 390 CE

1.3 Culminating Events

End of *Nesi'ut* in 425 CE (coinciding with fall of Rome)
Sanhedrin prohibited from collecting regular tax from diaspora
Magi persecutions in Bavel   mid 5th century CE

2. CONSTITUTIONAL HISTORY

The final redaction of the *Mishnah* by Rabbi Judah ha-Nasi (*Rabi*) is the dominant constitutional landmark of Epoch VIII. Based on several previous compilations which were given form following Rabbi Akiva's organizational scheme during the founding generation of the epoch, the work confirmed the victory of the Pharisaic school, whose teachings it reflects. While the *Mishnah* is maintained as a separate corpus rather than being integrated into the scriptural canon, it follows in the classic Jewish tradition of the constitution as an authoritative "teaching" (as its very name indicates and thereby emphasizes). The *Mishnah* was designed as an explication and elaboration of aspects of *Torat Moshe*, which it considerably amplified and from whence it claimed legitimacy. As such, it won acceptance as an authoritative constitutional referent for the entire *edah* and the *locus classicus* for all subsequent constitutional discourse. Henceforth, it would be second only to the Bible itself as a basic Jewish constitutional text.

The content of the *Mishnah* incorporates teachings and regulations which touch upon the functions of all three *ketarim*. In its methodology, however, it reflects exclusively the viewpoint of the *keter torah*. The constitution, thus defined, was a codex of a series of *halakhot*, whose efficacy and applicability were determined solely by the *tannaim* (teachers; the generic title applied to *talmidei ḥakhamim* of the period). Differences respecting the meaning of a particular *halakhah*, or divergent opinions as to the claims of certain *minhagim* (customs) to be classified as common practices with halakhic status, were all ironed out entirely within the confines of the *keter torah*. Moreover, the rules of procedure and interpretation whereby such issues were debated were framed only from the perspective of that *keter*. Thus, by the founding generations of the epoch, the *keter torah* had demonstrated its ability to tie up many of the constitutional loose ends which had remained from Epoch VII when differences of opinion between various "schools" were still rife.

To say that is not to imply that the *keter torah* thus became the only functioning domain of Jewish governance during this epoch. While it is true that *kohanim* were now reduced to constitutional fossils, bereft of all political influence, and that the *keter kehunah* virtually disappeared, the same cannot be said of the *keter malkhut*. The point to be made, rather, is that it became an instrument of the *keter torah*, and figures who owed their prominence and authority to their proficiency in that sphere now occupied the principal roles within the *keter malkhut*, too. People and Torah thus replaced state and Temple as the focal points of Jewish constitutional interest.

This was most vividly illustrated by the composition and activities of the Sanhedrin, which in this epoch became the most authoritative body for the entire *edah*. Consisting of seventy *talmidei ḥakhamim*, its composition made no allowance at all for the influence of the High Priestly families, and apparently very little for that of the moneyed aristocracy. Instead, it was the sages who took control of the *edah* in its entirety. The Sanhedrin's affairs were administered by an *av bet din*, and its business presided over by the *Nasi*. These leaders thus straddled the *keter torah* and the *keter malkhut*. They acted as the high court of the *edah*, enacted *takkanot* (ordinances) which were universally binding, and certified all actions of constitutional importance to the *edah*.

Even so, the essence of the distinction in role between the *ketarim* was retained. The principle of constitutional power-sharing was maintained by the *av bet din* and various prominent *ḥakhamim* balancing (and sometimes contesting) the authority of the *Nasi*; they also developed separate seats of power in the various *yeshivot* (academies) where they counseled, taught, and debated points of *halakhah*. Moreover, although *semikhah* (ordination) was not valid unless conferred jointly by both the *Nasi* and the members of the Sanhedrin, the two parties to the process clearly operated from separate power bases.

Divisions between the *keter malkhut* and the *keter torah* became even more pronounced as the epoch progressed. The *Nesi'ut* became a dynastic appointment limited to descendants of the family of Hillel the Elder, and, through him, the royal house of David, confirmed by the Roman suzerain. This lineage reinforced the separate authority of the office. Increasingly, the *Nasi* became identified with the fulfillment of functions reserved to the *keter malkhut*—for example, the right to pass judgment in capital cases. The development reached something of an apogee under the rulership of Severus, who markedly extended Jewish autonomous rights and permitted Jewish *batei din* to replace Roman courts.

In due course, the *ḥakhamim* had to take steps to retain their independence from a *Nesi'ut* which was increasingly adopting the trappings of a court. They insisted, for instance, that one of their own number open and close sessions of the Sanhedrin (*Bet ha-Va'ad*)—even when the *Nasi* was present.

The framework outlined above was clearly oriented toward the continued role of Eretz Israel as the seat of authority and power for the entire *edah*. Throughout the epoch, it was Eretz Israel which housed those institutions of Jewish government which embraced the *edah* in its entirety. *Takkanot* enacted by the Sanhedrin of Eretz Israel (whose precise seat changed periodically, moving from Judea to Galilee and within Galilee) were communicated to the diaspora by *mumḥim*; the *Nesi'ut* was supported by funds collected from throughout the Jewish world by *apostoloi* and *neḥutei*. Judgments formulated in Eretz Israel were invariably authoritative. *Talmidei ḥakhamim* who generally originated from Eretz Israel acted as conduits for constitutional interpretation and thus helped to preserve the unity of the *edah*.

Nevertheless, it was during the course of this epoch that a perceptible shift of axis occurred toward Bavel. While Eretz Israel was divided by Diocletian into three provinces (of which two had Jewish settlement and the third—Judea—was still without a Jewish population) the populous and prosperous *medinah* of Bavel developed institutions and officers of growing authority and centrifugal influence. Principal among these—in the realm of *keter malkhut*—was the *Resh Galuta* (Exilarch), who, like the *Nasi* of Eretz Israel, was accepted as a descendant of the House of David and—in the realm of *keter torah*—the *rashei yeshivot* of Pumbedita, Nehardea, Meḥoza, and Sura. The influence of the *Resh Galuta* increased both absolutely and proportionately after 140; that of the *yeshivot* received particular impetus in 219 CE, with the return of Rav to Bavel to head the *yeshiva* of Sura.

Within Bavel, tension between these two domains was common. Although the *Resh Galuta* was superior from the perspective of the foreign suzerain, he did not have hegemony within the Jewish polity. From the first, the decisions of his own court had to accord with the teachings of the *rashei yeshivot*. As a self-contained *medinah*, however, Bavel's sense of separate corporate identity and independence was growing (and possibly fostered by the fact that, unlike Roman-ruled Eretz Israel, Bavel was under Persian sway).

The challenge thus implied was rarely made explicit during this epoch. The *Resh Galuta*—although careful never formally to acknowledge the superiority of the *Nasi*—generally did so in practice. Bavel thus accepted the liturgy standardized in Eretz Israel, as well as the calendar determined there. Nevertheless, the epoch did witness a progressive contraction of Eretz Israel's authority and influence. In part, this may be attributed to factors over which the *edah* exercised very little independent control: the economic and demographic decline of Palestine and the Roman division of the land into three provinces. Other influences, however, were also at work. The *yeshivot* of Bavel produced successive generations of scholars of authority and renown, who refused to accept without question the rulings of their colleagues in Eretz Israel (which is one reason why the *Talmud Yerushalmi*, completed in Eretz Israel during the climactic generation of the epoch, never gained the same *edah*-wide stature as the *Talmud Bavli*).

Another reflection of the various shifts of this epoch is to be found in the fact that it was a Babylonian (and a *Rosh Yeshiva*, not a *Resh Galuta*) who in this epoch formulated the seminal rule of *dina demalkhuta dina*—a formula which determined much Jewish political and diplomatic practice thereafter. This formula, a necessity in the diaspora, was resisted in the Land of Israel which was considered Jewish soil under foreign occupation, fundamentally bound by Jewish law no matter what.

3. CONSTITUTION

The constitution consisted of the *Torat Moshe* and *Mishnah* (the latter also referred to as *hilkhata* (T.B. *Kiddushin* 49a–b) and *mesekhta* (T.B. *Bava*

Kamma 102a). It was defined through a series of *halakhot*; but it was also often applied through *minhag*, by which it might be modified (e.g., *Mishnah: Pesaḥim* 4:1–5).

3.1 Constitutional Issues

Relations between Eretz Israel and Bavel. Formally, Eretz Israel was clearly the predominant *medinah*, its representatives possessing a range of powers which were sanctified by custom and reinforced by their constant contacts with other diaspora communities (especially Egypt). Thus, *semikhah* could only be granted in Eretz Israel (T.B. *Sanhedrin* 14a), and it was there that the calendar was fixed and the liturgy standardized (*Mishnah: Rosh ha-Shanah* 1:1, 3, 4; 2:1–4). Moreover, the sages of Eretz Israel were consulted, as a matter of course, on the appointment of a head of the Babylonian academy of Pumbedita (T.B. *Horayot* 14a).

Nevertheless, times of tension between the two *medinot* were not lacking (*Genesis Rabbah* 33:3); and the sages of Eretz Israel found it necessary to rebuke Ḥananiah (a Babylonian *amora*) when, in 145 CE, he presumed to proclaim a Jewish calendar (T.B. *Berakhot* 63a). Subsequently, relations between the two *medinot* were usually expressed through the balance of relationships between the *Nasi* and the *Resh Galuta*.

Relations between *keter malkhut* and *keter torah* as manifested in relations between *Nasi* and other members of the Sanhedrin in Eretz Israel (e.g., Gamliel and Joshua—*Mishnah: Rosh ha-Shanah*—and conspiracy by Meir and Natan vs. Simon b. Gamilel—T.B. *Horayot* 13b; see also the activities of the circle of Akiva's disciples referred to in T.J. *Hagigah* 3:1, 78d) and between *Resh Galuta* and *rashei yeshivot* in Bavel.

Relationship of the *edah* toward *minim* (schismatic sects, e.g., T.J. *Sanhedrin* 10:6), which otherwise threatened to undermine the authority of the institutions of the polity as a whole.

Relations between autonomous Jewish institutions and the foreign ruler. Formulated in this epoch through the principle of *dina demalkhuta dina* (the law of the kingdom is the law—formulated in 250 CE by the *amora* Samuel as a means of retaining Jewish autonomy under Sassanian rule; T.B. *Nedarim* 28a, *Gittin* 10b, *Bava Kamma* 113a, *Bava Batra* 54b–55a). This principle strengthened the fiber of the Jewish constitutional system and structure by laying down the limits of the powers of the foreign suzerain, restricting them to areas of civil jurisdiction, and establishing the modes of their application through the *halakhic* medium.

3.2 Camps and Parties

During the last generations of the previous epoch, the Sadducees and Essenes were eliminated and the Christians cut off. Hence, the Pharisaic camp attained hegemony. Parties within this camp were based on differences in interpretation of the *halakhah* and the proper distribution of power between *keter torah* and *keter malkhut*.

4. CONSTITUTIONAL STRUCTURE OF THE *EDAH*

A nonterritorial polity, united by shared law that became increasingly detailed and precise

4.1 Principal Instruments, Officers, and Functions

KETER TORAH

The *keter torah* greatly increased in constitutional weight. With the disappearance of the Sadducean camp, principal institutions of *keter torah* became exclusive interpreters of the constitution and also exercised functions in the domain of *keter malkhut*.

Sanhedrin: Now became the highest authoritative body of the *edah*, con-

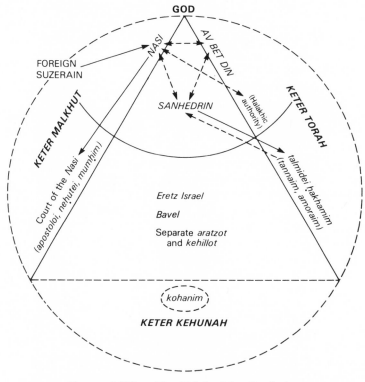

FIGURE VIII-1. The *Edah* of the *Sanhedrin* and the *Nesi'ut*

sisting of seventy members drawn from the domain of *keter torah*. The body retained and expanded its earlier functions: it acted as high court with power of law enforcement, interpreted the constitution and sharpened it by enactment of *takkanot*, and certified actions of constitutional import (e.g., date of new moon).

Av Bet Din: Appointed by the Sanhedrin, whose business as a court he administered. His office fell within the domain of the *keter torah*, in which capacity he balanced the *Nasi*. From the beginning of this epoch it became customary to appoint a scholar from Bavel to the office, as a means of including a representative of that *medinah* in the governance of the *edah*.

Talmidei Ḥakhamim: Recognized interpreters of the constitution (in Eretz Israel appointed by process of *semikhah*—T.B. *Sanhedrin* 14a), an intellectual meritocracy drawn from a widely popular base. Their opinions, framed within the context of *keter torah*, formed the basis of the *Mishnah* and later of the *Gemara*.

Neḥutei: Scholars who traveled between Eretz Israel and Bavel, thus helping to preserve the unity of the *edah* and common interpretation of the Torah, generally persons originally from Eretz Israel (e.g., Ulla—third century)

Mumḥim: (lit. "experts"); emissaries of *Nasi*, transmitted his halakhic judgments.

KETER MALKHUT

Limitations on possible forms of Jewish political organization imposed by foreign rule restricted the autonomy of the domain of *keter malkhut*. Most of its functions were now performed by principals whose claim to authority rested on their qualifications in the realm of *keter torah* and who were confirmed in their office by foreign suzerain.

Nasi: Nominally President of the Sanhedrin, chosen by that body and formally confirmed in office by Roman government as head of the *edah*. In fact a dynastic appointment, confined to descendants of Hillel I, and recognized as *nir le-vet David* (descendant of the [distaff line of the] House of David).

Empowered (by Sanhedrin and Romans) to administer province of Judea. Although first *Nesi'im* actively presided over the work of the Sanhedrin, after R. Judah ha-Nasi there was a separation of powers with *Nasi* confined to his principal domain of *keter malkhut*. Nevertheless he exercised his functions from a seat in *keter torah*, over which he consequently exerted influence.

Apostolai: Emissaries of the *Nasi*, whose task it was to collect voluntary taxes for the maintenance and support of the *Nesi'ut*.

The direction of constitutional decision-making for the *edah* was in the hands of a triumverate: the *Nasi*, the *Av Bet Din*, and a leading scholar with no formal institutional position other than membership in the Sanhedrin, reflecting the expanded role of the *keter torah*, its intrusion into the sphere of *keter malkhut*, and the mechanism developed by the Jews to continue the constitutional principle of power-sharing under these new circumstances. *Takkanot* and *halakhot* were enacted by the Sanhedrin in the name of the *Nasi*. *Semikhah* was granted jointly by both.

KETER KEHUNAH

No longer exercised constitutional functions and hence did not exert constitutional influence.

Kohanim: Retained limited ministerial functions exercised in the most immediately local arenas (blessing the congregation, redemption of firstborn); but as participants in governance reduced to fossils

5. *MEDINOT*

Two concentrations of Jews sufficiently constituted to function as *medinot* (Eretz Israel and Bavel), divided by the political boundary between Roman and Persian empires. Of these, Eretz Israel claimed—and was usually recognized as possessing—constitutional supremacy, with its institutional framework serving both the entire *edah* and its own *medinah*.

Aratzot—congeries of *kehillot* within recognized geopolitical entities but without permanent organizational frameworks (Mitzrayim, Cyrenaica, Syria, Asia Minor, Cyprus, Achea, Macedonia, Regnum Bospori, Italia, Arabia)

5.1 Eretz Israel (see *edah*)

Medinah institutions included *yeshivot*, self-contained academies of learning which also possessed legislative powers under *keter torah* at Lydda, Caesaria, and Akhbarei as well as Tiberias. Each *yeshiva* was semi-autonomous although superiority of Sanhedrin was always recognized. Ties among them were maintained through periodic conferences of *rashei yeshivot* and *talmidei ḥakhamim*. Principal *yeshivot*: Usha, Bet She'arim, Sephoris, Tiberias, Caesaria, Lydda.

5.2 Bavel

KETER TORAH

In Bavel, *yeshivot* fulfilled an even more important *medinah*-wide function than in Eretz Israel, since they also served as local equivalents of the San-

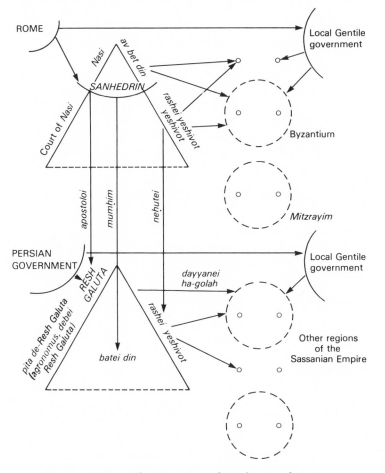

FIGURE VIII-2. The Structure of *Medinot* and *Aratzot*
in the Eighth Epoch

hedrin. Also known by the Aramaic term *metivta* and headed by a *rosh ye-shiva*, their development received a great impetus from the influx of scholars from Eretz Israel in the wake of the post–Bar Kochba persecutions. Subsequently, too, several of the principal instruments of the *keter torah* in Bavel received training at a *yeshiva* in Eretz Israel (e.g., Rav, who returned to Bavel in 219 and founded the great *yeshiva* of Sura where he instituted *yarhei kallah*). The influence of the *rashei yeshivot* reached its apogee under Rav Huna (Rav's successor at Sura and head of the *yeshiva* between 257 and 297), Abbaye (*rosh yeshiva* at Pumbedita), and Rava (*rosh yeshiva* at Meḥoza).

KETER MALKHUT

Resh Galuta (Exilarch): Principal instrument of *keter malkhut* for Bavel. A dynastic appointment limited to descendants of male line of David, ratified by foreign rule. Functioned as representative of the community in its dealings with foreign suzerain and was chiefly responsible for administering affairs of *medinah* of Bavel (e.g., appointment of tax collectors, *agronomus* (market inspector) and *rosh yeshiva* of Sura). With rise in importance of *yeshivot* (and consequent strengthening of *keter torah*), *Resh Galuta* was forced to share power with *rashei yeshivot*.

Pita de-Resh Galuta: Court of the *Resh Galuta*

Debei Resh Galuta: Clerks and police of exilarch

Dayyanei ha-Golah: Judicial authorities appointed by the Exilarch, also served as his emissaries to local communities

Agronomus: Superintendent of marketplace; appointed by *Resh Galuta*; set weights, measures, and prices and granted licenses

Batei Din: Courts consisting of three judges in small communities and twenty-three in large communities; appointment of judges by *Resh Galuta* and *yeshivot* with local involvement

6. *KEHILLOT*

Some local communities functioned within one or another of the two *medinot*, others as independent entities within the *edah*. Their autonomy was a function of their acceptance of the authority of the *Nasi* (in the Roman Empire) or the *Resh Galuta* (in the Persian Empire). Those within *medinot* were influenced by *dayyanei ha-Golah* and *mumhim*. Despite local variations, there was considerable commonality in construction of *kehillot* throughout the *edah*.

The government of the typical *kehillah* followed the following generalized model (see diagram).

KETER MALKHUT

Council (sometimes known as *Gerousia*) consisting of local notables (sometimes referred to as *havrei ha-ir* or *tuvei ha-ir*, usually ten in number). Chosen from among *ba'alei batim* (principal householders), they might be led by an *Archon* and usually appointed functionaries (*gabbaim*) to manage communal services (*gabbayei zedakah*, *soferim*).

KETER TORAH

Bet Din (court), usually consisting of three judges who met on Mondays and Thursdays; in some cases, these were the *mumhim* appointed by *Nasi* or Exilarch

Talmidei hakhamim, local scholars, serving as teachers of the Torah and heads of court

KETER KEHUNAH

Kohanim acquired ministerial function of blessing congregation. With the public and constitutional functions of the *kohanim* now reduced to an honor-

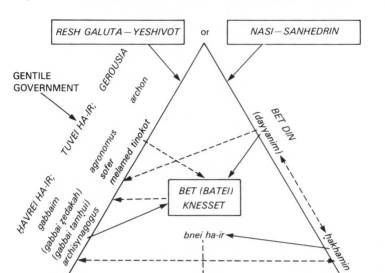

FIGURE VIII-3. The Structure of the *Kehillah*
in the Eighth Epoch

ific status, the need for the public expression of the ritual-cum-sacerdotal dimension of Jewish life had to be fulfilled by new functionaries, who operated in the arena of the *kehillah*. Prominent among these was the *ḥazzan*, who was responsible for the management of the *bet knesset* (the term may be related to the Akkadian *ḥazzanu*, "governor") and began to develop the function of the community in prayer.

7. REPRESENTATIVE PERSONALITIES

7.1 Constitutional Architects

R. Meir: (second century); *tanna* and principal instrument of *keter torah*; played decisive role in development of *Mishnah*, his collection forming basis of R. Judah ha-Nasi's work; all anonymous *halakhot* in *Mishnah* are attributed to him

R. Judah ha-Nasi: (*Rabi*—second–third century CE), *Nasi*, principal instrument of *keter torah*, also exerted great influence in domain of *keter malkhut*; redactor of *Mishnah*, henceforth to be regarded as a basic constitutional referent; also statesman

Samuel: (*Mar*—second–third century CE); Babylonian *amora*; *rosh yeshiva*, and in that capacity principal instrument of *keter torah*; author of constitutional principle *"dina demalkhuta dina"*

R. Ashi: (*Rabbana*—c. 335–427/8); *amora*, principal instrument of *keter torah*; began editing *Talmud Bavli*

7.2 Statesmen

R. Simeon ben   (second century), *Nasi*, strengthened Sanhedrin as most au-
Gamaliel II: thoritative institution of *edah* after Bar Kochba revolt

R. Joḥanan   (d. 279); *rosh* of the Sanhedrin in Tiberias; played major
bar Napḥa: role in transmitting teachings from Eretz Israel to Bavel, thus preserving unity of *edah*

R. Judah   *Nasi* and accomplished diplomat
ha-Nasi:

Rav: (*Abba Arikha*, third century), leading Babylonian *amora*, founder of *yeshiva* at Sura; ordained by Judah ha-Nasi, his *halakhot* helped to unify teachings of Eretz Israel and Bavel, introduced *yarḥei kallah*

Simeon bar   (second century), preserved unity of *keter torah* after failure
Yoḥai: of Bar Kochba revolt, emissary of people of Eretz Israel to Rome

7.3 Commentator

Onkeles: (second century), translator of Bible into Aramaic; his edition influenced understanding of text

8. TERMS

8.1 New

INDIGENOUS

Amora (one who explains); authoritative interpreter of the constitution in his capacity as instrument of *keter torah*; his authority was considered below that of his predecessors, the *tannaim*

Asmakhta (support); constitutional device, biblical text employed as a secondary exegesis (e.g., T.J. *Shevu'ot* 10:3, 39a)

Dayyanei ha-Golah, judicial authorities appointed by the *Resh Galuta* in his capacity as principal instrument of the *keter malkhut* in *medinah* of Bavel; they also served as his emissaries to local *kehillot*

Eduyot (evidences); prior to *mishnah* (T.B. *Berakhot* 28a)

Gabbai, official of the *kehillah* appointed to fulfill general or specific functions

Ḥazzan, functionary responsible for management of the *bet knesset*

Kabbalah, constitutional device, statement handed down by tradition (T.B. *Gittin* 36a)

Mi d'oraita, constitutional device, applied to statement whose source was in teachings of Torah

Mi de'rabbanan, constitutional device, applied to statement whose source was in sayings or teachings of authoritative instrument of *keter torah*

Mi divrei soferim, constitutional device, applied to statement handed down or interpreted from the days of the *soferim* (e.g., *Mishnah: Yevamot* 2:4)

Minhag (custom), now elevated to the status of a device whereby constitution could be modified and/or interpreted (e.g., T.J. *Peah* 7:5)

Minim, schismatic sects, regarded as a danger to the *edah* (e.g., T.J. *Sanhedrin* 10:6)

Mishnah, name applied to the legal codex compiled by Judah ha-Nasi, accepted by entire *edah* as constitution (T.B. *Kiddushin* 49a)

Mumḥim (experts); emissaries of *Nasi* (T.B. *Rosh ha-Shanah* 25b)

Pita de-Resh Galuta, court of the *Resh Galuta*

Rabban, Rav, titles denoting authority to interpret and apply Torah as constitution (*Tosefta Eduyot* 3:4)

Resh Galuta, Exilarch; principal instrument of *keter malkhut* in *medinah* of Bavel

Reshut, grant of authority (usually to judge; T.B. *Sanhedrin* 5a and 13b)

Rosh yeshiva, head of *yeshiva*; a principal instrument of *keter torah*

Tanna (one who teaches); authoritative interpreter of the constitution in his capacity as instrument of *keter torah*; his constitutional authority was superior to that of the *amoraim* (T.B. *Bava Metziah* 3a)

Zaken Mamre (lit. "rebellious elder"); a scholar who disregarded decision of superiors in *bet din* (*Mishnah: Sanhedrin* 11b)

Foreign Derivatives

Arnona, levy for maintenance of civil service (T.B. *Pesaḥim* 6a)

Apostoloi, emissaries of the *Nasi* in his capacity as principal instrument of the *edah* in the domain of *keter malkhut*; by collecting voluntary taxes for the maintenance of the *Nesi'ut*, they also strengthened ties within *edah*

Gushpanka, authority of office which had been constitutionally devolved (T.B. *Shabbat* 66b)

Kamara, sash of office (T.B. *Hor.* 13b)

Metivta, name used in Bavel for *yeshiva* (T.B. *Gittin* 8a)

Mar, title denoting authority to interpret and apply Torah as constitution (T.B. *Sanhedrin* 109b)

Neḥutei (Aram.: those who leave Israel temporarily for period of study), instruments of *keter torah* who traveled between Eretz Israel and Bavel thus helping to preserve unity of the *edah* and common interpretation of the Torah (T.J. *Shekalim* 8:51a)

8.2 Old—Change in Meaning

Dayyan, ordained judge, original appellation reserved only to God (e.g.,

1 Sam. 24:15, Psalms 68:6), now official title bestowed, via *semikhah*, on humans (T.B. *Sanhedrin* 5a)

Haverim, city dwellers, e.g., *Mishnah: Bava Batra* 1:5

9. BIBLIOGRAPHY

C. Albeck, "Ha-Sanhedrin u-Nesieiha," *Zion* 8 (1943), pp. 165–178.

S. L. Albeck, *Batei ha-Din Bimei ha-Talmud* (Ramat-Gan, 1980).

G. Alon, *The Jews in Their Land in the Talmudic Age* (70–640 CE), translated and edited by G. Levi, vol. I (Jerusalem, 1980).

S. Applebaum, *Jews and Greeks in Ancient Cyrene* (Leiden, 1979).

M. Avi-Yonah, *The Jews of Palestine, A Political History from the Bar-Kochba War to the Arab Conquest* (Oxford, 1976).

M. Baer, *Rashut Ha-Golah be-Bavel Bimei ha-Mishnah veha-Talmud* (Tel-Aviv, 1976).

A. I. Baumgarten, "The Akiban Opposition," *Hebrew Union College Annual* 50 (1974), pp. 179–197.

Y. Gafni, *Yahadut Bavel u-Mosdoteha Bitkufat ha-Talmud* (Jerusalem, 1975).

E. Goldenberg, "Darko shel R. Yehudah ha-Nasi Besidur ha-Mishnah." *Tarbitz* 28 (1959), pp. 260–269.

S. Lieberman, "The Publication of the Mishnah," in *Hellenism in Jewish Palestine* (New York, 1950), pp. 83–100.

J. Neusner, *There We Sat Down: Talmudic Judaism in the Making* (Nashville, 1972).

D. Rokeah, *Meridot ha-Yehudim Bimei Troyanus*, 115–115 C.E. (Jerusalem, 1978).

E. E. Urbach, "Halakhah u-Nevuah," *Tarbitz* 18 (1946–1947), pp. 1–27.

———. "The Talmudic Sage: Character and Authority," *Journal of World History* II (1968), pp. 116–142.

———. "Masoret ve-Halakhah," *Tarbitz* 50 (1981), pp. 136–163.

PART THREE

The Great Dispersion

EPOCH IX

c. 4185–c. 4500 AM (c. 425–c. 750 CE)

Ha-Yeshivot ve-Rashei ha-Golah
The Yeshivot and Exilarchs

1. DOMINANT EVENTS

1.1 Founding Events

Center of organized Jewish life moved from Eretz Israel to diaspora with Roman abolition of *Nesi'ut*, division of Sanhedrin, and suspension of Sanhedrin's right to levy taxes for its support in the diaspora   430 CE

Compilation of Babylonian Talmud   c. 499 CE

signified hegemony of Bavel over Eretz Israel

interpreted, codified, and instrumentalized by *savoraim*

Office of *Resh Galuta* regained status after century of upheaval

Note: Jewish rebellions against external government (e.g., rebellion of Mar Zutra in Bavel, 495–502) led to severe restrictions on Jewish autonomy (also, e.g., rebellion in Caesaria, 556, against Justinian Code).

1.2 Climactic Events

Application of Talmud as basic constitutional referent

Last Jewish effort to reestablish Jewish state by force of arms: in 614 Jews under "Nehemiah ben Hussiel ben Ephraim ben Yosef" helped Persians against Byzantium and were rewarded with right to rebuild Jerusalem, but by 617 Byzantines reconquered Eretz Israel

Islamic conquest of entire Middle East, replacing increasingly anti-Jewish Byzantine and Persian rulers   624–661 CE

1.3 Culminating Events

Decline of *Resh Galuta* as a political force

Last of the *savoraim*

Arab conquest of Spain, 711–712, completed process of bringing overwhelming majority of Jews under a single external government and under the influence of Arabic culture. After the Arab conquest of western Asia and Egypt, virtually the entire *edah* came under a single foreign government. The Arab conquest of North Africa and Spain left only a small percentage of Jews outside Moslem sphere.

2. CONSTITUTIONAL HISTORY

From a constitutional perspective, Epoch IX must be considered a period of consolidation. It witnessed no fundamental shifts of direction; rather, trends apparent in earlier epochs reached fruition and attained substantive form.

This characteristic was most pertinently apparent in the sphere of relations between the *medinot* of Eretz Israel and Bavel. As early as the founding generation of Epoch IX, the Roman government divided—and thus effectively disbanded—the Sanhedrin. This development, combined with the ending of the *Nesi'ut* in 425, facilitated the movement of the nexus of organized Jewish life to Bavel. Although Eretz Israel did remain the focus of Jewish pilgrimages—and even experienced a modest economic and cultural revival during the late fifth century—its institutions were clearly too weak to wield *edah*-wide authority. Justinian's unprecedented intrusions upon Jewish autonomy during the sixth century caused further damage, the extent of which was merely underlined by the short and brutal history of the Jewish effort to reestablish a polity (under Persian patronage) in Judea between 614 and 617.

By contrast, the *medinah* of Bavel, now under Sassanid dominion, experienced a period of steady—although not spectacular—growth. The Jewish communities of the region increased in both size and wealth, retaining and reinforcing the various institutional arrangements which had been developed during previous epochs. The process whereby Bavel's status—both relative and real—thereby grew was further reinforced by the completion of the *Talmud Bavli* during the founding generations of the epoch. The work soon became accepted as the basic constitutional referent for the entire *edah*. Essentially comprising the record of the discussions of several generations of Babylonian *amoraim*, the work indeed became the third classic Jewish text—superseded only by the Bible and the *Mishnah* (which it incorporated), both of which it was designed to mediate.

From a legal point of view, the *Talmud Bavli* undoubtedly sharpened the *halakhah* and determined the direction of its future development. From a constitutional point of view, however, the redaction of the work inaugurated a period of crystallization. It did not immediately lead to further significant departures. Rather, Jewish constitutional expression became inner-directed—intent more on providing glosses to established patterns of talmudic exegesis than on evolving new conceptions of a revolutionary nature. This became apparent during the second half of the epoch, in the work of the *savoraim*. It was they who codified, interpreted, and instrumentalized the Talmud; but they did so by amplifying existing decisions rather than by formulating new ones. The development of *aggadah* (through means of the sermon-discourse) and of the *piyyut* (in prayer) during the same generations provide indications of a similar trend. Both were significant cultural advances, not least because both employed the Hebrew language as their basic medium. Yet neither expression was intended (nor can it be regarded) as more than a buttress for a framework whose foundations had been laid in earlier, and more adventurous, times.

Another sphere in which the trend toward consolidation was apparent is that of the relationship within Bavel between the *keter malkhut* (as represented by the *Resh Galuta*) and the *keter torah* (as represented by the *rashei yeshivot*). With the disappearance of the *Nesi'ut* in Eretz Israel, the *Resh Galuta* assumed the role of *nasi ha-edah*—and was so regarded by both the Jewish people and the foreign suzerain. His was not, however, an authoritarian government but one based on power-sharing between the *keter malkhut* and the *keter torah*. For one thing, the prestige of the office was tarnished by a series of conflicts over the succession to the title during the first half of the epoch. For another, the *Resh Galuta's* power continued to be checked and balanced by that of the *rashei yeshivot*. By the end of the epoch, indeed, the arrangements whereby they shared authority (in the name of the *keter torah*) with the *Resh Galuta* were reformulated to the advantage of the latter, giving the *rashei yeshivot* superior status. Moreover, the popular authority of the *keter torah* was further increased during this epoch through the specific months of learning sponsored by the *yeshivot* (the *kallah* months) which served as annual periods of communication between the instruments of the *keter torah* and wide segments of the population.

Third, the epoch also witnessed the intensification of earlier trends toward the restructuring of the *edah*. Baldly stated, the dominant pattern is one of increasing dispersion and fission. The decline of Eretz Israel as the focus of all Jewish political life created something of a vacuum within which other *medinot* became virtually autonomous entities. Of these, Bavel was undoubtedly dominant; but its institutions never quite managed to attain the authority previously wielded by those of Eretz Israel. Equally unsuccessful were several attempts to establish politically independent entities. Armed Jewish uprisings at Meḥoza in the sixth century and in Judea in the seventh were abject failures. Only marginally more successful was the Jewish state of Himyar in the Yemen, which finally succumbed to the Ethiopians in 525.

It is significant that the rulers of Himyar did maintain contact with the Jewish community of Tiberias. This is a line of communication which reenforces the thesis that the *edah* continued to function as an operational organizing concept in this epoch. Indeed, the *edah* as a whole continued to be bound together by a shared adherence to its constitution as articulated through the

Talmud and—increasingly—by the common status of its members as *dhimmi* under Islamic rule (which, with the Islamic conquest of Spain in 711–712 toward the end of the epoch, came to embrace virtually the entire *edah*).

Nevertheless, the *edah* was clearly not a unified entity. By the end of the epoch it consisted, rather, of a congeries of three principal *medinot*—Eretz Israel, Bavel, and Mitzrayim—and a growing number of less articulated *aratzot* located in western Asia, north Africa, and southern Europe. Increasingly, Jewish communities were becoming more diffuse and more detached from contiguous territories. They were also falling under the sway of tribal and semi-nomadic cultures (Arabs, Slavs, and Germans), whose way of life was markedly different from the urban-centered civilizations which had hitherto shaped Jewish constitutional development.

3. CONSTITUTION

Torat Moshe as mediated through Talmud

3.1 Constitutional Issues

Continuing tension between Eretz Israel and Bavel for supremacy within *edah*; reflected in struggle over respective authoritativeness of *Talmud Bavli* and *Talmud Yerushalmi*. Only in matters relating to the calendar did Eretz Israel retain recognized supremacy. Otherwise shift apparent in the evidence which suggests that after 520 heads of the Sanhedrin in Eretz Israel were descendants of Mar Zutra, himself a former *Resh Galuta*.

Relationship between *Resh Galuta* and *rashei ha-yeshivot*

Adjustment to Islamic rule—especially to new status of Jews as *dhimmi* (members of a protected but subordinate community) under the terms of the covenant of Omar (634–644)

3.2 Camps and Parties

Resh Galuta and his party vs. the *rashei yeshivot* and theirs

Eretz Israel vs. Bavel

4. CONSTITUTIONAL STRUCTURE OF THE *EDAH*

Congeries of *medinot* and *aratzot* with seat in Bavel and headed by *Resh Galuta* and *rashei yeshivot*

4.1 Principal Instruments, Officers, and Functions

KETER MALKHUT

Resh Galuta: With disappearance of office of *Nasi* in Eretz Israel, the *Resh Galuta* assumed role of *Nasi ha-Edah*, and was so recognized

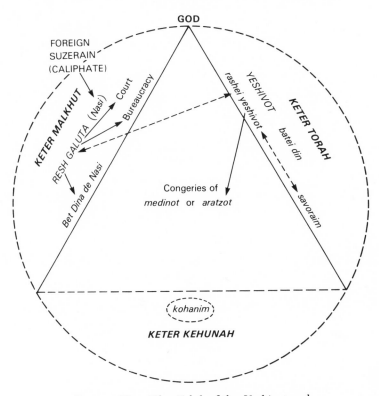

FIGURE IX-1. The *Edah* of the *Yeshivot* and
the *Rashei Ha-Golah*

by both the Jewish people and the foreign suzerain. His functions remained as before, except that power sharing arrangements with *rashei yeshivot* were now institutionalized; e.g.,
rashei yeshivot participated in designation of the *Resh Galuta*
from among the heirs to the position. Conversely, *takkanot* of
yeshivot required his signature. Furthermore, *Resh Galuta*
and *rashei yeshivot* consulted jointly in appointment of *dayyanim*. The *Resh Galuta* continued to have his own court, bureaucracy, and *bet din* (*Bet Dina de Nasi* or *Baba de Marata*).

KETER TORAH
Yeshivot: Assemblies (lit. seats) of scholars involved in the study and interpretation of the *keter torah*. The *yeshiva* was the place at
which they congregated in order to legislate in matters of constitutional and other import (hence, the *yeshiva* also known as
bet va'ad, literally "house of assembly"—a term which, as its

etymology indicates, retained the connotation of a constitutional gathering).

Yeshivot of Bavel inherited mantle of Sanhedrin of Eretz Israel, except in intercalation of the calendar. Their members formed an intellectual meritocracy, drawn from a widely popular base. The *rashei yeshivot* (now also called *adirah vemoshlah*) enacted *takkanot* for the entire *edah*.

Rashei yeshivot: Had now reached a position of political equality (and perhaps even more) with *Resh Galuta* and had their own *batei din*

Batei din: Served as appellate courts for entire *edah*

Savora'im: Recognized scholars in the domain of *keter torah*, successors to the *amoraim*. They were constitutionally competent to "render decisions" but administered private subjective judgments rather than authoritative ones. As a group they are credited with having completed the ordering of the Talmud, clarifying certain unsettled halakhic decisions. In so doing, they contributed to the wide acceptance of the *Talmud Bavli* as the basic constitutional referent of the succeeding epoch. Their own constitutional initiative, however, was extremely limited.

5. *MEDINOT*

Three concentrations of Jews, constituted as *medinot* (Eretz Israel, Miẓrayim, and Bavel, with latter now exercising the dominant influence)

Eretz Israel

The reduction of Eretz Israel to no more than *medinah* status is the direct result of, among other phenomena, the Roman abolition of *Nesi'ut* with its power and prestige and the abolition of the tax levied by the Sanhedrin on all diaspora communities for its support.

Rosh Perek was the successor to the *Nasi* with much reduced authority. Unlike the *Nasi* he was head of the Sanhedrin in fact as well as theory, functioning as its chairman rather than as an independent figure. Even so, an effort was made to preserve the office as a nucleus of political power by maintaining its dynastic character. The first family held it for nearly 100 years until replaced by Mar Zutra, son of the *Resh Galuta* who settled in Eretz Israel after fleeing Bavel. He succeeded to the office by virtue of his descent from the Davidic line, in other words, this was another means of strengthening the office. The office remained in his family for seven generations, until the Sanhedrin moved to Jerusalem in the seventh century.

Bavel

The same structure that governed the *edah* also governed Bavel.

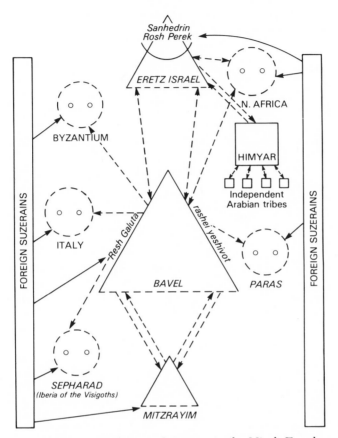

FIGURE IX-2. *Medinot* and *Aratzot* in the Ninth Epoch

Aratzot, congeries of *kehillot* within recognized geopolitical regions, without
permanent shared organizational framework (North Africa, Byzantium,
Hispania, Macedonia, Italy, Persia, North Arabia, South Arabia, Syria,
Asia Minor, Pannomia, Gaul)

Independent tribal and territorial entities. In this epoch, there existed a
number of politically independent Jewish tribes scattered through the Arabian and Saharan deserts, at least some of which maintained contact with
the centers of Jewish authority: Arabian Jewish tribes—Kheybar, Teyma,
Saharan Jewish tribes, and Berber Jewish tribes. All were destroyed with the
rise of Islam. For a period during the early sixth century, there existed a
Jewish kingdom of Himyar (Yemen) whose best known king was Joseph Dhu
Nuwas (c. 517–525), who maintained some contact with the *ḥakhamim* of
Tiberias.

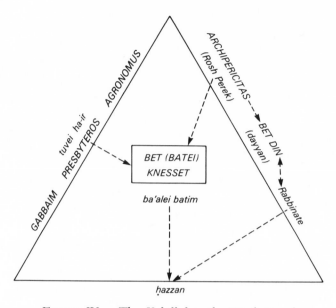

FIGURE IX-3. The *Kehillah* in the Ninth Epoch

6. *KEHILLOT*

Local communities, some within the two *medinot*, others as independent entities with the *edah*. Local variations persisted (although precise information is sparse) but the common pattern continued to be that observed during the previous epoch.

7. REPRESENTATIVE PERSONALITIES

7.2 Statesmen

Mar Zutra II: (c. 496–520); leader of revolt against Persians; established Jewish state in Maḥoza which lasted for seven years, subsequently fled to Tiberias and founded line of *rashei perek* to head Sanhedrin in Eretz Israel

Bustanai b. Ḥaninai: (c. 618–670); first *Resh Galuta* after Arab conquest of Bavel, accomplished diplomat who managed transition to new foreign suzerain

7.3 Constitutional Commentators

Aḥa (Aḥai) of Shabḥa: (680–752); author of *Sheiltot* (Questions), compilation of halakhic and aggadic material and first posttalmudic work to be attributed to its author

8. TERMS

8.1 New

ARAMAIC

Baba de Maruta ⎱ , court of the *Resh Galuta* (who is now referred to as
Bet Dina de-Nasi ⎰   *Nasi*)

Bet Va'ad (lit. "house of assembly"), a synonym for *yeshiva*. As indicated by
   its etymology, the term possesses the connotation of an authorized assembly
   which possesses right of constitutional modification

Dayyana de Bava, head of the court of the Exilarch

Hilkhata (the ruling is)   ⎫ legal terms with some political implications,
Mistabra (it is reasonable) ⎬ used as means of establishing authority of
Pashit (and he resolved it) ⎭ *Talmud Bavli*

Pitka de dinuta, letter of judicial authorization

GREEK

Archipericitas, head of the academy (as in Tiberias)

Presbyteros, member of the council of elders

9. BIBLIOGRAPHY

S. Asaf, *Batei Din ve-Sidreihem Aḥarei Ḥatimat ha-Talmud* (Jerusalem, 1924).

S. W. Baron, "Protected Minority," A *Social and Religious History of the Jewish People*,
   vol. 3 (New York, 1957), chapter 18.

Y. Dori, *Shilton Rashut ha-Golah veha-Yeshivot* (Tel Aviv, 1922).

M. Gil, "Ha-Mifgash ha-Bavli," *Tarbitz* 48 (1978), pp. 35–73.

D. M. Goodblatt, *Rabbinic Instruction in Sasanian Babylonia* (Leiden, 1975).

J. Neusner, *A History of the Jews in Babylonia*, 5 vols. (Leiden, 1965–1969).

   Vol. I: The Parthian Period
   Vol. II: The Early Sasanian Period
   Vol. III: From Shapur I to Shapur II
   Vol. IV: The Age of Shapur
   Vol. V: Later Sasanian Times

———. "The Rabbis and the Exilarch: Politics and Theocracy," in Neusner (ed.),
   Talmudic Judaism in Sasanian Babylon: Essays and Studies (Leiden, 1976),
   pp. 108–137.

A. Sharf, *Byzantine Jewry: From Justinian to the Fourth Crusade* (London, 1971).

EPOCH X

c. 4500–4798 AM (c. 750–1038 CE)

Yeshivot ve-Geonim
Yeshivot and Geonim

1. DOMINANT EVENTS

1.1 Founding Events

Establishment of *Geonut* (c. 760)
Compilation of first halakhic codes, *Halakhot Pesukot* (c. 760)
Beginning of a Karaite schism (762–767)

1.2 Climactic Events

Renewed tension between Eretz Israel and Bavel as representatives of former
   tried to regain leadership of the *edah*
Compilation of *Halakhot Gedolot* (c. 825)
Beginnings of large-scale Jewish migration to Europe

1.3 Culminating Events

Attempt of Eretz Israel to regain supremacy throughout *edah* by restoration of
   Nesi'ut
End of *Geonut* (d. of Hai Gaon—1038)
Decline of great *yeshivot* of Sura and Pumbedita
Emergence of rabbinical authorities in Europe, e.g., Rabbenu Gershom,
   c. 960–1028, known as *Me'or ha-Golah*

2. CONSTITUTIONAL HISTORY

The Karaite schism necessarily constitutes a predominant feature of Jewish
constitutional history during Epoch X. Not only did the controversy which it
provoked last for almost the entire course of the epoch, it also revolved around

issues of crucial importance for the *edah* as a whole. At stake was far more than the personal suitability of Anan ben David to be *Resh Galuta* (the rejection of his candidature being the ostensible cause of the schism in 767). His followers, by insisting on strict adherence to only a literal interpretation of the biblical texts (*mikra'ah*; hence the name Karaites) were in fact calling into question the entire body of rabbinic tradition. In so doing, they also raised an explicit challenge to the claims of the *Talmud Bavli* to be recognized as the basic constitutional referent for the entire *edah*. That, more than any other factor, must explain why their opponents (the Rabbanites) regarded the Karaites as dangerous schismatics whose potential influence was symbolically demonstrated by the establishment of their own center and synagogue in Jerusalem during the tenth century. For the first time since the Sadducees of Epoch VI (and for the only time until the thirteenth epoch), the essence of the accepted constitution itself was being called into question. Little wonder, therefore, that both parties perceived the struggle in terms of total conflict, nor that—by the end of the epoch—the Karaites had been forcefully cast out of the fold.

Clearly, the Rabbanites could not have emerged victorious had they not themselves taken steps to strengthen the efficacy of the talmudic corpus. This they sought to do on several occasions during the first half of the epoch by compiling codices which attempted to impose some order on the mass of talmudic material. The three compiled during this epoch were the *Halakhot Gedolot*, *Halakhot Pesukot*, and *Halakhot Ketzuvot*. Incorporating the teachings and decisions of the *savoraim*, they were also designed to make talmudic rulings more widely available. While these efforts had limited effect, they did serve as foundations upon which constitutional architects of succeeding epochs would construct new constitutional referents.

More effective, in immediate terms, were the steps taken during Epoch X to strengthen the rabbinic camp. The tenth epoch is notable for the fact that well over ninety percent of world Jewry (most of which was by now urbanized) were located under the common rule of the Arab empire. This, in turn, offered an opportunity to develop an *edah*-wide frame of governance unparalleled since the fall of the Persian Empire to Alexander the Great a millenium earlier. Bavel, the seat of the *Resh Galuta* and the locus of the great *yeshivot* of Sura and Pumbedita, took a decisive lead in this regard. In the domains of both the *keter malkhut* and the *keter torah*, instruments of *edah*-wide authority were sharpened and—where necessary—developed, with leadership being vested in a remarkably prolific and successful meritocracy and aristocracy. The task demanded relatively little change in the rights and obligations of the *Resh Galuta*. Not even the caliphate decree of 825, allowing any group of ten *dhimmi* the right to appoint their own communal leader (*rosh*), produced an immediate effect on the status of the office. Although the decree did portend the eventual splintering of the *keter malkhut*, the hemor-rhage was—during this epoch—contained by virtue of the ingrained respect of the entire *edah* for the descendants of the royal Davidic line.

Developments within the *keter torah* were more dramatic. There, the inter-nal governance of the *yeshivot* was entirely overhauled and consolidated dur-ing the course of the epoch. A completely new hierarchy emerged, replete with various titles and stations. At its apex stood the *Rosh Yeshivat Gaon Ya'akov*, generally known as the *Gaon*. Recognized as the principal instru-ment of the *keter torah* throughout the *edah*, the *Gaon* was empowered to issue halakhic decisions of absolute legal validity and to respond authori-tatively to halakhic enquiries from throughout the Jewish world. At the apogee of the office, he also functioned as the *edah's* chief legislator, chief justice, chief administrator, and chief spiritual mentor, all within a context whereby the *Resh Galuta* increasingly played a role approximating that of constitu-tional monarch, the *Yeshiva* that of legislature, and the *Gaon* that of prime minister. The epoch is studded with the names of *Geonim* who led the Rab-banite camp against the Karaites and who at the same time, and in so doing, reinforced the constitutional status of the *Talmud Bavli*. It was also character-ized by the flow of funds from throughout the *edah* to support the central institutions of the *Geonim* and *Resh Galuta*.

Not that the Rabbanite camp was itself entirely unified. There existed a sufficient number of issues of constitutional controversy to allow for the emergence of several separate parties within this camp. One such issue was the relative authority of the *Gaon* (representing the *keter torah*) and the *Resh Galuta* (representing the *keter malkhut*). The rise in influence of the former necessarily impinged upon the authority of the latter, much of whose power had in any case been curtailed by the developments noted during the previous epoch. Tension between the two was, accordingly, endemic; and power-sharing arrangements (as in the appointment of *dayyanim* to the *bet din*) rigidly enforced.

The intractable struggle for *edah*-wide hegemony between Eretz Israel and Bavel provided a further bone of contention which cut across otherwise clearly defined Rabbanite lines. The *medinah* of Eretz Israel experienced a modest revival during the ninth and tenth centuries. An attempt was made to reinstitute the *Nesi'ut* and to impose new calendrial regulations on Bavel. Both ventures failed (although not, in the latter case, without some fierce bickering); but while they lasted, the controversies thus engendered strained relations between the two rival centers.

By the end of the epoch, however, that particular confrontation had taken on a somewhat shop-worn and irrelevant appearance. By then, the *Geonut* was in itself in a state of decline as an institution with *edah*-wide influence. Partly, this may be attributed to the break-up of the Islamic empire and the consequent loosening of the political bonds which had embraced virtually the entire Jewish community; partly it was due to the shift of the Jewish demographic axis westward, taking with it the halakhic scholars who planted the seeds of future constitutional autonomy for the Jewish communities of Europe. (In this context, it is probably significant that the *Halakhot Pesukot* was compiled outside Bavel.)

For both reasons, the decisive movements which were subsequently to affect the course of Jewish constitutional history were taking place outside the traditional centers which had for the past three epochs dominated the *edah*'s affairs. Significant and important *medinot* began to emerge in North Africa, in Byzantium, and—perhaps most important of all—in the Iberian peninsula (Sepharad), in Narbonne, and in the Rhineland (Ashkenaz). The conversion to Judaism of the Kings of Khazaria centered in the Crimea also took place in this epoch. But despite the fascination which this event exerted on later writers, the incident had limited impact on the course of Jewish constitutional history. Contacts between Khazaria and the institutions of the *edah* apparently were sporadic though occasionally important—as in the case of Khazarian intervention on behalf of persecuted Jews in Byzantium (944).

Sepharad and Ashkenaz gradually broke away from the authority of the older centers during the course of this epoch. They were as yet unable to establish *medinah*-wide institutions of their own (hence their designation here as proto-*medinot*) but they were groping toward the construction of a framework which could embrace a large number of the local *kehillot*. In the realm of *keter torah* they produced (or imported) their own halakhic authorities; in that of *keter malkhut* they granted formal or informal authority to prominent courtiers in the service of foreign suzerains. They also benefited from grants of autonomy bestowed by local Gentile rulers (such as that proclaimed, as early as 825, by Louis the Pious, who entitled his Jewish subjects to live "in accordance with their own laws"). Thus, by the end of the epoch, their independence from the old centers of Jewish life was virtually assured. The *takkanot* enacted by Rabbenu Gershom in Ashkenaz were accepted throughout that area, thus providing it with a constitutional identity which both unified the local *kehillot* and set them apart from other segments of the *edah*.

3. CONSTITUTION

Torat Moshe, mediated through the Talmud with the addition of codices which must be viewed as experimental and which represented attempts to determine the effectiveness, applicability, and hierarchy of the talmudic corpus. These, however, had not yet gained authoritative status.

3.1 Constitutional Issues
Struggle between Rabbanites and Karaites, a sect founded by Anan ben David who (according to tradition) was slighted by not being appointed *Resh*

Galuta in 767. The Karaites rejected the Talmud and the entire body of Rabbinic tradition, insisting on strict adherence to a literal interpretation of the Scriptures (*mikra'ah*). The controversy spread throughout the *edah*, over whose history during this epoch it exerted a dominant influence. By the end of the epoch, however, the Karaites had been excluded from the *edah*.

Continuation of struggle for hegemony between Eretz Israel and Bavel (e.g., in determining date of *Rosh ha-Shanah* in 4683/922). Eretz Israel experienced a modest resurgence during the ninth and tenth centuries, when an attempt was made to reinstate the *Nesi'ut*. The failure of this venture finally moved the axis of authority away from Eretz Israel.

3.2 Camps and Parties

Rabbanites vs. Karaites

Parties within the Rabbanite camp, determined by allegiance to particular academies, teachers, and local traditions

4. CONSTITUTIONAL STRUCTURE OF THE *EDAH*

Congeries of *medinot* and *aratzot* with seat in Bavel, headed by *Gaon* and *Resh Galuta*

4.1 Principal Instruments, Officers, and Functions

KETER TORAH

Yeshivot of Sura and Pumbedita in Bavel continued to act as supreme interpreters of the Torah. They now also assumed role of supreme legislature in matters of *halakhah*. Members were drawn from various regions throughout the Islamic world and were recruited from broad popular base in accordance with their commitment to Torah scholarship.

In this epoch, the internal governance of the *yeshivot* became consolidated, with schools of authorities replacing individual opinions and a clear hierarchy emerging with the *yeshivot*.

Appropriate titles emerged accordingly, e.g.:

Bnei Tarbitzah:	Permanent students of the *yeshiva* (usually some 400)
Shevah shurot ha-ḥakhamim:	The group of seventy "prominent sages" occupying the first seven rows of the *yeshivot*. Seating in this hierarchy was fixed; places often passed as inheritance to the family of a deceased occupant.
Aluf:	A distinguished member of a *yeshiva*, who "commanded" a large territorial demesne

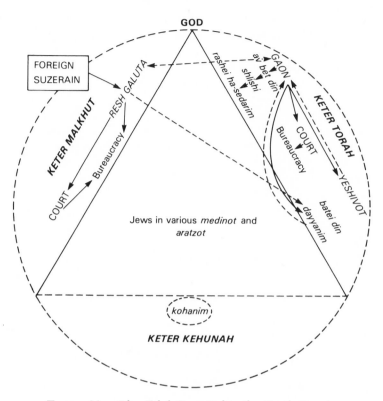

FIGURE X-1. The *Edah* Reunited in the Tenth Epoch

Rosh ha-Seder:	Officer delegated to apportion seats within the *yeshivot*
Tannaim:	(Recorders); charged with memorizing the entire Talmud, together with the appropriate vocalization and cantillation
Shlishi:	(Third); basically an administrative position. The title was accorded to the scholar immediately under the *av bet din* in the world of the *yeshivot*. The *shlishi* succeeded the *av bet din* when the latter died or was otherwise incapacitated. In turn, the *shlishi* was succeeded in the hierarchy by the *revi'i* (fourth) and *ḥamishi* (fifth). In view of the importance of the position, the *Gaon* would often attempt to appoint one of his own sons to the office of *shlishi*.
Sofer:	Administrative secretary to the bureaucracy of the *Geonut*. The *sofer* was responsible for formulating the *Gaon*'s replies to queries and was himself third in line to the *Geonut*.

Av *bet din*: (President of the high court); second in authority to the *Gaon* and his designated successor (also known as *dayyan de-bava*—guardians of the gate)

Gaon: Title of supreme authority within the *yeshiva* and its spokesman (officially known as *rav al metivta*—head of the academy).

Appointed by the *Resh Galuta* and confirmed by the foreign suzerain, the successful candidate had usually risen through the hierarchy of the *yeshivot*, and was drawn from a limited circle (known as *mishpaḥot ha-geonim*). Six such families existed in Bavel, one of which traced its descent back to the House of David (and hence was related to the *Resh Galuta*); a second traced its descent back to Aaron, the *Kohen Gadol*. One of the few *Geonim* to achieve office without belonging to one such family was R. Sa'adia, who was born in Mitzrayim and was *Gaon* of the *yeshiva* of Sura 928–930 and 937–942. The office was occasionally contested. At times, the spectacle was unsavory, but such contests nevertheless served as a good counterbalance to family rule and a potential overemphasis on hierarchy within the *yeshivot*.

At the apogee of the office, the *Gaon* functioned as the most authoritative instrument of *keter torah* for the entire *edah*. He was supported by contributions from the entire *edah*, for which he functioned as chief legislator, chief judge, chief administrator, and chief spiritual leader. He supervised marriages and divorces; was the guardian of the religious and moral conduct of the members of the *edah*; possessed the right to impose or cancel decrees of *ḥerem* (excommunication); and to appoint, and define the competence, of judges and to supervise *ne'emanim* (trustees) of the courts. In such capacities, he also shared some political roles with the *Resh Galuta*, and at times therefore conflict occurred between them (e.g., Sa'adia Gaon vs. the *Resh Galuta* David ben Zakkai, 930 CE).

In addition, the *Gaon* possessed three principal mechanisms for *edah*-wide constitutional revision and governance: (1) *takkanot*—halakhic ordinances of a binding legal validity (notably the *ḥerem*) promulgated by the *Gaon* from time to time; (2) *iggeret*—periodic letter of information and/or counsel to various communities (e.g., *iggeret* of R. Sa'adia Gaon to Egypt or of R. Hai Gaon to *kohanim* of North Africa); and (3) *teshuvot*—authoritative responses to halakhic

inquiries from throughout the Jewish world (surviving rec-
ords indicate such *teshuvot* to Balkḥ [Afghanistan], Kiev
[southern Russia], Tangiers, Lyon, and Cologne). In employ-
ing each of these mechanisms, the *Gaon* acted in conjunction with the senior members of the *yeshiva*. *Teshuvot*, for
instance, were not dispatched until they had been duly pro-
cessed. The procedure entailed (1) the tabling of inquiry before the *yeshiva* during the *kallah* months; (2) free debate
within the *yeshiva* on the subject; (3) the dictation by the
Gaon to the *Sofer* of a preliminary reply—in accordance
with the spirit of the debate and "by the authority of the
yeshiva"—here referred to as "the great Sanhedrin"; (4) further review of the draft reply at the end of the *kallah* month
by the entire *yeshiva*; and (5) consent by *yeshiva* and signature of the *Gaon*.

KETER MALKHUT

Resh Galuta: Although still chosen from among the descendants of *David
ha-melekh*, his appointment formally required the consent
of "the public"—(*da'at ha-kahal*). More important was
the ceremonious quiescence of the *Geonim* of Sura and
Pumbedita and—especially at times of contested elections—
of the *pinot ha-edah* (groups of wealthy families in Baghdad,
generally with contacts at the caliph's court). The *Resh
Galuta* continued to function as the supreme instrument of
the *keter malkhut* for the entire *edah*, as in the previous
epoch. However, he now shared some authority in this domain with the *Gaon*.

Batei Din: The judicial system reflected the power-sharing arrangement
between the *Gaon* and the *Resh Galuta*. *Dayyanim* were selected by *rashei yeshivot* and appointed by the *Resh Galuta*.
They adjudicated in accordance with principles laid down in
the *yeshivot*; but these decisions were made binding by virtue
of the authority vested in the courts and judges by the *Resh
Galuta*.

5. MEDINOT

Two principal concentrations of Jews constituted as *medinot*—in Bavel and
Eretz Israel. Of these, Bavel generally recognized to be supreme in con-
stitutional matters, although occasionally challenged by spokesmen for
Eretz Israel (e.g., ninth century—*paytanim*; tenth century—Nathan b.
Abraham; eleventh century—Palestinian *Geonim*). By the end of the epoch,
Mitzrayim and Sepharad became proto-*medinot*.

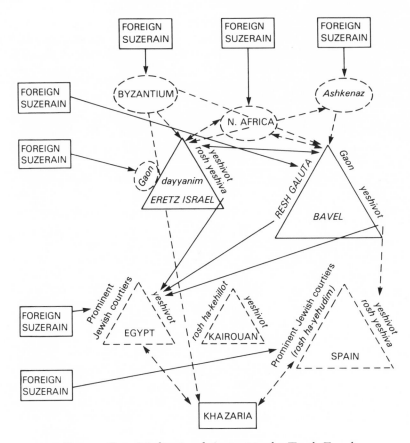

Figure X-2. *Medinot* and *Aratzot* in the Tenth Epoch

Proto-*medinot*. Lands of Jewish settlement in early stages of developing countrywide institutions, generally in response to strong, independent non-Jewish government with the region which encouraged that trend (e.g., Mitzrayim, particularly after the Fatimid conquest of 969 and Sepharad, after the establishment of the Umayyad Kingdom at Cordoba in 755).

Aratzot. Congeries of *kehillot* within recognizable geopolitical regions, but without permanent, shared organizational frameworks (e.g., North Africa, Byzantium, Germany [*Ashkenaz*]).

States with Jewish Rulers (e.g., the Kingdom of the Khazars, a politically independent entity, and the Jewish principality in Narbonne and the Spanish marches [768–901]).

Medinot

Bavel constituted the center of the *edah*, with the *Gaon* utilizing the *kallah* months to formally respond to halakhic inquiries from throughout the *edah*. It was from there that *Geonim* issued *teshuvot*, *igrot*, and *takkanot*, and thence that regional and local *dayyanim* and *alufim* received their letters of appointment (*minui*) from the *Gaon* and *Resh Galuta*. Such control, although initially very strong, became looser with the break-up of the caliphate. Authorities in Bavel then tended merely to grant formal assent to appointments determined by local communities who developed *yeshivot* and leaderships of their own.

Eretz Israel served as a secondary nexus of *edah*-wide halakhic communication—at times trying to compete with Bavel for primacy, at times sharing authority with it. Within the *medinah* of Eretz Israel, *Geonim* were designated by the *yeshivot* while *rashei yeshivot* were appointed from within the *yeshivot*. The *rashei yeshivot* appointed *ḥaverim*, who also served as *dayyanim*.

Mitzrayim was divided among adherents of the two Babylonian *yeshivot* and the *yeshiva* of Eretz Israel.

By the end of the epoch, Kairouan emerged as a *medinah* with a structure of its own and links with both Eretz Israel and Bavel.

Proto-Medinot and Aratzot

In the early part of the epoch, proto-*medinot* were virtually totally dependent on the instruments of the *edah* for constitutional determinants. As the epoch progressed, however, the proto-*medinot* tended to break away from the authority of the *Gaon* and to rely increasingly on their own halakhic authorities. Jewish government in these centers was further characterized by the emergence of prominent Jewish courtiers, who acquired formal or informal authority as instruments of the *keter malkhut* and/or *keter torah*. Ḥisdai ibn Shaprut, for instance, was granted the title *resh kallah* by the *yeshivot* of Bavel, and thus empowered to issue *teshuvot* and *igrot* of his own. In that capacity, he could also exert a substantial influence on the appointment of principal local instruments of the *keter torah* (e.g., Ḥisdai ibn Shaprut's influence on the appointment of Ḥanokh ben Moses and Moses ben Ḥanokh as *rosh yeshiva* of Cordoba successively).

Ashkenaz remained a congeries of local *kehillot*, but toward the end of the epoch began to develop a shared body of halakhic opinion (e.g., the *takkanot* of Rabbenu Gershom).

States

Khazaria, as an independent state, possessed institutions and officers which were peculiarly its own (e.g., the dual kingship) and which bore no relation to Jewish communal organization and government elsewhere. However, the kingdom of the Khazars might have been brought under talmudic law to some degree and was tied to other portions of the Jewish world by communications (which were probably not constitutional in character).

There is considerable evidence that some form of territorial vassal polity of the Carolingian Empire existed, under Jewish rule, in Narbonne and the northeastern Spanish borderlands, from the mid-eighth to possibly as late as the mid-eleventh centuries, covering Epoch X more or less precisely. (According to some later Narbonne traditions Pepin the Short granted Jews the right to elect Jewish kings when he conquered the town in 759.) This principality may have been headed by a descendant of the *Resh Galuta*, who was denominated *Nasi*. In any case it served as a bridge between the institutions of the *edah* in Bavel and the emerging Sephardic and Ashkenazic Jewries of Europe. Thus Barcelona, the major Jewish center in the principality in the ninth century, contributed to the support of the Gaonate and engaged in extensive official correspondence with that office. So, for example, R. Amram Gaon's classic *seder* (prayer formulary) was composed in response to a request from Barcelonian Jewry and transmitted to them in a *teshuvah* (c. 858–c. 878) and thence spread throughout Europe.

6. *KEHILLOT*

Local communities in Bavel, Eretz Israel, and Mitzrayim

Since *kehillot* were invariably small, the assembly of the entire local community was able to function—and usually did so—through the single *bet knesset*.

Thus, plenary sessions of the entire local community (which could also be attended by women and children who were residents) possessed authority to confirm the appointment of the *rav* of the community, to act as the board of appeals, and to elect a board of *zekenim* (elders—usually ten in number), some of whom were often nominated by the *Gaon* or *Resh Galuta*. Elections were frequent, although in some cases they tended to be *pro forma* affairs since offices remained in the hands of particular families (usually well-to-do in the case of *keter malkhut* and scholarly in the case of *keter torah*).

Executive authority was entrusted to the board of *zekenim*, from whose number were elected a *rosh ha-kahal* (who acted as the administrator of the local community's affairs) and *parnassim*, local magnates (sometimes referred to as *al shuyakh al-mush hurvim*, "noted elders"), who were responsible for the management of communal property and social services.

The board of *zekenim* appointed a wide range of local community functionaries. Some of these acted in an honorary capacity (and were entitled *batlanim*—those who could afford not to work), e.g., the *shamash*, the messenger of the local *bet din*. Others were salaried: e.g., the *dayyan* delivered public sermons, administered social services, represented the community be-

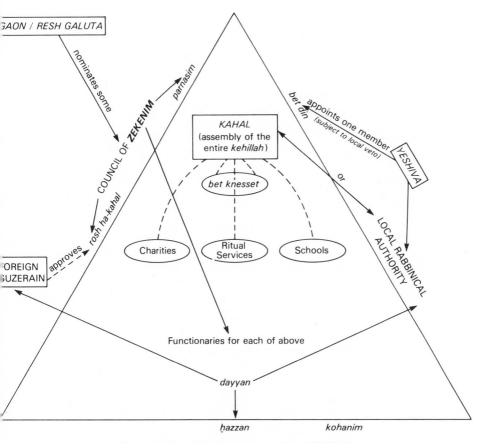

FIGURE X-3. The Structure of the *Kehillah*
in the Tenth Epoch

fore local and central officials of foreign suzerain; the *shokhet* slaughtered animals and inspected ritual fitness of meat; the *mashavit* was a tax assayer; and the *ḥazzan* led prayer services in the synagogue.

Elsewhere, the general pattern of local government was similar. However, instruments of the *edah* were referents only and did not play an authoritative role in the determination of communal leadership; titles varied from *kehillah* to *kehillah* and were influenced by local terminology (e.g., *muquammdim* in North Africa); Spain and Kairouan possessed *yeshivot* of their own, which stood between or served the local communities and the *yeshivot* of the *edah* in Bavel and Eretz Israel; and the emergence of a local *rav* or *ḥakham* is characteristic of *kehillot* within *aratzot* where *yeshivot* came to play a governing role (e.g., Ashkenaz).

7. REPRESENTATIVE PERSONALITIES

7.1 Constitutional Architects

Yehudai ben Naḥman:
(Yehudai Gaon; second half eighth century CE); the first *Gaon* to compile responsa and first to establish contact with Jewish communities of North Africa; author of *Halakhot Pesukot*

Simeon Kayyara:
Author of *Halakhot Gedolot*

Amram ben Shashnai Gaon:
(d. c. 875); first to compose a systematic arrangement of prayers and permanent laws for the entire annual cycle (*Seder Yesod ha-Amrami*, otherwise known as *Maḥzor de-Rav Amram*)

7.2 Statesmen

Anan ben David:
(eighth century); one of the most important schismatics in Jewish constitutional history; leader of sect whose members later became known as Karaites

Sa'adia (ben Joseph) Gaon:
(882–942); *Gaon* of Sura; 921–922 established calendar now in use and refuted claims of halakhic authorities in Eretz Israel to be final authority for entire *edah* in this matter; bitter opponent of Karaites

Sherira ben Ḥanina Gaon:
(c. 906–1006); *Gaon* of Pumbedita; historian and prolific writer of responsa; played key role in making *Talmud Bavli* supreme constitutional referent for entire *edah*

Ḥisdai (Ḥasdai) Ibn Shaprut:
(c. 915–c. 970); accomplished physician and diplomat; recognized as *rosh ha-Yehudim* in Cordoba, thus establishing right of *medinot* to develop independently of both Bavel and Eretz Israel; conducted correspondence with Joseph, King of Khazars, in conjunction with whom attempted to mitigate efforts at forcible baptism of Jews by the Byzantine Emperor Romanus Lecopenus (932–944)

7.3 Constitutional Commentators

Sa'adia Gaon:
Included in this category by virtue of both his *Kitab al-Amanat wa-al-l'tiquadat* and his halakhic works

Sherira Gaon:
His *iggeret* on the evolution of the Talmud a key source for constitutional history

8. TERMS

8.1 New

Shadarim and *Sheluḥei de-rabbanan*, emissaries from Eretz Israel to diaspora

Teshuva (response), formal opinion issued by *yeshiva* through *Gaon* in response to formal inquiry

FOREIGN DERIVATIVES

Muquaddim (Arabic), leader

8.2 Old—Change in Meaning

Aluf, distinguished member of a *yeshiva,* who "commanded" a large territorial demesne

Iggeret, official communication from *Gaon*; mechanism for *edah*-wide constitutional revision and government

9. BIBLIOGRAPHY

S. Abramson, *Be-Merkazim u-va-Tefutzot bitkufat ha-Geonim* (Jerusalem, 1965).

Z. Ankori, *Karaites in Byzantium: The Formative Years 970–1100* (New York, 1959).

E. Ashtor, *The Jews of Muslim Spain*, 2 vols. (Philadelphia, 1973).

S. W. Baron, "Sa-adya's Communal Activities," *Proceedings of the American Academy for Jewish Research* 11 (1943), pp. 36–47.

———. "Communal Controls," in *A Social and Religious History of the Jewish People*, vol. 5 (New York, 1957), pp. 3–81.

———. "Karaite Schism," *A Social and Religious History of the Jewish People*, pp. 209–287.

M. A. Cohen, "Anan ben David and Karaite Origins," *Jewish Quarterly Review* 68 (1978), pp. 129–145, and 69 (1979), pp. 224–234.

D. M. Dunlop, *The History of the Jewish Khazars* (New York, 1967).

L. Ginzberg, *Geonim*, 2 vols. (new edition, Philadelphia, 1968).

S. D. Goitein, *A Mediterranian Society: The Jewish Communities of the Arab World as Portrayed in the Documents of the Cairo Geniza*, 3 vols. (Berkeley, 1967).

S. N. Hoenig, "Halakhot Gedolot: An Early Halakhic Code," *Jewish Law Annual* 2 (1979), pp. 45–55.

J. Katz, "Rabbinical Authority and Authorization in the Middle Ages," in *Studies in Jewish History and Literature* (ed. I. Twersky; Harvard, 1979), pp. 41–56.

N. A. Stillman, *The Jews of Arab Lands: A History and Source Book* (Philadelphia, 1979), pp. 3–63; 113–254.

A. J. Zuckerman, *A Jewish Princedom in Feudal France, 768–900* (New York, 1972).

EPOCH XI

4798–5108 AM (1038–1348 CE)

Ha-Kehillot

The Kehillot

1. DOMINANT EVENTS

1.1 Founding Events

Dissolution of *edah*-wide organizational framework   mid 11th century
   Expansion of Jewish settlements in non-Islamic areas of Spain and in
      Rhineland on an autonomous basis
   Destruction of Jewish community in Eretz Israel by Crusaders   1099
Appearance of *Sefer Halakhot*, the first great code, by R. Isaac Alfasi, the *Rif*
   (1013–1103)

1.2 Climactic Events

Compilation of *Mishneh Torah* (1180) and ensuing first Maimonidean controversy. The *Rambam* played a key role in the build-up toward the epoch's
   climactic events. Following the *Rif*, he composed the *Mishneh Torah*,
   a grand code—the most comprehensive ever—and sought to have it accepted as authoritative. In the ensuing controversy, his position was rejected.
   The Jewish people, reaching heights of constitutional-making talents and
   powers not seen since the days of the redaction of the Talmud, rejected the
   imposition of a code which would have straight-jacketed that creativity. Instead, the case-law approach was adopted, with the *she'elah u-teshuvah*
   (responsum, or, in Hebrew abbreviation, *shut*) as its basic vehicle.
Flowering of *kehillah*-oriented constitutionalism. Exemplified and strongly
   influenced by the work of Meir b. Baruch of Rothenburg (*Maharam*),
   Solomon b. Abraham Adret of Barcelona (*Rashba*), and Asher b. Jehiel of
   Germany and Spain (*Rosh*); also strongly influenced by relative prosperity
   of Rhineland communities and silver age of Spanish Jewry.
Reestablishment of Jewish settlement in Jerusalem   1268

1.3 Culminating Events

Devastation of European communities by expulsions and as result of Black
   Death   1348–1349

2. CONSTITUTIONAL HISTORY

Jewish political history during Epoch XI is a chronicle of substantial structural
change, influenced, for the most part, by two simultaneous—but independent—clusters of phenomena. The first is the progression of events over
which the Jews as a polity exercised no control: the continued movement toward political separatism in the Islamic lands and the Holy Roman Empire,
the dislocations caused in the Iberian peninsula by the Reconquista, and the
chronic instability which affected much of west and central Europe during the
series of motley military ventures known to history as the Crusades. The second was expressed in the pattern of demographic movement within the Jewish
world. The epoch witnessed the numerical growth of Jewish settlement in
non-Islamic regions (Christian Spain and west-central Europe) and the steady
rise of the Ashkenazi proportion of the Jewish population. Whereas during
the first half of the epoch Ashkenazi Jewry comprised a little less than seven
percent of all Jewry (Arthur Ruppin estimated that, in 1170, Sephardi and
Oriental Jews constituted 1.4 million out of the total Jewish population of 1.5
million), by the end of the epoch that proportion had doubled, with the
number of Ashkenazi Jews increasing to some 300,000.

Even more dramatic was the transformation which took place in the organizational structure of the Jewish polity during this epoch. Bavel, which during the previous two epochs had constituted the nexus of organized Jewish
life, was gradually divested of its *edah*-wide influence and authority. Even
within the Islamic world it lost much of its influence to Mitzrayim. In Europe
its authority (always weak) eventually disappeared altogether.

No other single center arose to take its place and thereby serve as an authoritative focus of communal government for Jews either north or south of
the Pyrenees. Only during the founding generations of the epoch did new
Sephardi and Ashkenazi communities turn for guidance in the management
of their affairs to authorities located outside their immediate vicinity—especially Bavel for the Sephardim and Rome for the Ashkenazim. Narbonne, by
the twelfth century, had established its reputation as an independent center of
both academic excellence and halakhic jurisdiction. So, too, had various of
the communities in Spain and the Rhineland. In both Sepharad and Ashkenaz, moreover, individual *kehillot* tended to develop autonomous institutional forms and procedures and to produce their own, local, leaderships.

This was a trend which received further impetus as a result of the changing
nature of the uneasy relationships between individual *kehillot* and their local
foreign suzerains. The charters which regulated Jewish life during the epoch

tended to be imposed by the Gentile ruler—rather than (as had often been the case previously) negotiated with him. In much of northern Europe, especially, the Jews came increasingly to be regarded as unwelcome necessities rather than invited settlers. The one significant exception was Poland, which became an increasingly popular place of Jewish refuge and where, in 1264, Boleslav the Pious issued a model charter of protection and liberties. Elsewhere, however, Jews were often defined as *servi camerae regis* (servants of the royal household), a status which at once both reflected and exacerbated the extent to which their welfare depended upon the whim of their local ruler and/or his ability to withstand the popular spasms of anti-Jewish activities of his subjects.

Under these circumstances, the main task of the *kehillah*, in its external relations, centered upon the need to work out some sort of accommodation within the framework of the charter. Constant care was taken either to modify the terms of the document or—where necessary—to prevent its abrogation. The initiative, of necessity, had to be local; increasingly, moreover, it tended to devolve upon the *kehillah*'s own *shtadlan* (in Ashkenaz; in Sepharad, the parallel term was *mishtadel*), a person who had developed means of interceding on behalf of Jewish interests at the local court and—by virtue of his success—thereby tended to gain further influence within the local Jewish community. It was thus that the *keter malkhut* came to experience a resurgence of its local authority, at precisely the moment when it had lost its *edah*-wide form and expression.

The combined effect of these various pressures was to bring about the dissolution of the organizational frameworks and franchises which had previously embraced the entire *edah*. It was now reduced to an amorphous network of *kehillot* which were more widely scattered than even before and—as individual units—more autonomous than ever before. Jewish political life became regionally (*eretz*)-oriented and locally (*kehillah*)-defined. Jewish communities were bound together as a collectivity by a common faith and shared adherence to the *halakhah*. But they lacked a visible overarching structure which expressed the manner in which they did so. The *edah*, by this epoch, was reduced to a communications network, resting primarily upon the application of Jewish law as expressed through extensive and pervasive correspondence between *posekim* (authoritative sages) and a modicum of interregional travel and migration.

Even the concept of the *medinah* was similarly affected. Some regional centers of Jewish communal life did, certainly, retain their fully articulated forms. This was most noticeably so in Islamic lands. In Bavel, for instance, the traditional distinction between the *Resh Galuta* (as the principal instrument of the *keter malkhut*) and the *rashei yeshivot* (as principal instruments of the *keter torah*) was retained—formally, at least—throughout the first half of the epoch. Elsewhere in the Arab world, the *rashei yeshivot* shared power with the *Nagid*, who was locally recognized as the principal instrument of the *keter malkhut*.

In both Spain (by now known as Sepharad) and Germany (by now known as Ashkenaz), which in this epoch became the two most fecund centers of Jewish intellectual life, a sense of regional consciousness had emerged but had not yet acquired organizational expression. South of the Pyrenees, the concept of a *Nagid* for the entire Iberian peninsula did continue to carry some residual weight; in Ashkenaz, even such a theoretical framework was lacking. In both areas, the only region-wide authorities were outstanding individual *posekim*, who individually adjudicated matters of *halakhah* in response to public and private inquiries. Their emergence had been foreshadowed in Ashkenaz toward the end of Epoch X in the person of Rabbenu Gershon. During Epoch XI it was advanced by *Rashi*, Rabbenu Tam, and the *Maharam* of Rothenburg (in Ashkenaz) and by the *Rif* and the *Rashba* (in Sepharad). Nevertheless, their attainments did not lead to the establishment of organizational provisions for the effective region-wide governance. In Christian-controlled Spain, no intercommunal *va'ad* (synod) convened until 1354 (at Aragon), and even then the effort was in many respects abortive. In Ashkenaz, although the experiment was tried somewhat earlier, the meetings were sporadic and similarly indecisive.

In the absence of any *edah*- or *medinah*-wide institutions of communal governance, it was the individual *kehillah* which now became the principal repository of Jewish communal authority. Indeed, each *kehillah* during this epoch acted in place of the organized *edah*, its members constituting themselves into a *bet din* with complete jurisdiction over the local Jewish population. The propriety of these developments was repeatedly confirmed throughout the epoch by an impressive variety of Ashkenazi and Sephardi *posekim*, whose numerous responsa emphasized both the absolute autonomy of the local *kehillah* and the right of its members to develop their own forms of leadership selection and appointment.

In the arena of local organization, the development was further illustrated by the appearance, early in the epoch, of the *Sefer ha-Shtarot* by Judah Barceloni (late eleventh to early twelfth centuries). That work included among its contracts a collection relating to communal organization that essentially constituted a manual of communal government. Drawing upon the accumulated experience of *kehillah* governance in eleventh-century Spain, it outlined the organizational needs of Jewish communal life and specified the institutional procedures through which to meet them.

The important constitutional debates of the epoch reflected the Jewish polity's intensive interest in questions of organizational structure and procedural form. These were issues which clearly overshadowed dialogues on the balance among the three *ketarim*—hitherto a more fertile source of political discourse. To say that is not to disregard the changes, some of them seminal, which did take place at this time within the *ketarim* and which were ultimately to affect the *edah* in its entirety. Shifts within the *keter torah* were, by these standards, of particular significance. For one thing, the *yeshivot* began to change in character. They increasingly tended to function—almost exclusively—as academies of learning rather than as judicial and legislative bodies. Consequently, they must now be described as the repositories of different "schools" of halakhic interpretation rather than as the embodiments of a unified "seat" of halakhic application. Secondly, the epoch witnessed the emergence of classical kabbalism. Consisting of several strands of normative Jewish esoteric thought, the kabbalists added a third layer to the classic literature of the Jewish people. They provided a body of works whose intellectual content gradually came to inform the *keter torah* in its entirety and—in the course of time—spilled over into the *keter kehunah*.

Far more characteristic of the epoch was the heat engendered during its climactic generation by what are known as the Maimonidean controversies. At issue, in constitutional terms, were the respective merits of the codificatory and case-law approaches to Jewish practice. The main lines of the debate had been drawn during the very first generations of the epoch, with the appearance of the *Sefer ha-Halakhot* by R. Isaac Alfasi (the *Rif*). Controversy intensified, however, with the appearance in 1180 of Maimonides's own *Mishneh Torah* (much of which acknowledges the *Rif*'s precedence). Maimonides himself conceived of his work as a summary of the entire body of *halakhah*, a grand and comprehensive code which could replace the Talmud as a constitutional referent and be accepted as authoritative by the Jewish people in its entirety. It was precisely on those grounds that Maimonides and the *Mishneh Torah* were vilified. Critics questioned not only the validity of some of Maimonides's specific rulings (in itself a difficult exercise; his infuriating refusal to specify his sources necessitated much scholarly rummaging back and forth among the appropriate Talmudic texts) but more generally the constitutional propriety implicit in the imposition of a code which might straight-jacket the Jewish tradition of constitutional creativity. Significantly, therefore, the *Mishneh Torah* did not attain the constitutional status for which its author had originally hoped. Instead, the Jewish people continued to maintain and advance the case-law tradition. The *she'elot u'tshuvot* (responsa), not a code, became the vehicle of constitutional discourse; *takkanot* were the responsibility of various *posekim*, not the exclusive preserve of any single codifier.

The epoch is studded with the names of case-law constitutionalists, each of whom exemplified this approach: the *Maharam* (R. Meir) of Rothenberg, the *Rashba* (R. Shlomo ben Aderet), and the *Rosh* (R. Jacob ben Asher) are merely the most eminent and representative. No less significantly, the epoch is also characterized by the appearance of an entire range of new constitutional terms the most important of which represent modifications of earlier expressions. The concept of *herem*, for instance, was now expanded to include the new device of *herem ha-yishuv*; just as some *takkanot* were now classified as *takkanot ha-kahal*. The development was not entirely innovative. Its origins can be traced as far back as Mishnaic times. The terms and devices here referred to, it must be stressed, fall into the category of adaptations rather than inventions. But their general thrust is clear: in the constitutional realm, centripetal aspirations now frustrated centrifugal traditions, just as in the institutional domain, local autonomy superseded *edah*-wide uniformity.

The principal officers and instruments of each *keter* are summarized in the following text and need not be detailed here. What does need to be emphasized, however, is the reemergence of the *keter kehunah* as a factor in Jewish communal life in this epoch. This, as will have been noted, is not an entirely new development. Ever since the disappearance of the formalized priesthood in the last generation of Epoch VII, the Jewish political tradition had been groping toward a formula which might fill the vacuum thus created. The *hazzan* (an office which itself had its roots in its association with the temple service, see *Mishnah: Yoma* 7:1) had begun to play a role in communal life as early as Epoch VIII, when its incumbent began to act as *shaliah ha-zibbur* (the community's emissary) in prayer instead of manager of the ritual dimension of the synagogue, the original function of the office. A slow process of gestation had been under way ever since. It was in Epoch XI, however, that the *keter kehunah* as a whole attained additional influence. Individual *kehillot* were now also served by a *moreh horayah* (instructor) and *magid* (preacher), both of which offices dealt with matters of ritual first and foremost. The *hazzan*, too, attained greater authority, as was symbolized by his active participation in the ceremony of *herem*, which did not come into force until it had been formally pronounced by the *hazzan*.

Each of these officers derived his sanction and authority from the *keter torah*, within whose parameters of constitutional interpretation he was bound to act. Each, too, owed his appointment to the joint recommendation of the principal local instruments of both the *keter torah* and the *keter malkhut*. Nevertheless, their combined influence was of a degree which justifies their consideration as representatives of an essentially separate domain of government. Under the arrangement as it now emerged, the functions of the *keter malkhut* (as represented by nonrabbinic officials of the community) were to ensure good communal government and good relations with the foreign suzerain; those of the *keter torah* (as represented by the local *rav* or *hakham*) were to pass judgment on the halakhic legitimacy of communal *takkanot* and to judge cases and controversies. Those of the *keter kehunah* were to assist individual members of the *kehillah* to reach out for more personal contact with the Divine.

3. CONSTITUTION

Torat Moshe, mediated through Talmud and Codes (with commentaries) as *halakhah* and often communicated through ad hoc *she'elot u-teshuvot* (responsa) and local *takkanot* (ordinances)

3.1 Constitutional Issues
The authority of local communities to act in place of the *edah* and represent
   the local community in its dealings with non-Jewish suzerains
Controversy between codifiers and case-law constitutionalists
Unanimity as against majority rule in communal decision-making
Relations with local foreign suzerains (e.g., charters, informers)

3.2 Camps and Parties
Supporters of *Rambam* vs. his opponents
"Insiders" vs. "Outsiders." Conflicts and tensions between ruling elites (tending to be wealthy) of *kehillot* and their challengers (who tended to be less affluent). This was virtually an *edah*-wide phenomenon, which was manifested during the course of intra-*kehillah* struggles. In Sepharad and Provence, the alignment consisted of courtiers and their circle vs. middle-class merchants and poorer scholars (e.g., Barcelona and Saragossa). In Ashkenaz, its most interesting manifestation was the tension between the local elites and the *Ḥassidei Ashkenaz*. The latter constituted a small pietist sect which flourished in the Rhineland during the twelfth and thirteenth centuries. It was politically important because of its attacks on the standard (nonpietist) communal leadership (referred to by them as *ra'im*—wicked ones; *pesulim*—unfit) and the distinctions drawn between its own members (*tovim*—good ones; *ḥassidim*; *hagunim*—proper; *ẓaddikim*—righteous ones) and the masses (*peshutim*—simple people) and because of its effort to capture control of the communities or—failing that—to create its own. At some points, the sect came close to suggesting the coexistence of two Jewish constitutions: "The Law of the Torah" (to which the *peshutim* adhered) and the "Law of Heaven" (to which the *ḥassid* aspired).

4. CONSTITUTIONAL STRUCTURE OF THE *EDAH*

The *edah* consisted of autonomous regional and local communities, unevenly distributed over wide geographic areas, living under the jurisdiction of different foreign suzerains, and bound together as a collectivity by a common faith and shared adherence to the *halakhah*.

The beginning of the epoch marked the end of the authoritative position and significant powers of the *edah*-wide institutions and officers that had been centered in Bavel and Eretz Israel during the previous three epochs. Remnants of the network which had embodied those authorities and powers persisted only in Islamic lands during the first generations of the epoch. They were finally destroyed as the epoch approached its climax, at which time the new institutions which had been in the process of development since the dawn of the epoch became the only devices buttressing the *edah* in its entirety.

Increasingly, Jewish life became regionally (*eretz*) oriented, and almost entirely locally (*kehillah*) defined. This process was exacerbated by the tendency of non-Jewish suzerains to grant separate charters to individual Jewish communities (e.g., *aljamas*—assemblies—in Spain), which defined their obligations and rights.

Strong *edah*-wide institutions were restricted to the *keter torah*; in the domain of both the *keter malkhut* and the *keter kehunah* they were either seriously weakened or yet to be fully articulated.

Thus lacking several essential organizational components, the *edah* was re-

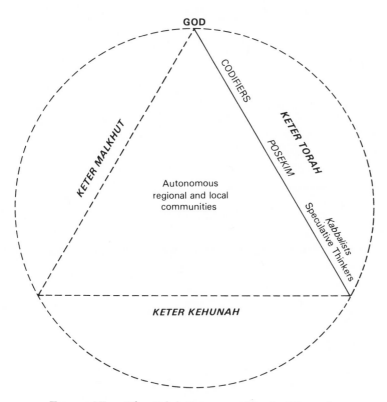

FIGURE XI-1. The *Edah* Fragmented in the Eleventh
Epoch

duced to a communications network, resting upon an extensive and pervasive halakhic correspondence between *posekim* (authoritative sages) and a modicum of interregional travel and migration. These cemented halakhic ties through personal contact and thus helped separate Jewish collectivities to retain a basic constitutional unity in fundamental matters of form and procedure and interpretation.

4.1 Principal Instruments, Officers, and Functions

Codifiers: Authors of *sifrei halakhot* who sought to ease access to halakhic matters for all members of the *edah* through systematic codifications of Jewish law

Posekim: Replied to halakhic queries through their responsa, which in outstanding cases had *edah*-wide influence

Speculative Thinkers: Architects of a systematic intellectual approach to matters of Jewish belief and doctrine

Kabbalists: Several schools of normative Jewish esoteric thought. These flowered during the course of this epoch and created a classic literature, including the *Zohar*, which became one of the three fundamental texts of Judaism (along with the Bible and Talmud). Their specific role with regard to the *edah* was to bring the transcendent God as ruler of the universe into the covenant of the community. Hence Kabbalists referred to themselves as *bnei meheimnuta* (children of the faith), *bnei heikhala dimalka* (children of the king's palace), and *ba'alei ha-avodah* (masters of the service).

5. MEDINOT

The *medinot* were regional centers of Jewish life.

Distinctions can be drawn between three categories: fully articulated *medinot* (with recognizable and recognized institutional framework, as in previous epochs), proto-*medinot* (where such frameworks were partial and unstructured but nevertheless broadly acknowledged), and *aratzot* (where there was a regional consciousness but no formal frameworks for region-wide governance). Of these, the proto-*medinot* are particularly worthy of note. Indeed, characteristic of the epoch is the emergence of proto-*medinot* in two specific cultural regions of Europe—Sepharad and Ashkenaz, each of which developed its own mode of halakhic (and liturgical) expression.

Within these regions, authority and power resided expressly in individual *kehillot*. However, representatives of the latter did occasionally convene on a regional basis (e.g., through *va'adim*, usually referred to as synods in English) and regularly communicated on a regional and transregional basis (via responsa, travelers, and the emigration of such eminent personalities as the *Rosh*) for *medinah-* and *edah*-wide purposes.

The diagram illustrates two facts:

1. Lines of "control" between the various arenas were absent. This phenomenon emphasizes the extent of the autonomy of the individual units.
2. Such lines of communication as did exist were predominantly between

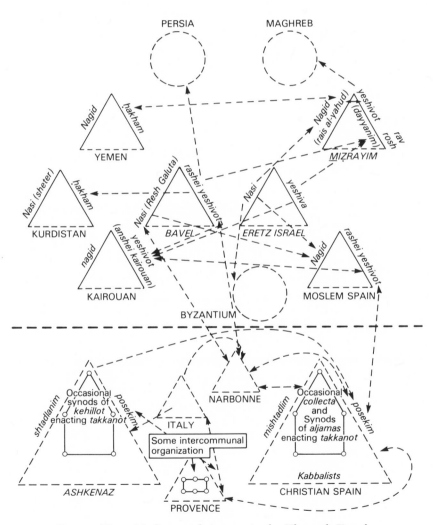

FIGURE XI-2. *Medinot* and *Aratzot* in the Eleventh Epoch

representatives of the *keter torah*. It was this *keter* which now carried the principal burden of maintaining the unity of the *edah*.

5.1 Instruments and Officers
KETER MALKHUT

Nagid: Principal instrument of the *keter malkhut* in *medinot* under Islamic rule (other than Bavel). The office and title seem first to have appeared in Tunisia toward the end of the previous epoch; but it was during the course of the present epoch that it became widespread, being found in Spain, Egypt, Yemen, and other centers of Jewish life in north Africa. The office reached its apogee in Fatimid Egypt, where it was also the most persistent and most fiercely contested (e.g., Zuta).

Appointed by the foreign suzerain on the recommendation of the community, the office of the *Nagid* could often be hereditary. In Egypt, for instance, it remained in the hands of the *Rambam's* descendants for four generations.

Essentially, the *Nagid* performed three functions. (1) He represented the foreign suzerain in its relations with the community and was therefore ultimately responsible for Jewish loyalty to the government, for the enforcement of the Covenant of Omar, and for the maintenance of law and order. (2) He represented the community in its relations with the foreign suzerain, often interceding on behalf of Jewish individual and communal interests. (3) He acted as the administrator of the community's internal affairs: he appointed *dayyanim* and *berurim* (arbitrators), maintaining the standards of Jewish moral and religious behavior and allocating funds for the upkeep of social and religious institutions.

KETER TORAH

Yeshivot: Centers of *keter torah*, whose membership was based on scholarly merit. Responsible for legal and constitutional decision-making for the *medinah* in response to local requirements.

With the decline and disappearance of the great *yeshivot* of Sura and Pumbedita (which were transferred to Baghdad at the beginning of the epoch, where they declined) and the enforced perambulations of that of Eretz Israel to Tyre and Damascus, *yeshivot* were now divested of their *edah*-wide functions. Instead, the *yeshivot*, at best, played a role in the *medinah* arena, with those of Fostat, Cordoba, Bari, and the Rhineland being among the most outstanding in this respect. At the same time, these *yeshivot* underwent a process of transformation. They no longer exhibited the exclusivism and aristocratic claims characteristic of the older *ye-*

shivot, which had been based on an aristocratic hierarchy of intellectual families whose profession was the study of the Torah and whose leadership derived from the sanctity of their study.

It is characteristic of the centripetal nature of the epoch that different "clusters" of *yeshivot* developed different "schools" of talmudic exegesis and halakhic method. The great codifiers of the period, for instance, tended to be products of *yeshivot* in Islamic lands (*Rif, Rambam, Rosh*). The Rhineland *yeshivot*, conversely, produced the *tosafists*, whose mastery of the classical texts found expression in a form of casuistry known as *pilpul*.

Despite these variations which broadly mirrored the emergent differences between the Sephardi and Ashkenazi worlds, respectively, each school nevertheless accepted the teachings and conclusions of the other, thus preserving the halakhic unity of the *edah*.

FULLY ARTICULATED *MEDINOT*

All *medinot* in west-central Asia were severely affected by the Mongol invasion during the middle generation of the epoch. These often devastated Jewish communities, which did not recover until the Sephardi migration of Epoch XII.

BAVEL

The *Resh Galuta* formally continued to function as regional leader of Jewish life in the Islamic middle east, but his position was essentially narrowed down to that of a symbol of Jewish unity in the Islamic world. The office came to an end during the middle generations of the epoch. For some time previously, however, effective influence and authority had passed to the *rashei ha-yeshivot* in Bavel who, after the death of David b. Ḥisdai IV (1174), inherited almost all of the powers of the *Resh Galuta*.

ERETZ ISRAEL

In this massively weakened *medinah*, such authority and power as there was to be had was divided between the *rashei yeshivot* (also known as *rashei beit va'ad*) and the *Nasi*. Nevertheless, Eretz Israel remained the fulcrum of the Jewish world until the combination of Crusader and Mongol devastation destroyed much of the *medinah* during the middle generations of the epoch. The arrival of several *aliyot* culminating with that of Moses b. Naḥman (Nachmanides, known in Jewish tradition as *Ramban*) in Eretz Israel in 1267 did, however, generate the beginnings of a restoration of organized Jewish life in the main centers.

MIẒRAYIM

While functions and authority of *keter malkhut* were generally unified in person of *Nagid*, the sphere of *keter torah* was divided between separate *yeshivot*, which maintained independent ties with either Bavel or Eretz Israel.

MOSLEM SPAIN (UNTIL TWELFTH CENTURY)

In this *medinah*, prominent Jewish courtiers and advisers to the foreign suzerain exercised a predominant influence on the *keter malkhut* while local *yeshivot* exercised the powers of the *keter torah*.

PROTO-*MEDINOT*

SEPHARAD

The epoch witnessed a shift away from even theoretical countrywide organization, as Spain itself was fragmented into individual polities and ravaged during the period of the Reconquista. By the end of the epoch, Christianity had come to embrace almost the entire Iberian peninsula.

Nevertheless, Sepharad did grope toward some form of unity. In Navarre and Castile the *aljamas* (Arabic word meaning assembly, the formal title of the *kehillah*) of the entire realm were occasionally placed under the authority of a *rab de la corte*, appointed at royal command, who supervised Jewish communal leadership and the apportionment of taxes among the communities (whence he was also known as *repartidor de todas las aljamas*). Moreover, individual *aljamas* also formed themselves into *collecta* (tax districts) which occasionally also acted as courts of appeal. Finally, and above all, individual *aljamas* showed themselves willing to accept the authority of outstanding *posekim* (e.g., *Rashba*), whose decisions were generally considered binding on the entire region.

ASHKENAZ

All attempts to create *medinah*-wide institutional ties within this region were necessarily frustrated by the chronic political fragmentation which characterized the external (non-Jewish) environment of the times. Hence, there existed neither a recognized regional *Nagid* or *Nasi* nor any organization. Consequently the autonomous powers of the individual *kehillah* here reached its apogee, and even such regional synods as did take place (notably, at Troyes in 1150; Mayence in 1196; and the *va'adei shum* [Speyers, Worms, Mainz] of 1220–1223) did not manage to overcome the particularism of the region by establishing permanent juridical and administrative councils.

Nevertheless, the very existence of such synods is indicative of the move toward regional confederation which would become stronger during the next epoch. Moreover, the trend was further encouraged and exemplified by the regional acceptance of specific *takkanot*—especially those attributed to R. Gershom b. Judah of Mainz (c. 920–1028), the regional recognition of the halakhic authority of such outstanding *posekim* as *Rashi* (referred to as *gadol ha-dor*) and the *Maharam*, and the regional influence of the Rhineland *yeshivot*.

ARATZOT

Byzantium, Persia, Italy, Provence

6. *KEHILLOT*

Autonomous local communities were the principal repositories of Jewish communal authority during this epoch.

The dominant constitutional characteristic of the epoch was the authorization of the local *kehillot* to act in place of the organized *edah* and represent Jewish interests on an individual basis via-a-vis foreign suzerains. It is in keeping with this development that various constitutional devices were either expanded or initiated (e.g., *hefker bet din*, the power of the local community to claim jurisdiction; *takkanot ha-kahal*, communal ordinances which were binding upon each and every member of the *kahal* and which might—according to some authorities—even override traditional *halakhah*; *herem bet din* [*gadol*], expressed *kehillah*-based primacy by insisting that justice be dispensed within the *sha'arei ha-ir*—the city limits [Explicitly excluded, therefore, was recourse to either a "college" of scholars, or even a *bet din* in another territorial demesne]; and *herem ha-yishuv*, ban on settlement in the community of Jews who had not been accepted into the local *kahal*—and who were occasionally referred to as *nokhrim*). Notwithstanding the differences in the external environments of separate Jewish communities (which were occasionally reflected in the differences in terminology employed), most *kehillot* of the epoch exhibited remarkable similarities in constitutional form and substance.

Throughout, government was vested in the *kahal* in its entirety, which was regarded as a partnership (*shutfut*) of every individual resident. Theoretically, all residents (*bnei ha-ir*) participated in elections to communal offices, although invariably—and perhaps inevitably—the principal offices were limited to a select group of wealthy and distinguished families.

KETER MALKHUT

Administration of the community was the responsibility of the appointed communal councils, composed of local *parnassim* (also known as *hashuvim* in Spain) and the communal rabbi (also known as *morenu* in Ashkenaz). The principal tasks of this body were to assess communal taxes (by means of *shamayim* or *borerim*); to supervise the community's various social, philanthropic, educational, and religious institutions; to appoint functionaries to administer those institutions; to enact communal ordinances (*takkanot* in Ashkenaz, *haskamot* in Sepharad); to send delegates to inter-*kehillah va'adim*; and to maintain contact with the foreign suzerain. This last duty gave rise to the phenomenon of local—and sometimes regional—"intercessionaries" (*mishtadlim* in Spain and Maghreb, *shtadlanim* in Ashkenaz).

KETER TORAH

The local *rav* or *hakham* reviewed all *takkanot ha-kahal* for their conformity with the *halakhah*. He served as the local *posek* who might appeal to greater

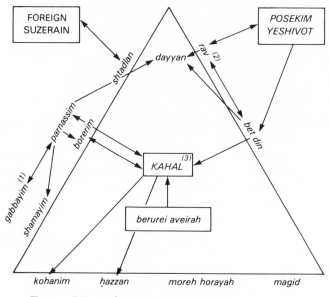

FIGURE XI-3. The *Kehillah* in the Eleventh Epoch

authority at his discretion. In larger communities there was a local *bet din* (court) to adjudicate cases and controversies.

KETER KEHUNAH

Within the sphere of the *keter kehunah*, the most significant offices were occupied by the *ḥazzan* (as in previous epochs), the *moreh horayah* (instructor), and the *magid* (preacher, in Sepharad known sometimes as *mokhiaḥ*). Note also the appointment in some instances of *bururei aveirah* (a board of officials charged with ensuring the enforcement of moral standards within the community).

Alternative Terminologies

1. *Avenanti* (directors, Catalonia), *Adelantados* (parnassim), *Viejos* (elders), *Mishtadlim* (*shtadlanim*)
2. *Morenu* (communal rabbi)
3. *Bnei Ha-ir* (citizens), *Aljama* (community assembly)
4. *Mokhiaḥ* (preacher)

7. REPRESENTATIVE PERSONALITIES

7.1 Constitutional Architects

Isaac ben Jacob Alfasi: (*Rif*, 1013–1103); author of *Sefer Halakhot*, first comprehensive codex of Jewish law

Moses ben Maimon:	(*Rambam*, 1135–1204); author of *Mishneh Torah*, designed to replace Talmud as constitution of entire *edah* but not accepted as such
Meir ben Barukh of Rothenburg:	(*Maharam*, c. 1215–1293); supreme halakhic authority in Ashkenaz; major proponent of *kehillah*-based constitutionalism
Solomon ben Abraham Adret of Barcelona:	(*Rashba*, c. 1235–c. 1310); leading *posek* of Sephardi Jewry; major proponent of *kehillah*-based constitutionalism
Solomon ben Isaac:	(*Rashi*, 1040–1105); principal instrument of *keter torah* for Ashkenazi *kehillot*; major proponent of *kehillah*-based constitutionalism; also commentator
Samuel ben Isaac Sardi:	(c. 1185–c. 1255); author of *Sefer ha-Terumot*, first code of Jewish civil law

7.2 Statesmen

Jacob ben Netanel ben (al)-Fayyumi:	(twelfth century); *Nagid* of Yemenite Jewry; his inquiry to Maimonides inspired the *Iggeret Taiman*
Jacob ben Meir Tam:	(c. 1100–1171); leading tosafist; major proponent of *kehillah*-based constitutionalism
Mevorakh ben Sa'adiah:	(c. 1079–1119); *Nagid* of Egyptian community
Moses ben Naḥman:	(*Ramban*, 1194–1270); probably *rav rashi* of Catalonia; leading Jewish spokesman in 1263 Disputation of Barcelona (also commentator)
Todros ben Joseph ha-Levi Abulafia:	(c. 1220–1298); Spanish rabbi and kabbalist; considered "Spanish exilarch"
Zuta:	(twelfth century); thrice appointed (and thrice deposed) *Nagid* of Egyptian Jewry

7.3 Constitutional Commentators

Abraham ben David Ibn Daud:	(c. 1110–1180); author of *Sefer ha-Kabbalah*, a history of talmudic scholarship, written in 1160–1161; defender of Rabbanite tradition and independence of *medinah* of Sepharad
Judah he-Ḥasid:	(c. 1150–1217); leader of Ḥassidei Ashkenaz
Abraham ben	(*Rabad*, c. 1125–1198); author of *hassagot* on *Mishneh*

David of Posquières:	*Torah* and one of the work's most outspoken critics
Moses ben Naḥman:	(*Ramban*); author of influential biblical commentary conveying philosophical ideas; his kabbalistic knowledge is also woven into his *Sha'ar ha-Gemul*
Solomon ben Isaac:	(*Rashi*, 1040–1105); leading commentator on Bible and Talmud; his interpretations became basic guide for understanding prime constitutional referents
Meir Abulafia:	(c. 1170–1244); one of the leading Spanish rabbis to polemicize with *Rambam*
Judah ben Barzillai ha-Barceloni (Bargeloni):	(late eleventh–early twelfth centuries); *Ha-Nasi*, rabbi of Barcelona; author of *Sefer Ha-Shetarot*
Judah ha-Levi:	(c. 1075–1141); leading Hebrew poet and philosopher of Sephardi Jewry; composed both Zionides and *Kuzari*

8. TERMS

8.1 New—Indigenous

Bitul ha-tammid (interruption of prayers), means of seeking redress of wrong; in Sepharad sometimes referred to as *Ikuv Tefilah*

Gadol ha-Dor (great man of the generation), accepted term for a *posek* with *edah*-wide or regional influence

Gezerot ha-Kahal (decree of the community), constitutional device; expresses constitution-making powers of the *kehillah*

Haggahot (glosses, corrections), constitutional device; means of commenting, and correcting, halakhic decisions

Hassagot (strictures, animadversions, supplements), constitutional device; form of expressing disagreement with decisions of codifiers (used, e.g., by *Rabad* on *Rambam*)

Ḥerem ha-yishuv (ban on settlement), constitutional device; designed to preserve autonomy of *kehillah*

Mishtadel (one who lobbies), representative of Jews in Sepharad who lobbied on their behalf with foreign suzerain; based in *keter malkhut*

Morenu (our teacher), title accorded to principal local instruments of *keter torah*; came into use in Ashkenaz

Pinkas (minute book), official chronicle of communal decisions; no *takkanah* was valid unless entered therein and signed by principal local instuments of *keter torah* and *keter malkhut*

Shtadlan (one who lobbies), representative of Jews in Ashkenaz who lobbied on their behalf with foreign suzerain; based in *keter malkhut*

Takkanot ha-kahal, local communal ordinances; binding throughout the area of jurisdiction of the *kehillah*

Tosafot (additions), constitutional device; often employed by its exponents as means of adapting Talmud to local conditions

9. BIBLIOGRAPHY

I. A. Agus, *Rabbi Meir of Rothenburg* (2 vols., Philadelphia, 1947).

————. *The Heroic Age of Franco-German Jewry* (New York, 1969).

A. Ashtor, *Korot ha-Yehudim bisfarad ha-Muslemit* (2 vols., Jerusalem, 1969).

E. Ashtor, *The Jews of Moslem Spain* (translated by A. Klein and J. Machlowitz; 3 vols.; Philadelphia, c. 1973, c. 1979, 1984).

S. W. Baron, "Reign of Law," in *A Social and Religious History of the Jewish People*, vol. 6 (New York, 1958), chapter 27.

H. H. Ben-Sasson, *Yahadut Ashkenaz* (Jerusalem, 1963).

Y. Baer, "Ha-Yesodot veha-Hathalot shel Irgun ha-Kehillah ha-Yehudit Bimei ha-Beinayim," *Zion* 15 (1950), pp. 1–41.

————. *A History of the Jews of Christian Spain* (translated by L. Schoffman from the Hebrew; 2 vols.; Philadelphia, 1961).

M. R. Cohen, *Jewish Self-Government in Medieval Egypt. The Origins of The Office of the Head of the Jews, 1065–1126* (Princeton, 1980).

S. Dubnow, *History of the Jews in Russia and Poland*, vol. 1 (new edition; Philadelphia, 1975).

L. Finkelstein, *Jewish Self-Government in the Middle Ages* (New York, 1924).

M. P. Golding, "The Juridical Basis of Communal Association in Medieval Rabbinic Legal Thought," *Jewish Social Studies* 28 (1968), pp. 25–33.

H. Z. Hirschberg, *A History of the Jews in North Africa*, vol. 1 (Leiden, 1974).

G. Kisch, *The Jews in Medieval Germany* (second edition; New York, 1970).

L. Landman, *The Cantor: An Historical Perspective* (New York, 1972).

I. G. Marcus, *Piety and Society: The Jewish Pietists of Medieval Germany* (Leiden, 1981).

S. Morrel, "The Constitutional Limits of Communal Government in Rabbinic Law," *Jewish Social Studies* 33 (1971), pp. 87–119.

L. Rabinowitz, *The Herem Ha-Yishub* (London, 1945).

B. Rosenweig, *Ashkenazic Jewry in Transition* (Waterloo, 1975).

C. Roth, *The History of the Jews in Italy* (Philadelphia, 1946).

A. Schochat, "Berurim be-Farashat ha-Pulmus ha-Rishon al Sifrei ha-Rambam," *Zion* 36 (1971), pp. 27–60.

B. Septimus, "Piety and Power in Thirteenth Century Catalonia," in *Studies in Medieval Jewish History and Literature* (ed. I. Twersky; Harvard, 1979), pp. 197–230.

E. Shereshevsky, *Rashi: The Man and His World* (New York, 1982).

I. Twersky, *Introduction to the Code of Maimonides* (*Mishneh Torah*), (New Haven, 1980).

E. E. Urbach, *Ba'alei ha-Tosafot* (Tel-Aviv, 1955).

EPOCH XII

5108–5408 AM (1348–1648 CE)

Ha-Va'adim

Federations of Kehillot

1. DOMINANT EVENTS

1.1 Founding Events

Reconstitution of Jewish communal life after the persecutions and upheavals of the Black Death (e.g., attempt to confederate the Jewish communities of the kingdom of Aragon at Council of Barcelona, 1354)

Regularization of the constitutional status of Polish Jewry in charter to Jews issued by Casimir the Great, 1364

General acceptance of *Arba'ah Turim* (compiled by the *Rosh* before 1340)

1.2 Climactic Events

The period was dominated by a shift of demographic and administrative axis from western Europe to eastern Europe, the Middle East, and north Africa.

Expulsion from Spain (1492) and spread of Sephardic diaspora throughout the world

Settlement in Ottoman Empire and attempt to establish empire-wide authority

Establishment of *Va'ad Arba Aratzot* in Poland

First full printing of *Arba'ah Turim* (1475)

Rise of Safed as spiritual center and compilation there of *Shulḥan Arukh* (1567). For a brief time, kabbalist tradition of Safed promised to restore Eretz Israel to prominence throughout *edah*. As it was, accomplishments in Safed were to exert a major influence on Jewish life until middle of next epoch.

1.3 Culminating Events

Chmelnitsky massacres of 1648–1649

High-water mark of Ottoman Empire (mid 17th century) and Jewish prosperity within it

2. CONSTITUTIONAL HISTORY

Jewish history during Epoch XII (very much like non-Jewish history) constitutes a tale of social turbulence, intellectual ferment, and political upheaval. It was a period when western European civilization undertook the passage from the medieval to the modern world, when eastern European and Mediterranean civilizations became backwaters—and when Jewish communities in both regions often served as the barometers of change. As such, they were made to suffer many of the hardships with which such major transitions are usually associated. The epoch was, indeed, punctuated by the periodic destruction of local and regional Jewish communities by massacre and/or expulsion. Among its most prominent benchmarks were the Black Death upheavals (at the beginning of the founding generation), the mass expulsions from the Iberian peninsula (during the climactic generation), and the Chmelnitsky massacres (at the end of the culminating generation).

Even when conditions were not quite so critical, Jewish communal life depended upon the maintenance of a delicate balance. In part, this was due to the increasing hardships imposed on the Jews by the conditions of what were euphemistically termed their "Charters of Privileges." More often, it was the result of their wider social and cultural marginalty—characteristics which, in Europe, were emphasized by the peculiarities of their occupations, their places of enforced residence, their language, and their mores. In older areas of Jewish settlement these conditions were compounded by the tensions generated by the Renaissance, the Reformation, and the Counter-Reformation to produce a spate of unprecedentedly vicious anti-Semitic outrages. In new regions (such as Poland) they combined with largely exogenous social currents to produce equally violent spasms of anti-Jewish terror. Only in the Ottoman Empire (which provided sanctuary for many of the Iberian refugees) were Jewish communities permitted to develop more or less uninhibited. But, by the end of the epoch, that empire had spent itself in vain efforts to conquer Christendom and had begun its lengthy process of decline.

As a result of persecutions, expulsions, and plague, the Jewish population fell drastically at the beginning of the epoch (as did that of Europe as a whole). The subsequent recovery was slow, sure—and not altogether even. The proportion of Sephardim within the *edah* dropped from an estimated 85 percent (1.7 million) in the mid-fourteenth century, to about 60 percent (1,050,000) in 1650. During the same period, the number of Ashkenazim increased from about 300,000 to some 700,000 souls.

Equally significant was the gradual and perceptible shift of Jewry's demographic axis. Throughout most of the epoch the majority of Jews were being pushed away from the Atlantic seaboard and pulled toward Ottoman and Slavic lands. This development did ensure the newer communities of a measure of temporary physical security and economic improvement. Ultimately, however, it proved contrary to the trend of economic and political power in the larger world, which during this epoch moved inexorably westward. Not until the very end of the epoch were Jewish communities established in the Netherlands (1602) and on the Atlantic seaboard of Germany and Denmark. Even so, these were small and fragile, and could not balance the isolation of the majority of the *edah* from the major new nexi of power and wealth.

From an organizational point of view, significant Jewish leaders were willing to try to fashion *edah*-wide instruments which might have facilitated the harmonization of Jewish response to the turmoil of the age and the coordination of appropriate action, but Jewry was still incapable of doing so. The gap between the highly particularistic *kehillah*-centric orientations of previous generations and the worldwide perspectives that were to emerge in modern times was, it appears, too wide to be bridged within a single constitutional epoch. Most blatantly, the *edah* continued to lack a recognized operational center. During the latter half of the sixteenth century, the kabbalists of Safed did attempt to reinstate Eretz Israel to its classical preeminence. The experiment was unsuccessful but, ultimately, the result of their efforts was to transform the kabbalah into a popular—as well as elite—phenomenon and thereby to fashion some of the ideas and doctrines which were ultimately to affect Jewish constitutional perspectives. Most important, the *Shulḥan Arukh* of R. Joseph Caro, conceived and written in Safed, was to become the basic constitutional referent of the *edah* in the next epoch. All this is testimony to the importance of an Eretz Israel center, however short-lived. These, without doubt, were important influences, but they were not to come to full fruition until the next epoch.

Meanwhile, the *edah* continued to consist of a number of scattered and diverse *medinot* and *aratzot*, within each of which the *kehillah* continued to constitute the principal locus of organized Jewish life. This characteristic, clearly predominant in Epoch XI, was in some regions even strengthened with the construction of enclosed areas of enforced Jewish settlement (ghettos in Germany and Italy, mellahs in some Islamic lands). It was taken to extremes in some of the lands in which the victims of expulsion found refuge; in Salonika, to take only the most blatant example, the newcomers reconstructed *kehillot* within *kehillot*.

Fluctuations in Jewish demographic patterns necessarily brought about changes in the construction, character, and size of *medinot*—and in their relative weight. During the course of the epoch, some *medinot* disappeared (notably in the Iberian peninsula), others were given new form (e.g., in the Ottoman Empire), and still others emerged for the first time (e.g., in the Netherlands). Hence, the distinction between *aratzot* (localities of Jewish settlement without recognized or recognizable institutional affiliations) and fully constituted *medinot* continued to be relevant.

The epoch did witness increasing attempts on the part of several *kehillot* to enter into formal ties of regional association through the medium of the *va'ad* (synod). By any standards, these were significant constitutional developments; by the standards of their own age, they were outstanding experiments in confederal governance. The *va'adim* were not necessarily designed to encroach upon the established liberties of individual *kehillot*. On the contrary, and in strict conformity with the covenantal traditions of Jewish polities, they were federal in principle and consensual in practice. Thus, decisions of the *va'ad* had to be read and affirmed by local communities, who were also responsible for their enforcement. Moreover, the *va'ad* itself did not (initially) constitute either a standing body or a continuing institution. Rather, it was designed to act as a periodic regional assembly of permanently constituted *kehillot*, all of whom would benefit from the better management of their political affairs, both internal and external.

As a Jewish phenomenon, the *va'ad* was not entirely new. Sure signs of its emergence had been apparent in both Sepharad and Ashkenaz during the previous epoch. In both regions, however, the tendency gained distinct momentum during this epoch, becoming a dominant feature of Jewish communal life throughout the *edah*. *Va'adim* were convened in Aragon (Barcelona, 1354), Castile (Valladolid, 1432), Italy (Bologna, 1416; Gorlin, 1418; and the Synod of the Marches, 1420), and Germany (Mainz, 1381; Nuremberg, 1477; Frankfort-am-Main, 1603).

Admittedly, in none of these regions were the experiments overly successful—some *va'adim* failed to overcome the particularism of their constituent Jewish *kehillot*; others aroused the suspicions of the foreign suzerains (the participants in the Frankfort *va'ad* of 1603, for instance, were charged with high treason and their effort to confederate the communities of Ashkenaz was thereby quelled). Still others could not prevent the expulsion of the Jews from the countries or regions in which they were located (e.g., Spain).

Nevertheless, the process of regional collaboration was not therefore stultified. On the contrary, it reached its apotheosis during the second half of the epoch in those Slavic lands which were soon to become the most populous and intensive centers of Jewish life. The *Va'ad Arba ha-Aratzot* (Council of the Four Lands: Great Poland, Little Poland, Podolia, Volhynia) was established in the mid-sixteenth century; and the *Va'ad Lita* (Lithuanian Council of Brest-Litovsk, Grodno, Pinsk) in 1623. A central *va'ad* of Bohemia–Moravia (Upper Territories, Lower Territories, and Third Territories) was fully functioning by 1651. Unlike their precursors, these bodies were both continuing in form and permanent in structure. They also wielded unchallenged authority in regional affairs, possessing accredited officers in the domains of both the *keter malkhut* and the *keter torah* to give effect to their decisions and recognition by the foreign suzerain.

Despite these regional developments, some of which were to reach fruition in the next epoch, the *edah* continued to lack an operational organizing device. Significantly, the conventional histories record not a single instance of inter-*va'ad* consultation. The *edah* did continue to function as a communications network in the sphere of the *keter torah* (especially after the invention of printing). Somewhat more spasmodically and erratically, it also did so in the sphere of the *keter kehunah* (particularly when kabbalist influences became strong). But in neither of these domains—nor, of course, in that of the *keter malkhut*—had it yet found full expression.

The extent to which this was so was illustrated by the failures of the various—and very different—attempts which were made during the epoch to repair this situation. In 1538, during the climactic generations of the epoch, Jacob Berab attempted to provide the entire *edah* with a centralized meritocracy by reinstituting the procedure of *semikhah* in Safed but was stopped cold by the opposition of the Jerusalem rabbinate. Less than one generation later (in 1558), the leadership in the Ottoman Empire failed in their endeavor to organize a punitive Jewish commercial boycott of the port of Ancona, where Pope Paul IV (reversing previous policy) suddenly condemned to the stake Marrano refugees from Portugal, because of local Jewish opposition. Both efforts, the former in the domain of the *keter torah* and the latter in that of the *keter malkhut*, floundered on the rocks of conflicting Jewish interests; neither, indeed, was to be emulated until the climactic generations of the succeeding epoch.

Even more traumatic, and dramatic, were the fates of the various messianic movements which attempted to straddle all three *ketarim* and which were led by such charismatic figures as David Reubeni, Solomon Molcho, and Shabbetai Zevi. Each set out to act as spokesman for the entire *edah*. Sooner or later, all three failed because of the intervention of foreign powers.

Characteristically, the one massive exception to this general rule of Jewish constitutional disparity took the form of the universal Jewish acceptance of a basic framework of halakhic codification which laid down the ground rules for the evolution of the polity's fundamental constitutional referents. The composition of the *Arba'ah Turim* by R. Jacob Asher of Toledo (the *Rosh*) at the very end of the previous epoch (1340) was, in this respect, a constitutional landmark of enduring significance. The *Rosh* gave posterity not only the first consolidated summary of the manifold local *takkanot* of the previous epoch but also a basic constitutional text which itself provided a new literary structure and form, with its own characteristics and methods of procedure. Both came to exercise a singularly tight hold on the subsequent development of the genre in the hands of his successors, of whom Joseph Caro (author of the *Shulḥan Arukh*), Moses Isserlis (Author of the *Darkei Moshe*), and Ḥayyim Benveniste (author of *Knesset ha-Gedolah*) are the most renowned. The conclusions of the *Rosh* constituted the basis for the *Shulḥan Arukh* which, by the end of the epoch, had gained recognition as the fundamental halakhic compilation of the entire *edah*.

And yet, as the long list of commentaries and supercommentaries to each of these works themselves indicates, the great codes did not replace the *posekim* in this epoch. As yet, there was no acceptance of the Maimonidean approach which had threatened to stifle local freedom. The *edah* was far too diversified for that. Differences between Ashkenazic and Sephardic customs and usages (and for that matter, differences between various subgroups within each of these two main cultural segments of the Jewish world) were far too deep to be thus easily overcome; so, too, was the independence of individual *kehillot*. Local *minhagim* had by this epoch themselves already attained something of the status of *halakhot*; so much so that in some communities (e.g., Frankfort) they were enscribed in local compilations in order that they might be rigidly maintained. These were not trends which the *Rosh* or his successors sought either to obstruct or to modify. Their contribution, rather, lay in that they provided an intellectual framework within which all later constitutional adaptations could be accommodated and in accordance with which they might also be classified.

3. CONSTITUTION

The constitution consisted of *Torat Moshe*, mediated through Talmud and commentaries, and as structured at the end of the previous epoch in *Arba'ah Turim* by R. Jacob ben Asher of Toledo. The *kehillah*-based *takkanot* which characterized the constitution of the previous epoch were now coordinated and consolidated in a series of monumental codes which collated the entire body of contemporary *halakhah*. The early efforts in this direction by Jacob ben Asher (*Ba'al ha-Turim*) were reinforced during the course of later supplements (often initially in the form of commentaries and supercommentaries), all of which employed the basic structure mapped out in the *Arba'ah Turim*: e.g., *Haskamot* of Valladolid (1432) which provided the foundation for the constitutional governance of Sephardic communities everywhere; *Bet Yosef* by Joseph Caro (1488–1575), later simplified and condensed in his *Shulḥan Arukh*; *Mappah* and *Darkei Moshe* by Moses ben Israel Isserles (*Rema*, c. 1525–1572) which added Ashkenazi usage to Caro's code and thus made it universally acceptable; and *Knesset ha-Gedolah* by Ḥayyim Benveniste (1603–1673), accepted as authoritative by both Ashkenazim and Sephardim.

3.1 Constitutional Issues
The authority of the *va'adim*, necessitated by reorganization of Jewish communities

The authority of the codes

The constitutional status of local *minhagim* (customs) and the attempt to compile local collections of *minhagim* (e.g., in Frankfort)

Rabbinical ordination. The attempt to revive the ancient practice of *semikhah* by Jacob Berab in Safed in 1538 failed. The epoch did, however, witness a growing insistence that candidates for communal rabbinical office furnish written proof of their competence from a recognized rabbinical authority. In Ashkenaz this trend especially pronounced (e.g., opinion of R. Meir ben Barukh ha-Levi of Vienna, fourteenth century).

The Jewish status of the Marranos

The authority of self-proclaimed messianic harbingers—e.g., David Reubeni (d. 1538), Solomon Molcho (c. 1500–1532), and Shabbetai Zevi (1626–1676)

3.2 Camps and Parties

Pro-messianists vs. anti-messianists

Local groupings within *kehillot*, often defined by differences in origins (e.g., *megorashim*—groups of Jews expelled from Iberia after 1492—vs. local inhabitants, in Maghreb, whom the newcomers termed *forasteros*—aliens)

4. CONSTITUTIONAL STRUCTURE OF THE *EDAH*

The *edah* continued to function as a communications network. In the absence of a formal structure embracing the entire *edah*, ties between its various component *medinot* and *aratzot* were maintained by halakhic correspondence, migration, and shared experiences and aspirations (e.g., messianic expectations at the end of the epoch).

The most significant new development of the epoch in this realm was the emergence and extension of comprehensive and authoritative codes. Their acceptance was greatly facilitated by the invention of printing during the climactic generation of the epoch, assuring their near-universal availability (the *Arba'ah Turim* was the second complete work to be printed in Hebrew, 1475; *Rashi*'s commentary on the Bible being the first).

4.1 Principal Instruments, Officers, and Functions

Halakhic Authorities:	Made their major constitutional contribution by the compilation of monumental codes, which incorporated both earlier commentaries on the Talmud and more recent *piskei din*
Kabbalists:	The wide study of the Zohar moved Kabbalistic ideas, systems, and methods to a central position along the axis of *keter kehunah*. This trend culminated in the institutionalization of the Kabbalah school of thought by Isaac ben Solomon Ashkenazi Luria (*ha-Ari*; 1534–1572) in Safed and by the Spanish Kabbalists. Increasingly, Kabbalistic influences permeated liturgy (e.g., the rite of *kabbalat Shabbat*), speculative thought, and *minhagim*.

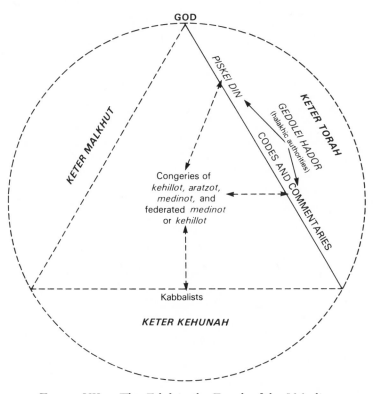

FIGURE XII-1. The *Edah* in the Epoch of the *Va'adim*

5. *MEDINOT*

The *medinot* were regional groupings of *kehillot* which followed political boundaries established by the foreign suzerain; now they were increasingly exemplified by the construction of local federations, with the instrument of the *va'ad* (area-wide council) as their formal expression.

While the major regions of Jewish settlement were now organized as articulated *medinot*, most of the others remained in the category of *aratzot*, notably Eretz Israel and Iraq/Persia. The scattered groups of Marranos in Central and South America formed communities which were linked into what might be described as crypto-*aratzot*.

5.1 Instruments and Officers

KETER TORAH

Yeshivot: Continued to constitute the principal repositories of the *keter torah* throughout the epoch, and in every *medinah*. Moreover, it was from the ranks of the *talmidei yeshivot* (also known as *bakhurei yeshiva*) that the principal instruments of this *keter* were recruited.

Posekim: Served as transmitters of the constitution to the *medinah* (and, in outstanding cases, to the *edah* in its entirety), generally in response to inquiries from rabbis whose constituency was essentially local. Thus, the principal medium of the *posekim* remained the *teshuvah* (responsum) in response to a *she'elah* (inquiry).

Chief Rabbis: Indicative of the crystallization of a *medinah*-wide consciousness in various regions (particularly northern and central Europe) was the emergence of persons aspiring to supreme and formally recognized rabbinical jurisdiction for entire geographical areas. They transposed the informal authority wielded by *posekim* (a tradition still maintained in North Africa) into formal power.

Among the titles employed to describe the position were (in Ashkenaz) *landrabbin, rav medinah, gaon, rosh ha-Golah, ha-rav ha-manhig*, and (in the Ottoman Empire) *Ḥakham Bashi*. Attainment of the office could be the result of either election by peers or appointment by the foreign suzerain (e.g., Jacob Pollack by King Alexander of Poland in 1503)— or a combination of the two processes.

Despite some severe opposition, such titles gained recognition by the climax of the epoch and heralded the reinstitutionalization of the *keter torah* on a *medinah*-wide basis. Where such "chief rabbis" existed, they participated in regional *va'adim*, whose *takkanot* had to receive their sanction (and were invariably formulated by them). Within the *keter torah*, they were empowered to preside over the *bet din* (in their capacity as *av* of that institution), to counsel, to teach (in the capacity of *rosh yeshiva*) and grant *semikhah*, and to decide matters of local halakhic in accordance with the decisions of *posekim*.

KETER MALKHUT

The epoch witnessed the extension of the territorial franchise of several principal instruments of the *keter malkhut* and their expansion to encompass entire *medinot*. This tendency to an extent paralleled the emergence of "new monarchies" in western Europe and the expansion of the Ottoman Empire.

Shtadlanim/   Tended to possess wider briefs to intercede on behalf of Jewish
Mishtadlim: interests at the local court (the mitigation of the terms of some charters, the prevention of the abrogation of others). Often

Va'adim:

contracted by *kehillot* and *va'adim* of an entire region or political unit for this purpose.

(synods or congresses). Initially neither a standing body nor a continuing institution, a *va'ad* was designed to act as a periodic assembly of representatives of permanently constituted *kehillot* on a confederated basis. Membership was by invitation, with larger *kehillot* often regulating the proportional representation of the satellite *kehillot* in their respective locales. In Slavic regions, during the second half of the epoch, *va'adim* became permanent federations with continuing forms.

Convened either at the behest of the constituent *kehillot*, at the initiative of a local *shtadlan*, or at the command of the foreign suzerain, the *va'ad* was empowered to enact *takkanot* regulating inter- and intra-communal affairs and to represent local Jewry in its dealings with the foreign suzerain.

Decisions of the *va'ad* had to accord with the *halakhah*. Hence all *va'adim* contained representatives of the *keter torah*, who usually formulated its *takkanot* and *gezerot*. However, enforcement was left to representatives of the *keter malkhut* and interpretation of specifics to local instruments of the *keter torah*, often now possessed of *semikhah* (see later section *Kehillot*). Proceedings of the *va'ad* were based upon the kind of powersharing and consensual politics noted in covenantal systems. Decisions of the *va'ad* had to be read and affirmed by local *kehillot*, who were responsible for their enforcement.

A principal expression of the authority of the *va'ad* was its power to levy taxation on individual *kehillot* for regional purposes. In the *va'adim* of east-central Europe, seventy percent of the income thus obtained was expended on "defense" (i.e., payments to the foreign suzerain and/or his representatives); fifteen percent on administration; and fifteen percent on *tzedakah* (welfare).

5.2 Individual Medinot and Aratzot

ERETZ ISRAEL

Spanish persecutions of 1391 and subsequently stimulated new waves of settlement in the country. From then until the nineteenth century, there was at least one wave every two generations. In the fifteenth and early sixteenth centuries, there were new waves in each generation as Sephardic exiles sought new places of settlement. Thus, by the climax of the epoch, there were significant Jewish communities in the four Holy cities of Jerusalem, Hebron,

Tiberias, and Safed, as well as scattered settlement in other towns and villages. Of these, Safed was the most important—and the most idiosyncratic; most of the inhabitants constituted an *agudah* of kabbalists, formed out of groups of *ḥavurot*. The dispute between R. Judah Berab and R. Levi b. Jacob ibn Habib of Jerusalem concerning *semikhah* reflected difficulties of linking the several communities within the country. Rather than establish their own overarching authority, they preferred to refer major controversies to the *Nagid* in Mitzrayim, as long as that office existed.

ARAGON (UNTIL 1492)

Va'ad of 1354 attempted to construct a confederation of all communities of Aragon, Catalonia, Valencia, and Majorca (the kingdom of Aragon) on the initiative of the provincial oligarchies. Proceedings gave rise to a constitution of two parts dealing with internal matters and external affairs, respectively, of which only the latter is extant. Among the internal matters discussed were taxation, the treatment of informers, confederal arrangements, and their maintenance.

The *va'ad* also proposed the election of a confederal body of six *nivrarim* (selectmen), two each for Catalonia and Aragon and one each for Valencia and Majorca.

CASTILE (UNTIL 1492)

Va'ad kehillot Castilla (Vallidolid, 1432). Convened by Abraham Benveniste in his capacity as *Rab de la Corte* of Castile, this *va'ad* resulted in a detailed list of *haskamot* which, taken together, amounted to a constitutional code for the region. Matters dealt with included Torah study and its support, the choice of *dayyanim*, the appointment of communal functionaries and the definition of their duties, relations with the foreign suzerain and the maintenance of Jewish autonomy, taxation, and sumptuary laws.

The goal of the *va'ad* was to federate communities of the kingdom of Castile and Leon by appointment of permanent council of *anashim tovim morshim* (including representatives of *keter torah* and *keter malkhut*—*mishtadlim*—sometimes referred to as *resh galuta* of Spain) under general directorship of *ha-sar ha-rav* (e.g., Don Abraham Benveniste himself). The proposal initially received blessing of foreign suzerain, but had not succeeded fully by time of expulsion.

ITALY

Several communal *va'adim* convened during the fourteenth, fifteenth, and sixteenth centuries; but there was opposition to attempt by R. Messer Leon to impose his spiritual authority on all Italian Jewry and form Chief Rabbinate (1416).

OTTOMAN EMPIRE

Separation between the *keter malkhut* and *keter torah* was institutionalized with appointment of *Kehaya* (supervisor of Jewish taxes) in 1519 and with expansion of scope of office of *Ḥakham Bashi* (originally established 1453).

Nevertheless, attempts at further *medinah*-wide development were hindered by differences between local and immigrant communities after 1492 (see *Kehillot*).

ALGERIA/TUNISIA

Zaken ha-Yehudim, principal instrument of *keter malkhut*; appointed by Muslim authorities (as quadi) on recommendation of local community from among its notables. He was in possession of discretionary powers (and sometimes of police force and prison, too); appointed main functionaries of the community (*gedolei ha-kahal, ziknei ha-kahal*); and was charged with the collection and administration of its funds.

His authority was tempered by that of local halakhic dignitaries (e.g., Isaac bar Sheshet of Algiers), who constituted principal instrument of *keter torah* and supervised *bet din*.

EGYPT

As in the previous epoch, the *keter torah* was represented by local halakhic authority (*rav rosh*), who also acted as *dayyan*. The principal instrument of *keter malkhut* continued to be the *Nagid* (although after Turkish conquest of 1517, the latter was often an Ottoman appointment). The office fell into disrepute in the mid-sixteenth century and was discontinued after 1560.

YEMEN

GERMANY

Va'adim were convened on an ad hoc but frequent basis, occasionally at instigation of foreign suzerain (especially between 1431 and 1471 when they followed the local pattern of diets) and at other times at instigation of Jews. Nevertheless, the pattern of autonomous *kehillot* continued to be the dominant one, not least because it was preferred by the foreign suzerains. Thus, *va'adim* were tolerated only as long as they restricted their jurisdiction to the territories of the independent principalities.

In this context, particular note should be taken of the *Va'ad Frankfort* of 1603, the last of the German *va'adim*. Convened with the intention of establishing a permanent body, the *va'ad* passed *takkanot* imposing a national tax system in order to support the efforts of *shtadlanim*, and requiring the maintenance of strict business ethics in dealing with non-Jews. It also renewed an old *takkanah* regulating the conferment of *semikhah*, reaffirmed the local rights of each *bet din* and *rav*, and passed sumptuary laws. The members of the *va'ad* were accused of treason by the Gentile authorities and barely escaped punishment. Given this opposition to Jewish efforts at attaining unity across existing political boundaries, the effort was not repeated.

Instead, the *va'adim* were replaced, within each principality, by the *Landjudenschaft* (known in Hebrew as *kehal medinah*), membership in which remained compulsory for all "protected" Jews within the autonomous territories comprising the Holy Roman Empire until emancipation. This body generally convened a *Landtag* (*yom ha-va'ad*), an assembly of all deputated heads of families within the local territory, once every three or four years. There ordinances were passed, taxes assessed, and elections held for the principal communal posts—which were then subject to government approval.

In the domain of the *keter torah*, there was an *av bet din ha-medinah* and *dayyanei ha-medinah*; in that of the *keter malkhut*, a treasurer, scribe, *parnasei ha-medinah*, and *Oberparnass* (usually the local court Jew—who also acted as *shtadlan*).

Notwithstanding this clear tendency toward particularism, informal instruments of confederal unity did emerge. In the realm of the *keter torah*, eminent *posekim* of the stature of Isserles wielded *eretz*-wide authority; in that of the *keter malkhut*, similar authority was held by Joseph (Yossele) of Rosheim (c. 1478–1554), a *shtadlan* to whom the foreign suzerain accorded the title of "*Befehlshaber der ganzen Juden*" and who styled himself *shaliaḥ kelal yisrael*. The epoch also witnessed the development of metropolitan arrangements whereby major *kehillot* served as government centers for smaller, subsidiary ones nearby.

BOHEMIA-MORAVIA

A confederation of communities in three regional *gelilot* (territories) known as the upper, central, and third. *Va'ad Bohemia-Moravia* was fully functioning some time before 1651. The *va'ad* contained representatives of both major *ketarim*, whose principal instruments thus wielded *medinah*-wide authority.

Members of the *va'ad* were elected by means of a complicated procedure which attempted to preserve both the independence of each *galil* and the unity of the whole. Individual communities which did not possess the right of election to the *va'ad* of their territory possessed the right of appeal (*tiyyun*) to the confederate *va'ad*.

POLAND

The most fully developed example of a federated *medinah*, it was organized to promote unity from the smallest to the largest arenas, each with its own government. The various communities in each locality were divided among *kehillot rashiyot* and *kehillot ketanot*, with the former retaining jurisdiction over their environs (*sevivah*). In turn, these were grouped into *gelilot* (provincial circuits), which were combined in four separate *medinot* or *aratzot*, which were federated as the *Va'ad Arba ha-Aratzot*.

Three *aratzot* of the region were constituted by 1570. By 1580 they had established a supreme court (*bet din*, composed of *dayyanei ha-aratzot*), to which was later added the *va'ad* or congress, comprised of instruments of the *keter malkhut*.

Both bodies, together constituting the *Va'ad Arba ha-Aratzot*, met regularly (often twice yearly) at one of the great trade fairs. There they elected representatives to a permanent council of thirty (six *dayyanei aratzot* elected annually and twenty-four *rashei medinot*—one of whom was also elected for a three-year term as *parnas bet yisrael*). The *va'ad* also maintained a regular

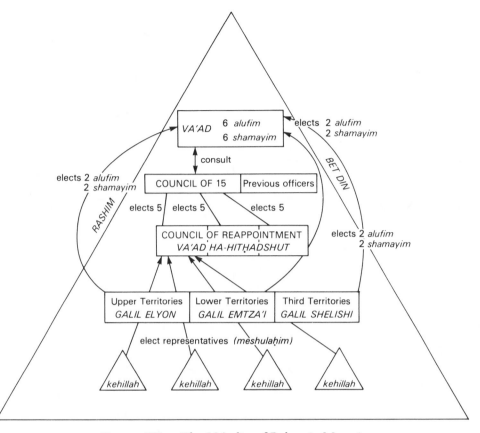

FIGURE XII-2. The *Va'adim* of Bohemia-Moravia
(early 17th Century)

and orderly communications network between *gelilot* and *medinot* in inter-
vals between its regular sessions. When in session, the *va'ad* functioned as the
supreme legislature and judiciary for the region in its entirety. Its *takkanot*
were initiated by the *keter malkhut*, drafted by the *keter torah*, and adopted by
the two domains combined. They were enforced by each constituent *va'ad
ha-galil* and acted on by the *kehillot ketanot* through the *kehillot gedolot*.

Elections to the *Va'ad Arba ha-Aratzot* were conducted on a constituency
basis. *Kehillot* of a region (*sevivah*) could send representatives to a regional
va'ad (*va'ad ha-galil* or *va'ad ha-medinah*), which would then elect delegates
to the central *va'ad*. Within *kehillot*, elections were usually determined by
the local *borerim*, although sometimes they were determined by thirty-two
outstanding wardens from the entire district.

Elections of delegates were usually controlled by local magnates and accorded with the logic of economics and status.

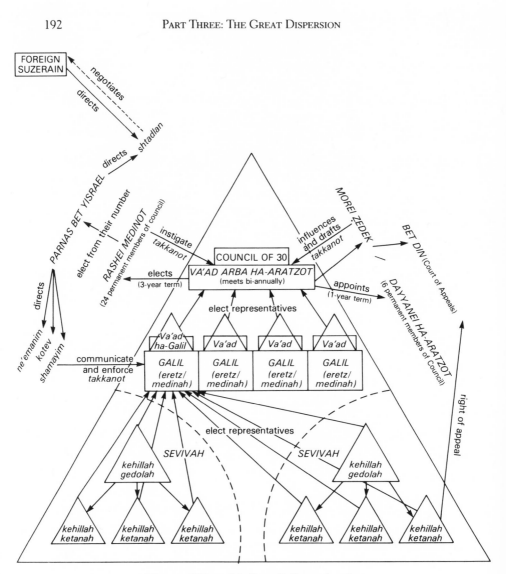

FIGURE XII-3. *Medinat Polin* under the
Va'ad Arba Aratzot

The composition of the *va'ad* reflected the division between the two dominant *ketarim*. Of its thirty permanent delegates, twenty-four were representatives of the *keter malkhut* (termed *rashei medinot*) and six outstanding
halakhic authorities (*morei zedek* or *dayyanei ha-aratzot*), in accordance with
whose teachings all decisions were taken.

The principal officers were *parnass bet yisrael*, one of the *rashei medinot* who presided at *va'ad* meetings; *ne'eman*, treasurer and chief secretary, a salaried position open to candidates drawn from representatives of the *keter torah*; *shtadlan*, a highly paid officer who represented the community in its dealings with the foreign suzerain; *kotev*, clerk to the *va'ad*; and *shammayim*, assessors.

The functions of the *va'ad* were particularly wide and included the distribution of taxes among *kehillot*; the maintenance of relations with the foreign suzerain and the enforcement of its edicts; the prevention of the infringement of copyright; the supervision of the system of education within its entire sphere of jurisdiction; the regulation of local industry; the passage of sumptuary laws (enforcing moderation in dress and social life); and the arbitration of disputes between the various components of the federation.

LITHUANIA

A confederation of *kehillot* in the region existed by 1569. The *va'ad* then consisted of nine *rashei medinot* (acting as a parliament) and three *dayyanei aratzot* (acting as a supreme court). It was headed by the *av bet din* of Brest-Litovsk.

In 1623 the principal communities of the region (Brest-Litovsk, Grodno, Pinsk, Brzesc—later also joined by Vilna) signed an agreement establishing *va'ad eretz Lita*, which thereafter usually met once every two years (until disbanded by the foreign suzerain in 1724). Its composition and functions were similar to those of the *Va'ad Arba ha-Aratzot*, except for the absence of regional *va'adim*. Moreover, the *va'ad Lita*, too, established clear channels of communication for consultation in between formal sessions of the *va'ad*.

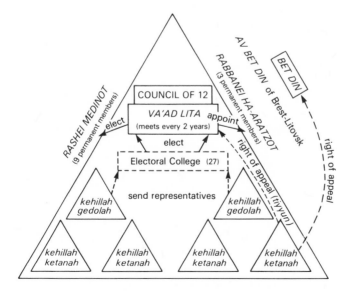

FIGURE XII-4. *Va'ad Lita* (after 1623)

Representation of the *va'ad* was restricted to the major *kehillot*. Smaller *kehillot* had only the right of appeal—a fact which led them to revolt against the *va'ad* by establishing their own tax network (the *korolka*—shopping basket). Elections were managed by an oligarchy, which also established and controlled an electoral college of eleven to sixteen (later twenty-seven) local notables.

CRYPTO-ARATZOT

Jewish settlement in Latin America began with the arrival of Marranos, who accompanied conquistadores and established themselves as traders. Concentrations of "New Christian" communities were recognizable in Mexico and Brazil by the 1530s, and in Peru by the 1580s. Some of these maintained clandestine contact with European *kehillot* and with Eretz Israel.

The Marranos were soon harassed by the Inquisition (established in Mexico in 1571) and subjected to spectacular *autos da fe* (Peru, 1639; Mexico, 1641). The short-lived Dutch conquest of northeast Brazil (1627–1654) afforded some relief, enabling the establishment of *kehillot* on the Sephardi model and the construction of a synagogue (1636).

6. *KEHILLOT*

Despite the tendency for many *kehillot* to form confederative arrangements during this epoch, the individual *kehillah* continued to constitute the principal cell of Jewish life. Moreover, the construction of enclosed areas of enforced Jewish settlement (*ghettos* in Italy and Germany, *mellahs* in some Islamic lands) tended to make communal life within *kehillot* in those regions more self-contained and particularistic. The simultaneous development of specifically local *minhagim* (customs which attain semi-constitutional force and even some degree of sanctity) added a further dimension to the autonomy of the *kehillah*, which had already gained halakhic sanction during the previous epoch.

Nevertheless, it is characteristic of Epoch XII that in many *medinot* the unity and uniformity of *kehillot* became fractured. In some cases, this circumstance is attributable to the growing diversification of Jewish economic life, which emphasized and exacerbated income differentials within *kehillot* and led to chronic social conflict. In constitutional matters, this found expression in two ways:

1. Disputes over the apportionment of taxes and the consequent need to devise arrangements commensurate with local economic circumstances. A prime early example is to be found in the *kehillah* of Barcelona, where *takkanot* passed in 1386 provided for a three-tier style of council, composed of *ashirim* (rich), *benoni'im* (middle), and *dalim* (poor).

2. The selection of community officers. The dominant characteristic was a patrician tendency to limit electoral arrangements and—through various election clauses incorporated in local *takkanot*—to make the ruling circle a closed and self-perpetuating clique of those members of the community who were rich, learned, or *persona grata* with the foreign suzerain (or, better still, all three).

The expulsion of the Jews from Spain in 1492 added yet another layer of intracommunal diversification. The *megorashim* insisted on retaining their distinctive customs and constitutional arrangements (and individual forms of worship in separate synagogues) in their new countries of residence. Consequently, separate *kehillot* (defined by place of origin) often existed within the same urban settlement throughout the Mediterranean basin, where they also retained their traditional halakhic and leadership traditions (e.g., conflict between eastern and western communal administrative styles in the responsa of R. Isaac b. Sheshet Perfet and R. Simon b. Zemah Duran, Spanish rabbis who, after 1393, took over the management of Algerian communities.

The broad outlines of *kehillah* government remained as they were during the previous epoch, with the division of functions and authorities between the three *ketarim* not changing in any substantial degree. The one significant exception was the *kehillah* of kabbalists of Sefad (who termed themselves an *agudah*), within which preponderate authority and influence resided within the *keter kehunah*. Elsewhere, local franchises became more clearly demarcated.

KETER TORAH

In the case of the *keter torah*, the trend found expression in the emergence (particularly within Ashkenazi *kehillot*) of the *marah d'atrah* (lit. "master of the place"—communal rabbi). Once elected by his community—usually during the intermediate days of *Pesah* (Passover)—the rabbi possessed full authority to decide halakhic issues locally. In many cases, demarcation between this personage and the rest of the community was emphasized by his attain-

FIGURE XII-5. The *Kehillah* of Safed (16th Century)

ment of *semikhah* (granting him the right to the title of *morenu*), which clearly set him apart from his *kahal* of *ba'alei batim* (householders). In some (extreme) cases, hereditary claims to the office of local *rav* were put forward. His position was further strengthened by the convention which entitled the local rabbinical authority to undivided authority within his own demesne, from which all other halakhic authorities of equal standing were denied rights of access. He was, of course, expected to refer inquiries beyond his ken to rabbinical authorities of greater competence.

In Sephardi *kehillot*, the formal rabbinate was less entrenched. *Semikhah* was not practiced (other than in the particular—and brief—instance of Safed, where the introduction of the rite was motivated by other concerns) and the separation of rabbinical and other authority was less sharp. Moreover, challenges to rabbinical rule by a broader base of *ba'alei batim* were more frequent.

KETER MALKHUT

Shtadlanim (in Sephardi *kehillot* termed *mishtadlim*) continued to act as local instruments of the *keter malkhut*.

Instruments of this *keter* continued to be recruited from a narrow stratum of Jewish society, especially in Ashkenaz, and elected to office on the basis of a restricted franchise. The *kehillot* of the Sephardic world underwent a revolution at the beginning of the epoch and thenceforth were governed from a broader base. Whatever the base, they continued to appoint local functionaries, who were responsible for the assessment and collection of communal taxes and the maintenance of good relations with the local foreign suzerain (or his representatives). Where *medinah*-wide *va'adim* existed, in all three capacities they were subject to the *takkanot* (*haskamot*) and *gezerot* there enacted.

KETER KEHUNAH

Other than in the kabbalist *kehillah* of Safed (noted earlier), this *keter* continued to lack extensive institutional expression. Its main instruments were the *ḥazzan* (who by this epoch had often become a salaried official and also entitled *shaliaḥ ha-ẓibbur*), the *magid* (preacher), and the *darshan* (lit. exegete, also preacher). The latter could be appointed to permanent posts by the *kehillah*; more often, however, they tended to be itinerant.

The scattered and fluid nature of Jewish settlement in this epoch ensured that varieties of local communal arrangements abounded. Distinctions between Sephardi and Ashkenazi communities were now compounded by the effects of social and organizational transformations within those two broad sections of the *edah*. Figures XII-6, 7, 8, 9, and 10 present some of the more prominent (and more fully documented) of the possible forms. (Figure XII-6 shows Barcelona before and after popular revolt at beginning of epoch, which led to greater representation of middle and lower classes).

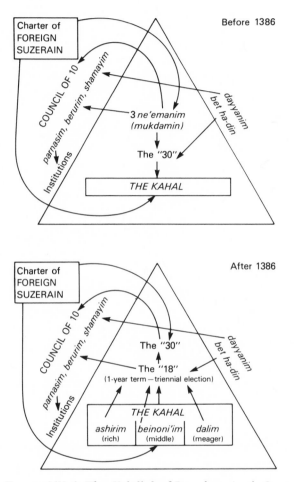

FIGURE XII-6. The *Kehillah* of Barcelona (14th Century)

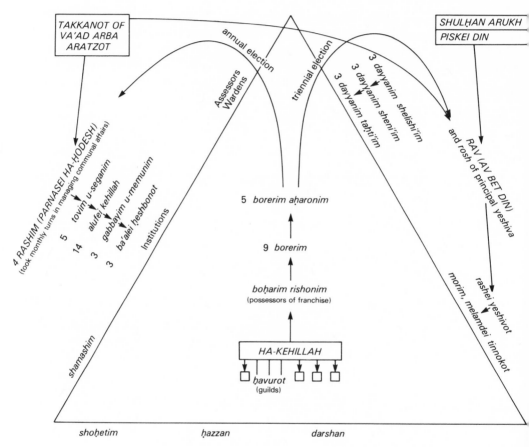

FIGURE XII-7. The *Kehillah* of Cracow (16th Century)

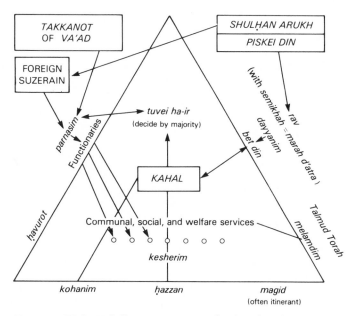

FIGURE XII-8. *Kehillot Ketanot* in Poland and Lithuania

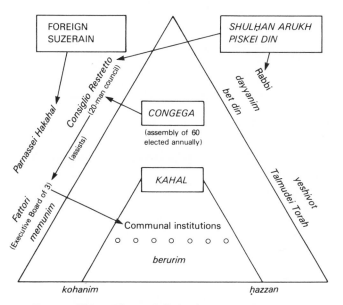

FIGURE XII-9. The *Kehillah* of Rome (16th Century)

The constitution of the Rome community as drawn up in 1524 by Daniel de Pisa

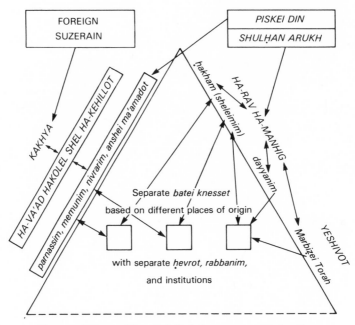

FIGURE XII-10. The *Kehillah* Structure of Salonika,
Constantinople, and Other Ottoman Centers

7. REPRESENTATIVE PERSONALITIES

7.1 Constitutional Architects

Jacob ben Asher:	(c. 1270–1340); author of *Arba'ah Turim,* which served as basis for halakhic codes throughout the epoch
Abraham Benveniste:	(1406–1454); *Rab de la Corte* of Castile; prime instigator of *va'ad* of Valladolid
Joseph Caro:	(1488–1575); author of *Shulhan Arukh*
Moses Isserles:	(*Rema,* c. 1525–1572); amplified *Shulhan Arukh* to encompass Ashkenazi rites

7.2 Statesmen

Jacob Berab:	(c. 1373–1541); attempted to reintroduce *semikhah* in Safed
David Reubeni:	(d. 1538); messianic leader; sought a political solution to Jewish situation (as distinct from Shabbetai Zevi, who sought a Divine solution through human devices)

Joseph   (c. 1478–1554); greatest of Ashkenazi *shtadlanim*; opposed
(Joselmann)   messianic movement of Reubeni
of Rosheim:

Moses   (1420–1496?); outstanding *dayyan* of Constantinople com-
Capsali: munity

Isaac   (1437–1508); greatest of Spanish *mishtadlim*; also com-
Abrabanel: mentator

Israel ben   (1390–1460); principal instrument of *keter torah* in Ash-
Pethahiah   kenazi Jewry and *posek* for entire region; author of influen-
Isserlein: tial responsa *Terumat ha-Deshen*; also commentator

Samuel ben   (*Maharashdam*, 1506–1584); principal instrument of *keter
Moses di   torah* in Salonika; his halakhic decisions also influenced
Medinah: eastern Europe

Elijah   (c. 1450–1520); principal instrument of *keter torah* in Ot-
Mizrahi: toman Empire and *posek* for entire region; active in absorp-
                          tion of exiles from Spain and Portugal

Gracia   (c. 1510–1569); Portuguese-born Marrano; influential in-
Mendes: strument of *keter malkhut* in Ottoman Empire; organized
                          escape of Marranos from Portugal and boycott of Ancona; se-
                          cured grant of Tiberias from Sublime Porte

Joseph Nasi: (c. 1524–1579); Portuguese-born Marrano, nephew (and
                          later son-in-law) of Gracia Mendes; principal instrument of
                          keter malkhut in Ottoman Empire; created Duke of Naxos,
                          obtained extension of concession in Tiberias

7.3 Constitutional Commentators

Simeon ben   (*Rashbaz*, 1361–1444); b. Majorca, emigrated to Algeria,
Zemah Duran: where he became leading *posek*

Isaac ben   (*Ribash*, 1326–1408); Spanish rabbi; frequently involved in
Sheshet   communal controversies in Spain and Algiers; his responsa
Perfet: influenced *Shulhan Arukh*

Israel ben   Sought to restore study of Talmud and other ancient sources
Pethahiah   to their former importance because of a growing tendency to
Isserlein: rely mainly on the *posekim*

Joshua Falk: (c. 1555–1614); outstanding Polish *posek*

Judah Loew   (*Maharal*, c. 1525–1609); moralist, scholar, and leader of
ben Bezalel: Ashkenazi Jewry; renowned for piety and asceticism

Isaac Luria: (*ha-Ari*, 1534–1572); kabbalist; leader of Safed kabbalist
                          community; founder of new and influential trend of kab-
                          balist thought; transmitted his teachings orally

Joel Sirkis: (*Bah*, 1561–1640); author of *Bayit Hadash*, comprehensive
                          and influential commentary on *Arba'ah Turim*; opposed to
                          codification of *halakhah*

8. TERMS

8.1 New—Indigenous

Gelilot (regions), as areas of governance (as in Poland)

Ḥillukim (disagreements), constitutional device, expressed differences of opinion with *posek* or halakhic code

Kesherim (those who are fit), term used in Polish *kehillot* to describe worthy candidates for communal office

Marah d'Atra (master of the place); title given to local representative of *keter torah* in Ashkenazi *kehillot*

Nivrarim (selectmen), representatives of *keter malkhut* as provided for by *Va'ad Aragon* of 1354

8.2 Old—Change in Meaning

Agudah (organized body) consociation; term used to describe polity of sixteenth-century Safed

Ḥavurah, association of members of the *kehillah* for specific communal purposes

Semikhah (ordination), during this epoch rabbinical ordination increasingly transmitted through a document which contained a fixed formula

9. BIBLIOGRAPHY

A. Atlas, "Kiryat Arbah (al Va'ad Arba ha-Aratzot)," *He-asaf* 2 (1886), pp. 383–406, 451–454.

Y. Baer, *A History of the Jews in Christian Spain*, vol. 2 (Philadelphia, 1961).

S. W. Baron, "Destruction of Iberian Jewry," *A Social and Religious History of the Jewish People*, vol. 10 (New York, 1965), pp. 167–219.

———. "Marrano Dispersion," *A Social and Religious History of the Jewish People*, vol. 13 (New York, 1969), pp. 64–158.

———. "Poland-Lithuania 1500–1650," *A Social and Religious History of the Jewish People*, vol. 16 (New York, 1976), pp. 3–239.

———. "North Africa and Muslim Spain," *A Social and Religious History of the Jewish People*, vol. 17 (New York, 1980), pp. 224–296.

———. "Turkey's Golden Age," *A Social and Religious History of the Jewish People*, vol. 18 (New York, 1983), pp. 45–121.

H. H. Ben-Sasson, *Ha-Kehillah ha-Yehudit bimei ha-Benayim* (Tel Aviv, 1969).

———. "The Middle Ages," in H. H. Ben-Sasson (ed.), *A History of the Jewish People* (Cambridge, Mass., 1976), part 2:

Y. Ben-Zevi, *Eretz Yisrael vi-Yeshuvah bimei ha-Shilton ha-Ottomani* (Tel Aviv, 1967).

M. Benayahu, "Ḥiddushah shel ha-Semikhah bi-Tsefat," *Sefer Yovel l'Yitzhak Baer* (Jerusalem, 1961).

D. Cohen, "Ha-Va'ad ha-Katan shel B'nei Medinot Aschenbach," *Sefer Yovel l'Yitzak Baer*.

S. Dubnow, *History of the Jews in Russia and Poland from the Earliest Times to the Present Day*, vol. I (new edition, Philadelphia, 1975).

S. Eidelberg, *Jewish Life in Austria in the 15th Century* (New York, 1962).

M. Elon, "Le-Mahutan shel Takkanot ha-Kahal be-Mishpat ha-Ivri," *Meḥkarei Mishpat le-Zekher Avraham Rosenthal* (Jerusalem, 1964), pp. 1–54.

———. "On Power and Authority: Halakhic Stance of the Traditional Community and its Contemporary Implications," *Kinship and Consent: The Jewish Political Tradition and its Contemporary Uses*, ed. D. J. Elazar (Ramat-Gan, 1981).

I. Epstein, *The Responsa of Simon ben Zemah Duran as a Source for the History of the Jews of North Africa* (Oxford, 1930).

L. Finkelstein, *Jewish Self-Government in the Middle Ages* (New York, 1924).

J. Gerber, *Jewish Society in Fez* (New York, 1972).

Y. Harozen, *Dona Gracia u-Medinat ha-Yehudim be-Tiveryah asher be-Galil* (Jerusalem, 1980).

Y. Heilprin, "Reshito shel Va'ad Medinot Lita ve-Yaḥaso el Va'ad Arba ha-Aratzot," *Ẓion* 3 (i), 1938, pp. 439–445.

———. "Mivneh ha-Va'adim be-Eyropa ha-Mizraḥit be-Meah ha-17 veha-18," *World Conference of Jewish Studies*, vol. 1 (Jerusalem, 1972), pp. 439–445.

A. H. Hershman, *Rabbi Isaac ben Sheshet Perfet and his Times* (New York, 1943).

H. Z. Hirschberg, *Yisrael Be-Arav* (Jerusalem, 1950).

———. "Sidrei ha-Tzibur," in *Toldot ha-Yehudim be-Afrika ha-Ẓefonit* (Tel Aviv, 1965), vol. 1, pp. 152–183.

Y. Katz, "Maḥloket ha-Semikhah bein R. Ya'akov Berav veha-Ralbah," *Ẓion* 16 (1951), pp. 28–45.

C. Roth, *A History of the Marranos* (London, 1932).

———. *The History of the Jews in Italy* (Philadelphia, 1946).

———. *The House of Nasi* (Philadelphia, 1948).

S. Simonsohn, "Ha-Getto be-Italia u-Mishtaro," *Sefer Yovel le-Yitzhak Baer* (Jerusalem, 1961), pp. 270–286.

S. Stern, *Josel von Rosheim* (New York, 1959).

A. Straus, *Toldot ha-Yehudim be-Mizrayim ve-Suryah taḥat Shilton ha-Mamelukim*, 2 vols. (Jerusalem, 1944, 1951).

R. J. Z. Werblowsky, *Joseph Caro* (New York, 1962).

E. Zimmer, *Harmony and Discord: An Analysis of the Decline of Jewish Self-Government in 15th Century Central Europe* (New York, 1970).

PART
FOUR

Modernity and the
Restoration of Statehood

EPOCH XIII

Hitagduyot
Voluntary Associations

1. DOMINANT EVENTS

1.1 Founding Events

Rise and collapse of Sabbateanism brought an end to messianism in its medieval form. Henceforth, all Jewish authorities looked with deep suspicion upon any trend (including Zionism) which threatened to restore the messianic impulse.   1649–1666

Creation of modern Jewish diasporas in western world (Great Britain, North America, Scandinavia)   mid 17th century

1.2 Climactic Events

Abolition of autonomous constitutional status and reorganization of emancipated communities on voluntary basis   from early 18th century

Grant of emancipation to Jews as individuals by host state: e.g., 1776 New York (full citizenship); 1791 France; 1796 Holland; 1797 Venice; 1798 Rome; 1812 Prussia; 1858 United Kingdom; and 1870 Germany, Italy, Algiers.

Haskalah (enlightenment) and the search for new political status by individual Jews in their countries of residence   from late 18th century

1.3 Culminating Events

Shift of Jewish political and demographic axis away from Europe signified and generated by mass migration westward and *halutzic aliyah* to Eretz Israel in late nineteenth century and by rise to prominence of Eretz Israel and large non-European diasporas in twentieth century

Destruction of European Jewry during twentieth century (most savagely in territories dominated or conquered by Nazis)

Zionist movement and establishment of State of Israel in 1948

2. CONSTITUTIONAL HISTORY

Epoch XIII opened in a mood of compelling high drama, with the proclamation of Shabbtai Zevi as the Messiah in 1665. It ended on a note of unprecedented tragedy, with the murder of over six million Jews and the destruction of their communities by the Nazis and their collaborators. Between these two *edah*-reshaping events, the Jews experienced vicissitudes of regime, residence, and referent at a pace—and to a degree—hardly equaled in any previous constitutional epoch.

So marked was the transformation that the *edah* of the mid-twentieth century was, in several respects, almost unrecognizably different from that of the mid-seventeenth century. On a physical plane, it had grown enormously in both numerical size and geographical extent. At the beginning of the epoch, the largest concentration of Jews under any one government was still to be found in the Ottoman Empire where several hundred thousand Sephardic Jews had settled. Sephardim, moreover, continued to represent a majority of the Jewish world. Soon after 1700, however, Ashkenazic Jewry surged ahead, experiencing a population explosion (especially during the nineteenth century) which gave it some 14 million (91.8 percent of the entire *edah*) by 1930. Even at the end of the epoch—and despite the Holocaust—Ashkenazim outnumbered Sephardim within the *edah* by seven to one (9.5 million vs. 1.35 million).

Not all of the Ashkenazi masses remained in the traditional centers of Ashkenaz. On the contrary, one of the distinctive features of the epoch—and one contributing cause of its turbulence—was the extent of their migration. Moving steadily westward, initially across Europe and after 1881 (and in greater numbers) to the Americas, South Africa, the Antipodes, and, for the minority of *halutzim*, Eretz Israel, they created new centers which were in every way to rival their mother communities in both virility and influence. Table 3 delineates this demographic change.

At the same time, the *edah* also became increasingly concentrated in big cities. Although Jews in the diaspora always represented a disproportionate percentage of the urban population, during the previous epoch they for the most part lived in small and scattered settlements. By the end of Epoch XIII Jews had been largely drawn toward the major cities of both the old and the new worlds. There Jews settled in distinctive residential quarters, pursued a widely divergent range of economic activity, and perforce experimented in the adaptation of traditional forms of communal organization and government to their new mass-based and generally postemancipation environments.

As one generation followed another, the general and the Jewish environments within which the *edah* functioned progressively merged, with the result that organized Jewish life—even when still conducted on traditional lines—tended to adopt new modes and structures in accord with local circumstances.

This, too, was a divisive force. Altogether, issues of continuity and discontinuity in Jewish life and thought became central to the *edah* and its parts. Consequently, the *edah* tended at times to resemble a battleground of divergent—and often conflicting—constitutional norms, no one of which managed to attain commanding institutional authority.

The tone of dissonance which was to characterize the epoch in its entirety was set during its founding generations. These were deeply affected by the experience of *Shabta'ut* (Sabbateanism). Although it was, in its character, the last of the medieval messianic movements (which began with David Alroi at the beginning of Epoch XI), its meteoric rise and fall caused deep rifts within the *edah*, fostering schismatic manifestations whose residual traces were still apparent when the epoch came to an end. In retrospect, no less than at the time, the political dimension of *Shabta'ut* is not hard to find. Among its other aspects, the movement in effect raised the entire issue of the fabric of constitutional determination. Visionaries—whatever the magnetism of their personal appeal—were bound to be distrusted. Claiming to receive their revelation directly from God, they challenged the established lines of authority. They also presented intractable problems of recognition. Charlatans were not easily distinguishable from men sincerely inspired—and even if they were so inspired, was it by God?

As far as most of the *edah* was concerned, Shabbetai Zevi's conversion to Islam in 1666 obviated the need to confront the issue. Crypto-Sabbateans and Frankists continued to exist, with the suspicion of their presence exciting comment and controversy—notably during the Emden-Eybeschuetz controversy of 1751–1764. However, the influence of *Shabta'ut* continued in much modified and redirected form in various guises within the *edah*.

As the epoch built up during the eighteenth century, a more lasting division emerged in eastern Europe between Hassidim (who derived their original inspiration from the *Ba'al Shem Tov*) and their opponents, the *mitnagdim*. Hassidism as a movement only attained full institutional form in its third generation (late eighteenth century). It was organized in the form of several clusters of *hatzerim* (courts), spread over relatively large areas of northeastern Russia, Poland, and White Russia, and did not possess a single, compact leadership. Individual *admorim*, also known as *zaddikim* or *rebbe'im*, were endowed with regional authority by their regional adherents, and in exceptional cases attained *edah*-wide renown—although only occasionally recognition—by virtue of their charisma and intellectual prowess.

Even more pressing, during the climactic generations of the epoch, were the divisions generated by the emergence of *maskilim* (proponents of Jewish "enlightenment") and emancipationists. Increasingly, these were the camps which shaped Jewish life until the epoch came to a close. Their advocacy of the personal emancipation of the individual Jews—as much from the *edah* as from the ghetto—divided the *edah* as rarely before.

Table 3   Jewish Population of Selected Countries: 1820–1948.

	1820–25	1900	1939	1948
Eretz Israel	4,500	50,000	450,000	650,000
Ottoman Empire and Successor States				
Turkey	—	75,000	78,000	72,000
Romania	80,000	267,000	850,000	428,000
Yugoslavia	—	—	72,000	10,000
Greece	—	10,000	77,000	8,500
Bulgaria	—	—	50,000	45,000
Iraq	—	—	75,000	116,000
Syria	—	20,000	15,000	15,000
Lebanon	500	—	5,000	5,000
Yemen	—	30,000	50,000	45,000
Egypt	—	27,000	65,000	65,000
Morocco	—	103,000	162,000	286,000
Algeria	20,000	51,000	117,000	130,000
Tunisia	30,000	62,500	60,000	71,500
Russian Empire and Successor States				
Russia-Poland	1,600,000	5,190,000	—	—
USSR	—	—	3,020,000	2,000,000
Poland	—	—	3,250,000	100,000
Lithuania	—	—	158,000	20,000
Latvia	—	100,000	95,000	5,000
Estonia	—	4,000	4,500	5,000
Austro-Hungarian Empire and Successor States				
Austro-Hungary	568,000	—	—	—
Austria	—	190,000	182,000	31,000
Hungary	—	900,000	450,000	200,000
Czechoslovakia	—	—	360,000	44,000
Western Europe				
Germany	223,000	587,000	234,000	153,000
Italy	25,000	35,000	51,000	53,000
Britain	20,000	200,000	340,000	345,000
France	50,000	115,000	320,000	235,000
Netherlands	55,000	104,000	130,000	28,000
Belgium	2,000	20,000	100,000	45,000
Switzerland	2,000	12,500	25,000	35,000
Denmark	2,000	3,500	7,000	—
Ireland	—	3,700	4,000	—
Spain	—	—	4,500	—
Sweden	800	3,500	7,500	—
North America				
United States	6,000	1,000,000	4,975,000	5,000,000
Canada	100	16,000	155,000	180,000

Latin America				
Mexico	—	1,000	9,000	25,000
Argentina	—	30,000	275,000	250,000
Brazil	—	2,000	52,000	111,000
Uruguay	—	1,000	12,000	37,000
Chile	—	—	—	25,000
Venezuela	—	300	—	3,000
Colombia	—	—	3,500	6,000
South Africa and Australasia				
South Africa	100	25,000	90,700	106,000
Australia	100	15,000	23,600	35,000
New Zealand	—	1,600	2,700	3,500
Asia and Orient				
Iran	—	35,000	50,000	95,000
India	—	18,200	24,000	28,000
China	—	2,000	10,000	15,000
Japan	—	—	2,000	2,000

Emancipation—the principal instrument of the proposed reform—was, it must be stressed, an uneven and irregular process. Oases of enlightenment existed even during the founding generations of the epoch (Jews were granted civic status in the Netherlands in 1657); elsewhere (as in Russia and Arab lands) emancipation was not to be effected even by its close. In yet a third category (as in early nineteenth-century Germany), the relevant decrees could be revoked by arbitrary action or (as in interwar Hungary and Poland) made meaningless by additional legislation. In still others (e.g., Great Britain and the United States), no formal emancipation was required, only the elimination of specific restrictions on full participation in the body politic.

Although the spread of emancipation and its consequences was well-nigh completed by the time of the establishment of the State of Israel at the beginning of Epoch XIV, it is significant for understanding the continuity of Jewish political life that there never was a moment when there was not some part of the world where Jews lived in autonomous communities. Nevertheless—and even when due account is taken of such variations—the issue, as an issue, clearly constituted a watershed in Jewish constitutional development. Where introduced, emancipation granted Jews civic equality as individuals, but required them to surrender their corporate identity in return. Accompanied as it invariably was by a cultural and economic mobility hitherto unprecedented in either its scope or pace, emancipation demanded a thorough reexamination of the nature of the Jewishness of Jews—what was to become known as

Jewish "identity"—and a restructuring of the framework of corporate Jewish institutions.

Emancipation transformed the context and character of two questions of particular constitutional importance. One was the nature of the relationship to be pursued with non-Jewish governments. Hitherto, this had been an issue limited to a matter of external relations with the "majority outside the walls"; it now became a subject of discourse with one's fellow-citizens of different religious persuasions. Second, and perhaps more insidious, was the question of the relationship which emancipation demanded of the Jew and his community. The state, after all, now regarded the emancipated Jew as an individual, not as a member of a particular national community; indeed, it was on an individual basis that emancipation had been granted. But for precisely that reason it allowed Jewish affiliation to become optional, while demanding that Jewish identity be religious or at most cultural in content rather than political.

This definition of Jewishness suited the newly strong nation-states of the West which rejected the corporate structures of the medieval past in their search for national unity and identity. Indeed, the new nation-states often abolished Jewish corporate autonomy long before granting the Jews emancipation as individuals; hence the change was hardly an exchange as it is sometimes viewed. From the perspective of Jewish constitutional history, this was a revolutionary development which raised far more questions than the first generations of emancipated Jewry were equipped to answer.

Hence, the dominant constitutional characteristic of Epoch XIII is the progressive decline in commitment on the part of Jews to a common authoritative constitutional framework. This was a development of revolutionary—and unprecedented—proportions, which had concomitant consequences for both the *am* (the Jews as a people) and the *edah* (the Jewish polity). Hitherto, the various classical texts which had mediated, interpreted, or refined *Torat Moshe* had been accorded a universally compelling influence which traversed otherwise clearly defined boundaries between most camps and parties within the Jewish polity. In some cases, the growth of their influence had been uneven and beset by constitutional disputes which had occasionally delayed their broad acceptance. In general, however, such differences had been confined to matters of detail, not fundamental substance. During the course of Epoch XIII, this situation changed drastically, so that by its end, a majority of Jews, while still accepting *Torat Moshe* as a personal or group referent in a way which was often undefined, no longer felt themselves bound by the normative constitutional framework which had been developed over the previous generations and epochs.

The most significant constitutional consequence of this situation was the emergence, particularly during the last third of the epoch, of a wide variety of Jewish political doctrines and statements. Admittedly, large segments of the *edah*, especially in the massive Jewish concentrations of eastern Europe, western Asia, and North Africa (thus no doubt a majority of the Jewish people until the twentieth century) continued to regard the *Shulḥan Arukh* as their guiding constitutional referent. But others—who claimed to be regarded as equal partners in the Jewish polity and who, indeed, assumed leadership roles as spokesmen for the *edah* in religious and political affairs—adopted different referents which, while claiming traditional justification, departed from established constitutional norms. Differentiating their views were not only questions of means (how to react to the forces of change) but—more fundamentally—of ends (what was the most appropriate or legitimate goal of Jewish action). The "Jewish Question," as Aḥad Ha'am was to put it, could not properly be tackled unless the "Question of Judaism" was addressed first.

The range of proposed "solutions" (and, indeed, combinations of solutions) bears striking testimony to both the seriousness of the issues and the fertility of the minds who discussed them. Political Zionism (as envisioned by Mordecai Manual Noah in the USA; as formulated by Alkalai, Kalischer, Hess and Pinsker; and as instrumentalized by Herzl—whose range of backgrounds indicates the *edah*-wide genesis of the notion) proposed a territorial solution based upon Eretz Israel. Autonomism (as advocated by Simon Dubnow) and Territorialism (as expressed by Israel Zangwill) were territorial solutions centered in the diaspora. These ideas were challenged by both the traditional Orthodox (who posited a nonpolitical existence even in Eretz Israel) and the emancipationists (in both their Reform and Bundist manifestations) who sought a nonterritorialist diaspora existence. Each of these "schools" developed singular interpretations of *Torat Moshe*. Each was invigorated by the literary and political activities of their founding fathers. Each transmitted its ideas to the *edah* by means of a growing press (in both Hebrew and the variety of local languages spoken by Jews). Each also gave rise to the formation of different (and often rival) parties and camps within the *edah*—some of which (such as the Mizrachists) attempted to yoke together otherwise irreconcilable opposites. The whole can be diagrammed simply in the following manner:

	Eretz Israel	*Diaspora*
Territorial	Zionist	Autonomist/ Territorialist
Nonterritorial	Traditional (*Agudat Yisrael*/ neo-Orthodox)	Emancipationist (Reform/Bund)

The effects of this situation were felt on every plane of organized Jewish life, and within every sphere. Most particularly, however, did it affect the *keter torah* and the *keter kehunah*, in both of which authority became particularly diffuse. The influence of the traditional *yeshivot* and their products (the eminent *posekim*) became increasingly limited, both geographically and substantively. Their authority was challenged by a range of rabbinical academies (Orthodox, Conservative, and Reform) whose adherence to the tenets of the *Shulḥan Arukh* was either filtered through a different prism or ceased to exist altogether. Similarly, officers within the *keter kehunah* were now distributed across a wide spectrum of approaches to the understanding of the Divine, stretching from the Hassidic *ẓaddik* to the theologians of the Reform school.

The fragmentation of the *keter torah* took an even more drastic turn during the climacfic generation of the epoch with the emergence in Germany of the *haskalah* (enlightenment) movement. As formulated by Moses Mendelssohn (1729–1786), the *haskalah* attempted to adapt Judaism to the new universalism of the age of reason by first recognizing and then abandoning its political dimension. His theses were later sharpened—often to the extent of distortion—by the Reform school of thought (although the thrust of Reform arguments was to be more fully felt in the realm of the *keter kehunah*—see later discussion). Mendelssohn's theses were, later still, adopted by the exponents of the more commonly accepted "Science of Judaism" and its outgrowth ("the historical school" and Conservative Judaism—which broke from the Reform school in 1845).

The function of the proponents of the Science of Judaism was not to interpret laws in the traditional mold. Rather, they posited a new intellectual framework which might enable Jews to act in a manner consistent with both modern mores and the "spirit" of the Jewish constitution as it seemed previously to have evolved. They thus offered an alternative approach to interpreting the Torah in its constitutional dimension, as in other spheres, by those Jews who chose to accept their assumptions and conclusions.

Equally significant were the organizational devices developed in order to facilitate this acceptance. Reform synods were held at Raunschweig in 1844, Frankfort in 1845, Leipzig in 1869, and Augsburg in 1871 and a Conservative Seminary established at Breslau in 1853. Both developments were transplanted to the United States in the 1840s—particularly after the 1848 revolutions—with the Hebrew Union College being established at Cincinnati in 1871 and the Jewish Theological Seminary (Conservative) in Philadelphia in 1888 (reorganized and moved to New York in 1902).

These developments spurred traditional Jews to undertake a similar program of retrenchment and organization in this *keter*. The lead was taken as early as 1819 when the Sofer family (led by Moses, the Ḥatam Sofer, 1762–1839) founded a massive *yeshiva*—the largest since those of Bavel—in Pressburg, and by the rabbinic scholars of Lithuania (notably Ḥayyim b. Isaac, 1749–1821), who established the prototype of the Litvak non-Hassidic centers of learning at Volozhin. What we know as Orthodoxy grew out of these efforts. In Germany, which remained the principal battleground, Orthodoxy gained further impetus under Azriel Hildesheimer (1820–1889), who established the Berlin (Orthodox) Rabbinical Seminary in 1873, and Samson

Raphael Hirsch (1808–1888), who founded an entire "school" of neo-Orthodoxy. These trends, too, were transplanted to the United States where they gained additional organizational forms.

The importance of these developments did not lie solely in the ideological content of the debates which they generated. As institutionally organized, the various factions of the *keter torah* also engaged in a struggle for the control of the *edah*—a struggle which was expressed during the course of numerous skirmishes throughout all of the western world and much of eastern Ashkenaz, too.

This state of affairs has to be contrasted, however, with the gradual reconstruction of the *keter malkhut* as an operative organizing device. This development, too, had its roots in the founding generations of the epoch, with the emergence in central Europe of what were termed "Court Jews"—Jewish factors who served individual princes and emperors as contractors, bankers, diplomats, and civil servants. Men of this type were exemplified as early as the end of Epoch XII by Jacob Bassevi von Treuenberg of Prague (1570–1634), and in Epoch XIII by Joseph ben Issachar Suesskind Oppenheimer (c. 1698–1738). These men were not *shtadlanim* in the traditional sense. They did pioneer several breaches in the walls of anti-Jewish restrictions, securing residence permits and trading licenses for increasing numbers of their coreligionists. Their accomplishments, however, were essentially personal. Their wealth, their prestige, and their political attainments endowed them with a far greater influence on Jewish communal fortunes than had been possessed by their nominal predecessors, thereby endowing the *keter malkhut* with a degree of authority and influence which—however localized—was sufficiently well entrenched to provide the foundations upon which their successors might build.

Such a development did indeed take place during the last third of this epoch, when the initial impact of emancipation was at its height. The lead was taken by a small number of individual Jewish statesmen (especially Sir Moses Montefiore and Adolphe Cremieux), who were simultaneously figures of influence in their respective countries and committed advocates of Jewish interests, each of whom possessed international influence on a personal basis. These latter-day *shtadlanim* were succeeded by, first, shtadlanic countrywide institutions established on a multicountry basis to reunite emancipated Jews, at least with regard to their common international agenda. The establishment of such a framework was an early aspiration of the *Alliance Israelite Universelle*—which stimulated the formulation of such parallel and satellite organizations as the *Israelitische Allianz zu Wien* (1873). The AIU's sphere of influence was, however, restricted by the prevalence of imperial rivalries during the nineteenth century. The AIU did act as a metropolitan organization during the 1878 Berlin Congress, when it coordinated Jewish representation via separate Jewish national organizations. The World Zionist Organization explicitly aspired to bring the *edah* back into the political arena as a collectivity. Under the leadership of Herzl, Nordau, Weizmann, and Ben Gurion, it succeeded in so doing.

Another significant step in this direction was the establishment, during the 1919 Versailles Conference, of the *Comité des Delegations Juives*. Consisting of representatives of the American Jewish Committee, of the National Councils of Jews in Eastern Regions, of Jewish associations in Italy, Germany, and White Russia, of the WZO and the *Va'ad Leumi* (but not of the AIU or the Conjoint Foreign Committee of Anglo-Jewry), the Committee—led by Julius Mack, Louis Marshall, and Naḥum Sokolow—submitted a Jewish Bill of Rights to the Conference and helped formulate the minority clauses of the treaty. Although it continued to function after 1919 in order to safeguard minority rights, it failed to gain permanency. The culmination of these developments can be seen in the founding of the World Jewish Congress in 1936, almost at the end of the epoch.

The rise of political Zionism similarly affected the corporate structure of the *edah*. The founding of the World Zionist Organization in 1897 marked another major step in the reconstitution of the *edah* through the *keter malkhut*, by moving the Jewish people from a reliance on shtadlanic organizations to active involvement in a popular, representative body which claimed to speak in the name of the *edah* as a collectivity. For the avowed Zionists, of course, all forms of Jewish life elsewhere than in Eretz Israel and especially political life, were necessarily deficient. For them, therefore, that *Medinah* was the unequivocal center of the entire *edah*. But by the last generation of the epoch, even non-Zionists within Jewry came to appreciate the importance of the *Yishuv* (whose institutions in spheres appertaining to the *keter malkhut* and *keter torah* became increasingly well-organized in response to successive *aliyot*). The expansion of the Jewish Agency to include non-Zionists in 1929 was, in this respect, a sign of both the appeal of the Zionist ideal and of the growing influence of the Zionist enterprise.

The impact of Zionism on Eretz Israel was immediately apparent. Despite the immigration restrictions imposed by the British mandatory authorities before and during World War II—and notwithstanding the continued reluctance of the majority of the *edah* to make their homes in Eretz Israel— the Jewish population of this *medinah* had grown to nearly 700,000 by the last generation of the epoch. Its spiritual and cultural influence was even greater. On the eve of Jewish statehood, Eretz Israel had regained much of its ancient status as the nexus of Jewish life and the fulcrum of future Jewish development.

To say that is not to disregard the importance of other major areas of Jewish settlement and life. Following the eighteenth-century partition of Poland, Russia had risen to undoubted prominence as the largest concentration of Jews in the world. Despite successive waves of persecution and emigration, it retained this position until the last generation of the epoch. Notwithstanding the acute distress of most of the Jewish population (vast numbers of whom were confined to the "Pale of Settlement"), Russia was also an active source of Jewish constitutional ideas. It did not, however, constitute a fully articulated *medinah* because the authorities refused to allow the Jews to organize beyond the local plane. Russian resistance to Jewish communal organization intensified after the Bolshevik revolution. The Communist regime was even more opposed to Jewish communal expression than its Czarist predecessor. Hence, throughout the epoch, the Jewish community remained amorphous. After 1917, the former Russian possessions which gained independence did allow the development of quasi-autonomous Jewish communities, albeit with the greatest reluctance.

The Jewish community of the United States—whose rise to prominence constitutes one of the culminating events of the epoch—also had difficulties in developing a *medinah*-wide organizational framework, albeit for very different reasons. This center of Jewish settlement was to become the largest in Jewish history by the last generation of the epoch. Voluntary countrywide bodies did emerge during the epoch's last three generations, under the aegis of both the *keter malkhut* and the *keter torah*. Nevertheless, the overriding picture remained one of locally anchored particularism, whose major expression was congregational for most of the period.

Other "new worlds" of Jewish settlement did manage to construct somewhat wider frameworks. The foundation of the South African Jewish Board of Deputies in 1912 and the establishment of the Canadian Jewish Congress in 1919 were early indications of a trend which was complemented with the establishment of the Executive Council of Australian Jewry in 1944 and of the DAIA (1933) and AMIA (1940) in Argentina.

This situation must be compared with that prevailing in the classical *medinot* of Europe. For the most part, these developed new structures, each adapted to the particular state under which it was constituted. In most cases, those structures reflected the processes of modernization, although in some the forces of disintegration were stronger than those of reintegration, almost invariably as a result of external government pressures. Only certain Jewish communities in the Muslim world retained their classic form and structure until the end of the epoch. Otherwise, however, and especially in western Europe, the dominant pattern was one of diversity and change. Some *medinot* evolved state-recognized communal structures (here referred to as the *Kultusgemeinde* model of Germany); others, state-recognized religious structures (the *Consistoire* model of France); or, in a third category, representative bodies (the Board of Deputies model of Great Britain). Despite their marked individuality, all of these structures did possess certain characteristics in common, most notably in that they shared the division into three *ketarim* which has throughout been characteristic of the Jewish constitutional world. Clearly, however, each was influenced by the differing political structures prevailing in the contemporary Gentile environment with which the Jews increasingly interacted and of which, increasingly, they felt themselves a part.

3. CONSTITUTION

Torat Moshe, now open and subjected to various simultaneous interpretations, some of which overlapped: via Talmud and *Shulḥan Arukh* by traditionalists, via "liberal-humanistic" prism of Reform school, via political prism of Zionists, and via mystical-halakhic prism of Ḥassidic *rebbe*

3.1 Constitutional Issues

Messianism: Suppression of active or suspected manifestations of traditional messianism (e.g., in attitude toward Frankists in former case and Emden-Eybeschutz controversy in latter) gave way to modern forms of messianic expression, first through universalism and then through Zionism—which reached fruition by the end of epoch.

Emancipation: An uneven and irregular process, it was never granted to the entire *edah* and even where it was formally bestowed, it was often breached in practice. The phenomenon affected different *medinot* at different times throughout the epoch (e.g., Jews were granted civic status in the Netherlands as early as 1657, but even by the end of the epoch were not regarded as full citizens in most Arab lands).

Where enacted, however, emancipation was of momentous constitutional importance. Since it gave Jews civic equality as individuals but required them to surrender corporate autonomy, emancipation demanded a thorough examination of the nature of Jewish "identity" and the restructuring of corporate Jewish institutions.

In so doing, it raised two issues of constitutional import: the relationship to be pursued with the general government (hitherto this had been strictly a question of external relations) and Jewish identity, which became not only optional but also more cultural than political in content.

Extent of authority of Jewish communal organizations: For the same reasons, Jewish communal organizations lost most, if not all, of their *coercive* power (e.g., 1876 *Austrittsgesetz* in Germany permitted Jews to leave their local communities for reasons of conscience). By the end of the modern epoch (end of World War II), the last of the autonomous diaspora Jewish communities in the traditional mold came to an end.

The internationalization of the "Jewish problem," facilitated by the technological revolution in communications and the spread of modern anti-Semitism in its racial form. This necessitated the recreation of the *edah*—albeit under modern conditions.

The status and authority of worldwide Jewish representatives (individuals and/or organizations) aspiring to lead the *keter malkhut* for the entire *edah*

3.2 Camps and Parties

Greatly increased in number and kind (e.g., religious camps such as Reform, Orthodox, and Conservative; parties within Orthodoxy such as Ḥassidim vs. Mitnagdim; political camps such as Zionists vs. anti-Zionists, Bundists, and Territorialists; cultural camps such as assimilationists vs. anti-assimilationists, Autonomists)

4. CONSTITUTIONAL STRUCTURE OF THE *EDAH*

The progressive decline of the previously existing communications network embracing the *edah* in its entirety, based on common allegiance to *Torat Moshe* as traditionally interpreted through the Talmud, left the *edah* without a commonly accepted framework during the latter generations of this epoch.

Three particular developments contributed toward the liquefaction of the arena. Two of these were (1) fissures within the *keter torah* (the communications network of *piskei din*, which had previously cemented the *edah* and provided it with an almost monolithic interpretation of *halakhah*, began to lose its authority for increasing numbers of Jews) and (2) drastic reduction in the scope of Jewish corporate autonomy, progressively—albeit unevenly—affected by the processes of absolutism, toleration, and emancipation. These trends (which although often simultaneous were also conflicting and uneven) called into question the premises upon which the corporate status of the Jews had hitherto rested. Circumstances differed from *medinah* to *medinah*; hence synoptic generalizations were unapplicable.

As the epoch unfolded, however, it was becoming increasingly clear that, for the non-Jews, natural religion was replacing Divine religion, thereby delegitimizing the separate status of Jewry as a nation-in-exile whose preservation was a Divine command; natural rights were replacing Divine rights, thereby denying the basis for the separation of Jews from humanity at large; and natural man was replacing covenanted man, thereby eliminating the binding character of group demands. These perspectives necessarily affected Gentile as well as Jewish attitudes toward the status of the Jewish community, requiring also a revision of the Jews' legal status.

The third development was a sharp divergence in external cultural and political influence and circumstances. These precluded uniform Jewish responses to situations of rapid change. Instead, and increasingly, the *edah* tended to be divided into three spheres of influence, each forming a grand regional cluster: the traditional Ashkenazi world, consisting essentially of eastern Europe; the traditional Sephardi world, consisting essentially of the Mediterranean basin and southwest Asia—with its center increasingly in Jerusalem; and the new "western" world, of western Europe, the Americas, and the new Jewish settlements of the southern hemisphere.

Some crucial *edah*-wide reorganization did take place during the last third of the epoch. Particularly was this so within the sphere of *keter malkhut*, where *medinah*-based officers and organizations adopted *edah*-wide agendas. Nevertheless, the *edah*, rather than presenting a unified structure, continued to consist of a number of elements, each of which imposed itself upon (and at times came into confrontation with) the other.

KETER MALKHUT

Edah-oriented institutions of this *keter* reemerged and began to play an *edah*-wide role. One harbinger of this development emerged during the founding generation of the epoch. Shabbetai Zevi, proclaimed *mashiaḥ* by Nathan of Gaza in 1665, claimed to speak on behalf of the entire *edah*. In order to buttress that claim, he invoked both liberation motifs and Davidic associations.

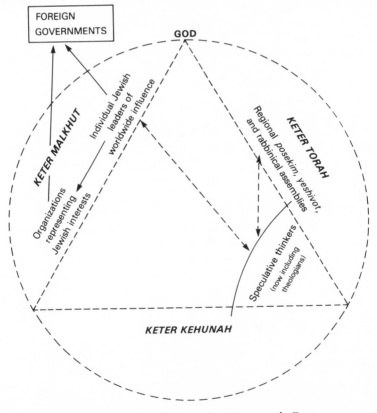

FIGURE XIII-1. The *Edah* in the Nineteenth Century

His movement embraced both the Sephardi and the Ashkenazi worlds, thus reestablishing communication between them in the sphere of the *keter malkhut*. The collapse of Sabbateanism stultified this development until such time as it received new impetus under the very different circumstances of emancipation.

In countries where Jews were granted civic equality, the non-Jewish state took over many of the functions of *keter malkhut* previously within the civil and criminal jurisdiction of Jewish communal government. Hence the Jewish people were faced with the necessity of reconstructing the institutions of *keter malkhut* in all arenas on a new basis. Perhaps paradoxically, this led to the reemergence of the *edah*-wide functions of this *keter*.

The latter third of the epoch witnessed the first steps toward the reconstitution of the *keter malkhut* with postemancipation characteristics. The institutions established for that purpose claimed no mandate or authority from either heaven or tradition; hence they are the first organizations in Jewish history which can be defined as secular (although some included components who sought to justify their function on religious grounds—e.g., the Mizrachists in the WZO). This was an evolutionary phenomenon, which developed in three main stages:

1. The emergence of international Jewish spokesmen (Moses Montefiore and Adolph Cremieux being the most outstanding examples). Self-appointed Jewish notables who had attained success and recognition (and in some cases titles) in the non-Jewish world, they voluntarily assumed the tasks of *edah*-wide *shtadlanim*. They derived their authority from the interplay of their standing within the Jewish and non-Jewish worlds: they were recognized by foreign governments as spokesmen for the Jews and the prestige they thus gained further enhanced their status in the eyes of their "co-religionists" (a new term coined after emancipation to describe Jewish ties to avoid suggesting that the Jews are a nation).

2. The creation of countrywide shtadlanic organizations with an international agenda (Alliance Israélite Universelle, 1860; Anglo-Jewish Association, 1871; Hilfsverein der Deutschen Juden, 1901; American Jewish Committee, 1906). The establishment of these organizations was stimulated by the desire of emancipated Jews to secure the emancipation of their brethren in less enlightened countries and by the appearance of anti-Semitism in its modern, racial form. They were founded on the initiative of the outstanding *edah*-wide *shtadlanim* of the previous generation, who tended to view them as institutional extensions of their individual activities. They were self-selected bodies composed and financed by a patrician class of Jewish notables. The principal functions of such organizations were to secure the rights of Jews in countries where emancipation had not yet been granted; to secure the ultimate (and presumably inevitable) emancipation of those Jews; to protect the newly won civic rights of Jews in emancipated states; and to educate the Jews toward

"good and productive citizenship" (by the foundation and maintenance of schools and vocational training centers).

Each of these organizations retained its independence and developed its own territorial sphere of operations (usually corresponding to the imperial interests of the state in which it was located). However, their individual officers coordinated activities in matters of shared Jewish interests through regular meetings, joint missions, and combined interventions.

These organizations occasionally directed the activities of a variety of other bodies, whose work was more strictly defined as being philanthropic, and which acted as relief agencies: e.g., ORT, established in Russia in 1880; ICA, founded by Baron Maurice de Hirsch in 1891; HIAS, founded in New York in 1909 as an immigrant aid service, established offices in eastern Europe and Far East; OSE, a worldwide organization for child care, health, and hygiene among Jews, founded in Paris in 1912; American Joint Distribution Committee, founded 1914; HICEM (an amalgam of HIAS, ICA, and EMIGDIREKT), established in 1927 to help refugees from eastern Europe, and later Nazi Germany; and Central British Fund, founded in 1933 in the United Kingdom to assist refugees from Nazism.

3. The establishment of worldwide Jewish organizations with international status. Responsibility for the development of truly *edah*-embracing institutional frameworks devolved upon a range of separate organizations. First among these was the Bnai Brith (founded USA, 1843), which by the 1880s attempted to unite Jews throughout the world on a fraternal basis. Officially, the Bnai Brith did not aspire to a political role; in fact, some individual lodges and chapters, due to the nature of the local community, actually became the informal instruments of local Jewish governance. It was followed by other organizations which explicitly aspired to bring the *edah* back into the political arena as a collectivity—and succeeded in so doing: e.g., Chovevei Zion (founded at Kattowice, Russian Poland, in 1884); the World Zionist Organization (founded at Basel, Switzerland, in 1897), which sought the restoration of the Jews to their homeland in Eretz Israel, as a polity "secured by public law"; and the World Jewish Congress (founded in Geneva, 1936), which sought to place the protection of Jewish rights in their countries of residence in the hands of a body chosen more democratically than existing Jewish organizations.

Institutions in this category claimed to be progressively more representative of Jewry at large, holding formal elections and congresses. As grassroots organizations, they thus became popularly based—albeit not comprehensive—in their constituencies.

KETER TORAH

This domain became progressively fragmented, with dichotomies and conflicts emerging between traditional *posekim* on the one hand and proponents of the new "science of Judaism" on the other.

The influence of the *posekim* remained substantial during the first two-

thirds of the epoch; their functions, modes of recruitment, and forms of ac-
quiring recognition were hardly altered. During the latter third of the epoch,
however, their role became increasingly circumscribed, with their authority
often being confined to matters of ritual import. Only among increasingly
limited circles did they retain their previous functions in civil and criminal
affairs. More generally, however, emancipation reduced their sphere of authoritative influence in these matters, especially once increasing numbers
of Jews began to drop away from what in this epoch became defined as
"Orthodoxy."

The emergence of the Science of Judaism and its outgrowths (Reform and
the "historical school," later Conservative Judaism) offered an alternative approach to interpreting the Torah in its constitutional dimension, as in other
spheres, by those Jews who chose to accept its assumptions and conclusions.
Hence, at their points of contact, confrontation became endemic between the
traditional earning of the *yeshivot* and the new approach to "Torah" and
"Jewishness."

The function of the proponents of the Science of Judaism was not to interpret laws in the traditional mold. Rather, they posited a new intellectual
framework which might enable Jews to act in a manner consistent with both
modern mores and the "spirit" of the Jewish constitution as it seemed to have
previously evolved.

Those who embraced the Science of Judaism gained recognition and office
by adopting the canons and trappings of the western academic community.
They acquired their knowledge in universities or rabbinical assemblies which
granted degrees and/or ordination and thus empowered their graduates to
transmit teachings in their name. Jewish congregations in the western world
increasingly demanded that candidates for rabbinical posts possess degrees or
certification from recognized academies (which they supported financially,
but over which they possessed no scholastic jurisdiction).

KETER KEHUNAH

This *keter* was revived in radically new forms that were also extraordinarily
polarized. The range of instruments in this sphere stretched from the hassidic
admorim (who established *shalshalot*—dynasties—of territorially circumscribed demesnes) to Reform rabbis (who emphasized the sacerdotal dimensions of Judaism at the expense of the political and halakhic) to Jewish theologians (who generated schools of thought). In all cases, their perceived
function was to bring God closer to the Jews by sharpening their awareness of
the transcendental and shaping their awareness of the Divine.

HASSIDISM

Hassidic *zaddikim* were endowed with formal authority by their regional adherents (*kehillah*) and in exceptional cases attained *edah*-wide renown—
although only occasionally recognition—by virtue of their charisma and intellectual prowess.

The *zaddik* unified the principal functions of all three *ketarim* within a

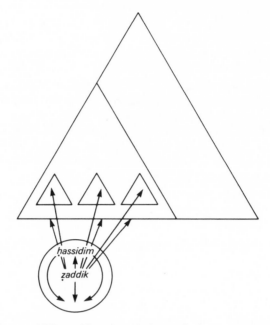

FIGURE XIII-2. The Late Eighteenth-Century Eastern
European Model

De facto rival to *Va'ad ha-Aretz*

> protect *ḥazakot*
> ransom captives
> collect funds for Eretz Israel
> organize opposition to Foreign Suzerain oppression

Strengthened Jewish autonomy in last analysis by adding
sociological dimension capable of resisting *haskalah*

single personage (see also *Kehillot*). Hence, whatever his scholastic attainments and/or shtadlanic prowess, the basis of his power basically rested upon
his enhancement of the status of the *keter kehunah* which, in Hassidic centers, was raised to the status of the principal arm of Jewish government.

At its broadest level, Hassidism thus introduced a distinctive subcategory
into the existing structure of Jewish self-government, causing friction and endemic strife within and between camps of *ḥassidim* and *mitnagdim*. Its position, however, was intrinsically stronger than that of previous sectorian movements (the Essenes, Karaites, Frankists), since it could not be attacked on
halakhic grounds. Hassidic *kehillot* thus became "states within states," performing all the essential functions of organized Jewish life within the confines
of the existing framework.

THE REFORM MOVEMENT

In constitutional terms, this was an attempt to flatten the traditional triangle of Jewish government by rejecting the *keter malkhut* and transforming the *keter torah* into a vague set of ethical teachings denominated "prophetic Judaism." Organizationally and doctrinally, the movement was based solely on *keter kehunah*. Thus, Reform temples (the first of which was established at Hamburg in 1818) omitted all references to the political restoration of Jews in prayers—which were conducted in the vernacular to be intelligible to assimilated Jews. (In this connection, the leading exponent of Reform during its initial stages advocated the restriction of the rabbis to ritual functions.) The emergence of the modern synagogue was an expression of the *keter kehunah*. This was reflected in the new name "temple" applied to that institution, first by the Reform movement and then later by the Conservative movement in North America as well. The Reform movement adopted the term to suggest that the ultimate sacerdotal functions of Judaism could now be performed anywhere and not simply in Jerusalem. In fact, the name reflects their emphasis on the sacerdotal dimension and, in general, the functions originally associated with the *keter kehunah*.

JEWISH THEOLOGIANS

Jewish theologians (e.g., Claude Montefiore, Rosenzweig, Buber, Kaplan) gained recognition by their ability to attract adherents to their respective views. They possessed no formal authority, but rather strengthened the attachment of Jews to the several systems of constitutional interpretation now claiming to be authoritative.

5. *MEDINOT*

The *medinot* were regional groupings of *kehillot*, increasingly within boundaries of European nation-states and their empires, or new states in the Americas, Africa, and Australasia.

Until the last third of the epoch, the majority of Jews still lived in those regions of settlement which had predominated during the previous epoch (the Ottoman, Russian, Austro-Hungarian, and German empires). Despite the differences in the respective political weights of these centers within the *edah*, their combined influence was unquestionable. By the second half of the nineteenth century, revolutionary changes in the Jewish birth rates (particularly in eastern Europe), together with massive migrations (especially after 1881), generated significant shifts. The relative weight of the Sephardi *medinot* (particularly in Asia Minor and North Africa) declined; that of Eretz Israel, North and South America, South Africa, and Australasia experienced a sudden rise. Some of the latter adopted the characteristics of fully articulated *medinot* (e.g., especially Eretz Israel); others (notably the USA) groped toward that status but—by the end of the epoch—had not quite attained it. In each case, however, these all became major new centers of Jewish life in every respect, and accordingly developed new structural modes and institutional processes.

It is possible to distinguish between six classes of *medinot* or *aratzot* during the epoch:

1. Eretz Israel, *sui generis* by virtue of the development of both the old *yishuv* (lit. "settled community") and the new as well as its traditional status in the Jewish polity

2. Traditional medinot which retained their older patterns and structures of communal organization, perhaps with minor changes

3. Segregated Jewries, countrywide congeries of *kehillot* whose members remained excluded from the general body politic until the very end of the epoch, and even after being made citizens had something less than equality as individuals. Collectively these Jews had some measure of official status as members of a minority group. Jewish communal organization reflected this situation.

4. Integrated Jewries, countrywide congeries of *kehillot*, usually enjoying some measure of formal recognition by the host state—generally on religious grounds—whose members came to enjoy full rights of citizenship in the course of the epoch. These *aratzot* transposed traditional Jewish communal structures by adopting a variety of new forms and processes, each of which reflected the ambience of their host environment.

5. The USA, where Jewish communal life was organized on an entirely voluntary and pluralistic basis—albeit without an all-embracing country-wide framework of institutions

6. Autonomous Jewish territories in the Diaspora, compact territories formally under Jewish government within the framework of a larger Gentile state

Eretz Israel

Eretz Israel was a *medinah* organized in the traditional manner under Jewish law as sanctioned by the Ottoman Sultan and (after 1920) the British mandatory government.

During the epoch's early generations, the land became little more than a stagnant backwater of the Ottoman Empire as a result of economic and population decline which began in the last generations of the previous epoch. The eighteenth century witnessed sporadic attempts at revival, markedly the arrival of various groups and individuals, whose migration bore testimony to the continued centrality of Eretz Israel in Jewish thought (e.g., Judah Ḥasid from Germany, 1700; R. Shalom Sharabi from Yemen, 1737; R. Ḥayyim Abulafia from Izmir, 1740; R. Ḥayyim b. Atar from Morocco, 1742; Moshe Mendel of Vitebsk, 1770; and *Talmidei ga-Gaon mi-Vilna*, 1808–1810).

By the end of the century, several thousand Jews lived in scattered villages in the Galilee, as well as such urban centers as Jerusalem, Tiberias, Hebron, Safad, Gaza, and Acco. Their numbers were further augmented during the nineteenth century by Sephardi immigrants from the Balkans and by some Ashkenazim. Thus, between 1848 and 1881 the Jewish population grew from some ten thousand to some 24,000, of whom 14,000 were concentrated in Jerusalem, 5,000 in Safad, and 2,000 in Tiberias.

During the last third of the epoch, this *medinah* underwent four successive transformations.

Until the 1850s, the organization of communal government reflected both Ottoman rule and Sephardi supremacy. Management of the affairs of the country as a whole was the responsibility of the Ottoman representatives in the *vilayets* of Beirut and Damascus and the *sanjak* of Jerusalem; the pre-eminent Jewish official was the *Rishon le-Zion*. This office, originally established during the seventeenth century, was in 1840 given a status equivalent to and independent of the *Ḥakham Bashi* in Constantinople—and thus became the supreme local instrument of the *keter torah*. It was paralleled, in the sphere of the *keter malkhut*, by a council of notables with whom the *Rishon le-Zion* shared effective power.

After the middle of the century, this structure was altered by four factors:

1. The establishment of foreign consulates in Jerusalem with capitulatory rights to intervene on behalf of European subjects (British, French, Austro-Hungarian, Russian)
2. The formation of various independent institutional networks by recent arrivals (e.g., the *Kolel Hod* of Ashkenazim from Germany and Holland

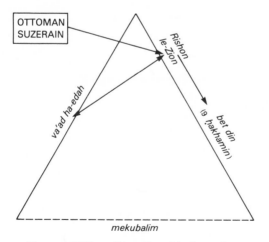

FIGURE XIII-3. *Eretz Israel* before 1850

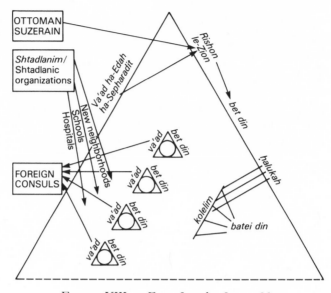

FIGURE XIII-4. *Eretz Israel*, 1850–1880

and the *Edah Mugrabit* of North African Sephardim). These gained *de facto* if not *de jure* autonomy within the formal framework, establishing their own *yeshivot* and *batei din* and possessing independent incomes by means of the *ḥalukah*.

3. The growing involvement in the affairs of Eretz Israel of both individual international *shtadlanim* (e.g., Moses Montefiore) and shtadlanic organizations (e.g., the AIU) who assisted the local communities in the establishment of modern schools and hospitals

4. Developments within the *yishuv* itself—such as the establishment of new settlements (e.g., Yemin Moshe outside the walls of Jerusalem and Motza in the Judean hills) and the foundation of modern institutions, such as Hebrew newspapers

The emergence of modern Jewish nationalism in Europe, which stimulated *aliyot* as early as the 1880s, brought about the creation of the *Yishuv he-Ḥadash* (new *Yishuv*), which developed its own modes and procedures of communal organization and came into conflict with the *Yishuv ha-Yashan* (old *Yishuv*), some of whose members were in any case beginning to reject older habits and authority. The new settlers received substantial support from such external individuals as Baron Rothschild and such new organizations as the ICA, the Ḥovevei Zion Association, and (after 1897) the Zionist Organization. They established new institutions (e.g., the Technion, high schools, hospitals) and new forms of organization (the *kvutza*, *Ha-Shomer* self-defense

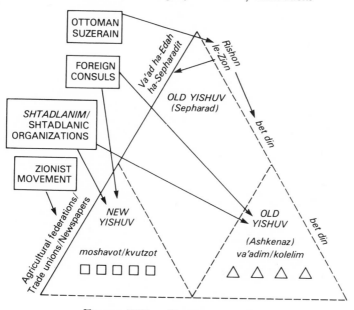

FIGURE XIII-5. *Eretz Israel*, 1881–1917

groups, *moshavot*, trade unions, and federation of agricultural settlements), all of which decreased the influence of the traditional frameworks.

The new *Yishuv* became dominant after 1917, in the last generation of the epoch, under the British mandate. The Jewish community was recognized by law (1927) as *Knesset Yisrael* and, as such, it represented a modernized version of the traditionally autonomous *medinah* under a foreign suzerain. It developed increasingly diversified organs of association and governance. These included the *Histadrut* (labor federation), *Haganah* (militia), *batei mishpat ha-shalom* (magistrates courts), and municipal councils—all of which were supported by voluntary taxes (*kofer ha-yishuv*).

The supreme organ of the *yishuv* in the conduct of its communal affairs was the *Asefat ha-Nivḥarim* (Elected Assembly), a parliament democratically elected by the entire *yishuv* on the basis of proportional representation and along party lines. It elected a *Va'ad Leumi* (National Council), with each party represented in proportion to its electoral strength, which was responsible for matters falling within the jurisdiction of the *keter malkhut*. Mapai (*Mifleget Poalei Eretz Israel*—founded 1930) within a year won supremacy in this body; despite the foundation of the Revisionist Party in 1925, it continued to hold sway until the end of the epoch, for most of the period in alliance with the Mizrachi party (constituted in Eretz Israel in 1918).

Supreme authority in the domain of *keter torah* was wielded by the *Moetzet ha-Rabbanut* (Rabbinical Council), consisting of two *Rabbanim Rashi'im*

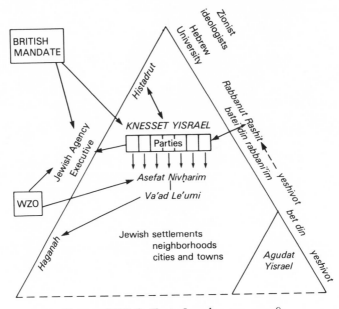

FIGURE XIII-6. *Eretz Israel*, 1917–1948

(Chief Rabbis), one Ashkenazi and one Sephardi—the latter still known as the *Rishon le-Zion*; six additional rabbis (three Ashkenazi and three Sephardi), all of whom were elected by an assembly consisting of seventy-one members (two-thirds rabbis and one-third laymen).

Throughout the last generation of the epoch, the activities of both *ketarim* were supplemented and supported by the work of two *edah*-wide institutions: the Jewish Agency, established under the terms of the League of Nations mandate and enlarged in 1929 to include non-Zionists, and the WZO, which controlled the Jewish Agency. Both of these bodies were focused on Eretz Israel as the nexus of the entire *edah*.

Traditional Medinot

These possessed recognized and recognizable organizational frameworks which bore the characteristics evident in the previous epochs. As such, they constituted state-recognized communal structures in which the Jewish community possessed authority, but in which Jews as individuals did not possess equal rights.

THE OTTOMAN EMPIRE

As in the previous epoch, Jewish autonomy was considerable, with the *Ḥakham Bashi* constituting the principal representative of the community in its dealings with the Sublime Porte.

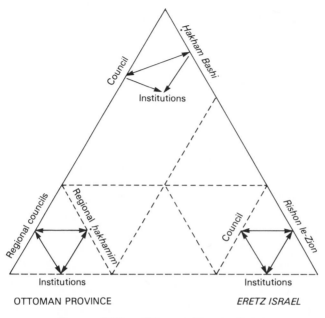

FIGURE XIII-7. Ottoman Empire Jewries

BAVEL

Notwithstanding the political changes in the government of this *medinah*, the Jewish community retained its traditional structure and, in some cases, nomenclature.

Segregated Jewries

RUSSIA

In this most outstanding and consistent example of segregated Jewries, rulers consistently opposed any Jewish organization beyond the local arena. Even in local affairs, the Russian government sharply restricted Jewish autonomy. Russia's peculiarity was emphasized by the fact that, after the successive annexations of Polish territory during the eighteenth century, it contained the largest single concentration of Jews in the world. This is the first epoch in Jewish history during which such a significant proportion of the *edah* lacked *medinah*-wide form and authority. In this way, Russia followed the pattern of the modern epoch even though its Jews were among the last to be emancipated.

Instead, this *eretz* was divided into three grand clusters of *kehillot*: the "Pale of Settlement," the Crimea, and the Caucasus. All *kehillot* within these regions were influenced, in varying degrees, by the decisions of contemporary *posekim* (*gedolei ha-dor*) and by the teachings inculcated in the growing

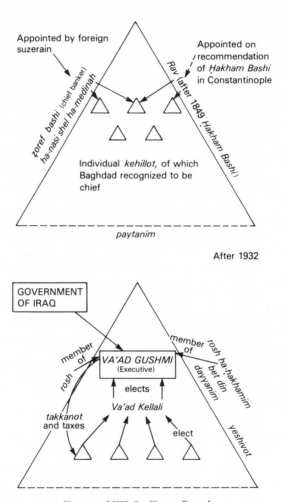

FIGURE XIII-8. *Eretz Bavel*

number of *yeshivot*. They tended, however, to develop norms of great particularity in view of the ideological differences which characterize the epoch in its entirety. Prominent among these are the differences in outlook between *mit-nagdim* (who looked to the *Gaon* of Vilna as their intellectual guide) and *ḥassidim* (who derived inspiration from the teachings transmitted in the name of the *Baal Shem Tov*); the divergent allegiances which separated *ḥavurot* of *ḥassidim* bound to the *ḥazerim* (courts) of various hassidic *ẓaddikim* (also known as *rebbeim* or *admorim*); the conflicts between traditionally Orthodox

Jews and groups of *maskilim* (followers of the enlightenment); and—during the last generations of the epoch—political divisions (Zionists, Bundists, Social Democrats, Communists, etc.).

All attempts to bind these conflicting camps and parties together were further hindered by the official abolition of the *kahal* in Russia in 1844 (abolished in Polish regions in 1822, when it was replaced by a synagogue board—*Dozor boznicy*). Despite attempts by Baron Horace Guenzberg (1833–1909) to overcome such obstacles by establishing a countrywide organization of Russian Jews in 1881–1882, no permanent organizations or institutions were established and representatives of certain Jewish communities convened together in St. Petersburg only occasionally.

The Russian revolutions of March and November 1917 led to a second attempt to establish a countrywide organization. An all-Russian Jewish conference (on which the Zionists controlled two-thirds of the seats) was convened in 1917, and in 1918 it elected a Central Bureau. The experiment was, however, soon aborted by the Bolsheviks. The Communist regime, like its Czarist predecessor, refused to allow the Jewish community the right to organize for anything more than the most limited purposes and then only locally.

POLAND

UNTIL 1795

The *Va'ad Arba ha-Aratzot* continued to exist until the partitions of Poland in the late eighteenth century but never fully recovered from the impact of the massacres of 1648–1649. It became increasingly obligarchic in character and lost the confidence of the population it served. Its status as representative of Polish Jewry before the foreign suzerain was abolished by the Polish government in 1764.

AFTER 1919

Jewish rights in the reconstituted state were guaranteed by the minority clauses of the Versailles Treaty. Formally binding, they were systematically breached by the Polish government (and, indeed, every other government in the successor territories).

By 1919 a Jewish National Council was formed and attempts were made (with the assistance of the JDC and ORT) to establish *medinah*-wide welfare and education services. Tensions within the Jewish population, however, precluded the establishment of a unified Jewish framework. While many of the *kehillot* were dominated by the *Agudat Yisrael*, much of the proletariat was under the influence of the Bund. The Zionist movements (which were themselves not united) constituted yet another axis of allegiance.

The result was the increasing organization of communal life within the *medinah* on specifically Jewish party lines. General Zionists, Mizrachists, the Agudat Yisrael, Folkists, and Autonomists all sought to control Jewish education and to maintain their own welfare agencies. All, accordingly, claimed the right to levy taxes for that purpose.

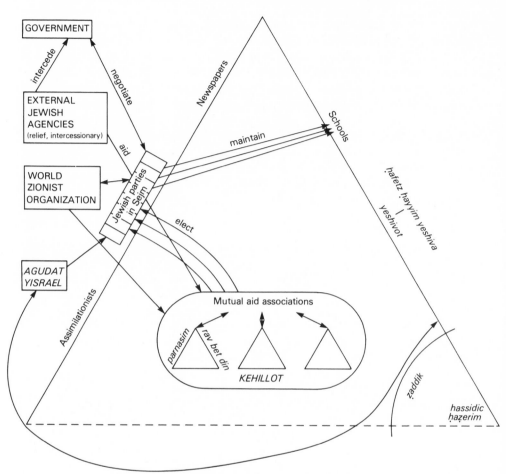

FIGURE XIII-9. *Medinat Polin* after 1919

External relations with the state authorities were similarly diffuse. A Jewish bloc of Zionists and Mizrachists (*"Ha-Moetzah ha-Leumit"*) was organized in elections to the Sejm as early as 1918, and Jewish representatives reached a much-criticized minorities-*bloc* compromise with the government in 1925. Thereafter, however, the Jewish vote split among various "lists," and consequently lost much of its bargaining power.

OTHER CENTRAL AND EASTERN EUROPEAN STATES

A similar situation prevailed in the other states of central and eastern Europe. Even where central Jewish organizations did exist, their composition was largely determined on party lines—e.g., Lithuania, where the Jewish community possessed legal status between 1920 (when a Jewish National Council was appointed) and 1925; Estonia, where a Cultural Council (dominated by the Zionists) was established in 1926; Rumania, where a chief rabbinate was established in 1919 and a Union of Rumanian Jews (embracing all but the Hassidic communities of Transylvania) in 1928; Austria, where—on Zionist initiative—a Jewish National Council was formed in 1919; Yugoslavia, where Ashkenazim and Sephardim were united in the Federation of Jewish Religious Communities (1919) and nominally accepted the jurisdiction of a single chief rabbi (appointed by the government after 1923); and Czechoslovakia, where a Jewish party was formed in the parliament, a Supreme Council of Jewish Religious Communities was established in 1926, and the Chief Rabbi of Prague (ex-officio a member of that body) was generally recognized to speak on behalf of the entire community.

Integrated Jewries
STATE-RECOGNIZED COMMUNAL STRUCTURES, THE *KULTUSGEMEINDE* MODEL (Germany and Central Europe)

Jews as individuals acquired civil rights which, in time, formally became equal rights, but, unless they converted to Christianity, were legally bound to be members of a recognized Jewish community within the framework of which they organized themselves in local and regional arenas (*Landjuden-schaft*) and to which they paid internal taxes. Each local community elected representatives to these bodies, which maintained the Jewish institutions and tended to be oligarchic in character.

No alternative organizational frameworks could be established until state law provided for them: e.g., in 1871 in Hungary the government approved a

FIGURE XIII-10. German Jewry (Early 20th Century)

threefold division of independent community unions consisting of Liberal, Orthodox, and "status quo" congregations; and in 1876 Prussia adopted the *Austrittsgesetz* ("Law on the withdrawal from the Jewish community") and thus gave sanction to the independent neo-Orthodox congregations earlier established in Frankfurt by S. R. Hirsch.

The patterns of internal organization thus consisted primarily of the formalization and modernization of earlier models and their adaptation to non-Jewish political formats. A principal result was to place new emphasis on the *keter kehunah* functions which suited the image of "religion" of the non-Jewish world and, increasingly, the Jews who had assimilated within it. Nevertheless, the distinction between the *keter torah* and the *keter malkhut* was formally maintained.

STATE-RECOGNIZED RELIGIOUS STRUCTURES, THE *CONSISTOIRE* MODEL

In France Jews as individuals possessed equal rights and were not legally required to affiliate with the Jewish community—even in its congregational form. From the point of view of the authorities, the Jewish community was considered to be a "church," whose principal responsibilities were to provide facilities for religious worship and observance. The community could undertake ancillary activities only insofar as they could be justified from that perspective.

In the *consistoire* model as introduced by Napoleonic legislation, a statewide authority was established in France for the first time and was highly centralized in its administration. After the Napoleonic regime, the Central Consistoire consisted of a Grand Rabbin and a representative of each of the regional consistoires; each of the latter consisted of a Grand Rabbin and five laymen. Centralization remained the rule.

During the course of the nineteenth century, the *consistoire* model was adopted by the Netherlands, Belgium, Italy, and Rumania as well as France. Under it, the organizational functions of the community veered heavily toward the domain of *keter kehunah*, with the rabbis playing a predominantly pastoral role in halakhic guise. The Jews in these *medinot*, however, used the instrumentality thus provided by the state (and, indeed, financed by it) to keep alive the conventional functions of the other *ketarim*, too, and adapted established modes and procedures of Jewish government to the new situation. In the course of time, therefore, cultural and welfare institutions were established, each of which was administered by a board of lay and clerical governors.

Modes of election to official Jewish bodies were a matter of dispute between the non-Jewish authorities (who favored an electoral college) and the Jews (who desired democratic suffrage). This is a good reflection of their differences in approach to communal organization.

In France, the *consistoire* remained the only authoritative Jewish communal organization until the legal separation of Church from State in 1905. In

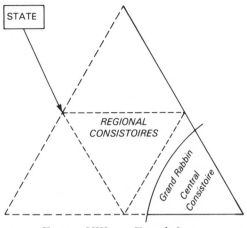

FIGURE XIII-11. French Jewry

the Netherlands, the *consistoire* was established under Napoleonic rule in 1808; it underwent several changes until, in 1870, a central commission was established for ten districts, each with an independent rabbi. In Belgium, the *consistoire* was reestablished in 1835 (after Belgium won its independence from the Netherlands), and membership in the community was made compulsory. In Italy, the *consistoire* was originally established by Napoleon and in the mid-nineteenth century was recreated along the pattern prevalent in Piedmont; in 1911 it was reconstituted under the name of Consorzio fra le Communite Israelitische Italiana; its status was reconfirmed under Fascist rule during the interwar generation.

REPRESENTATIVE BODIES

Jews as individuals possessed equal rights and were not legally required to maintain affiliation with the Jewish community in any form. Those who wished to retain their Jewish identity organized themselves into specific institutions, each of which had a particular purpose (political, religious, cultural, welfare), few of which were comprehensive, but most of which possessed *medinah*-wide scope or aspired to *medinah*-wide comprehensiveness— although in very few cases did they manage to achieve that aim. The influence of these bodies was generally acknowledged by the non-Jewish authorities (in the case of Britain's United Synagogue, by act of Parliament), but they possessed no coercive powers over those who chose to establish parallel, or even rival, organizations (e.g., Sephardi congregations, the Orthodox Federation of Synagogues, Bnai Brith, United Council of Jewish Friendly Societies).

The separation of powers between the three *ketarim* was maintained, although consultation and contact between their representatives and officers was frequent.

In the United Kingdom the Board of Deputies (established 1760) consti-

tuted the informal "parliament" of the community, to which individual congregations throughout the country and other Jewish organizations might elect
delegates if they so chose. The Board (headed by an elected president and executive) represented the community in its dealings with the government.

Ashkenazi synagogues (almost exclusively in the capital) clustered around
the United Synagogue (founded 1870) whose Council elected a president and
arranged for the appointment of a Chief Rabbi (who possessed ritual jurisdiction throughout the British Empire). His functions (paralleled in the Sephardi
congregations by the Ḥakham) included the approval of appointment of
ministers to many congregations and the supervision of Jewish elementary
education within the synagogue framework.

This model was adopted in several of the territories constituting dominions
within the British Empire. Some established chief rabbinates (often subordinate to London) and most established representative boards (e.g., South African Board of Deputies, 1912; Canadian Jewish Congress, 1919; and the Executive Council of Australian Jewry, 1944—a confederation of state Boards of
Deputies). All, too, possessed Zionist Federations (the influence of which was
particularly strong in South Africa) and a countrywide Jewish press.

CULTURALLY SEPARATIST JEWRIES

These were found principally in the new diasporas of South America. Since
most of the Ashkenazi immigrants were secularists, congregational affiliation
among the majority was weak. The principal means of Jewish association were

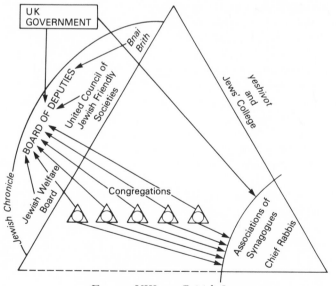

FIGURE XIII-12. British Jewry

mutual aid societies (notably the *landsmanschaft*) and cultural bodies. Only among the large Sephardic minority was congregational life of central importance. It was these which, by the culminating generation of the epoch, had formed the community's principal representative bodies.

The outstanding example of *medinot* of this type was Argentina. Despite its initial tendency to congregational organization (the Congregacion Israelita de la Republica Argentina was established in 1868), the arrival of large numbers of immigrants from eastern Europe toward the turn of the century (some of whom settled on Baron Maurice de Hirsch's colonies) led to a new organizational form achieving preeminence. The newcomers, instead of affiliating to the community's existing organs, founded *landsmanschaft*, cultural societies, synagogues, and parties of their own. It was these which constituted the principal building blocks of the community's representative organs: The DAIA (Delegacion de Associaciones Israelitas Argentinas), founded in 1933 and organized on the basis of representative local, regional, and national cultural and synagogual bodies, became the officially recognized representative body of Argentinian Jewry; and the AMIA (Associacion Mutual Israelita Argentina), founded as the *Hevra Kadisha* in 1893, was reorganized in 1940 as the roof organization of the Buenos Aires Ashkenazi communities.

The Sephardic Jews who arrived at the turn of the century and who were far more traditional combined the congregational and mutual aid molds by establishing *batei knesset* based upon their countries or cities of origin. Their links with the Ashkenazi community were tenuous in the extreme.

The United States
This was a community organized on an entirely voluntary basis from the first. Under American law, its institutions were deemed to be private, incorporated under the laws of each state like any other nonprofit corporation. No Jew was required to affiliate with any Jewish body and any group might establish a synagogue or other organization simply by fulfilling the terms of state law. Moreover, with minor exceptions, Jews possessed full civil rights in the United States from its very establishment.

The American Jewish community developed from several (later numerous) local communities, at first having only one congregation embracing all Jews who cared to affiliate and later adding others as groups of Jews from other countries and regions arrived and wished to organize themselves separately. There existed, at this stage, no authoritative translocal bodies performing functions which fell within the domain of *keter malkhut*. The *keter torah* was represented by the occasional rabbinical figure, not always possessing *semikhah* (e.g., Gershon Mendes Seixas in the late eighteenth century and Isaac Leeser in the mid-nineteenth century), with countrywide influence, who drew upon the teachings and decisions of the classic texts and rabbinical authorities elsewhere in the *edah*. The *keter kehunah* became the most pronounced of the three as the *hazzanim* emerged as the central figures in the local congregations, and the first efforts to unite American Jewry revolved around the development of a *minhag America*, a common American Jewish synagogue ritual. When these assumed the title "rabbi," that office became identified with the tasks of that *keter* far more than the *keter torah*.

The first countrywide organization was Bnai Brith (1843), established as a fraternal society. The first to concern itself with political matters was the Board of Deputies of American Israelites (1859) which later merged with the Union of American Hebrew Congregations (1873), the first synagogue confederation.

Countrywide bodies emerged in the last two generations of the epoch, and consisted of Bnai Brith, including the eleemosynary institutions founded and sponsored by it; synagogue leagues (UAHC, United Synagogue, Union of Orthodox Jewish Congregations of America) each with its rabbinical seminary and assembly; community relations organizations (American Jewish Committee, Anti-Defamation League of Bnai Brith, American Jewish Congress); cul-

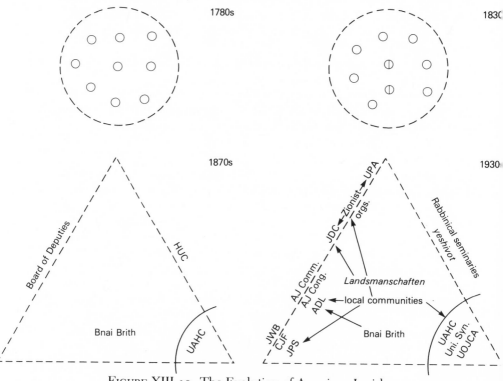

FIGURE XIII-13. The Evolution of American Jewish Community Organization, 1780–1935

tural institutions (e.g., Jewish Publication Society of America, Yiddish, English and Hebrew newspapers and magazines); countrywide arms of local communal and welfare bodies (e.g., Council of Jewish Federations, National Jewish Welfare Board); and Joint Distribution Committee (a union of Zionist, religious, and *landsmanschaft* relief bodies to provide assistance to Jews outside the USA). Each of these bodies was formally organized on the basis of democratic elections but, in fact, their offices were in most instances filled by slated candidates drawn from those willing to serve, as appropriate to each organization. Some (e.g., American Jewish Committee) included only notables; others (e.g., Bnai Brith) were open to almost all comers.

Autonomous Jewish Territories in the Diaspora
At least four such phenomena appeared in the modern epoch: two quite real and the other two quite fraudulent. For three generations, from the late seventeenth to the late eighteenth century, there was an autonomous Jewish region in Surinam, in northeastern South America, known as *Joden Savanne* (Jewish Savannah). This area, in the interior of the Dutch colony, consisted of a compact network of Jewish plantations and towns serving them, which acquired autonomous status under the Dutch, with its own political and religious institutions, including a *beth din* recognized by the Dutch authorities, and a Jewish militia. Its population ranged from several hundred to several thousand Jews at different periods and for at least a generation it represented the controlling power throughout Surinam.

The fraudulent examples were to be found in the USSR in the interwar generation. The first comprised the Jewish agricultural settlements in the Crimean peninsula. Two Jewish national districts were organized in the Crimea, Freidorf in 1930 and Larendorf in 1935. In 1938 there were six Jewish *kolkhozes* (collective farms) operating within them with some 20,000 Jewish inhabitants. All were annihilated when the Germans occupied the area in 1941, after having been turned into shells in the late thirties as a result of the Stalinist purges. The second was Birobidzhan, which was set aside as an area of settlement for Jews in 1927 and proclaimed an autonomous Jewish region (Oblast) in 1934: a kind of Potemkin village established to compete with Zionism and to win Jews for Communism. Its Jewish population reached a maximum of 30,000 by about 1948 and declined to about one-third of that by the end of the postwar generation. While the Jews there managed to establish something of a Communist Jewish culture in Yiddish from the mid-1930s until the end of World War II, the Stalinist persecutions of the postwar period destroyed virtually all but vestiges of that culture. Birobidzhan still remains technically an autonomous Jewish region, but the Stalinist purges of 1948 were directed to systematically eliminating all collective Jewish effort and expression there.

The fourth example was to be found on the local plane in the form of Jewish agricultural colonies in Argentina, Canada, and the United States established in the late nineteenth century. While real enough, only in Argentina did such colonies take hold and become autonomous communities for as much as a generation; but they, too, ceased to be separate communities after World War II as a result of assimilation and the migration of their members to the cities.

6. *KEHILLOT*

Local community organization varied from *medinah* to *medinah* and (sometimes more frequently still) from *kehillah* to *kehillah* within various *medinot* and *aratzot*. Such diversity was exacerbated by the impact of the modern era, which added new forms of governance in some cases while allowing others to persist alongside it in others.

The dramatic growth in the Jewish population of the world (which commenced in Europe in the mid-seventeenth century) was accompanied by the phenomenon of increasing Jewish urbanization. The largest local communities became far larger and more complex in their organization than ever before in Jewish history. Such urban centers did not experience a steady growth but expanded in spasms, in response to waves of migration.

By 1914, New York already had a Jewish population of 1,350,000 (thus constituting the largest single local center of Jewish population—a position which it still retains). Other major centers were Warsaw, 350,000; Chicago, 350,000; Budapest, 200,000; Philadelphia, 175,000; Odessa, Vienna, Lodz, 160,000; and London, 150,000. No less significant than the size of these

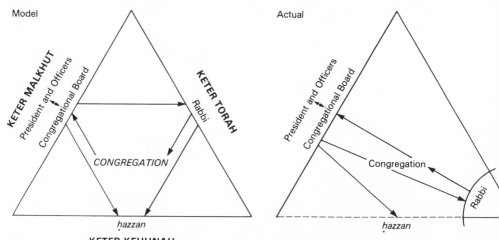

Figure XIII-14. The Modern *Bet Knesset*

kehillot is the fact of their newness. Very few of the large *kehillot* antedated the epoch; most were founded during its founding or climactic generations.

Under these new circumstances, the medieval pattern of the single congregation gave way to one of many, or at least several, *batei knesset* which in some places served as building blocks of the community, in others competed with one another because of ideological differences, and in still others were paralleled by a separate set of organizations not related to the synagogue. In every case, however, the *bet knesset* retained the formal division of its governing instrumentalities among the three *ketarim*, viz:

Distinctions are here made between *kehillot* in Eretz Israel; the traditional *kehillah* in Islamic lands almost totally unaffected by modernity (e.g., Sa'ana in Yemen); the traditional *kehillah* of *mitnagdim* in Europe, where functions and offices were divided between the three *ketarim* in the manner apparent during the previous epoch (titles, too, hardly differed); the hassidic *kehillah*, in which the *zaddik* was the principal instrument of all three *ketarim*; *kehillot* in the modern integrated *medinot* (e.g., Boston, Frankfurt-am-Main; Marseilles, and Manchester), where the community included a number of *batei knesset* (synagogues) of different kinds, each independent in its own right; and *kehillot* in the *medinot* whose Jewries are segregated.

Kehillot in Eretz Israel

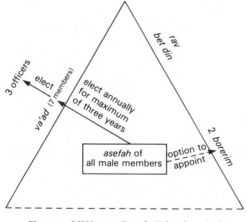

FIGURE XIII-15. *Petah Tikvah*, 1878

The government of the *moshava* as ordained by the *brit* of its founding members

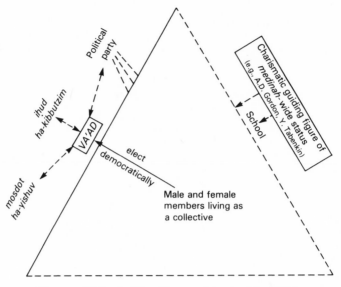

FIGURE XIII-16. The *Kevutzah* in the New *Yishuv*

Traditional *Kehillah*—Islamic World

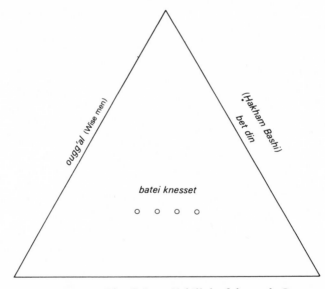

FIGURE XIII-17. The Sa'ana *Kehillah* of the 19th Century

Ougg'al—supervised activities of community, formulated legislation, served as scapegoats

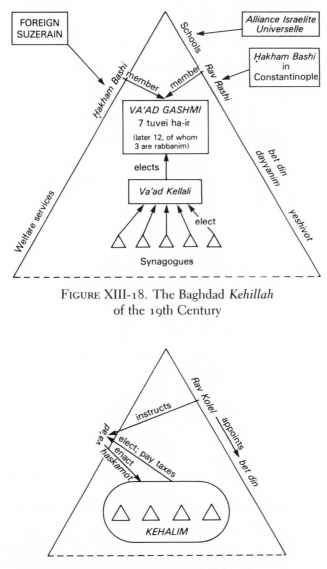

FIGURE XIII-18. The Baghdad *Kehillah*
of the 19th Century

FIGURE XIII-19. The Izmir *Kehillah*, 1650–1772

In Ismir, the modern Jewish community came into existence as a result of renewed Jewish settlement at the beginning of the epoch. Under the leadership of R. Joseph Ishkafa (the *Rav Kolel*), the community established a federation of congregations (*kehalim*), organized by external place of origin. Each was represented on a central council (*va'ad*), controlled by notables, which handled all taxation (internal and external) and enacted *haskamot*. Attempts on part of poorer section of community to gain separate representation failed.

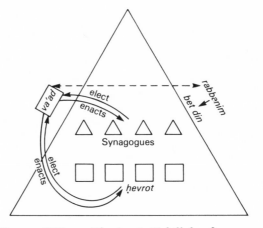

FIGURE XIII-20. The Izmir *Kehillah*, after 1772

The great fire of 1772 destroyed the synagogues in the town and ended the traditional residential pattern, thereby dispersing the *kehalim* based upon external place of origin. Attempts by the *va'ad* to restore the old pattern were frustrated by Ottoman restriction on reconstruction of central synagogue (until 1781) and the development of new congregations in the interim, based upon new residence patterns.

The federation of congregations framework remained unchanged, however, until the influx of refugees—especially after the Greek War of Independence of 1821—who developed new forms of association (*hevrot*) and refused to be subject to an oligarchy. This led to midcentury electoral reforms.

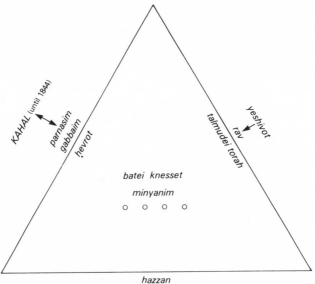

FIGURE XIII-21. The *Kehillah* of the *Mitnagdim*

Traditional *Kehillah*—Eastern Europe

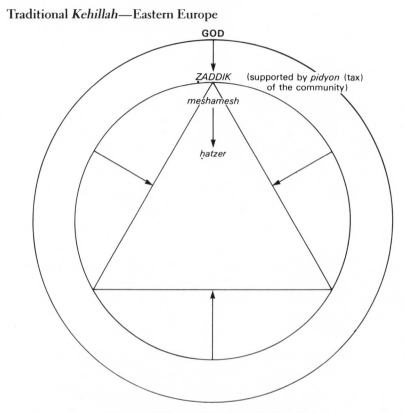

FIGURE XIII-22. The Hassidic *Kehillah*

In the Hassidic community the *Zaddik* functioned in all three spheres, as *posek, maggid,* and *parnass.*

Kehillot in Modern Integrated **Medinot** ₁

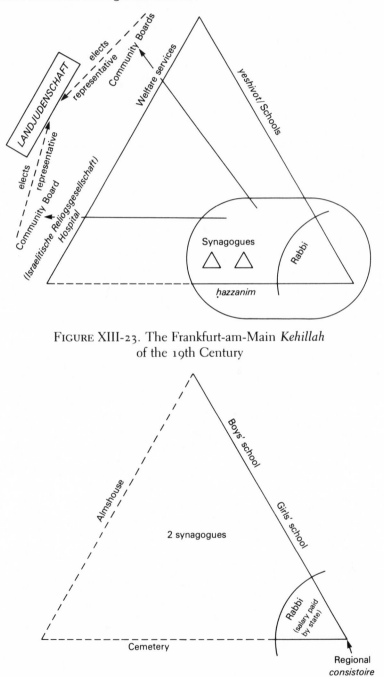

FIGURE XIII-23. The Frankfurt-am-Main *Kehillah*
of the 19th Century

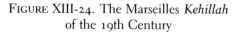

FIGURE XIII-24. The Marseilles *Kehillah*
of the 19th Century

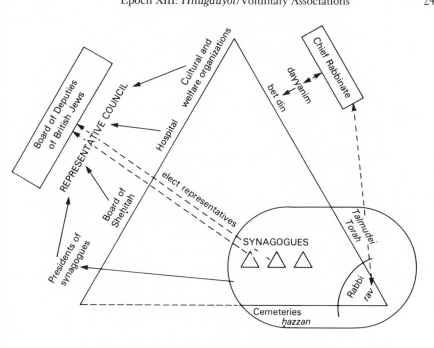

FIGURE XIII-25. The Manchester *Kehillah*, 1890s–1940s

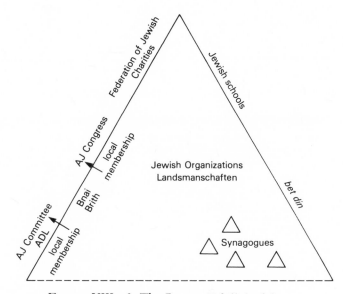

FIGURE XIII-26. The Boston *Kehillah* of the 1920s

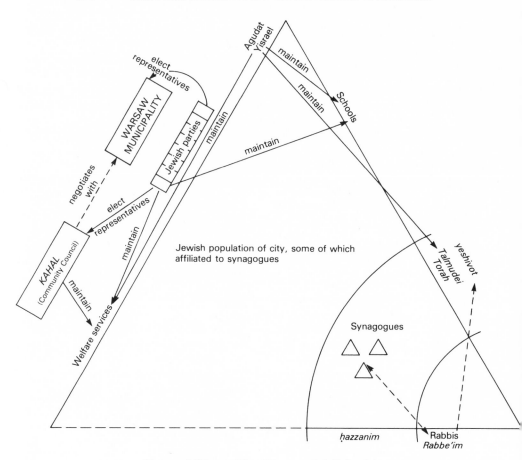

FIGURE XIII-27. The Warsaw *Kehillah* of the 1920s

7. REPRESENTATIVE PERSONALITIES

7.1 Constitutional Architects

Dov Baer: The *Maggid* of Meźhirech (d. 1772); disciple of *Ba'al Shem Tov* and his successor as leader of Hassidic camp; played crucial role in formation and expansion of this camp

Theodor Herzl: (1860–1904); most influential proponent of political Zionism (although not first advocate of the idea), considerably strengthened nationalism as element of constitution; founder of World Zionist Organization, also statesman

Samson Raphael: (1808–1888); principal ideologist of neo-Orthodoxy and architect of *Austrittsgemeinde*

Hirsch: Mordecai Menachem Kaplan:	(1881–1983); a founder of New York *kehillah*, created the idea of the synagogue center, conceived and founded Young Israel; defined Judaism as an evolving religious civilization, provided modern definition of Jewish peoplehood, and suggested institutional arrangements suitable to the new situation of the Jews; also commentator

7.2 Statesmen

David Ben Gurion:	(1886–1973); leader of Mapai and person chiefly responsible for building the political structure of the *Yishuv* on the eve of statehood
Louis Dembitz Brandeis:	(1856–1941); principal, though unofficial, instrument of *keter malkhut* in *medinah* of USA; his personal contacts with President Wilson influential in securing American support for Balfour Declaration
Isaac Adolphe Cremieux:	(1796–1880); prominent in the reconstruction of the *edah*-wide *keter malkhut* in the nineteenth century; a founder of the Alliance Israélite Universelle
Theodor Herzl:	Principal instrument of the *keter malkhut* on an *edah*-wide basis; first Jew of modern times to negotiate with a great power for the establishment of a Jewish state, first to be offered a territory (in East Africa) as a Jewish homeland
Baron Maurice de Hirsch:	(1831–1896); prominent figure in reconstruction of *keter malkhut* during last third of the epoch. The Jewish Colonization Association (ICA), which he founded in 1891, financed Jewish settlement in North and South America, Eretz Israel, eastern Europe, and elsewhere
Vladimir (Ze'ev) Jabotinsky:	(1880–1940); Zionist leader; obtained British sanction for formation of Jewish battalions in World War I; formed and headed World Zionist Revisionists, 1925; established New Zionist Organization, 1935; commanded *Irgun Zvai Leumi*, 1937–1940
Menasseh ben Israel:	(1604–1657); prominent instrument of *keter torah* and *keter malkhut* in *medinah* of Holland in seventeenth century; forerunner of scholars who attempted to present Judaism in manner acceptable to Christian world; played prominent role in negotiating return of Jews to England, 1656
Louis Marshall:	(1856–1929); prominent in reconstruction of *edah*-wide *keter malkhut* during culminating generations; a founder and president (1919–1921) of American Jewish Committee; key non-Zionist figure in expanding Jewish Agency in 1929
Moses	(1784–1885); prominent in reconstruction of *edah-wide*

Montefiore: *keter malkhut* in nineteenth century; president of the Board of Deputies of British Jews for over forty years

Nathan of Gaza: (1643/4–1680); principally responsible for giving organizational impetus to Sabbatean movement

Joseph ben Issachar Suesskind Oppenheimer: (c. 1698–1738); outstanding example of principal instrument of *keter malkhut* in *medinah* arena during founding generations; court Jew and financial adviser to Duke of Wuerttemberg

Baron Edward James de Rothschild: (1845–1934); philanthropist; his patronage contributed to revival of status of *medinah* of Eretz Israel (where he became known as "*Avi* (father of) *ha-Yishuv*"

Shneur Zalman of Lyady: (1745–1813); founder of Ḥabad Hassidism; pupil of Dov Baer of Mezherich; outstanding example of manner in which hassidic *ẓaddik* united in his person principal functions of all three *ketarim*

Moses Sofer: (*Ḥatam Sofer*, 1762–1830); principal instrument of *keter torah* in Hungarian Orthodoxy and founder of Orthodoxy as a separate camp; established famous *yeshiva* in Pressburg, largest since those of Bavel; undisputed leader of rabbis of Europe opposing Reform movement

Chaim Weizmann: (1874–1952); key figure in negotiations culminating in Balfour Declaration, 1917; president of WZO, 1920–1930, 1935–1946; culminated his career (at the beginning of next epoch) as first *Nasi* (president) of State of Israel

Stephen S. Wise: (1874–1949); a founder and first secretary of Federation of American Zionists; a founder and first president of American Jewish Congress; founded Free Synagogue, where he served as outstanding example of manner in which, in modern *medinot*, rabbi fulfills principal functions of *keter kehunah*

7.3 Constitutional Commentators

Ba'al Shem Tov: (Israel ben Eliezer, c. 1700–1760); founder and principal mentor of Hassidism, a major camp emphasizing virtues of devotional joy in worship of God; principal instrument of *keter kehunah* for this camp

Martin Buber: (1878–1965); influential exponent of a spiritually grounded Zionism and biblically based socialism, both rooted in a kind of neo-Hassidism; for culminating generations of epoch, major spiritual figure

Simon Dubnow: (1860–1941); founder of sociological method in Jewish history; propounded doctrine of Jewish national autonomy (Autonomism) anchored on social and cultural rather than political or territorial independence

Elijah ben Solomon:	(the "*Gaon* of Vilna," 1720–1797); led camp of opponents to *Hassidim* (*mitnagdim*); principal instrument of *keter torah* in the traditional sense
Abraham Geiger:	(1810–1874); major proponent of Reform Judaism; added to the constitutional dimensions of the *edah* by proposing that Judaism be regarded as a religion with a world mission and that its national element should therefore be eliminated
Heinrich Graetz:	(1817–1891); author of first comprehensive attempt to write history of Jews as history of living people and from Jewish point of view
Aharon David Gordon:	(1856–1922); spiritual mentor of pioneering labor Zionism
Moses Hess:	(1812–1875); precursor (albeit totally without operational influence) of political Zionism
Mordecai Kaplan:	Articulator of non-halakhic, peoplehood-oriented Judaism
Berl Katznelson:	(1887–1944); ideologist of Zionist labor movement
Abraham Isaac Kook:	(1865–1935); outstanding exponent of mystical trend in religious Zionism; during culminating generation of epoch, a principal instrument of *keter torah*, with influence in sphere of *keter kehunah*
Moses Mendelssohn:	(1729–1786); seminal philosopher of the *haskalah*; added large cosmopolitan dimension to constitutional framework of a considerable proportion of the *edah*, making possible Jewish assimilation of emancipation
Franz Rosenzweig:	(1886–1929); theologian; principal instrument of *keter kehunah* for many German Jews of his generation
Ben-Zion Meir Ḥai Uziel:	(1880–1953); *Rishon le-Zion*, 1939–1953; outstanding instrument of *keter torah* in formative period of new *yishuv* in Eretz Israel
Leopold Zunz:	(1794–1886); pioneer of modern scientific methods in Jewish studies, thereby generating emergence of camps and parties who adopted his approach

8. TERMS

Note: During this epoch, terms used in reference to the Jewish polity bear one of two main characteristics. They are generally *either* foreign derivatives *or* Hebrew revivals, usually adapted for use in modern Eretz Israel by the Zionists.

8.1 New
INDIGENOUS

Admor, abbreviation of "*adonenu, morenu, rabenu*"; title conferred on leaders of Hassidic groups

Bet Mishpat, court of law; term used in Eretz Israel to distinguish civil court from *bet din*

Histadrut, organization

Rav Rashi (chief rabbi), term used to designate principal instrument of *keter torah* in various *medinot*

Rebbe, version used in Hassidic communities of term "rabbi"; but here applied to person whose functions extended over all three *ketarim*

Sochnut, agency; as Jewish Agency, principal instrument of *keter malkhut* of Zionist camp in dealings with British mandatory government of Eretz Israel

Tenuah, movement

Tzionim (Zionists), used specifically to refer to followers of movement founded by Theodor Herzl

FOREIGN DERIVATIVE

Anti-Tzionim, opposed *Tzionim*

Board, governing body of organization or institution

Chairman, presiding officer of a modern organization or committee

Congress, term introduced into Jewish polity by Herzl

Conservative/Traditional/Neolog, movement which sought to modernize Judaism within framework of *halakhah* through liberal interpretation and selective observance

Consistoire (Fr.), form of religious organization; term introduced by Napoleon

Executive, in Hebrew *executivah*

Gemeinde (Ger.), association

President, highest office of a modern Jewish organization

Reform/Liberal/Progressive, movement which rejected halakhic Judaism as norm in favor of modern liberalism which it defined as reinterpretation of "Prophetic Judaism"

Synagogue, Jewish house of worship

8.2 Old—Change in Meaning

Agudah, association

Aliyah (ascent), process of migration to Eretz Israel

Brit, federation

Dayyan (judge), in *medinah* of Eretz Israel, a judge in religious courts, deriving his authority entirely from *keter torah*

Ḥaredim (lit. zealous), advocates of unbending adherence to traditional patterns of behavior and thought, and therefore opponents of *maskilim*

Ḥassidim (lit. loving fulfillers of the covenant obligation), here specifically signifies those who followed the teachings originating with the *Ba'al Shem Tov* as interpreted by his successors, the *zaddikim* (see later)

Ḥatzer, "court" of hassidic *rebbe*

Ḥaver (lit. comrade, in the sense of partner), in Eretz Israel used as a common greeting among members of the socialist camp or to refer to a member of an official institution, e.g., *ḥaver ha-Vaad ha-Poel ha-Tzioni*; a corporative body, e.g., *ḥaver kibbutz*; or an organization, e.g., *ḥaver ha-Histadrut ha-Tzionit*

Ḥavurah, community of *ḥassidim* or Jews seeking more intimate religious experience

Ḥalutz (lit. "one in the vanguard"—e.g., Num. 32:27), here applied to pioneers in Eretz Israel who presumably stood in the vanguard of Jewish national revival

Iggud, organization

Knesset, assembly

Kibbutz, Hassidic gathering (in Europe) or collective settlement (in Eretz Israel)

Kofer, levy; self-imposed tax employed in Eretz Israel during mandate to support the institutions of the *yishuv*

Maskilim (enlightened), followers of teachings originating with Moses Mendelssohn

Mazkir, secretary

Memshalah, government

Miflagah, party

Minyan, quorum; now used in a secular sense and thus emptied of its specifically ritual content

Mitnagdim (lit. opponents), specifically used to denote those who rejected implications and characteristics of Hassidism

Moetzah, council

Moledet, fatherland; applied by Zionists only to Eretz Israel

Moshav, cooperative settlement

Moshavah, settlement

Nasi, president

Netziv, commissioner

Pidyon (lit. redemption money), used in Hassidic *ḥavurot* to refer to tax levied to pay for upkeep of the *rebbe's ḥatzer*

Sar, used to refer to government minister

Shofet (judge), in *medinah* of Eretz Israel, a judge in a civil court, who was appointed solely by *keter malkhut*

Va'ad, council

Yishuv, settlement, specifically used to describe *medinah* of Eretz Israel

Yeridah (descent), process of migration from Eretz Israel

Zaddik (lit. righteous person), here used to refer to leader of Hassidic group, with authority in all three *ketarim*

9. BIBLIOGRAPHY

A. Altman, *Moses Mendelssohn: A Biographical Study* (Alabama, 1973).

H. Avni, *Argentina: Ha-Eretz ha-Ye'udah* (Jerusalem, 1973).

S. W. Baron, "Dutch Jerusalem," *A Social and Religious History of the Jewish People*, vol. 15 (New York, 1973), pp. 3–73.

N. C. Belth (ed.), *Not the Work of a Day* (New York, 1965).

G. Berger, *The Jewish Community Center: A Fourth Force in American Jewish Life* (New York, 1961).

J. L. Blau and S. W. Baron, *The Jews of the United States: A Documentary History* (New York, 1965).

N. W. Cohen, *Not Free to Desist. The American Jewish Committee, 1906–1966* (Philadelphia, 1972).

R. Cohen (ed.), *The Jewish Nation in Surinam: Historical Essays* (Amsterdam, 1982).

S. A. Cohen, *English Zionists and British Jews: The Communal Politics of Anglo-Jewry: 1895–1920* (Princeton, 1982).

M. Davis, *The Emergence of Conservative Judaism* (Philadelphia, 1963).

D. J. Elazar, *Community and Polity: The Organizational Dynamics of American Jewry* (Philadelphia, 1974).

D. J. Elazar and P. Medding, *Jewish Communities on the Great Frontier* (New York, 1982).

M. Eliav, *Eretz Yisrael Vi-Yishuvah be-Meah ha-19* (Jerusalem, 1978).

S. Ettinger, "The Modern Age," in *A History of the Jewish People* (ed. H. H. Ben-Sasson, part III; Cambridge, Mass., 1976).

H. P. Friedenreich, *The Jews of Yugoslavia: A Quest for Community* (Philadelphia, 1979).

A. Gal, *Brandeis of Boston* (Harvard, 1980).

A. A. Goren, *New York Jews and the Quest for Community: The Kehillah Experiment, 1908–1922* (Columbia, 1979).

O. Handlin, *Adventure in Freedom: Three Hundred Years of Jewish Life in America* (New York, 1954).

A. Hertzberg, *The French Enlightenment and the Jews* (New York, 1968).

P. Hyman, *From Dreyfus to Vichy: The Re-Making of French Jewry, 1906–1939* (Columbia, 1981).

A. Karp, "New York Chooses a Chief Rabbi," *Publication of the American Jewish Historical Society* 43 (3), March 1955, pp. 129–198.

J. Katz, *Tradition and Crisis* (Harvard, 1974).

———. *Out of the Ghetto* (Harvard, 1976).

N. Katzburg, *Hungary and the Jews* (Ramat-Gan, 1981).

J. Levitats, *The Jewish Community in Russia, 1772–1844* (New York, 1943).

M. Lissak and D. Horowitz, *Origins of the Israeli Polity: Palestine Under the Mandate* (Chicago, 1978).

J. R. Marcus, *Early American Jewry* (Philadelphia, 1953).

E. Markovitz, "Henry Pereira Mendes: Architect of the Union of Orthodox Jewish Congregations of America," *American Jewish Historical Quarterly* 55 (1966).

E. Mendelsohn, *The Jews of East Central Europe between the World Wars* (Bloomington, Indiana, 1983).

J. Niewyk, *The Jews in Weimar Germany* (Manchester, 1980).

Y. Nini, "Ha-Kehillah ha-Yehudit be-Taiman: Nosei ha-Tafkidim Shebah u-Mosdotehah miṭhilat ha-Meah ha-19 ad Teḥilat ha-Meah ha-20," *Hebrew Union College Annual* 51 (1979), pp. 9–20.

W. G. Plaut, *The Rise of Reform Judaism* (2 vols.; New York, 1963–1965).

J. Reinharz, *Fatherland or Promised Land: The Dilemma of the German Jews, 1893–1914* (Ann Arbor, 1975).

C. Reznikoff (ed.), *Louis Marshall: Champion of Liberty* (Philadelphia, 1957).

J. P. Roche, *The Quest for the Dream* (New York, 1963).

C. Roth, *A Life of Menasseh Ben Israel* (Philadelphia, 1945).

———. *The House of Nasi* (Philadelphia, 1948).

———. *History of the Jews in England* (3rd ed.; Oxford, 1964).

M. V. Schappes, *A Documentary History of the Jews in the United States, 1654–1875* (New York, 1979).

G. Scholem, *Shabbetai Zevi* (London, 1976).

G. Shimoni, *Jews and Zionism: The South African Experience* (Cape Town, 1980).

D. Shohat, *Mosad ha-Rabbanut Mi-Ta'am* (Haifa, 1976).

S. Stern, *The Court Jew* (Philadelphia, 1953).

S. Temkin, "A Century of Reform Judaism in America," *American Jewish Year Book* 74 (1973), pp. 3–75.

D. Vital, *The Origins of Zionism* (Oxford, 1975).

———. *Zionism: The Formative Years* (Oxford, 1982).

C. Vitelis, *A History of the Co-Operative Movement in Israel* (7 vols.; Jerusalem, 1966).

M. Waxman (ed.), *Tradition and Change: The Development of Conservative Judaism* (New York, 1958).

B. D. Weinryb, *The Jews of Poland* (Philadelphia, 1972).

R. Weisbord, *The Jews of Argentina: From the Inquisition to Peron* (Philadelphia, 1979).

C. Weizmann, *Trial and Error* (London, 1944).

M. Wilensky, *Hasidim u-Mitnagdim* (Jerusalem, 1970).

Y. Zimmer, *Perakim be-Toldot ha-Yehudim bi-N'sikhat Ansbach be-Meah ha-17 ve-ha-18* (Ramat-Gan, 1975).

EPOCH XIV

5708 AM–   (1948 CE–   )

Medinah ve-Am
State and People

1. DOMINANT EVENTS

1.1 Founding Events
Establishment of State of Israel (1948)
USA Jewish community becomes preeminent diaspora community
Virtual liquidation of Jewish settlement in Arab lands

2. CONSTITUTIONAL HISTORY

The Second World War marked the culmination of all the trends and tendencies of the modern era and the end of the era itself for all mankind. (The dates 1945–1948 encompass the benchmark of the transition from the modern to the postmodern eras.) For the Jewish people, the Holocaust and the establishment of the State of Israel provided the pair of decisive events that marked the crossing of the watershed into the postmodern world. In the process, the entire basis of the Jewish polity was radically changed, the locus of Jewish life shifted, and virtually every organized Jewish community was reconstituted in some way.

Central to the reconstitution was the reestablishment of a Jewish commonwealth in Israel. The restoration of a politically independent Jewish state added a new factor to the *edah*, creating a new focus of Jewish energy and concern precisely at the moment when the older foci had reached the end of their ability to attract a majority of Jews. As the 1967 crisis demonstrated decisively, Israel was not simply another Jewish community in the constellation but the center of the world for Jews.

The Jewry that greeted the new state was no longer an expanding one which was gaining population even in the face of the attrition of intermarriage and assimilation. On the contrary, it was a decimated one (even worse, for decimated means the loss of one in ten; the Jews lost one in three); a Jewry whose very physical survival had been in grave jeopardy and whose rate of loss from defections came close to equaling its birth rate. Moreover, the traditional strongholds of Jewish communal life in Europe (which were also areas with a high Jewish reproduction rate) were those that had been wiped out.

At the end of the 1940s, the centers of Jewish life had shifted decisively away from Europe to Israel and North America. By then, continental Europe as a whole ranked behind Latin America, North Africa, and Great Britain as a force in Jewish life. In fact, its Jews were almost entirely dependent upon financial and technical assistance from the United States and Israel. Except for those in the Muslim countries that were soon virtually to disappear, the major functioning Jewish communities all had acquired sufficient size to become significant factors on the Jewish scene only within the previous two generations. In effect, the shapers of those communities were still alive, and in many cases still the actual community leaders. The Jewish world had been willy-nilly thrown back to a pioneering stage.

This new epoch is still in its early years, hardly more than a single generation; hence its character is still in its formative stages. Nevertheless, with the establishment of the State of Israel in 1948 the Jewish polity began a constitutional change of revolutionary proportions, inaugurating a new epoch in Jewish constitutional history. For the first time in almost two millenia, the majority of the Jewish people were presented with the opportunity to attain citizenship in their own state. Indeed, Israel's very first law (*Hok ha-Shevut*—the Law of Return) specified that citizenship would be granted to any Jew-per-Jew wishing to live within the country.

To date, only a fraction of the *edah* have taken advantage of Israel's availability. The majority continue to live (in most cases, of their own free will) in the various *medinot* of the diaspora. Hence the dominant structural characteristic of the *edah* continues to be the absence of a binding, all-embracing political framework, although it now has a focus. The State of Israel and its various organs have a strong claim to preeminence in fields which touch upon the political, educational, and philanthropic aspects of Jewish communal life. David Ben Gurion, probably the only constitutional architect to have emerged hitherto during this epoch, was a particularly articulate exponent of the justice of that claim. However, as his correspondence with Jacob Blaustein (president of the American Jewish Committee) indicated, both the premises and the substance of Israel's statements were often contested. American Jewry (whose simultaneous rise to diaspora preeminence constituted the epoch's second founding event) has in many areas taken a different position which has, for certain purposes at least, made Israel no more than first among equals. Nevertheless, the reestablishment of a Jewish state has crystallized the *edah* as a polity, restoring a sense of political involvement among Jews and shaping a new institutional framework within which the business of the *edah* is conducted.

The diffusion of authority and influence which continues to characterize the structure of the *edah* has taken various forms. Some of these need be touched upon only in passing, since in essence they seem to constitute no more than overspills from developments already apparent toward the close of the previous epoch whose transformation is still under way. Most noticeably is this so in the case of the differentials pertaining within and between various *medinot* and *kehillot*. At this level of inquiry, many of the structural patterns previously noted in Latin America, western Europe, and the countries which once comprised the British Empire have not altered substantially. Virtually all, however, underwent some serious degree of reconstitution after World War II, itself one of the *edah*'s principal tasks after the war. In Israel and the United States, this reconstitution involved major institutional changes.

More striking is the reflections of the *edah*'s diffusion of authority as reflected in each of the three *ketarim*. In the sphere of the *keter malkhut*, for instance, influence and power are here described as being spread over a comparatively large network of single- and multi-purpose functional authorities, most of which do not aspire to be more than functional authorities, but all of which acknowledge the place of the State of Israel at the fulcrum of the network. The *keter kehunah*, similarly, is portrayed here as a conglomeration of synagogue movements and their rabbinates (who are mainly responsible for ritual and pastoral functions), each of which manages—independently—various ritual functions in a manner which it deems appropriate to its own traditions, perspectives, and environment. The fact that these movements have combined themselves into frameworks with worldwide aspirations such as the World Union for Progressive Judaism and the World Council of Synagogues merely underlines the new organizational character of the *edah*.

Sectoralism is most pronounced, however, in the instance of the *keter torah*. Some circumscribed factions within the *edah* do continue to abide by the decisions of the traditional rabbinate—as expressed, for instance, by the occasional pronouncements of the *Moetzet Gedolei ha-Torah* or its individual members. Far more, however, take their cue in this domain from a kaleidoscopic spectrum of authorities. Their range stretches from the professorial community of Jewish scholars who influence Jews' understanding of what is expected of them as Jews to the rabbinical seminaries of the Orthodox, Conservative, and Reform camps, who may use traditional devices for ruling on matters of Torah but often in untraditional ways, and thence to the *yeshi-*

vot and the *rebbes* of various emigre Hassidic communities who have re-established themselves in the principal cities of Israel and the United States from which they have developed multicountry networks.

The dissonance of the *keter torah* which has resulted from this situation can perhaps best be understood as a reflection, and expression, of the absence as yet of a uniformly acceptable constitutional referent for the entire *edah*. The tendency toward various—and variant—interpretations of *Torat Moshe*, already noted during the culminating generations of the previous epoch, has now become exacerbated. Indeed, it is a singular sign of the times that if a single empirical definition of the constitution is to be identified at all, the term *Torat Moshe* (which has here been used continuously since Epoch III) has to be reinterpreted for a majority of Jews, if used at all. The empirical reality is that the norms by which self-confessing Jews would like to live their lives are interpreted through various prisms of which the traditional prism is now only one among several. While most Jews may still perceive *Torat Moshe* to be their guide, most no longer understand it in traditional ways.

As much is further reflected in the multiplicity of camps and parties which now attempt to exert an influence on the life of the *edah*, and of its various constituent *medinot* and *aratzot*. Broadly speaking, the principal camps can be termed: the Orthodox, the non-Orthodox religious, and the Zionist. These camps are separate but not mutually exclusive. Presented diagrammatically, they ought to be viewed as a triangle (a device which stresses their points of overlap as well as their distinctiveness). The Mizrachi party, for instance, straddles both the Zionist and the Orthodox camp, viewing its Zionism as one expression of its orthodoxy. Increasingly, too, do the Conservative and Reform movements find themselves linked with Zionism. At the same time, the Neturei Karta, the secularist Zionists, and the surviving classical Reform elements remain separated in their respective camps.

Whatever its form of organization, the primary fact of Jewish communal life today is its voluntary character. While there are some differences from country to country in the degree of actual freedom to be Jewish or not, the virtual disappearance of the remaining legal and even social or cultural barriers to individual free choice in all but a handful of countries has made free association the dominant characteristic of Jewish life in the postmodern era. Consequently, the first task of each Jewish community is to learn to deal with the particular local manifestation of this freedom. This task is a major factor in determining the direction of the reconstitution of Jewish life in this generation.

The new voluntarism extends itself into the internal life of the Jewish community as well, generating pluralism even in previously free but relatively homogeneous or monolithic community structures. This pluralism is increased by the breakdown of the traditional reasons for being Jewish and the rise of new incentives for Jewish association. At the same time, the possibilities for organizing a pluralistic Jewish community have also been enhanced by these new incentives and the communications network; a set of interacting institutions which, while preserving their own structural integrity and filling their own functional roles, are informed by shared patterns of culture, activated by a shared system of organizations, and governed by shared leadership cadres. The character of the matrix and its communications network varies from community to community with particularly sharp variations separating the six basic types. In some cases, the network is connected through a common center which serves as the major (but rarely, if ever, the exclusive) channel for communication. In others, the network forms a matrix without any real center, with the lines of communication criss-crossing in all directions. In all cases, the boundaries of the community are revealed only when the pattern of the network is uncovered. The pattern itself stands revealed only when both of its components are—namely, its institutions and organizations with their respective roles and the way in which communications are passed between them.

The pattern itself is inevitably a dynamic one. That is to say, there is rarely a fixed division of authority and influence but, rather, one that varies from time to time and usually from issue to issue, with different elements in the matrix taking on different "loads" at different times and relative to different issues. Since the community is a voluntary one, persuasion rather than compulsion, influence rather than power, are the only tools available for making and executing policies. This, too, works to strengthen its character as a communications network since the character, quality, and relevance of what is communicated and the way in which it is communicated frequently determine the extent of the authority and influence of the parties to the communication.

The reconstitution of the *edah* is only in its beginning stages; its final form for this epoch cannot yet be foreseen. At this writing, the Jewish people is in the buildup period of the second generation of the postmodern epoch and is actively engaged in trying to work through a new constitutional synthesis, both political and religious.

3. CONSTITUTION

Torat Moshe as variously understood and interpreted in traditional and nontraditional ways, with a new emphasis on the rest of the *Tanakh*—in the diaspora emphasizing "prophetic Judaism" and in Medinat Israel, the national history and culture of ancient Israel—plus the unwritten commitment to Jewish unity and peoplehood as embodied in the network of institutions serving the *edah*

3.1 Constitutional Issues
Reconstitution of organized Jewish life after World War II
Israel–diaspora relationships

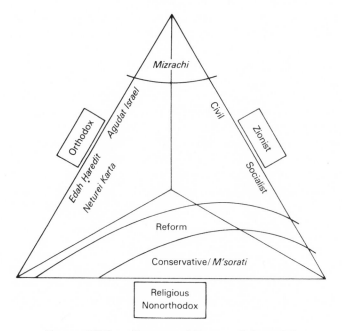

FIGURE XIV-1. Camps and Parties of the *Edah*

Security and welfare of State of Israel
Assimilation in its various facets and citizenship in the *edah*

3.2 Camps and Parties

Orthodoxy in its various aspects (e.g., Agudath Israel, Hassidic groups, modern Orthodox)

Zionists or New Sadducees (those, particularly Israelis, seeking to express their Judaism through a Jewish civil religion)

Non-Orthodox religious movements, seeking a path between Orthodoxy and modernism (e.g., Conservative and Reform Judaism)

4. CONSTITUTIONAL STRUCTURE OF THE *EDAH*

There is a network of single- and multi-purpose functional authorities, no single one of which encompasses the entire gamut of Jewish political interests, although several have attempted to do so in specific areas: "national institutions"—e.g., Jewish Agency, World Zionist Organization, Jewish National Fund; multicountry associations—e.g., ORT, World Jewish Congress; educational institutions defined as under the auspices of the entire Jewish people—e.g., the universities in Israel; and organizations under more specific local sponsorship whose defined sphere of activity is multicountry—e.g., the Joint Distribution Committee.

Another way of grouping the multicountry associations is by their principal goals. Here are the broad categories, with prominent examples for each (a more inclusive list appears later in Table 4):

Principal Goal Characteristics	Organization
Political—general purpose	World Zionist Organization (WZO)
	World Jewish Congress (WJC)
Political—special purpose	World Conference on Soviet Jewry
Distributive	Conference on Jewish Material Claims Against Germany
	Memorial Foundation for Jewish Culture
Services—operational	World ORT Union
Services—coordinating	European Council of Jewish Communities
Religious	World Union for Progressive Judaism
	Agudas Israel World Organization
Association—fraternal	Bnai Brith International Council
Association—special interest	World Sephardi Federation
	World Union of Jewish Students

The political associations listed here as "general" are those concerned with the status of the Jewish people as a whole; in this they are both outer-directed to the non-Jewish world and inner-directed to the Jewish community. Although the Israeli government has largely preempted political activity on the world scene, it has not explicitly claimed to act as the diplomatic agent for the Jewish people beyond its borders. This leaves some room for diplomatic activity by the Jewish nongovernmental organizations, especially where Israel is not represented or is particularly limited in its access.

4.1 Principal Instruments, Officers, and Functions
KETER MALKHUT

The outstanding features of this epoch are the shift to preeminence of the *keter malkhut* and the emergence of a coherent set of institutions embodying the *keter malkhut* on an *edah*-wide basis. While power and influence are dispersed among a number of authorities, most of which lay claim to preeminence in particular spheres which fall within the provenance of the domain, they are increasingly tied together by a sense of common purpose, shared leadership, and programmatic collaboration. Most of these can be perceived as outgrowths or continuations of the organizations which emerged toward the end of the previous generation, including those discussed in the following text.

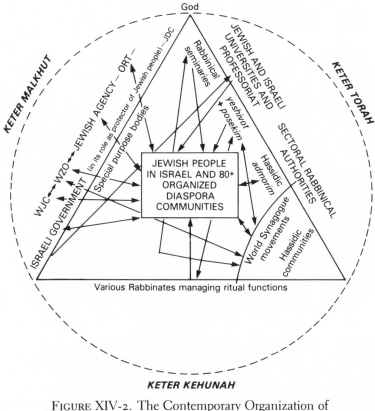

FIGURE XIV-2. The Contemporary Organization of
the *Edah*

JEWISH AGENCY FOR ISRAEL (JAFI)
Originally established by the World Zionist Organization in 1922 to represent
world Jewry in Mandatory Palestine, it became the governing body of the Jewish "state within a state" prior to 1948. Its status as the arm of world Jewry was
reaffirmed by the Israeli Knesset in 1952 through legislation which was formalized through a covenant between the Jewish Agency and the State of Israel. Its principal responsibility under the covenant was to handle the mass
immigration of Jews into Israel and various aspects of their settlement. Essentially an instrument of the WZO until 1971 (except for a brief period after
1929), it was then reconstituted to include the "Non-Zionist" representatives
of the diaspora communities and their fund-raising arms, as equal partners.
The 1952 covenant was further revised in 1979 to strengthen JAFI as an instrumentality of the Jewish people and the diaspora role within it.

JAFI functions in the fields of education, housing, immigration, settlement, and urban rehabilitation, and provides certain social services. It remains closely tied to the WZO which is, in many respects, its alter ego for work in the diaspora. It is governed by an Assembly of several hundred members, a Board of Governors of over sixty, and an Executive.

WORLD ZIONIST ORGANIZATION (WZO)

The WZO was founded at the first Zionist Congress (1897) to obtain a "legally secured, publicly recognized national home for the Jewish people." That goal was reached formally when the Balfour Declaration became part of the League of Nations Mandate for Palestine (1922). The WZO was acknowledged by Britain as the "Jewish agency" charged with representing the world Jewish interest in the implementation of the Mandate. It then turned to mobilizing support for building the national home and securing a Jewish state in Eretz Israel.

Today the WZO is charged with implementing the "Jerusalem Program" of 1968, defining as one of the aims of Zionism "The Unity of the Jewish People and the Centrality of Israel in Jewish life; . . . the Preservation of the Identity of the Jewish People through the Fostering of Jewish and Hebrew Education and of Jewish Spiritual and Cultural Values; the Protection of Jewish Rights Everywhere." This makes explicit WZO's new role as a diaspora-oriented body, where its original purpose had been to harness world Jewry's efforts on behalf of the *yishuv*. Its functions are ideology- or diaspora-oriented, or deal with areas that cannot be subsumed under the headings for which tax-exempt philanthropic funds in the United States and elsewhere are being allocated. Although agricultural settlement work on behalf of new immigrants is the domain of the Jewish Agency, it is WZO which finances agricultural projects in the administered territories, since philanthropic funds cannot be used for these.

WZO retains a fifty percent partnership in the Jewish Agency, thereby preserving for itself the legitimacy that comes with responsibility for the practical work of immigration and absorption. It was also given exclusive responsibility for encouraging and implementing immigration from the countries of the free world.

Structurally, WZO is a federation of countrywide Zionist organizations. Most of these constituent bodies are, in effect, extensions or affiliates of Israeli parties, whose ideologies, however, became frozen at a certain point and, as a rule, do not reflect the evolution, mergers, and splits occurring in the Israeli party system. The World Confederation of General Zionists, for example, retains nomenclature that ceased to exist in Israel two decades ago.

The WZO is governed by the World Zionist Congress, which, in the Jewish world, comes closest to being an elected parliament (apart from Israel's Knesset). Seats in the Congress, which meets every four years, are allocated geographically in the following proportion: thirty-eight percent for Israel, twenty-nine percent for the United States, and thirty-three percent for the other diaspora countries. In Israel delegates were chosen by the political parties in proportion to their representation in the Knesset. The voting outside Israel is largely by party lists, so that the 559-member Congress reflects, to a considerable extent, the party-political spectrum in Israel. The Congress elects the Executive, in which the major parties are represented, and the General Council. The latter meets once a year between congresses.

The party composition of the Zionist movement long antedates the establishment of the state. From its very inception, the movement was fragmented, so that the congresses were assemblies of parties, as well as of delegates. Despite a widespread desire for structural changes after 1948, WZO found it impossible to transcend the party structure, which undoubtedly reduced its effectiveness as a mass movement in the diaspora. (In Israel, WZO's function as a representative body was superfluous after 1917 when democratically elected parliamentary bodies were introduced to speak for the Jewish *yishuv*). Reform was achieved by separating the Jewish Agency—the implementing machinery —from WZO—the political-ideological structure. An attempt was also made to dilute the political character of WZO by permitting individuals to affiliate directly with countrywide Zionist federations without first joining political groups. Furthermore, nonpolitical groups, such as WIZO (Women's International Zionist Organization), the Maccabi World Union, the World Sephardi Federation, and American synagogue movements, are enrolled in WZO as associate members. Full membership, however, remains reserved for the political groups.

In the federated structure that is WZO, the influence of the center is greater than that of the sum of all its parts. This is because the center represents Israel to the diaspora bodies: it originates programs, has a highly articulated bureaucracy, and allocates the financial resources. On the other hand, WZO's status in the diaspora is weakened by the lack of clarity about its tasks in the era of statehood. The impact of the late David Ben Gurion's openly critical attitude toward WZO has not yet worn off. WZO's aims are broad enough and its apparatus wide-ranging enough for it to assume the character of a conglomerate among multicountry Jewish organization; but its political structure sets limits to its acceptance on a broad popular basis.

WORLD JEWISH CONGRESS (WJC)

The World Jewish Congress has as its main purpose the defense of Jewish rights, and to that end it aims to be representative of the widest possible spectrum of world Jewry. Its specific activities in recent years have included intervention on behalf of Jews in Arab countries; pressure for the prosecution of Nazi war criminals and for indemnification payments to their victims; contacts with Christian church bodies on questions of Israel and anti-Semitism; assistance to small Jewish communities for cultural needs; relations with international organizations, including the International Committee of the Red

Cross, the Organization of American States, and the Council of Europe; espousal of the cause of Soviet Jewry; and, above all, support of Israel in its diplomatic struggles.

Like the WZO, the World Jewish Congress has a federative structure. In theory it is a confederation of countrywide representative community bodies, with the central body deliberately limiting itself in scope. The members—independent community organizations—are free to determine their own policies locally. WJC's constitution prohibits it from operating or speaking in a given country unless its local constituent agrees, except where no organized community exists or where a community cannot freely express its will.

On the other hand, WJC may set up branches in countries without a "representative" organization or where the leading groups are unwilling to participate. Thus, when the Board of Deputies of British Jews refused to affiliate, WJC established a British Section. In the United States, the American Jewish Congress was intended to function as the American arm of WJC, but when differences arose between the two groups, WJC established a North American Section, which has recently begun to enroll the rabbinical and congregational associations as affiliates. On the other hand, the Canadian Jewish Congress and DAIA (the representative organization of Argentine Jewry) are, as representative organizations, directly affiliated with the WJC.

The WJC Executive functions through four regional branches, each with its own constitution—in North America, South America, Europe, and Israel—that mediate between the parent body and affiliates. The European branch, which operates primarily in Western Europe, also maintains ties with community organizations in the Communist bloc. The Israeli branch does not have constituent organizations. Composed in keeping with the ubiquitous "party key," its eighteen members are drawn from the spectrum of parliamentary parties.

Since its members are organizations, the number of individuals actually connected with WJC is relatively small. Some 400 to 500 delegates attend the WJC quadrennial assemblies. Between assemblies, an executive committee of 120 meets annually, and every member organization sends at least one delegate. There is also a governing council of 35, a secretary-general in Geneva, and a director-general in New York. The WJC is officially headquartered in Geneva. Its cultural department is headquartered in Israel, the political department in Paris, and its policy research institute is in London. In 1981, the center of its governance was transferred to New York. Among the members of the governing council is a strong contingent of prominent rabbis and diaspora Zionist leaders.

WJC has complemented WZO in areas where the latter could not operate, but, at the same time, has also been its potential rival. For this reason, the Zionist leadership's attitude toward WJC from the beginning has been one of ambivalence. In the 1930s, Dr. Weizmann, as WZO president, stayed away from the founding assembly of the Congress, persisting in his resolve to eschew Jewish politics in the diaspora. Although a majority of the Zionist Congress voted to designate WJC as the most suitable instrument for the protection of Jewish rights, thereby ensuring WZO representation in (and in recent years, subsidization of) WJC, the concern that diaspora interests might compete with those of the *yishuv* was never far submerged and came to the fore again in the era of the state. The notion of an organization representing world Jewry which might espouse a position independent of Israel had little appeal to the state's policymakers. A second, equally substantial factor in WJC's inability to become the representative organization of world Jewry was the unwillingness of the major Jewish organizations in the United States and Britain to become part of WJC structure.

CONFERENCE ON JEWISH MATERIAL CLAIMS AGAINST GERMANY

The Conference on Jewish Material Claims Against Germany (Claims Conference) is an effective, special purpose, multicountry association with two tasks: (1) to press (in conjunction with the government of Israel) Jewish claims against Germany and (2) to distribute the funds received among eligible beneficiaries. The Conference was established in 1951, and ended its active role in 1965 with the fulfillment of its stated goal. Its formal existence is being maintained for the performance of certain ongoing tasks. Among these are monitoring the implementation of German legislation on restitution, pressing for further legislation (also in East Germany), administering a fund for former community leaders, and supporting non-Jews who had helped rescue Jews and who are in financial straits.

By 1965 the Claims Conference had allocated $110 million, of which three-fourths was applied to the relief, rehabilitation, and resettlement of Nazi victims outside Israel and the balance was used mainly for cultural and educational reconstruction. Grants were made to some 250 Jewish communities and institutions in 30 countries, primarily in Europe, as well as for research and publications by authors who were Nazi victims. Institutions for the commemoration of the Holocaust were also beneficiaries.

The Conference was founded on 21 October 1951 in New York on the initiative of the Israeli Government and the WZO–Jewish Agency and with the assistance of the WJC. Twenty-two organizations from the United States, England, Canada, Australia, South Africa, France, and Argentina participated. Protracted negotiations led to separate agreements by the German Federal Republic with Israel and with the Claims Conference. According to them, the Claims Conference had three functions: (1) to distribute the funds it received for the relief, rehabilitation, and resettlement of Jewish victims of Nazi persecution living outside of Israel; (2) to seek enactment of better and more extensive legislation in Germany for the indemnification of victims of Nazism; and (3) to participate with the Jewish Agency in distributing funds for the relief and other needs of refugees in Israel.

In the distributive phase that followed there was remarkable consensus among the many divergent organizational interests represented. This was despite strong ideological opposition to the idea of accepting payments from Germany, which only gradually receded in the "Jewish street." The success of the Claims Conference in both its diplomatic and its distributive tasks can be attributed to the following factors: its representative character; its clearly delimited goal; the challenge of *bona fide* diplomatic activity with two sovereign states in place of the lobbying and shadowboxing that is normally the lot of nonsovereign entities; the opportunity to be a full-fledged partner of Israel in the negotiations; the high caliber of the negotiators; the early agreement on criteria and priorities for the distribution of the funds; and the utilization of established facilities rather than becoming an operating agency or creating new instrumentalities.

MEMORIAL FOUNDATION FOR JEWISH CULTURE

In 1964, the Claims Conference established the Memorial Foundation for Jewish Culture to serve as a living memorial to the six million who perished in the Holocaust and transferred to it the funds which had remained after German payments ceased. This base endowment of about $10 million was augmented by additional amounts in subsequent years, so that the Foundation has been able to distribute about $1.25 million annually. The Memorial Foundation maintains quite an elaborate apparatus for the implementation of a financially rather modest program. It has forty-seven member organizations, each of which sends three representatives to the board of directors. Eighteen organizations are of the multicountry type (thirteen have the word "World" in their names) and twenty-nine are territorial, the latter including five academic and cultural groups in Israel. Thus the Memorial Foundation is even more inclusive than the Claims Conference. Like the latter, it has a small professional staff, whose job consists mainly of sifting applications for support (these amount to several times the available financing) and making recommendations for allocations to the board and the twenty-five-member executive committee.

WORLD ORT UNION

The World ORT Union (Organization for Rehabilitation through Training) is a service agency which is multicountry in all respects: functional, administrative, and financial. Originating as a small operation in Eastern Europe before World War I, ORT developed programs that met essential needs in countries of resettlement after World War II and now trains Jews in sophisticated technological specialties. Operations are conducted in twenty-four countries and over 100,000 students are enrolled in vocational-training courses of a wide variety, making ORT the largest nongovernmental system of vocational education in the world. Its major center of activity is Israel, with an enrollment of some 60,000. Other programs are conducted in Iran, Ethiopia, Morocco, and India; in Argentina, Venezuela, and Uruguay; in France, Italy, and the United States.

The World ORT Union, which has its seat in Geneva, is a federation of autonomous national organizations, constituted as an association according to the Swiss civil code. It makes available to the local groups financial subsidies, training of personnel, and overall planning. The Union is governed by a congress meeting every six years, to which member organizations send elected delegates. A central committee of 150 meets between congresses; it, in turn, elects an executive committee of twenty to forty members, which convenes biennially. The president of the World ORT Union is an American, as is its executive director; the executive committee chairman is French. In the lower administrative echelons, the staff is multinational.

ORT also conducts training programs in third-world countries; these are sponsored and financed by the United States foreign aid program and by international institutions, primarily the World Bank. The Central ORT Training Institute in Anières, Switzerland, has been asked by the Swiss Foreign Ministry to train teaching personnel for countries to which Switzerland wishes to give technical assistance.

JOINT DISTRIBUTION COMMITTEE (JDC)

A major share of multicountry activity in the fields of education, welfare, and community organization is performed by organizations sponsored by individual *medinot*. Outstanding among them is the Joint Distribution Committee, the chief overseas welfare agency of American Jewry. The JDC was founded in 1914 as a union of three separate American overseas relief bodies and is confederated for fund-raising purposes with the U.S. United Israel Appeal in the United Jewish Appeal. Its headquarters are in New York.

While sponsored and governed by American Jews, its staff is multicountry. Its range of operations is probably greater than that of any other Jewish body. The JDC organizes and finances rescue, relief, and rehabilitation programs for imperiled and needy Jews throughout the world; conducts a wide range of health, welfare, education, and rehabilitation programs; and provides aid to cultural and religious institutions. It serves some 430,000 Jews in 25 countries, including Israel. Its funds contribute to the support of many other Jewish organizations and it works with most of the other *edah* bodies in the fulfillment of its mission.

ALLIANCE ISRAÉLITE UNIVERSELLE

The France-based Alliance Israélite Universelle has an illustrious record of establishing educational institutions in the Muslim world. With the demise of Jewish communities in those countries, it has been on the decline although it continues to do important work in Israel and France as well as in the remnant communities it has traditionally served.

EUROPEAN COUNCIL OF JEWISH COMMUNITY SERVICES

The most recently established multicountry association of consequence is the European Council of Jewish Community Services, a regional body which serves as a forum for community leaders from some seventy communities in eighteen European countries. The Council is the successor to the Standing Conference of European Jewish Communities, which was organized by JDC in the 1950s and functioned in close liaison with JDC's European office in Geneva. Its purpose was to stem the slow disintegration of Jewish life in postwar Europe and to help the communities transcend their local preoccupation in the search for common solutions. When the Conference transformed itself into the Council, its offices were moved to Paris, and the appointment of a French communal worker as secretary general, in place of a JDC staff member, completed the agency's "Europeanization." The Jewish community of Great Britain is part of the new organization; the Council's publication, *Exchange*, is written in English. A meeting of the Council in Berlin, in May 1972, was considered the point of its "turning from a liaison body into a large international Jewish organization." The assembly adopted a five-year program, which provided for commissions on fund-raising, young leadership training, and social services, and activated a Europe-wide Community Center Association. In its scope and functions, the European Council is not dissimilar to the U.S. Council of Jewish Federations (CJF) and, indeed, maintains consultative contact with its American counterpart.

These bodies have developed a more or less common institutional structure which can be diagrammed as follows:

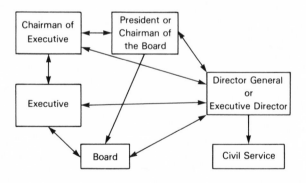

GOVERNMENT OF ISRAEL

The government of the State of Israel now acts as a principal defender of the physical welfare of the entire Jewish people under certain circumstances and claims to do so in the name of the entire *edah* (e.g., the capture and trial of Adolph Eichmann). Thus, the security forces of Israel sometimes defend all Jews, the Knesset of Israel plays a major role in defining their status as Jews, and the Prime Minister or President speaks in their name. The government of

| Goals | | | Structure and Membership | | | | Mode of Operation | | |
| Fraternal | | Youth | Federative | | | | | | |
General	Special Interest	Sports	Roof Organization	New Body	Autonomous	Individual Membership	Operational	Consultative	Distributive
					X		X		
					X		X		
X			X				Y	X	
				X					X
			X					X	
			X					X	
			X					X	
X						X		X	
					X		X		
					X				X
		X	X				X		
				X					X
					X		X		
			X				X		
					X		X		
			X				X		
				X				X	
			X					X	
		X	X					X	
				X				X	
	X		X				Y	X	
	Y	X				X	Y	X	
			X				Y	X	
			X				X	Y	
		X					X	Y	

the State of Israel is also exceptional in that it possesses an institutional structure which is a direct reflection of the workings of parliamentary democracy
within *Medinat Yisrael*.

KETER TORAH

Due to simultaneous multiplicity of interpretations of the constitution, this
domain is clearly sectoral. Within it, older institutions and officers continue
to serve various segments of the *edah* in more or less traditional ways at the
same time as some new institutions emerge to serve other groups in new ways,
some changing to maintain traditional patterns. Further characteristic of the
lack of unity of the *keter* is the fact that some of these institutions overlap in
both competence and thrust. For example, both the Agudas Israel World Organization and the Mizrachi World Union were founded essentially for political purposes; the first to safeguard the interests of Orthodox Jewry outside the
Zionist framework, the second to do so within it.

Outstanding among the survivors from the previous epoch are a limited
number of *posekim* with *edah*-wide influence within their own camp, and a
number of similarly placed *yeshivot*. The chief *posekim* of the ultra-Orthodox
are organized as *Moetzet Gedolei ha-Torah* (Council of Torah Sages). Hassidic
groups, whose centers are now transplanted either to Israel or to the USA also
survive (although their principal officer is now generally a *rebbe*, rather than a
zaddik). Conspicious among the latter are the Chabad (Lubavitcher) Hassidim,
one of the very few Hassidic sects who attempt to reach out to the *edah* in its
entirety.

Non-Orthodox representatives of this *keter* are found primarily in the theological seminaries of the respective movements, reflecting the combination of
rabbinical and professorial status which marks the effort of the non-Orthodox
to combine modern and traditional forms. Since the Reform movement is
much less oriented to the very concept of the *keter torah* than the Conservative, this phenomenon is more pronounced among the latter.

Prominent among the new institutions in this *keter* are the professors of
Jewish studies at Israeli and other universities. These, and certain others
drawn from the intellectual community, address themselves to Jewish concerns in an academic fashion, and in so doing lay the groundwork for new
interpretations of the constitution.

KETER KEHUNAH

The *keter kehunah* is comprised of various rabbinates and synagogue bodies
who essentially occupy themselves with ritual functions and their management. In some cases, instruments of this *keter* have become more highly organized than at any time since the destruction of the Second Temple. The world
synagogue movements, together with the organized rabbinates in the UK and
Israel, provide outstanding examples. The latter are especially important because they provide examples of the manner in which *medinah*-based instruments of this *keter* now attempt to perform an *edah*-wide function, e.g., the

A Typology of Jewish Multicountry Associations

Name of Association	Goals				
	Religious	Service		Political	
		Education Culture	Welfare Community Organization	Rights	Ideology
1. Agudas Israel World Organization	X*				Y*
2. Alliance Israelite Universelle[1]		X		Y	
3. Bnai Brith International Council		Y	Y		
4. Conference on Jewish Material Claims Against Germany		X	X		
5. World Conference of Jewish Organizations (COJO)		Y		X	
6. Consultative Council of Jewish Organizations				X	
7. European Council of Jewish Community Services			X		
8. International Conference of Jewish Communal Service			Y		
9. Jewish Agency for Israel		X	X		
10. Jewish Colonization Association		X	X		
11. Maccabi World Union					
12. Memorial Foundation for Jewish Culture		X			
13. Mizrachi World Union	X				Y
14. ORT (World ORT Union)		X			
15. OSE (Oeuvre de Secours aux Enfants)[2]			X		
16. Women's International Zionist Organization		X	X		Y
17. World Conference on Soviet Jewry[3]				X	
18. World Council of Synagogues	X				
19. World Federation of YMHAs and Jewish Community Centers					
20. World Jewish Congress				X	
21. World Sephardi Federation					
22. World Union of Jewish Students					
23. World Union for Progressive Judaism	X				
24. World Zionist Organization					X
25. Zionist Youth Movements Bnei Akiva, Habonim, etc.)					Y

*X = primary; Y = secondary.

[1] Although no longer multicountry by our criteria, the Alliance began its career in 1860 as the first "universal" Jewish association in modern times; it therefore deserves a place in this table.

[2] OSE is included because of its historic multicountry character; today, to all intents and purposes, it is a French organization.

[3] This is an *ad hoc* association with a single purpose. Unlike the more permanent multipurpose political associations, it has been able to enlist across-the-board participation.

Israeli Chief Rabbinate provides services for a number of small communities (e.g., Iran, India), as does the UK rabbinate of the United Synagogue for some of the communities in countries which once comprised the British Empire. The World Council of Synagogues (Conservative, established 1957) and the World Union for Progressive Judaism (Reform, established 1926) are basically associations of countrywide congregational bodies.

5. *MEDINOT*

Jews are known to reside in 121 countries, 82 of which have permanent organized communities. At least three and perhaps as many as twelve others are remnant communities where a relative handful of Jews have custody of the few institutions that have survived in the wake of the emigration of the majority of the Jewish population. A number are transient communities where American or Israeli Jews temporarily stationed in some Asian or African country create such basic Jewish institutions (e.g., religious services, schools) as they need. Only 21 countries with known Jewish residents have no organized Jewish life.

The largest *medinot/aratzot* are as follows:

United States	5.9 million
Israel	3.4 million
USSR	2.1 million
France	650,000
United Kingdom	400,000
Argentina	350,000
Canada	310,000
Brazil	150,000
South Africa	120,000
Hungary	80,000
Australia	70,000

In the late 1940s and the 1950s the reconstruction and the reconstitution of existing communities, and the founding of new ones, were the order of the day throughout the Jewish world. The Jewish communities of continental Europe all underwent periods of reconstruction or reconstitution in the wake of wartime losses, changes in the formal status of religious communities in their host countries, emigration to Israel, internal European migrations, and the introduction of new, especially Communist, regimes. Those of the Muslim countries were transformed in response to the convergence of two factors: the establishment of Israel and the anticolonial revolutions in Asia and Africa. The greater portion of the Jewish population in those countries was transferred to Israel and organized Jewish life beyond the maintenance of local congregations virtually came to an end in all of them except Iran, Morocco, and Tunisia.

The English-speaking Jewries and, to a somewhat lesser extent, those of Latin America were faced with the more complex task of adapting their organizational structures to three new purposes: to assume responsibilities passed to them as a result of the destruction of European Jewry, to play a major role in supporting Israel, and to accommodate internal changes in communities still in the process of acculturation. Many of the transient Jewish communities in Asia and Africa were actually founded or given organized form in this period, while others, consisting in the main of transient merchants or refugees, were abandoned.

At first, the patterns of *medinah*-wide Jewish communal organization followed those of the previous epoch with some modifications, but as the postmodern epoch begins to plant its own imprint on the *edah*, the differences in status and structure are diminishing. A common organizational pattern is emerging, consisting of certain basic elements, including the following:

1. Government-like institutions, whether "roof" organizations or separate institutions serving discrete functions, that play roles and provide services on all planes (countrywide, local, and, where used, intermediate) which, under other conditions, would be played, provided, or controlled—predominantly or exclusively—by governmental authorities (for instance, external relations, defense, education, social welfare, and public—that is, communal—finance), specifically, a more or less comprehensive fund-raising and social planning body; a representative body for external relations; a Jewish education service agency; a vehicle or vehicles for assisting Israel and other Jewish communities; and various health and welfare institutions

2. Localistic institutions and organizations that provide a means for attaching people to Jewish life on the basis of their most immediate and personal interests and needs, specifically, congregations organized into one or more synagogue unions, federations, or confederations, and local cultural and recreational centers, often federated or confederated with one another

3. General-purpose mass-based organizations, operating countrywide on all planes, that function to articulate community values, attitudes, and policies; provide the energy and motive force for crystallizing the communal consensus that grows out of those values, attitudes, and policies; and maintain institutionalized channels of communication between the community's leaders and "actives" ("cosmopolitans") and the broad base of the affiliated Jewish population ("locals") for dealing with the problems and tasks facing the community in the light of the consensus, specifically, a Zionist federation and its constituent organizations, as well as fraternal organizations

4. Special interest organizations which, by serving specialized interests in the community on all planes, function to mobilize concern and support for the various programs conducted by the community and to apply pressure for their expansion, modification, and improvement

Politically Independent State—Israel

The State of Israel is *sui generis* in the Jewish world, not only because it is politically sovereign but because of its character as a Jewish society functioning in a self-consciously Jewish manner in an epoch which witnessed the disappearance of the last of such societies in the diaspora. Thus, although most of its governmental institutions are adapted from liberal European models, they are described in Israel in a political terminology which, for the most part, invokes the slogans and symbols of the earlier epochs (IV–VII) of Jewish national sovereignty.

Israel constitutes a focal point for the entire *edah* in the domains of both the *keter torah* and *keter malkhut*. In both, its institutions serve the entire *edah*, often claiming preeminence throughout the *edah*.

Keter Malkhut

Knesset (Assembly): Israel's supreme legislative body, elected by universal adult suffrage on a party (*miflagah*) basis through proportional representation

Memshalah (Government): The government of Israel is organized as a cabinet with collective responsibility. It must have the confidence of the Knesset; hence it is invariably based on a coalition of parties and is constituted through a formal coalition agreement

Rosh Memshalah (Head of government): Prime Minister, must be member of the Knesset

Sarim (Ministers; singular: *sar*): Members of the government, most of whom are also the political heads of *misradim* (departments); can be members of Knesset and most are

Misradim (Departments; singular: *misrad*). Major ones include:
   Otzar (treasury)
   Ḥutz (foreign affairs)
   Bitaḥon (defense)
   Pnim (interior)
   Datot (religions)

Nasi (President): Head of the Israeli state; elected by the Knesset for a fixed term

Batei Mishpat (courts; singular: *bet mishpat*): Civil courts ranging from *Bet Mishpat Elyon* (supreme courts) through district and magistrates courts

Keter Torah

Moetzet ha-Rabbanut ha-Rashit (Council of the Chief Rabbinate): Supreme state body governing Jewish religious activities

Rabbanim Rashi'im (Chief rabbis): Sephardic (formally titled *Rishon le-Zion—*

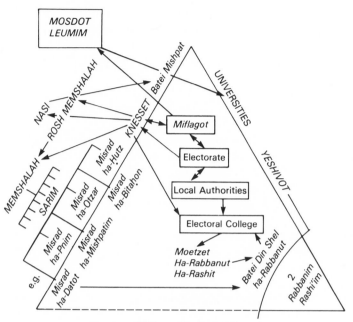

FIGURE XIV-3. *Medinat Yisrael*

the first of Zion) and Ashkenazic; preside over *Moetzet ha-Rabbanut ha-Rashit* and supreme halakhic authorities in ritual matters for their respective communities; elected by an electoral college composed of state and local religious and governmental officials

Batei Din (courts; singular: *bet din*): Rabbinical courts established under state law with exclusive jurisdiction in personal status matters and concurrent jurisdiction in most civil matters

Yeshivot: Informal centers of halakhic authority, some of whose heads sometimes intervene in political matters

Universities: Generally secular institutions, certain of whose professors have become the principal articulators of non-Orthodox Jewish visions and the teachings associated with them, especially Zionism

Keter Kehunah

Tasks essentially handled by various instrumentalities of *keter torah* plus *Misrad ha-Datot*

Diaspora medinot or aratzot

The diaspora *medinot* or *aratzot* have almost invariably retained (or restored) the tripartite structure of the three *ketarim*. In most cases, functions in each domain are now fulfilled by a variety of institutions, headed by formally elected officers and staffed by a professional civil service. Despite the general adherence to this pattern, distinct organizational variations can be discerned.

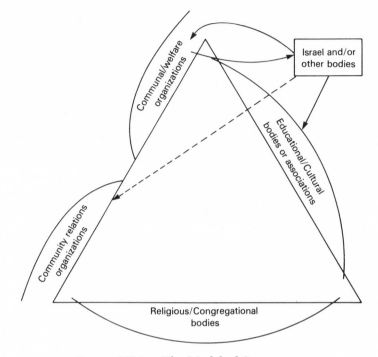

FIGURE XIV-4. The Model of Contemporary
Diaspora *Aratzot*

Of these, the most important is the distinction between those *medinot* in which Jewish association is voluntary (as in communities of the western world) and those in which Jewry constitutes a subjugated minority.

UNITED STATES (5.9 MILLION)

The United States, with over half of all the Jews in the diaspora, stands in a class by itself. The combination of a very large, fully modern society, established from the first on individualistic principles, pluralistic in the full sense of the word, settled by several significantly different waves of very adventurous Jewish immigrants who shared a common commitment to seeking new lives as individuals was not conducive to the development of sufficient homogeneity to permit the formation of a neat communal structure.

The organized American Jewish community is entirely built upon an associational base. That is to say, not only is there no inescapable compulsion, external or internal, to affiliate with organized Jewry but all connections with organized Jewish life are based on voluntary association with some particular organization or institution, whether in the form of synagogue membership, contribution to the local Jewish Welfare Fund (which is considered to be an act of joining as well as contributing), or affiliation with a Bnai Brith Lodge or

Hadassah chapter. Indeed the usual pattern for affiliated Jews is one of multiple association with memberships in different kinds of association reinforcing one another and creating an interlocking network of Jewish ties that binds the individual more firmly to the community. Without the associational base, there would be no organized Jewish community at all; with it, the Jewish community attains the kind of social—and even a certain legal—status that enables it to fit well into the larger society of which it is a part.

The associational basis of American Jewish life is manifested in a wide variety of local and national organizations designed to suit every Jewish taste. While these organizations may be confined to specific localities or may reflect specific interests, classes, or types on a strictly supralocal basis, the most successful ones develop both countrywide and local facets. It is no accident that Bnai Brith, a countrywide (now worldwide) federation of multistate districts and local lodges, and the Hadassah, a countrywide organization that emphasizes the role of its local chapters (which are further divided into almost neighborhood groups) are the two most successful mass Jewish organizations in the United States. The key to their success is that they provide both an overall purpose attuned to the highest aims of Jewish life and local attachment based on the immediate social needs of the individual Jew in such a way that people can be members for either or both reasons. Sooner or later, all large country-wide Jewish organizations have found that their survival is contingent upon developing some sort of serious local dimension to accommodate the very powerful combination of American and Jewish penchants for organizational arrangements on federal principles.

While certain of its organizations sometimes succeed in developing from the top down, the institutions of the American Jewish community are essentially local and, at most, loosely confederated with one another for very limited purposes. The three great synagogue movements, for example, are essentially confederations of highly independent local congregations, linked by relatively vague persuasional ties and a need for certain technical services. The confederations function to provide the requisite emotional reinforcement of those ties and the services desired by their member units. As in the case of the other countrywide organizations, they combine countrywide identification with essentially local attachments. With the exception of a few institutions of higher education (and, once upon a time, a few specialized hospitals, now nonsectarian), all Jewish social, welfare, and educational institutions are local in name and in fact, some loosely confederated on a supralocal basis and most not.

The demands placed upon the American Jewish community beginning in the late 1930s led to a growing recognition of the need to reconstitute the community's organizational structure at least to the extent of rationalizing the major interinstitutional relationships and generally tightening the matrix. These efforts at reconstitution received added impetus from the changes in

American society as a whole (and the Jews' place in it) after 1945. They signaled the abandonment of earlier chimeral efforts to create a more orthodox organizational pyramid in imitation of foreign patterns which, given the character of American society as a whole, would have been quite out of place.

What has emerged to unite all these highly independent associations is a number of overlapping local and supralocal federations designed for different purposes. The most powerful among them are the local federations of Jewish agencies and their countrywide confederation, the Council of Jewish Federations (CJF), which have become the framing institutions of the *medinah* and its *kehillot*. They are the only ones able to claim near-universal membership and all-embracing purposes, though not even the CJF has the formal status of an overall countrywide "roof body." Other federal arrangements tend to be limited to single functions and their general organizations rarely have more than a consultative role or power or accreditation.

This unity on a confederative basis, which characterizes American Jewry, is very different from unity on a hierarchical one; what emerges in front of the viewer's eye is not a single pyramidal structure, not even one in which the "bottom" rules the "top" (as in the case of most of the communities with representative boards), but a matrix consisting of many institutions and organizations tied together by a criss-crossing of memberships, shared purposes, and common interests, whose roles and powers vary according to situation and issue.

Keter Malkhut

Council of Jewish Federations (CJF): Confederation of 211 Jewish community federations in the United States and spokesman for them in matters of *medinah*-wide concern. Secretariat of Large Cities Budgetary Conference, American Jewry's major instrument for promoting fiscal accountability. Speaks for local federations in relations with UJA, Jewish Agency, and *medinah*-wide functional confederations. Annual General Assembly of CJF is most important single gathering of American Jewry.

Conference of Presidents of Major Jewish Organizations: Confederation of over thirty organizations organized to speak for American Jewry before the United States Government in matters relating to Israel

United Jewish Appeal: Major fund-raising instrumentality for general Israel and overseas purposes, including refugee resettlement. Jointly established and governed by Joint Distribution Committee (JDC) and United Israel Appeal (UIA) with Hebrew Immigrant Aid Society (HIAS) as third beneficiary

National Jewish Education Service: *Medinah*-wide service agency for Jewish education

Jewish Welfare Board: *Medinah*-wide service agency for Jewish community centers, also handles various *medinah*-wide social service responsibilities directly

National Foundation for Jewish Culture: *Medinah*-wide service agency for

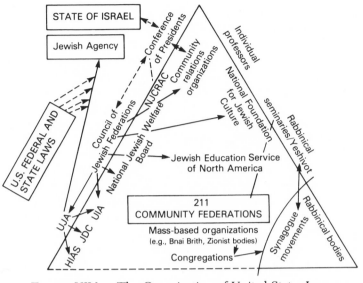

FIGURE XIV-5. The Organization of United States Jewry
Today

Jewish cultural activities; manages Joint Cultural Appeal which funds nine
specialized cultural agencies

National Jewish Community Relations Advisory Council (NJCRAC): *Medinah*-
wide confederation and service agency for local Jewish community relations
councils and most "national" Jewish community relations organizations

Keter Torah

Principally in the hands of the rabbinical seminaries of the major religious
movements and, to a lesser extent, their rabbinical bodies. For Orthodox
camp, *yeshivot* and individual *posekim* (most heads of *yeshivot*) are authoritative. For non-Orthodox, certain professors of Jewish studies also play an authoritative role.

Keter Kehunah

Principally in the hands of the synagogue movements and their rabbinical
bodies which concern themselves with sacerdotal matters and ritual observance.

JEWRIES OF THE BRITISH COMMONWEALTH

While there are variations among them, characteristic of all of the Jewries
whose origin is in the British Commonwealth is an ambivalence in defining
Jewishness. On one hand there is the sense on the part of both the community
and the larger society of which it is a part that Jewish attachment is a form of
religious affiliation and that every individual has free choice in the matter. On
the other, there is an equally strong feeling that somehow Jews stand apart
from the majority "Anglo-Saxon" population and can never bridge that gap.

Regardless of the intensity of their Jewish attachments, the overwhelming majority of the Jews in these countries have culturally assimilated into the wider society's way of life. Thus the associational aspects of Jewish affiliation are far more important than the organic ones, however real the latter may be, and the community structure is built around associational premises from top to bottom.

The communities themselves have no special status in public law. At most, there is a roof organization which is formally or tacitly accepted as the address of the Jewish community for certain limited purposes and subsidiary institutions which are occasionally accorded government support (along with similar non-Jewish institutions) for specific functions. Nor do the communities have any strong tradition of communal self-government to call upon. All are entirely products of the modern era; hence their founders were either postemancipation Jews or Jews seeking the benefits of emancipation and desirous of throwing off the burdens of an all-encompassing corporate Jewish life.

The larger communities in this category, at least, were created by successive waves of immigration, the greatest of which arrived in the past 100 years; hence the history of their present communal patterns does not go back more than three or four generations, if that. Most of their present leaders are sons of immigrants, if not immigrants themselves.

Eleven of these *medinot* have representative boards, usually called Boards of Deputies, as their principal spokesmen. These representative boards in most cases formally embrace virtually all the other Jewish institutions and organizations in the community. Those other organizations, however, while nominally associated with the Board, are, for all practical purposes, independent of and even equal to it in stature and influence. Fund-raising, religious life, and social services tend to be under other auspices. The Board tends to be pushed in the direction of becoming the ambassador of the Jewish community to the outside world rather than its governing body. This tendency has been accelerated since the Second World War by the coming of age of the last great wave of immigrants and the consequent diminution of the monolithic character of most of the communities. The increase in competing interests, the decline in religious interest, and the growth of assimilatory tendencies have all contributed to this change.

Communities with representative boards are also constructed on federal lines. At the very least, the Boards become federations of institutions and organizations; and in the federal or quasi-federal countries, they become territorial federations as well.

UNITED KINGDOM (410,000)

The rise of the last wave of immigrants and a new native-born generation has led to challenges to the communal status quo from both left and right, weakening traditional institutions and strengthening new ones that reflect the community's greater diversity. The Board of Deputies remains the most distinguished body of the *medinah* but is either unable or uninterested in extending

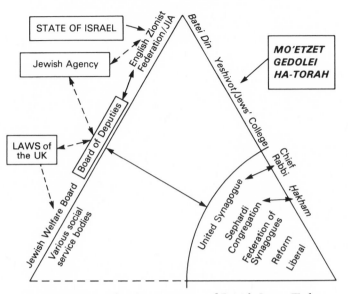

FIGURE XIV-6. The Organization of British Jewry Today

its sphere of activity, thereby allowing other bodies to play major roles in all spheres but that of community relations.

Keter Malkhut

Board of Deputies of British Jewry: Representative body in which virtually all of British Jewry is represented; established by Act of Parliament as the vehicle for Jewish relations with UK government

Joint Israel Appeal (JIA): Principal instrumentality for general Israel fundraising; part of British Zionist Federation and linked to Keren ha-Yesod

Jewish Welfare Board: Principal confederation of social service agencies

Keter Kehunah

Divided among five synagogue bodies: (1) the mainstream Orthodox United Synagogue, a centralized union of congregations under the authority of the Ashkenazi Chief Rabbi; (2) the Sephardi congregations under the authority of the *Ḥakham* (Sephardic Chief Rabbi); (3) the ultra-Orthodox Federation of Synagogues which accepts the authority of the *Moetzet Gedolai ha-Torah*; (4) the Liberal congregations; and (5) the Reform congregations. The first three maintain *batei din.*

Keter Torah

Consisting of the Chief Rabbi and the *Ḥakham* and, to a lesser extent, the *yeshivot*

AUSTRALIA (70,000)

The postwar influx of refugees enhanced Jewish life and necessitated changes in its organizational structure to encompass a widened scope of Jewish activity and more intensely Jewish Jews. State boards of deputies, particularly in Vic-

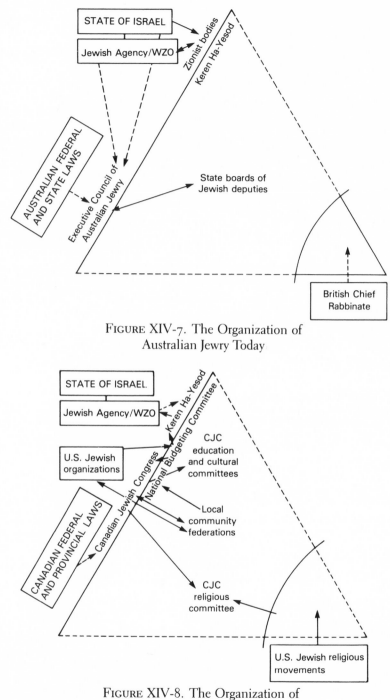

FIGURE XIV-7. The Organization of
Australian Jewry Today

FIGURE XIV-8. The Organization of
Canadian Jewry Today

toria (Melbourne) and New South Wales (Sydney) are principal loci of power. The Executive Council of Australian Jewry plays a limited role, confined to countrywide and international community relations.

CANADA (310,000)

Pressures of "Americanization," suburbanization, and general homogenization of Canada have led to reconstitution of the traditional Canadian communal structure and introduction of an American-style model in conjunction with the Canadian Jewish Congress.

IRELAND (1,900)

Little significant constitutional change has occurred, but a native-born generation has come to the fore. Population is declining through emigration.

NEW ZEALAND (5,000)

Continued emigration of younger generation has prevented increase in Jewish population. Community structure remains unchanged.

SOUTH AFRICA (118,000)

Change in the regime and rise of native-born generation within the community has shifted the emphases of the communal institutions and dominant mode of Jewish identification while encouraging maintenance of high level of communal cohesion. South African Jewish Board of Deputies remains strong countrywide union of Jewish communities.

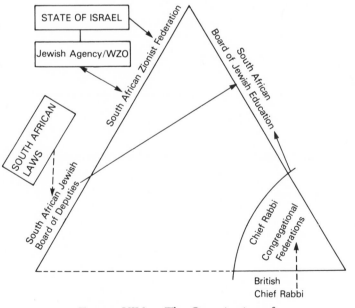

FIGURE XIV-9. The Organization of
South African Jewry Today

ZIMBABWE (1,800)

After period of growth due to influx from other African countries, Jews began emigrating during civil war and, at accelerated pace after black victory in 1980. Community appears to be in process of self-liquidation.

CARIBBEAN ISLAND COMMUNITIES

Nine small island communties are organized primarily as local congregations or congregation-centers. Most combine Sephardim, whose families have been in the islands for generations, and newly arrived American Jews and combine the characteristics of both, namely full voluntarism and identification primarily through religious institutions. Their lack of size and the low level of interest of most local Jewish residents keep organized Jewish life within a more or less neat framework that may mask grave weaknesses of morale and commitment. They have been affected somewhat less than the larger communities by postwar changes. While the process of assimilation has been hastened, the rise of Israel has given them a previously lacking interest (which they cultivate assiduously) and an anchor. They include

Aruba (130)	
Barbados (70)	
Cuba (1,500)	Declining as a result of Castro; organized life limited
Curacao (700)	Only Sephardic Reform congregation in the world
Dominican Republic (200)	Remnant of refugee community
Haiti (150)	Remnant of refugee community
Jamaica (350)	
Surinam (500)	
Trinidad and Tobago (500)	

LATIN AMERICA

The Eastern European Jews who migrated to Latin America in the twentieth century established replicas of the European *kehillah*, without official status but tacitly recognized by Jews and non-Jews alike as the organized Jewish community. The central institutions of these communities have a distinct public character but no special recognition in public law. Founded in the main by secularists, these communities were built in the mold of diaspora nationalism and emphasize the secular side of Jewish life. Since they function in an environment that provides neither the cultural nor the legal framework for a European-model *kehillah*, they must rely on the voluntary attachment of their members. The Latin American communities were relatively successful in maintaining this corporate pattern until recently because the great social and cultural gap between the Jews and their neighbors aided in giving the Jews a self-image as a special and distinct group, but it has become increasingly difficult to do so as the gap disappears.

Ashkenazim and Sephardim organized their separate communities, in some cases by country or city of origin. Just as the Jewish immigrants did not assimilate into their host societies, so, too, they did not assimilate among themselves. In the course of time, these communities loosely confederated with one another to deal with common problems that emerged in their relations with their external environment, essentially those of immigration, anti-Semitism, and Israel. At the same time each country-of-origin community retains substantial, if not complete, autonomy in internal matters and control over its own institutions.

In three of the larger Latin American countries (Argentina, Brazil, and Colombia), the indigenous federal or quasi-federal structures of the countries themselves influenced the Jews to create countrywide confederations based on territorial divisions (officially uniting state or provincial communities which are, in fact, local communities concentrated in the state or provincial capitals). In the others, the local community containing the overwhelming majority of the Jewish population itself became the countrywide unit, usually by designating its federation as the council of communities. The community councils of the six Central American countries (total Jewish population 7,250) have organized the Federation of Central American Jewish Communities to pool resources and provide common services.

None of the tacitly recognized communal structures has been in existence more than three generations, and the communities themselves originated no more than four generations ago. Most of the smaller ones are just now entering their third generation since they were created by the refugees of the 1930s and 1940s. Consequently, many, if not most, are still in the process of developing an appropriate and accepted communal character.

The great postwar adjustment that has faced the Latin American communities centers on the emergence of a native-born majority. This new generation has far less attachment to the old country way of life with its emphasis on ideological and country-of-origin ties; hence the whole community structure is less relevant to them.

Moreover, the 625,000 Jews living in Latin America are located in unstable environments that do not necessarily encourage pluralism. Many of them are already beginning to assimilate into their own countries of birth, or at least into the local radical movements, in familiar Jewish ways. For an increasing number of Jews, the *deportivo*, or community recreational center, often seems the most relevant form of Jewish association and the building block for Jewish organizational life.

Not surprisingly, then, the elements of a constitutional crisis of the first magnitude are already present in the Latin American communities. To the extent that a communal structure, based on local territorial divisions rather

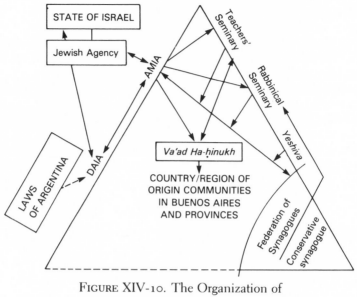

FIGURE XIV-10. The Organization of
Argentinian Jewry Today

than on the *landsman* principle is emerging in these communities (with its accompanying substructure of associational activities whose participants are drawn in on the basis of common interest rather than of common descent), this constitutional crisis is being overcome through the rise of new institutions.

The estimated Jewish population of Latin American *medinot* (1980) is as follows:

Argentina (350,000)   Honduras (200)
Bolivia (750)   Mexico (37,500)
Brazil (150,000)   Nicaragua (200)
Chile (30,000)   Panama (2,000)
Colombia (12,000)   Paraguay (1,200)
Costa Rica (2,500)   Peru (5,200)
Ecuador (1,000)   Uruguay (50,000)
El Salvador (350)   Venezuela (15,000)
Guatemala (2,000)

FREE EUROPE
In the wake of their destruction in World War II and subsequent reconstruction (facilitated in every case by the JDC), the *aratzot* in this region have developed new forms of communal association while at the same time retaining

the formal structures of governance of the previous epoch. Most obviously is this so in the case of those which in Epoch XIII had exhibited either the characteristics of a *Kultusgemeinde* (comprehensive state-recognized communal structure) or a *consistoire* (state-recognized or semi-official religious structure).

The only examples of the *Kultusgemeinde* model are to be found in central Europe or areas influenced by central European culture before the First World War. Even these communities have undergone basic constitutional changes in recent years. They have, by and large, lost their power to compel all Jews to be members and must now build their membership on a consensual basis. This usually means that all known Jews are automatically listed on the community's rolls but have the right to opt out if they choose to do so.

Structurally, the *kehillah* communities remain neat and all-embracing. All legitimate institutions or organizations function within their overall framework, except where the state has allowed secessionist groups to exist. As *medinot*, they are generally organized along conventional federal lines with either "national" and "local" or "national" "provincial," and "local" bodies, each chosen through formal elections and linked constitutionally to one another with a relatively clear division of powers. In some, authority remains in the local community, perhaps with some loose confederal relationships uniting the various localities. The greatest source of strength of the state-recognized communities lies in their power to tax or to receive automatically a portion of their members' regular taxes from the authorities.

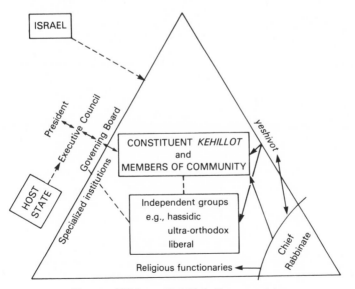

FIGURE XIV-11. *Kehillah* Communities

The state-recognized community, once the basis of Jewish life, is losing ground in size and importance in the Jewish world at the same time it is losing its compulsory character. Most are declining communities, decimated by war, emigration, and assimilation. Moreover, an increasing number of Jews within those communities may be opting out of community membership (and the taxes that go with it). In 1980, 150,000 Jews lived within such structures:

Austria (13,000)	Reconstructed and reconstituted after World War II with a substantially different population
Denmark (7,500)	Reconstructed along prewar lines. Absorbed refugees from Poland in 1968
Finland (1,000)	Reconstituted with additions of refugee population
German Federal Republic (38,000)	Reconstructed and reconstituted with substantially different population including Eastern European refugees and "Israelis"
Greece (6,000)	Partially reconstructed and reconstituted around remnant population
Italy (41,000)	Partially reconstructed after formal restoration of prewar constitution
Norway (900)	Reconstructed with addition of some refugees
Sweden (17,000)	Reconstituted with addition of refugees and abolition of state-required community membership
Switzerland (21,000)	Reconstituted to include wartime refugees
Yugoslavia (5,500)	Reconstructed and reconstituted under Communist regime after substantial emigration to Israel

Despite its importance during the nineteenth century, only a remnant of the *consistoire* pattern still exists in France. Somewhat more faithful models are to be found in those countries within the orbit of French culture in Europe and Africa. In some, the *consistoire* has a certain legal status as a religious body and its officials are usually supported by government funds, but affiliation with it is entirely voluntary. It is distinguished by its emphasis on the exclusively religious nature of Judaism (even emphasizing the *keter kehunah* over the *keter torah*) and its centralized character.

The *consistoire* is a casualty of the growing pluralism within the Jewish community. The refugees from eastern Europe and, later, North Africa, who became major—if not the dominant—forces in so many of the *consistoire* communities after the Second World War rejected its exclusively sacerdotal emphasis while the growth of secularism made Jewish identification via a state-recognized religious structure increasingly incongruous. The new ultra-

Orthodox congregations created by certain of the refugees rejected the laxity of the official orthodoxy of the *consistoire* and the tasks of communal reconstruction in the aftermath of the war proved too much for the consistorial bodies to handle alone. Above all, the rise of Israel generated demands for mobilization of diaspora resources that went beyond the capabilities of the *consistoire* structure, necessitating more appropriate organizational arrangements. In a larger sense, the times themselves conspired against the old system, as committed Jews the world over rediscovered the national-political aspects of Jewish existence.

New entirely voluntary organizations began to emerge within the framework of the *keter malkhut*, to reach those elements which were otherwise not part of the official community. In the process, they began to assume the functions of roof organizations to the extent that their local situation encourages such organizations and within the context of an emerging pluralism in Jewish communal life. Consistorial bodies survive but without the centrality they once had in Jewish life.

Today, countries with state-recognized religious structures contain 722,000 Jews. In fact, if France had not received the large migration from North Africa, that number would have been fifty percent smaller.

FRANCE (650,000)

Reconstructed and reconstituted with substantially new population from Eastern Europe; subsequently further reconstituted after North African influx.

Keter Malkhut

Fonds Social Juif Unifié (FSJU): Founded in 1949 with the assistance of the JDC to serve as the internal fund-raising and social planning arm of French Jewry, it has since risen to a dominant position in the community. Originally restricted to a narrow elite, it has been undergoing democratization since the beginning of the epoch's second generation. It manages the Appel Unifié Juif de France which unites local fund-raising and fund-raising for Israel.

Conseil Représentatif des Juifs de France (CRIF): Founded in 1944 "to protect the rights of the Jewish community in France," it is composed of religious, Zionist, secularist, and political bodies cutting across the entire range of French Jewry.

Jewish Agency: An arm of the *edah* which functions directly within France to organize and serve French Jewry in matters pertaining to Israel and certain educational activities

Keter Kehunah

Consistoire Central Israélite de France: The official representative of French Judaism. Moderate Orthodox in orientation, it is responsible for training and appointment of rabbis, religious education, *kashrut* supervision, and the application of religious law in personal status matters.

Three regional consistoires of Alsace-Lorraine: Semi-independent of Consis-

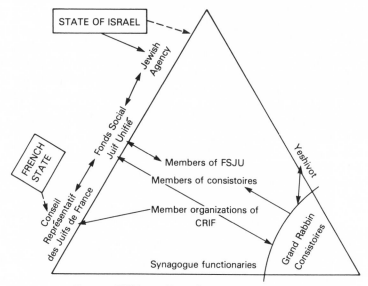

FIGURE XIV-12. French Jewry since 1948

toire Central for historic reasons, they perform similar functions but are supported by state funds.

Conseil Représentatif du Judaisme Traditionaliste de France (CRJTF): Founded in 1952 to represent more traditional Orthodoxy in France

Union Libérale Israélite: Affiliated with the World Union for Progressive Judaism

Keter Torah

Consisting of the Chief Rabbi of the Consistoire General; regional chief rabbis, especially in Alsace-Lorraine; rabbinical *posekim* of the bodies affiliated with the CRJTF; and prominent Jewish intellectuals who define Judaism for the basically areligious French Jews.

BELGIUM (41,000)

Reconstructed and reconstituted after significant new settlement by Eastern European refugees. *Aretz* divided into ultra-Orthodox community constituted by postwar immigrants, based in Antwerp; and basically areligious community composed of long-time Belgian Jews based in Brussels and other French-speaking cities. This division, while based on Jewish issues, parallels the division of Belgium into Flemish and Walloon communities.

LUXEMBOURG (1,000)

Reconstructed and reconstituted.

NETHERLANDS (30,000)

Partially reconstructed and reconstituted with remnant population and the addition of some refugees. Divided into Ashkenazic, Sephardic, and Liberal communities.

CONGREGATIONAL COMMUNITIES

All located in the Mediterranean world (the Iberian peninsula and Malta), these were organized in the late modern or early postmodern epochs in polities which initially did not formally recognize Jewish religious bodies. Once recognized, they remained voluntary in character, based on local congregation-community centers which either embrace the entire community or serve as its building blocks on a confederal basis.

Gibraltar (600)   Four congregations and various community organiza-
                   tions; no significant constitutional change in this
                   epoch
Malta (50)   Remnant community
Portugal (600)   One congregation in Lisbon; reconstituted to include
                   remnants of wartime influx of refugees; declining in
                   population
Spain (12,000)   Local congregation-community centers in five cities
                   confederated into a countrywide body for represen-
                   tational purposes. Spanish Jewry gained formal sta-
                   tus as community in this epoch. Wartime refugee
                   settlers founded first communal institutions and
                   were subsequently replaced by Sephardim from
                   North Africa, particularly from Morocco.

COMMUNIST EUROPE

The communities located in the Communist countries of eastern Europe are basically remnant communities, most of whose earlier residents either died in the Holocaust or emigrated to Israel. They are also subjugated in the way all potential rivals for the citizens' interest are curbed in totalitarian societies. The communities in Czechoslovakia, Hungary, and Rumania actually have a formal status similar to that of their sister communities in other continental European countries and, within the severe limits imposed upon them, function through state-recognized communal or religious structures. The communities of Bulgaria and Poland are organized under Communist-imposed structures. In the USSR, Jews are forbidden any organization beyond occasional synagogues and a few "showcase" institutions. In any case, whatever organized Jewish life there is, exists on sufferance of the authorities, and the authorities are fully willing to intervene in Jewish affairs in every way as a matter of ideology and policy. With the exception of the USSR, all these communities became subjugated ones after the Second World War. Russian Jewry, subjugated since the First World War, lost the last remnants of its organized communal life in the Stalin purges that came in the aftermath of the Second World War. Some 2.5 million Jews live in these subjugated communities.

Albania (300)   Disappeared as organized community after
                           Communist take-over

Bulgaria (7,000)	Jewish population survived war and migrated en masse to Israel, leaving a remnant to function in a severely limited way under Communist regime, governed by central committee for cultural activities
Czechoslovakia (12,000)	Partial reconstruction and limited reconstitution under Communist regime
German Democratic Republic (1,200)	Postwar remnant barely organized, principally in congregations
Hungary (80,000)	Partial reconstruction and limited reconstitution under Communist regime; flight of refugees in 1956. Community maintains only *yeshiva* behind Iron Curtain
Poland (6,000)	Extremely limited reconstitution under Communists with successive emigrations of surviving Jews; shadow central committee remains
Rumania (33,000)	Limited reconstitution under Communist regime; substantial and continuous emigration to Israel; organized as *consistoire* under chief rabbi
USSR (2,100,000)	Exists as an organized community only in the most limited sense because of Communist regime

THE MOSLEM WORLD

The communities located in the Islamic countries of the Middle East are the remnants of what were, until the rise of Israel, flourishing traditional *kehillot*. Their present state of subjugation or dissolution dates from their host countries' attainment of independence or from the establishment of Israel, and therefore reflects another kind of postwar reconstruction. The character of the subjugation varies from virtually complete suppression of all communal and private Jewish activities (Iraq) to government appointment of pliable leadership to manage the community's limited affairs (Tunisia). Only Morocco and Turkey have allowed their Jewish communities to continue to function with a minimum of disturbance, albeit under close government supervision.

In every case, the situation has deteriorated after each Israeli victory and the number of Jews remaining in the communities has decreased. Since emigration from the larger ones is not impossible, it seems clear that they, too, are fated to disappear or to become no more than very small remnant communities in the near future. In the meantime, communal life proceeds up to the limits of the possible in each of them. This usually means some form of religious life, increasingly limited opportunities to provide children with a Jewish education, and a few limited social services.

Aden	Entire community emigrated during decolonization
Afghanistan (200)	Majority of Jews emigrated to Israel leaving behind small oppressed community with no countrywide institutions
Algeria (1,000)	Virtually all Jews fled country in wake of French evacuation, moving to France and essentially ending Jewish communal life except for a few synagogues
Egypt (400)	Successive oppressions and migrations to Israel after 1948 virtually ended community's existence except for a few synagogues; the peace treaty with Israel has stabilized their situation
Iran (30,000)	Community reduced in size by emigration to Israel after 1948 and again after Iranian revolution; now declining and oppressed; until revolution governed by community council of notables and *bet din*
Iraq (450)	Mass migration to Israel reduced community to a tiny oppressed minority without right to organize
Lebanon (400)	Community weathered Arab-Israel conflicts until Lebanese civil war; at present in process of self-liquidation through emigration but not to Israel; a single synagogue remains
Libya (20)	Migration to Israel accelerated after each Arab-Israel crisis; community finally ceased to exist after 1967 war
Morocco (22,000)	Slow decline through emigration to Israel and elsewhere accelerated after Moroccan independence and picked up momentum after 1967 war; community organization remains more or less intact as do contacts with larger Jewish world
Pakistan (250)	Most of small community emigrated leaving very small group to carry on minimal communal life
Syria (4,500)	Oppression after 1948 led to migration of majority to Israel; government pressure increased against remnant after Six-Day War
Tunisia (7,000)	Despite official attempts to keep Jews, most emigrated to Israel in successive waves after independence
Turkey (24,000)	Remains structurally intact after mass emigration to Israel in 1949 and 1950; headed by chief rabbi and council of notables
Yemen (500)	All but tiny handful left for Israel immediately after establishment of state; no contact with remnant

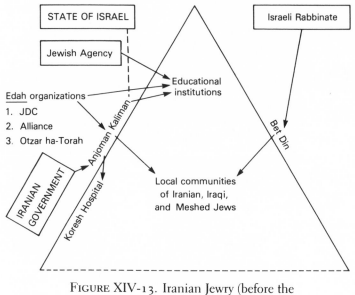

FIGURE XIV-13. Iranian Jewry (before the
Khomeini Revolution)

SOUTH AND EAST ASIA

These communities were established or constituted in their present form (India) in the nineteenth century by Sephardic Jewish businessmen moving eastward with the British Empire. Disrupted by World War II, these communities have been reconstituted by American and other Jewish businessmen, often with greatly reduced populations and, with the exception of India, are declining. Their basic structure is congregational with a few ancillary organizations.

Burma (50)	Small Jewish community abandoned after Japanese invasion (1942) and never restored
China (30)	Jewish communities, consisting principally of refugees, abandoned in wake of Chinese civil war, with most Jews emigrating to the United States or Israel
Hong Kong (250)	Small community populated by successive waves of Jewish businessmen
India (8,000)	Most Jews emigrated to Israel after 1948; now stable community concentrated in Bombay and other major cities
Indonesia (100)	Small community destroyed by World War II and Indonesian revolution; no known organized Jewish life

Japan (400)	Reconstituted in three localities in post–World War II years, primarily by American Jewish businessmen
Philippines (200)	Reconstituted after World War II, primarily by American Jewish businessmen
Singapore (450)	Reconstituted after World War II but slowly declining
Thailand	Small organic Jewish community reconstituted into a congregation-center by United States military chaplains, now continuing in that framework after United States withdrawal

AFRICA

Except for Ethiopia, these are small communities established later in the modern epoch in the wake of the European colonial division of the continent. Most experienced considerable outmigration when the new African states became independent so that what remains are small congregational communities with limited Jewish life in the following countries:

Ethiopia (22,000)	The Falasha Jews of Ethiopia are in a situation similar to their brethren in the Muslim world, although there the oppressors of the Falashas are Christians. The Jewish population is being steadily reduced and Jewish communal life is suffering accordingly
Kenya (450)	Community remained generally stable after independence
Zaire (200)	
Zambia (400)	

QUASI-COMMUNITIES

Quasi-communities are temporary concentrations of Jews with some attributes of an organized community but with no permanent institutions or settled Jewish population. Most are outposts established by Israeli or American Jews in the course of missions given them throughout the postwar world. Those established or given organizational form by Jews serving in the American armed forces are generally built upon religious facilities provided through the military chaplaincy. American Jewish chaplains and soldiers with religious and communal interests have even managed to mobilize the indigenous Jewish civilian populations wherever any exist and, in some cases (Japan, Thailand, Okinawa, Taiwan), have been instrumental in transforming quasi-communities into permanent ones. Nevertheless, the survival of the existing quasi-communities appears to depend upon the continued presence of the American Jews.

Those established by Israelis serving in countries on diplomatic, technical, or military assistance missions are generally built around the provision of educational facilities for the Israelis' children. Since they are located in countries with virtually no other Jews, they are even more dependent upon transients than are the American outposts. No population figures are available for most of these communities since their numbers are constantly fluctuating, but the total cannot exceed several thousand.

6. *KEHILLOT*

Local communities are organized in a manner suitable to each country following regional patterns. In most cases they are organized as federations of local organizations and/or institutions. Increasingly, they share a basic tripartite structure based on (1) synagogues, (2) welfare institutions, and (3) representative or Zionist institutions; only the emphasis is different in each *medinah/eretz*.

Prominent variations: formal municipal organizations functioning according to laws of the state (Israel); *kehillot* integrated around Jewish community federations which link functional agencies for fund-raising and community

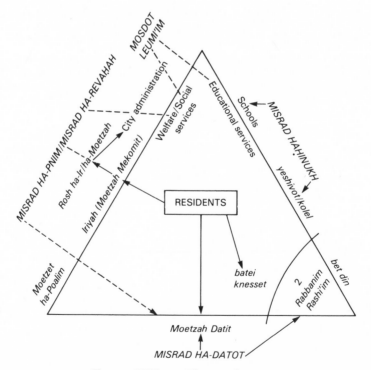

FIGURE XIV-14. The Israeli *Kehillah*

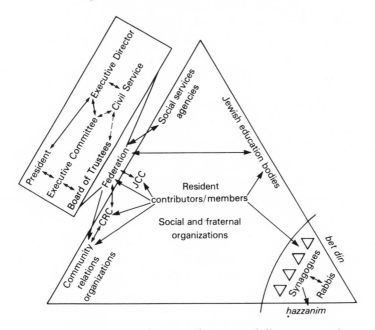

FIGURE XIV-15. The United States *Kehillot* since 1948

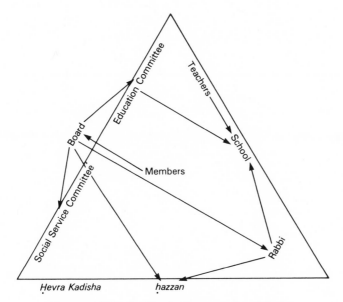

FIGURE XIV-16. Single Congregation Model

planning (United States, Canada); single congregations (e.g., New Zealand); *kehillot* integrated around community boards (e.g., Stockholm); *kehillot* integrated around federations of congregations (e.g., Istanbul); and *kehillot* integrated around specific welfare institutions (e.g., Buenos Aires).

7. REPRESENTATIVE PERSONALITIES

7.1 Constitutional Architects

David Ben Gurion:
(1886–1973); first *Rosh Memshalah* (Prime Minister) of Israel; man chiefly responsible for establishing the institutional framework, norms, and characteristics of Israel as an independent state; also played a dominant role in the development of the present framework of Israel-diaspora relations

7.2 Statesmen

Max Fisher:
(1908–   ); United States industrialist and community leader; one of the architects of the reconstituted Jewish Agency and leader of the UJA

Nahum Goldmann:
(1895–1982); a leading spokesman for the Jewish people since World War I; president WZO, 1955–1968; one of the founders and long-term president of WJC; founder and president of Conference of Jewish Organizations (COJO); founded United States Conference of Presidents of Major Jewish Organizations; largely responsible for negotiating reparations and indemnification for victims of Nazism; founder and president of Memorial Foundation for Jewish Culture

Golda Meir: (Myerson)
(1898–1979); *Rosh Memshalah* of Israel, 1969–1974

Louis Pincus:
(1912–1973); Chairman of the Jewish Agency Executive and principal architect of its reconstitution

Pinhas Sapir: (Koslowsky)
(1907–1979); Israeli minister of commerce and industry, 1955–1967; minister of finance, 1953, 1963–1967; 1969–1974; helped to create strong Israel–diaspora links, especially after 1967

Menahem Mendel Schneerson:
(1902–   ); leader of Lubavitch Hassidim; largely responsible for expansion of movement in United States and Israel

8. TERMS

Nagid, principal trustee
Rosh Memshalah, prime minister

Sar, minister of State of Israel
Shaliaḥ, emissary of one of the national institutions
Yoetz, counsellor of government (as in *yoetz mishpati* to *memshalah*)

9. BIBLIOGRAPHY

A. Avi-hai, *Ben Gurion: State Builder. Principles and Pragmatism, 1948–1963* (New York, 1970).
D. Avni-Segre, *Israel: A Society in Transition* (Oxford, 1971).
———. *A Crisis of Identity: Israel and Zionism* (Oxford, 1980).
H. Avni, *Yahadut Argentina: Ma'amadah ha-ḥevrati u-demutah ha-irgunit* (Jerusalem, 1972).
A. G. Brotman, "Jewish Communal Organization," in *Jewish Life in Modern Britain* (ed. J. Gould and S. Esh; London, 1964).
D. J. Elazar, "The Reconstitution of the Jewish Communities in the Postwar Period," *Jewish Journal of Sociology* (December 1969).
———. *Community and Polity: The Organizational Dynamics of American Jewry* (Philadelphia, 1976).
———. "The Jewish Agency and the Jewish People after Caesarea," *Forum* (Winter 1981).
D. J. Elazar with Peter Medding, *Jewish Communities on the Great Frontier* (New York, 1982).
S. Esh (ed.), *Yehudei Europa ha-Ma'aravit* (Jerusalem, 1967).
Z. Gitelman, *Jews in the USSR: Prospects and Policies* (New York, 1978).
J. Gutwirth, "The Jews of Antwerp Today," *Jewish Journal of Sociology* (June 1968).
I. Greilsammer, "Democratization of a Community: The Case of French Jewry," *Center for Jewish Community Studies, Working Paper* 1 (Jerusalem, 1978).
R. J. Isaac, *Israel Divided: Ideology and Politics in the Jewish State* (Johns Hopkins, 1976).
N. Lerner, "Irgun ha-Am ha-Yehudi bi-m'lot Esrim ve-Ḥamesh Shanim le-Medinat Yisrael," *Gesher* 18 (1972), pp. 197–208.
C. Liebman, "Dimensions of Authority in the Contemporary Jewish Community," *Jewish Journal of Sociology* (January 1970).
———. *Pressure Without Sanctions. The Influence of World Jewry on Israeli Policy* (New Jersey, 1977).
S. Liebman, "The Communal Organization of Mexican Jewry," *Tefutsot Israel* (January 1978).
H. J. Matt, "Synagogue and Covenant People," *Conservative Judaism* (Fall 1968).
Golda Meir, *My Life* (Jerusalem, 1975).
T. Meizel, "Yehudim be-Mexico," *Gesher* 17 (1971), pp. 68–79.
S. Nudelstejer, "Jewish Communities in Central America," *American Jewish Year Book* (1974–1975).
E. Stock, "In the Absence of Hierarchy: Notes on the Organization of the American Jewish Community," *Jewish Journal of Sociology* (December 1970).
———. "The Reconstitution of the Jewish Agency," *American Jewish Year Book* (1972).
———. "Jewish Multi-Country Associations," *American Jewish Year Book* (1975).